THE ENCYCLOPEDIA OF

EASTERN MYTHOLOGY

MOSE

THE ENCYCLOPEDIA OF

EASTERN MYTHOLOGY

Legends of the East: the fabulous myths and tales of the heroes, gods and warriors of ancient Egypt, Arabia, Persia, India, Tibet, China and Japan

RACHEL STORM

LORENZ BOOKS

This edition is published by Lorenz Books

Lorenz Books is an imprint of Anness Publishing Ltd
Hermes House, 88–89 Blackfriars Road, London SE1 8HA
tel. 020 7401 2077; fax 020 7633 9499
www.lorenzbooks.com; info@anness.com

UK agent: The Manning Partnership Ltd,
6 The Old Dairy, Melcombe Road, Bath BA2 3LR;
tel. 01225 478444; fax 01225 478440;
sales@manning-partnership.co.uk

UK distributor: Grantham Book Services Ltd,
Isaac Newton Way, Alma Park Industrial Estate,
Grantham, Lincs NG31 9SD;
tel. 01476 541080; fax 01476 541061;
orders@gbs.tbs-ltd.co.uk

North American agent/distributor: National Book Network,
4501 Forbes Boulevard, Suite 200, Lanham, MD 20706;
tel. 301 459 3366; fax 301 429 5746; www.nbnbooks.com

Australian agent/distributor: Pan Macmillan Australia,
Level 18, St Martins Tower, 31 Market St, Sydney, NSW
2000;
tel. 1300 135 113; fax 1300 135 103;
customer.service@macmillan.com.au

New Zealand agent/distributor: David Bateman Ltd,
30 Tarndale Grove, Off Bush Road, Albany, Auckland;
tel. (09) 415 7664; fax (09) 415 8892

A CIP catalogue record for this book is available from the British Library.

Publisher: Joanna Lorenz
Managing Editor: Helen Sudell
Design: Mario Bettella, Artmedia
Map Illustrator: Stephen Sweet
Picture Researcher: Adrian Bentley
Editorial Reader: Richard McGinlay
Production Controller: Wendy Lawson

Previously published as *Myths of the East*

10 9 8 7 6 5 4 3 2 1

PUBLISHER'S NOTE

The entries in this encyclopedia are all listed alphabetically. Where more than one name exists for a character the entry is listed under the name used in the original country of origin for that particular myth. Names in italic capital letters indicate that that name has an individual entry. Special feature spreads examine specific mythological themes in more detail. If a character is included in a special feature spread it is noted at the end of their individual entry.

CONTENTS

PREFACE

THE MYTHS OF THE GREAT CIVILIZATIONS of Asia include some of the oldest, most powerful stories in the world. This book explores them in three sections, beginning with those of the Middle East, including the Sumerians and Babylonians; the ancient Iranians; the Egyptians; the Canaanites and Hebrews. The section on South and Central Asia deals with the Hindu and Buddhist deities of India, Sri Lanka, Tibet and Nepal. Daoist and Buddhist myths; the folk religion of China; the Shinto deities of Japan; and animist and shamanistic religions practised from Siberia to the South-east Asian archipelago are included in the final section on East Asia. The entries concern deities or semi-divine beings.

APIS, *the sacred bull of the Egyptians, is worshipped by a devotee. Said to be an incarnation of the god Ptah, Apis wears the sun-disc of Ra and the rearing cobra of royal authority between his horns to signify his divinity. Ra's falcon wings are spread protectively above him.* (PAINTED LIMESTONE STELE, LATE PERIOD, 664–332 BC.)

GILGAMESH *was the Assyro-Babylonian hero of a great epic poem dating from the second millennium* BC. *Here, flanked by centaur-like figures wearing the horned crowns of the gods, Gilgamesh supports the winged disc which represents the Assyrian creator god, Ashur.* (SYRIO-HITTITE STELE, 9TH CENTURY BC.)

From Mesopotamia, the cradle of Western civilization, come legends of which we are able to glimpse only fragments, while the belief systems of other ancient societies, such as the Egyptians, are far more readily accessible. Though the stories survive, the gods they describe have long since passed into history. Others, such as the deities of Hinduism and Buddhism, remain at the centre of living faiths, worshipped by millions of present-day devotees.

One of the most striking characteristics of these myths is the way they have been adopted and adapted by successive cultures, or have been carried by missionaries from one part of the continent to another, giving rise to subtle variations in archetypal legends, and different manifestations of important mythological figures. Buddhism, for instance, which arose with the teachings of Gautama Buddha in northern India around 500 BC, was introduced to China around the time of

Christ and to Japan in the sixth century AD. The buddha Amitabha, whose cult may in turn have been influenced by Iranian religion, became the leading figure of Japanese buddhism as Amida, more highly venerated than Gautama himself. Gautama, meanwhile, was accommodated in Hindu myth as an avatar of Vishnu.

These stories underline both the variety and the continuity of human nature. Though they concern gods, heroes and monsters, much of their fascination lies in the human values they illuminate. It is easy to identify with the grief of the widowed Isis or the bereaved Gilgamesh; with the disgust of Amaterasu at the bad behaviour of Susano-Wo; or with the happy family life of Shiva and Parvati.

The themes of the great myths are universal. Creation myths have evolved in every culture, often with striking similarities – such as the limitless ocean from which the universe arises. A major preoccupation is that of life after death, which is explained in terms of parallel worlds: the underworld to which the dead descend to be judged; and the heavens to which the righteous aspire.

__KRISHNA__, the divine hero and the most beguiling incarnation of the great Hindu god, Vishnu, is accompanied by musicians as he dances in the rain, holding a lotus flower, a Hindu symbol of life and consciousness. (MINIATURE, RAJASTHAN SCHOOL, 17TH CENTURY.)

__BAAL__, which means "Lord", was the name given to the chief god of the Canaanites to conceal his true name, which could not be uttered and was known only to initiates. As a weather god, Baal wielded thunderbolts and dispensed rain. (BRONZE AND GOLD STATUETTE FROM RAS SHAMRA, UGARITIC, 1400–1200 BC.)

Even within Hinduism and Buddhism, in which life is seen as a succession of reincarnations leading to the final release of nirvana, complex pictures of these unearthly realms have arisen. The idea of a catastrophic flood is another powerful and recurring theme, illustrating the potential power of the gods to destroy humankind, and arising from a universal awareness of the precarious nature of human existence. Thus do the myths peculiar to each culture and religion point to the essential truths common to all humanity.

THE MYTHS OF EGYPT AND WEST ASIA

Introduction

The Ancient Middle East, the so-called "cradle of civilization", was the birthplace of Judaism, Islam and Christianity, the three faiths that came to have such an immense impact on human culture and, by tradition, originated amongst the descendants of Shem, one of the sons of Noah. Zoroastrianism, probably the most powerful religion of its time, also arose in the Middle East, whereas the wider area of West Asia witnessed the rise of the powerful Egyptian and Hittite empires.

What was it about this region that enabled it to bear witness to such remarkable achievements? One answer at least lies in the geography of the area: it was here that crop farming first began, and with it the beginnings of a settled, civilized way of life, which proceeded to bear rich cultural fruits.

The annual flooding of the Nile inspired many of the myths of ancient Egypt. The people there depended on the revival of the parched land for their livelihood, a concern that was reflected in the myth of Osiris, their dying-and-rising vegetation god, who finally retired from life to rule over the underworld. A preoccupation with death haunts Egyptian mythology, prompted by this sense of man's vulnerability in the face of forces beyond his control. Even the great sun god, Ra, was believed to die each evening and be born again at dawn.

It was on the fertile land produced by the Nile's annual floodings that Egypt's first city states grew up, each with its own gods. Eventually, around 3100 BC, these separate states were unified under a succession of pharaohs. Many of the local gods were admitted into the national pantheon, giving rise to a vast

Symbolizing *the divine relationship between pharaohs and the gods, Horemheb, the last Egyptian pharaoh of the 18th dynasty, sits beside the god Horus, son of Isis and Osiris.* (c. 1320 BC.)

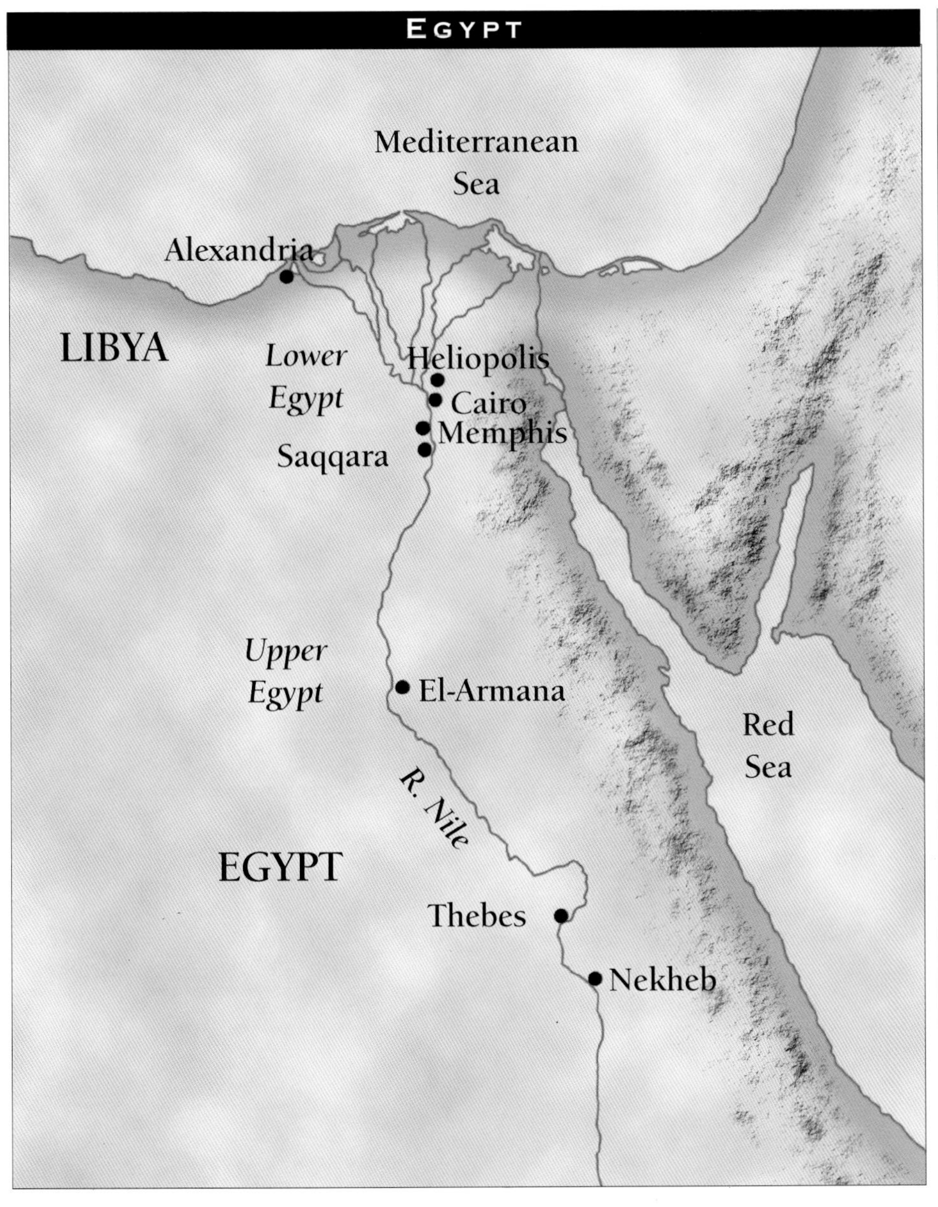

and splendid array of deities who flourished virtually unopposed by alien beliefs. Seen as divinely appointed mediators between the world of men and the gods, the pharaohs gave a political and religious focus to Egyptian civilization and culture. Their power was such that it came to extend into Canaan and Syria. However, in about 1387 BC the pharaoh Akhenaten instigated vast religious reforms, which, though eventually overturned when he died, began to weaken Egyptian power.

Like the Egyptians, the Mesopotamian settlers were attracted to the rich land left by the flooding of rivers. The Sumerians, a non-Semitic people (not descended from Shem), had settled in Mesopotamia, the area lying between the rivers Tigris and Euphrates, around 4000 BC. Some 2,000 years later, Babylon was made the region's capital and Sumer was gradually absorbed into Babylonia. The livelihood of these Mesopotamians, like that of the Egyptians, depended on the agricultural cycle, and their pantheon likewise featured dying and rising gods. The Mesopotamians' existence was, however, much more precarious than that of the Egyptians. Not only could the flooding of their rivers be sudden and unpredictable, but the people were also under constant threat from marauding tribes and foreign invaders. Their myths, therefore, tended to portray life as a constant battle against the forces of chaos.

Despite its political instability, ancient Mesopotamia produced an extensive written literature. As a result, the Mesopotamian deities and myths were transmitted to other West Asian peoples, including the Assyrians and Hittites. The Hittites, who originally hailed from Anatolia, came to be known in the Old Testament as one of the peoples occupying Canaan, the promised land of the Israelites. Many of the ancestors of the Israelites had themselves migrated from Mesopotamia to Canaan soon after 2000 BC; some of them continued into Egypt where, at a date which is uncertain, they were taken into slavery by a pharaoh. However, in the 13th century BC, Moses led the Israelites out of slavery in Egypt and back towards Canaan.

BAAL, an ancient fertility god, is a dying and rising god whose actions symbolized the growth and decay of vegetation. (BRONZE AGE, 1400–1300 BC.)

MOSES delivered the tribes of Israel from slavery in Egypt and led them through the desert to freedom. Here he strikes the rock to produce water. (19TH CENTURY ENGRAVING.)

13th century BC, Moses led the Israelites out of slavery in Egypt and back towards Canaan. On this journey, they made a solemn promise to worship only one god – Yahweh.

The Canaanite pantheon, which the Israelites encountered at the end of their journey, was dominated by the god of rain, fertility and storms, Baal. Many other gods also went under this name, which translates as "Lord", but the chief Baal was a warlike dying and rising god. His attributes reflected the Canaanite way of life which, like that of all the other peoples of the region, was closely bound up with the agricultural cycle.

As the tribes settled in Canaan, they united in their worship of Yahweh, who became the supreme god, although rites associated with other gods persisted for some time. The followers of the new faith were based around Jerusalem. In 587 BC, the city was conquered by the Babylonians, and the leading Israelites were taken into exile in Babylon. Nearly 50 years later, the Achaemenids of Iran, whom the Greeks called Persians, conquered Babylon in turn.

ZOROASTER, the great religious reformer of ancient Iran, receives fire and the law of reform, which is brought to him by Ahura Mazda, the principle of good. At the age of 30, Zoroaster received numerous revelations from the Amesa Spentas, or holy immortals. (19TH CENTURY ILLUSTRATION.)

The Persian conquerors introduced the Babylonians to their Zoroastrian faith, which, though often loosely adhered to, saw the world as in the grip of the forces of good and evil. Zoroaster, who founded the religion and who is now believed to have lived around 1200 BC, had preached of his vision of a single, supreme god. Faced with encroaching monotheism, and sometimes directly overthrown, the Mesopotamian gods finally began to lose their power. In 525 BC the Persians also occupied Egypt. Since the pharaoh Akhenaten had tried to bring about religious reform back in 1367 BC, the country had never quite recovered its harmony or strength, and its glorious pantheon of gods was becoming increasingly threatened by outside beliefs.

Monotheism, as preached by both the Israelites and the Zoroastrians, was thus beginning to threaten the vast and dramatic array of gods and goddesses until then prevalent across West Asia, and the region was to see yet more turmoil. Over the following centuries it was overrun by the Greeks and Romans. However, Cybele, the great mother goddess of Asia Minor, Isis, the great mother goddess of Egypt, and Mithra, originally an ancient Iranian sun god, all arrived in Rome. There they became the focus of mystery cults, which flourished in the early centuries of the Christian era. When many of the old gods of West Asia were losing their power, these ancient deities were believed to renew the spirit and put their devotees in touch with the divine.

Monotheism eventually triumphed in West Asia. By the time the prophet Muhammad was born, around AD 570, Judaism and later Christianity had already spread throughout the region, and had also encroached on the Arabian peninsula. With the arrival of the strictly monotheistic Islam, the days of the old gods were numbered.

Ancient Mesopotamia

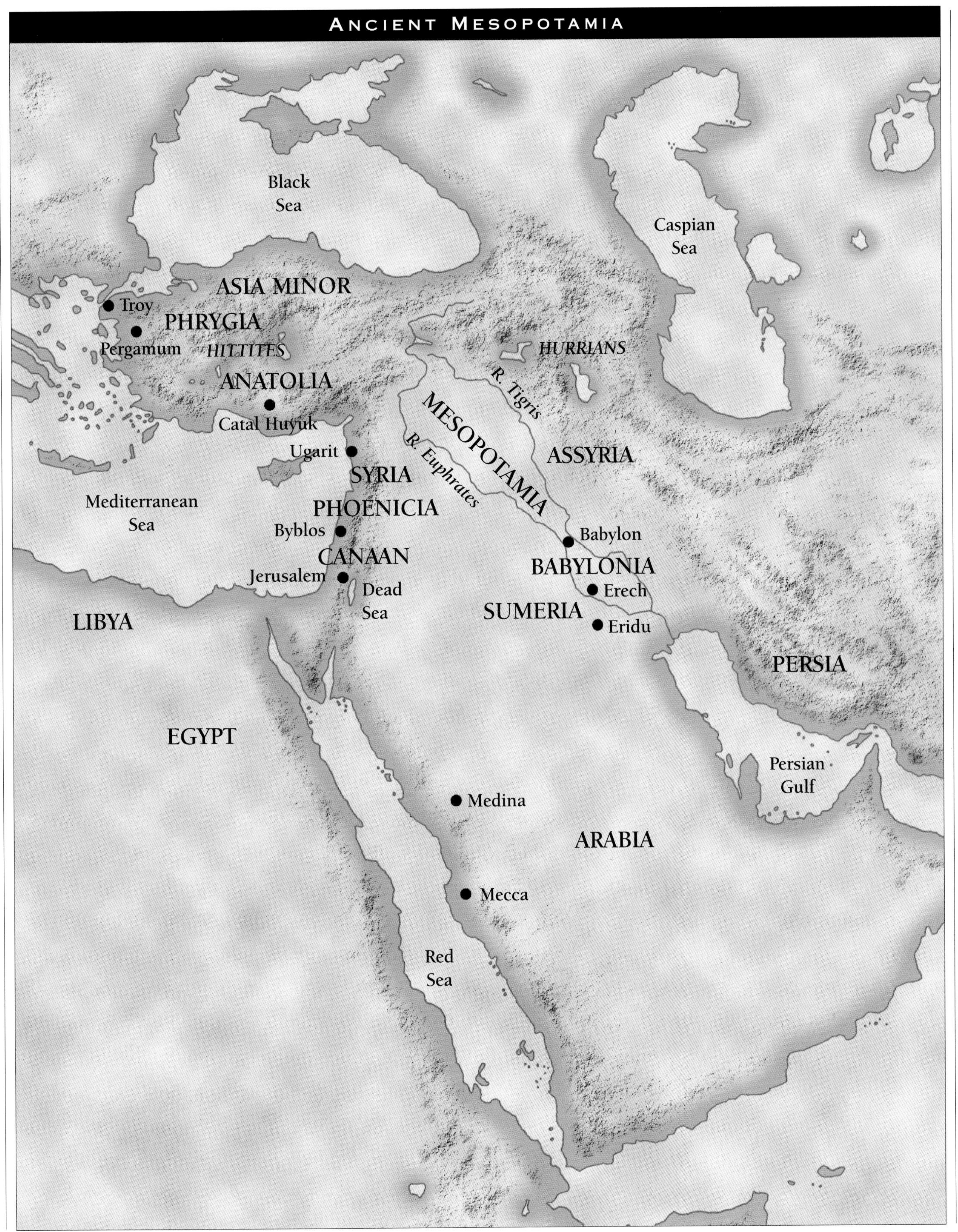

A

ABRAHAM, whose name means "Father of a Multitude", is a major character in the Old Testament, and is referred to in the earliest sources simply as "the Hebrew". The founder of the Hebrew people, he was the first patriarch, the husband of Sarah and the father of Isaac. He lived around 2000–1800 BC and was a devout believer of and subservient to God, representing an ideal for Hebrews to emulate. In Islam, Abraham, or Ibrahim, is known as the "Friend of God". He is regarded as the propagator of the original pure monotheism, the "religion of Abraham", which was restored and perfected by the Prophet Muhammad. Abraham is also said to have rebuilt the *KA'ABA*, the sacred shrine at Mecca, after it had been destroyed by the flood.

ABRAHAM (below), the father of the Israelite tribes, prepares to sacrifice his son, Isaac. (STAINED GLASS, ENGLAND.)

ABRAHAM (above) is known in Islam as Ibrahim, the "Friend of God". His son, Isaac, bears wood for the fire on which he is to be sacrificed. (19TH CENTURY ENGRAVING.)

ABZU see *APSU*.

ADAD was the Akkadian-Babylonian god of the wind, rain and thunder. He was usually said to be the son of *ANU*, and he was one of the deities who inflicted a deluge on humanity. However, he also brought helpful winds and rain and caused the annual flooding of the rivers, thereby bringing fertility to the land. As a result, Adad was often referred to as "Lord of Abundance". He could also see into the future. Adad was often represented standing on a bull and holding thunderbolts or lightning flashes in each hand.

ADAD (right), stands on the back of a bull, holding a bundle of thunderbolts in his hand. He is the Akkadian-Babylonian god of wind and rain. (NEO-ASSYRIAN BASALT RELIEF ON A STELE, 8TH CENTURY BC.)

ADAM, according to the Old Testament story, was the first man. God made him from dust and gave him a beautiful garden in which to live. Everything in the garden belonged to Adam, except for the fruit of one tree. Together with his consort *EVE*, Adam ate the forbidden fruit. As a result, the couple immediately lost their innocence and incurred the wrath of God. They were thrown out of the garden and had to work to survive.

According to the Jewish mystical system known as the Kabbalah, Adam both symbolized and embraced cosmic perfection. With Adam's fall, the material world was created and the light of his divine nature was broken up into countless minute sparks. These sparks are the lights that illuminate human souls. At the end of time, they will be reunited into perfection once more. (See also *SERPENTS AND DRAGONS*)

ADAPA, a wise man of Babylonian mythology, was created by the great god *EA* in order to be his priest in the holy city of Eridu and to rule over the people. Ea gave Adapa numerous good qualities, including wisdom and prudence, but did not make him immortal. Adapa spent much of his time fishing in the waters of the Persian Gulf.

One day, the south wind blew so strongly that it overturned his boat, sending him plunging into the depths. Adapa was furious and cursed the wind, causing it to cease blowing. Hearing what had happened, the supreme god *ANU* grew troubled that a mere mortal should have so much power. He summoned Adapa to his court and planned to send him to the land of the dead by giving him the food of death.

Ea, however, heard of Anu's plot and warned Adapa to accept no food or drink from the supreme god. Ea also told Adapa how to placate both Anu and the deities who lived with him. Adapa followed

ADAM and EVE were tempted by the serpent to eat the forbidden fruit. God banished them from the garden, and they had to work. (SPANISH SCHOOL, 12TH CENTURY.)

Ea's advice so punctiliously that Anu, rather than offering the food of death, offered him the food of life. However, Adapa remembered Ea's warning and refused the food, thereby losing his chance of becoming immortal.

Adapa, who was also credited with having invented speech, laid the foundations of civilized life.

ADONIS was a Phoenician deity who was later assimilated into the Greek pantheon. His name comes from the Semitic word *adoni*, meaning "My Lord, My Master". His worship was prevalent throughout Phoenicia, but it was most fervent in the city of Byblos, where his greatest temple stood.

Adonis symbolizes vegetation scorched by the heat of the summer sunshine. According to Greek legend, he was born from a myrtle or myrrh tree. His mother, Myrrha, had been changed into the tree by the gods who had sought to protect her from the wrath of her father, the king. Unbeknown to the king, Myrrha had seduced him and had conceived a child. Soon after Adonis was born, Aphrodite, the goddess of love, discovered the young deity. She hid him in a chest which she gave for safekeeping to Persephone, the goddess of the underworld. However, Persephone opened the chest and was so struck with the beauty of the child that she decided to keep him. Aphrodite appealed to Zeus, who decided that Adonis should spend a third of each year with himself, a third with Persephone and a third with the goddess of love.

When Adonis grew up, Aphrodite fell passionately in love with him. Out hunting one day, the god was killed by a boar. It is at this point, in some versions of the myth, that Aphrodite, mad with grief, managed to secure his release from the underworld for half of each year. In Byblos, it was said that he returned from the dead when the river ran red with soil brought down from the hills by rain.

The Adonia, the annual festivals that commemorated the god's death, were beautiful and opulent affairs in which the Phoenician women would ceaselessly repeat the word *adoni*. When the Greek writer Lucian visited Byblos in the second century AD he recorded the local belief that Adonis had been killed in a gorge. He also wrote that at the time of the god's return to the land of the living, pots of plants outside each house were tended to quickly blossom and wither, symbolizing Adonis's life and death. (See also *DYING AND RISING GODS*)

AGDISTIS was a hermaphrodite monster of Phrygian mythology. According to one tradition, he was born when some semen dropped from the great god Zeus on to Mount Ida, next to where the Great Mother *CYBELE* lay asleep.

The gods made Agdistis drunk by adding wine to the pool in which he bathed. The monster fell asleep, whereupon the gods tied his genitals to a tree. When he awoke and moved, he castrated himself and an almond or pomegranate tree grew from his sexual organs. One day Nana, the daughter of the river god gathered the fruit into her lap. One of the pieces of fruit disappeared, and the young woman discovered that she was pregnant. In due course, the nymph gave birth to *ATTIS*.

In one story, the adult Attis fell in love with a beautiful maiden. On the day of their wedding, Agdistis appeared at the feast in the form of the goddess Cybele. The maiden was furious to see Attis professing love to another woman and caused havoc. As a result, the bride died of self-inflicted wounds and Attis, mad with grief, castrated himself beneath a pine tree.

ADONIS was killed and consigned to the underworld, but Aphrodite secured his release for half of each year, symbolizing the renewal of vegetation. (VENUS AND ADONIS BY ANTONIO CANOVA, MARBLE 1794.)

AGLIBOL with Baal and the sun god Yarhibol, other members of the heavenly pantheon. (STONE, PALMYRA, 1ST CENTURY AD.)

AGLIBOL was a moon god from Palmyra in northern Arabia. He was depicted with a sickle moon either on his forehead or on his shoulders. His name is sometimes said to mean "Bull of Bol", suggesting that the sickle was originally intended to represent bull's horns.

AHAT, or Aqhat, according to Phoenician mythology, was the son of a local ruler, Daniel. Daniel had no children, but, prompted by the rain and fertility god *BAAL*, the supreme god *EL* gave him a son. When Ahat grew up, the divine craftsman *KOTHAR* gave him a splendid bow made from twisted horns. The goddess *ANAT* longed to possess the weapon and tried to persuade Ahat to give it to her. When Ahat refused, the goddess promised him immortality but Ahat replied that humankind's destiny was to die. Anat then sent Yatpan, her attendant, to kill Ahat. Though Yatpan killed the hero, the bow was lost in the struggle. In punishment, Baal stopped the rains falling, and so the crops failed.

Daniel mourned his son's death for seven years. Although the end of the myth is lost, it is believed that Ahat was resurrected and fertility was restored to the land. Ahat thus probably came to be regarded as a dying and rising god.

AHRIMAN see *ANGRA MAINYU*.

AHURA MAZDA, or Ohrmazd, was the supreme god and "Wise Lord" of ancient Iran. He was regarded as the all-encompassing sky. Until the time of the great religious reformer *ZOROASTER*, who lived around 1200 BC, the Iranians worshipped numerous gods. Zoroaster denounced the old gods and Ahura Mazda came to be regarded as the one true creator god who was constantly beleaguered by *ANGRA MAINYU*, or Ahriman, the principle of darkness.

After creating the *AMESA SPENTAS* and *YAZATAS*, Ahura Mazda made people, cattle, fire, earth, sky, water and plants. Zoroaster taught that Ahura Mazda made light visible, so the god was often depicted as the sun. Sometimes, however, the sun and moon are described as Ahura Mazda's eyes. Using the purifying quality of fire, Ahura Mazda was able to distinguish good from evil, and he bestowed fire, the symbol of truth, on his followers.

Under the Achaemenians, who ruled from 558 to 330 BC, Ahura Mazda was adopted as the patron of the royal house and was represented as a pair of vast wings. In the centuries following Zoroaster, a movement known as Zurvanism developed. Both Ahura Mazda and Angra Mainyu came to be regarded as descendants of *ZURVAN AKARANA*, or "Infinite Time". This helped to circumvent the problem of Ahura Mazda having created evil or, at least, having allowed it to exist. At the end of time, it was said that, "Ohrmazd will reign and will do everything according to his pleasure." (See also *ANGELS AND DJINN*)

AHURA MAZDA was the supreme god of ancient Iran, worshipped by Zoroaster and his followers. The world is the stage for the battle between Ahura Mazda and Angra Mainyu, the spirit of darkness; a battle in which Ahura Mazda will finally prevail. (ASSYRIAN RELIEF, 9TH CENTURY BC.)

AL-LAT, or Allat, was a pre-Islamic goddess of central and northern Arabia. Her following was particularly pronounced at Ta'if near Mecca, where she was worshipped in the form of a block of white granite. Women in particular would circle the stone in Al-Lat's honour, perhaps because she was regarded as a type of mother goddess. Al-Lat represented the earth and was said to be one of the three daughters of *ALLAH*, the supreme god. She is also believed to have been associated with the sun, moon or the planet Venus.

AL-UZZA, or El-'Ozza, was an Arabian goddess of pre-Islamic times who was regarded by the Bedouin tribes of central Arabia as the youngest daughter of *ALLAH*, the supreme deity. She was worshipped in the form of a black stone, on the surface of which lay a mark or indentation called the "Impression of Aphrodite". Al-Uzza was said to live in a tree and was identified with the morning star. She formed the centre of a sacrificial cult, and archaeologists have discovered recent evidence that human sacrifice was offered to her.

The tribe to which the prophet Muhammad belonged showed particular reverence for the goddess. The prophet himself was said to have taken the sacred Black Stone of Islam and placed it in the *KA'ABA*, the shrine in Mecca, Islam's holiest city. The cult of Al-Uzza was served by priestesses and, even after the arrival of Islam, the Ka'aba's guardians still continued to be called "Sons of the Old Woman".

According to the Qur'an, the sacred book of Islam, Al-Uzza, together with Arabia's other principal goddesses, *AL-LAT* and *MANAT*, "are not names which ye have named, ye and your fathers, for which Allah hath revealed no warrant. They follow but a guess and that which they themselves desire." In northern Arabia, Al-Uzza was known as Han-Uzzai.

ALALU, according to the Hittites, was the first king of heaven who came from south of the Black Sea. One myth tells how Alalu sat upon his throne and "the mighty *ANU*, the first among the gods, stood before him, bowed down at his feet and handed him the cup to drink". After nine years, Alalu was deposed by Anu and fled to the earth – possibly the underworld. Anu was in turn dethroned by *KUMARBI*, who was overthrown by his son *TESHUB*, the weather god.

ALLAH was the supreme, though not sole, deity in Arabia before the arrival of Islam. He lived, together with other deities, in the heavens and was said to have created the earth and bestowed water on it. In pre-Islamic times, animism was prevalent throughout Arabia: trees and springs were worshipped and certain stones were believed to contain sacred power. However, the prophet Muhammad (c. AD 570–632) adopted Allah as the one true god, to whom total submission was due, and proclaimed it blasphemous to worship any other deity. According to the Qur'an, polytheism is the greatest sin.

Allah is said to be supreme and transcendent; he is regarded as the creator of all life, the controller of all nature, the bestower of bounty and the judge of humankind in the last days. Although Allah can be terrifying, he is none the less righteous, just and merciful.

Because Allah is believed to be completely different from everything he has created, it is forbidden for anyone to attempt to portray him. In the Qur'an, he is given 99 names. The hundredth and greatest name is known to no mortal.

ALLAT see *AL-LAT.*

THE AMESA SPENTAS, or the Amesha Spentas, are the holy immortals of Zoroastrianism. They probably belonged to the pantheon of ancient Iranian gods which existed before *ZOROASTER*'s time. It is possible that, although the religious reformer denounced the old gods, he assimilated the Amesa Spentas into his teachings as aspects of *AHURA MAZDA*, the one and only true spirit set in opposition to *ANGRA MAINYU*, the spirit of evil.

The Amesa Spentas were said to serve Ahura Mazda, the "Supreme Lord". Otherwise known as Amshaspends or Ameshas Spenta, each of them ruled over a particular aspect of reality, such as a category of beings or a part of the year. *VOHU MANO* reigned over useful animals, including cattle. Asha-Vahishta looked after fire; Khshathra-Vairya moved the sun and heavens and ruled over metals; *SPENTA ARMAITI* ruled over the earth; Haurvatat governed the waters; and Ameretat governed plant life. Spenta Mainyu, who ruled over humanity, is either numbered among the Amesa Spentas or identified as Ahura Mazda himself.

AMON, wearing his plumed headdress, protects the young pharaoh, Tutankhamun, who reinstated him at the head of the Egyptian pantheon. (1350 BC.)

AMESHA SPENTAS see *AMESA SPENTAS.*

AMON, the Egyptian "King of the Gods", first came to prominence as the god of Thebes in Upper Egypt, where he was worshipped as a fertility deity. He grew in importance to become the god who looked after the most splendid of the *PHAROAHS.* Amon was often depicted wearing a headdress surmounted by two plumes, or sometimes with the head of a ram.

By the 18th dynasty, in the second millennium BC, Amon had become the supreme god of the whole of Egypt and was identified with the sun god as Amon-Ra, although *RA* continued to have his own separate following. The pharaohs Thuthmosis III and Amenhotep III described themselves as "Sons of Amon" and claimed that the god brought them victory over their enemies.

During the reign of Amenhotep's son, Akhenaten, worship of Amon was forbidden while *ATEN* was declared the true god. However, in 1361 BC, the succeeding pharaoh reinstated Amon and called himself Tutankhamun or "Living Image of Amon". Worship of Amon eventually spread beyond Egypt into Ethiopia and Libya. Amon's wife was Mut, whose son was called Khons.

AN see *ANU.*

ANAHITA, the Iranian goddess of water and fertility, was widely worshipped in Achaemenian times (558–330 BC) and was often associated with the great god *MITHRA.* In the fourth century BC, the ruler Artaxerxes II ordered that images of Anahita should be erected in all the principal cities of the empire. Her following later spread throughout Asia Minor and the West.

Anahita assisted *SPENTA ARMAITI* and was associated with *HAOMA*, the god who conferred immortality. Occasionally identified with the planet Venus, she is said to have originated from *ISHTAR*, the Babylonian fertility deity who is associated with the same planet. Her name means "Immaculate".

Anahita was often represented dressed in gleaming gold with a crown and jewels. The dove and peacock were her sacred creatures, and sacred prostitution formed part of her cult.

ANAHITA, the Iranian patroness of women and fertility, and an aspect of the "Great Goddess", crowns the ruler Narses. (BAS-RELIEF, LATE 3RD CENTURY BC.)

***ANGRA MAINYU** was the Zoroastrian principle of darkness, the antagonist of Ahura Mazda. He tried to thwart Ahura Mazda's plans to create an earthly paradise by sowing doubt and discord in the world, and even sought to destroy humanity.* (GOLD MEDALLION FROM THE OXUS TREASURE, C. 5TH CENTURY BC.)

ANAT, or Anath, was a goddess of the Canaanites and Phoenicians, and was the sister, and sometimes the consort, of *BAAL*. Her name is usually translated as "Providence" or "Precaution".

The goddess had a reputation for violence. According to one myth, she slaughtered Baal's worshippers and only ceased her attack when Baal promised to reveal the secret of lightning to her. Anat later asked the supreme god, *EL*, to give Baal a house, but it was the great mother goddess *ASTARTE* who eventually persuaded him to do so. After moving into the splendid palace, Baal boasted that he was now omnipotent and challenged *MOT*, the god of death, to a contest. However, it was Anat who eventually destroyed Mot, by killing, thrashing and burning him.

Anat was later assimilated into the Egyptian pantheon, where she was regarded as a goddess of war and a daughter of the sun god *RA*. The Egyptians usually depicted her carrying a spear, axe and shield, and wearing a tall crown surmounted by two ostrich feathers.

ANATH see *ANAT*.

ANBAY was a pre-Islamic god of southern Arabia who was known as the "Lord of Justice". Famed for his oracle, he spoke on behalf of the moon god, Amm, who ranked above him in the pantheon.

ANGRA MAINYU, or Ahriman, was the principle of darkness in ancient Iranian mythology. He was set in opposition to *AHURA MAZDA*, the principle of goodness and truth. Ahura Mazda planned to make Iran into an earthly paradise, but Angra Mainyu interfered, creating harsh weather conditions, smoke, darkness, sickness, disease and all manner of other evils. His was a world of death in which summer lasted for only two months whereas winter lasted for ten. Where people had faith, Angra Mainyu sowed the seeds of doubt, and where there were riches, he created laziness and poverty. Such was the extent of his evil-doing that he was sometimes accused of having killed *GEUSH URVAN*, the primeval bull. Angra Mainyu's symbol was the snake.

In later times, during the reign of the Sassanian kings (AD 226–652), the idea of *ZURVAN AKARANA*, or "Infinite Time" was developed. Both Angra Mainyu and Ahura Mazda were regarded as the offspring of Zurvan Akarana, who was said to have promised authority to the firstborn. As a result, Angra Mainyu tore his way out of the womb before his brother and held the reins of power for several thousand years. However, Zoroastrians believe that there will come a day when Ahura Mazda will succeed to power and Angra Mainyu will be destroyed, sinking into eternal darkness.

***ANAT**, the sister and sometimes the consort of Baal, was a Phoenician goddess with a reputation for violence. She later became a part of the Egyptian pantheon as a goddess of war.* (ASSYRIAN SEAL.)

ANSHAR was the male principle in Babylonian mythology. In the Babylonian epic *Enuma Elish* ("When on High"), he and Kishar, the female principle, are described as the second pair of deities, following Lahmu and Lahamu, the first divine couple. Both these couples originated when *APSU*, the primeval sweet water, mingled with *TIAMAT*, the primeval salt water. It is generally believed that the name Anshar means "Horizon of Heaven" and that the god represented the celestial world; Kishar, on the other hand, is thought to have been a terrestrial deity whose name means "Horizon of Earth".

Anshar and Kishar begat *ANU*, the sky god, and *EA*, the god of fresh water and wisdom. They also

ANSHAR *was a primordial deity of Babylonian mythology who represented the male principle. He was eventually equated with Ashur, a warrior god who ensured the victories of the Assyrians.*

begat the Igigi, the deities who inhabited the sky, and the Anunnake, the gods who lived on earth and in the underworld. From the ninth century BC onwards, Assur or Ashur, the national god of Assyria, was equated with Anshar.

ANU was the son of *ANSHAR* and Kishar, the male and female principles of Babylonian mythology. He formed one of a triad of creator gods which also included *EA*, the god of sweet and fertilizing waters, and *ENLIL* or Bel, lord of the wind.

The god of the sky, Anu was the supreme deity who reigned over the heavens. He was known as the father of the gods and had the power to judge those who committed misdeeds after summoning them before his throne, in front of which were placed the sceptre, the diadem, the crown and the staff of command. The stars were Anu's soldiers, whom he had created in order to destroy the wicked. He never descended to earth and had little to do with human beings. Rather, he stayed in the heavens and busied himself with the fate of the universe. In Sumerian mythology, Anu was known as An. He was sometimes represented by a crown on a throne.

Anu was introduced into the Hittite pantheon from Mesopotamia by way of the Hurrians. In the story of the divine kingship, *ALALU*, the king of heaven, was served by Anu, the first among the gods. Alalu reigned for nine years until Anu deposed him. After another nine years, Anu's minister *KUMARBI* seized the throne. Anu immediately flew up into the sky, but Kumarbi seized him by the foot and bit off his penis. However, Anu's semen impregnated Kumarbi and gave rise to three mighty gods, who are believed to be different aspects of the weather god, *TESHUB*.

ANUBIS was originally said to be the fourth son of the Egyptian sun god, *RA*. However, in later times, he came to be regarded as the child of the vegetation god, *OSIRIS*, and *NEPHTHYS*, the sister of *ISIS*. When Anubis was born, Nephthys hid the child in the marshes of the Nile delta in order to protect him from her consort *SETH*. The infant god was discovered there by Isis, the mother goddess, who subsequently brought him up.

When Osiris left Egypt in order to spread his teachings throughout the world, Anubis accompanied him on his travels. Later, when Osiris was killed by Seth, Anubis organized his burial, binding him with cloth and thereby creating the first mummy. As a result, Anubis came to be regarded as the inventor of funeral rites and was referred to as "Lord of the Mummy Wrappings". The god also assisted in the judgment of the dead and guided the honest dead towards the throne of Osiris. Anubis was depicted either as a jackal or as a man with the head of a jackal. (See also *GATEWAYS TO THE GODS; UNDERWORLDS*)

APEP was the eternal enemy of *RA*, the supreme god of the Egyptian pantheon. A terrifying serpent, Apep symbolized chaos and destruction. Each day, as the sun god, Ra, crossed the sky in his boat, Apep would viciously attack the vessel and occasionally, during a total eclipse, he was believed to have swallowed it whole.

Despite his ferocity, Apep never gained total victory over his enemy. However, at the same time, he himself was never believed to have been finally and completely conquered. However, the reddening of the sky at dusk was said to demonstrate that the serpent had been overcome by the sun's strength. According to one story, Apep was created when *NEITH*, the "Great Mother" associated with war and hunting, spat into *NUN*, the primal watery chaos. In later times, Apep came to be identified with *SETH*. He is often known by the Greek name of Apophis. (See also *SERPENTS AND DRAGONS*)

ANU, *Babylonian god of the sky, and Enlil, god of the earth, are symbolized by horned crowns on stylized thrones.* (DETAIL OF BABYLONIAN BOUNDARY STONE, C. 1120 BC.)

APEP *was the Egyptian symbol of chaos, a giant snake who occupied the Duat or underworld. The sun god, Ra, represented here as a falcon, battled daily with the snake.* (SMALL LIMESTONE PYRAMID, 19TH DYNASTY.)

SACRED ANIMALS

SURROUNDED BY A HOSTILE, DESERT landscape, people and animals alike depended on the great rivers that provided water and fertile soil. The ancient Egyptians were forcefully reminded of their close kinship with the animal world, as they had to share the fertile flood plain of the Nile with dangerous, powerful creatures such as lions, crocodiles, hippopotamuses and snakes. The association of these animals with the life-giving force of the river, and the fear and respect they commanded, gave rise to animal cults, which reached their peak during the Late and Ptolemaic Periods from 664–30 BC. Devotees did not worship the animals themselves but associated their qualities with a particular deity, who was portrayed in animal form. At shrines, offerings consisted of small animal figurines or mummified creatures. The temple officials turned this into a profitable business, breeding huge numbers of animals for mummification and sale to worshippers. The catacombs at North Saqqara, for instance, are thought to hold approximately four million mummified ibis.

THE COBRA *(left), or uraeus, rearing defensively, was a symbol that was both protective and potentially dangerous. The snake accompanied the deceased on his or her journey to the underworld in the sacred boat, and similar images were also placed protectively around shrines. A rearing female cobra formed part of the pharaoh's regalia, worn on the forehead, where it symbolically guarded both the pharaoh and the country. The Eye of Horus, a god often depicted with the head of a falcon, was another guarantee of protection in the afterlife.* (DETAIL FROM A BOOK OF THE DEAD, 21ST DYNASTY, HERUBEN PAPYRUS, C. 1000 BC.)

BASTET *(above) was the daughter (or sometimes sister and consort) of the Egyptian sun god, Ra. She was originally a fierce and vengeful goddess, portrayed as a lioness, but from around 1000 BC she became more peaceable and took on the shape of a cat. She was a goddess of fertility and love, and protected her devotees against disease and evil spirits. Her principal place of worship was at Bubastis, where thousands of mummified cats were dedicated to her. In the name of the goddess, cats were loved and respected by the Egyptians, to the extent that the killing of a cat was an offence punishable by death.* (EGYPTIAN BRONZE, 6TH CENTURY BC.)

RA-HERARHTY *(below), god of the rising sun, symbolized by his falcon wings and sun-disc headdress, is carved on the polished granite capstone of the pyramid of Amenemhet III. Coiled around the sun disc is the symbol of the cobra goddess Wadjet, representing the pharaoh's royal authority and power over the life and death of his people. The carvings below include a bee and an ibis, representing Thoth, the wise counsellor of the gods and the judge of the dead.* (PYRAMIDION, C. 1818–1772 BC.)

APIS *(above), the sacred bull, was worshipped as a living animal believed to be the reincarnation of the god Ptah at his temple at Memphis. Mythical bulls, symbols of strength and potency, occurred in many belief systems from the earliest times. Hathor, the Egyptian goddess of maternal and sexual love, took the form of a cow (above right) who nourished humankind with her milk. She was the protector of women, helping them to conceive and give birth, and was regarded as the mother of the pharaohs.* (EGYPTIAN BRONZE, 7TH–6TH CENTURY BC.)

DRAGONS *(right) symbolized Marduk, the tutelary god of the fabled city of Babylon. These composite creatures had the head and tail of a serpent, the body and forelegs of a lion and the hind legs of a falcon, and were emblazoned on the monumental Ishtar Gate at the climax of the ceremonial route through the city. The processional way was lined with rows of lions sacred to Ishtar, the goddess of love and fertility.* (GLAZED BRICK RELIEF, 6TH CENTURY BC.)

KHNUM *(above), the ram-headed god, took mud from the life-giving Nile and used it to create humanity on his potter's wheel. He was also responsible for supervising the annual flooding of the river. At his sanctuary near its mythical source, offerings of mummified rams decorated with gold leaf were buried in stone tombs. His consort was Satis, who was depicted pouring water on to the dry earth.*

SEBEK *(left), the crocodile god, represented the skill and strength of the pharaoh in battle. The qualities he needed to display could be seen in the crocodiles of the Nile, which inspired awe with their speed and agility in catching their prey and the fearsome strength of their jaws. The mortuary goddess Serket took the form of a scorpion, though she was sometimes depicted in human form with a scorpion headdress. Her role was to guard the canopic jars containing the vital organs of the dead, and to protect the throne of the pharaoh.* (EGYPTIAN BRONZES, 6TH CENTURY BC.)

APIS, or Hapi, was the most renowned of Egypt's sacred animals. He was worshipped at Memphis, where his temple lay opposite that of the great creator god *PTAH*. Apis, in the form of a real black bull, was believed to be the reincarnation or "glorious soul" of Ptah, who was said to have inseminated a virgin cow in the form of fire, and to have been born again as a black bull.

Each day, Apis was let loose in the courtyard attached to his temple, and the priests would use his movements as a means for divining the future. Usually, the Apis bull was allowed to die of old age, but he was drowned in a fountain if he reached the age of 25. The bull was twice assassinated by the Persians.

Ptah's priests were said to be able to recognize the next holy bull by discovering certain markings on the creature's body, including a white triangle on his forehead and a crescent moon on his right side. The extent of the reverence with which the sacred bulls were regarded can be gauged by the fact that their mummified bodies were buried with great ceremony in huge underground burial chambers. (See also *SACRED ANIMALS*)

APSU, in Mesopotamian mythology, was the watery abyss or primordial, fresh-water ocean, which existed at the beginning of time and which circled and supported the earth. Apsu spread happiness and abundance over the earth and was the source of knowledge and wisdom. Eventually, the waters of Apsu merged with those of *TIAMAT*, the primordial, salt-water ocean, and gave rise to Mummu, the waves, and the primal couple, Lahmu and Lahamu. *ANSHAR* and Kishar, the next divine couple to arise from the waves, were the male and female principles who bore the great gods *ANU* and *EA* as well as the other divinities who peopled the sky, the earth and the underworld.

In time, Apsu became troubled by the gods and plotted with Tiamat to destroy them. Tiamat was at first unwilling to take part in the battle, but, when Apsu was slain by the god Ea, she was prompted to seek revenge. Ea's son, the great god *MARDUK*, who had been born in the waters of Apsu, was chosen to challenge Tiamat. The bloody battle that ensued gave rise to the creation of the world and the sky. According to one tradition in Sumerian mythology, the goddess Nammu formed the first men from clay dug out of the waters of Apsu. In the epic of *GILGAMESH*, the hero descended into the waters of Apsu to find the plant of eternal life.

AQHAT see *AHAT*.

ARINNA was the name of a Hittite town. Its chief goddess was known as the "Sun of Arinna", or Ariniddu. The "Queen of Heaven and Earth", the goddess Arinna became the supreme patroness of the Hittite kingdom, protecting it from enemies and helping out in time of war. Her symbol was the sun disc. Arinna was identified with the Hurrian goddess *HEPAT*; both deities were said to be married to the weather god *TESHUB*.

The sun goddess Arinna was sometimes addressed as a masculine deity, the "Inspired Lord of Justice". The sun god was also an important figure in Hittite mythology, although his actual name has been lost. He was regarded as the king of the gods and a dispenser of truth and justice. In one prayer he was addressed as "Sun god of heaven, my lord, shepherd of mankind! Thou risest, O sun-god of heaven, from the sea and goest up to heaven. O sun-god of heaven, my lord, daily thou sittest in judgment upon man, dog, pig, and the wild beasts of the field." There was also a sun god of the water and a sun god of the underworld, through which the sun was believed to travel during the night.

ASTARTE was the principal goddess of the Phoenicians and the Canaanites. This figurine shows her, perhaps, as a fertility deity. She was associated with love and procreation. (CERAMIC FIGURINE, GATH, 8TH–7TH CENTURIES BC.)

ARSU see *RUDA*.

ASHERAT; ASHTORETH see *ASTARTE*

ASHUR see *ANSHAR*.

ASTARTE was the principal goddess of the Phoenicians and Canaanites. She was incorporated into Egyptian mythology as a daughter either of the sun god *RA*, or of *PTAH*, and she was often depicted naked, bearing weapons and riding a horse.

According to one story from Egyptian mythology, Ptah and the other great gods were forced to pay tributes to the sea. Gifts of silver, gold and precious stones were brought to the seashore, but the sea wanted more. The gods then told Astarte to take more offerings to the sea. When she arrived at the shore, Astarte mocked the sea, who responded by insisting that he have Astarte herself as a gift. The great gods covered Astarte with jewels and sent her back to the shore, but this time *SETH* accompanied her in order to fight the sea. Although the end of the story is missing, it is usually presumed that Seth fought the sea, and saved Astarte.

The name Astarte is sometimes translated as "Womb", or "That Which Issues from the Womb",

ATEN, the sun god, is symbolized by a sun disc whose rays fall on the pharaoh Akhenaten and queen Nefertiti as they perform a sacrifice to him. (FLAT RELIEF, AMARNA, C. 1350 BC.)

suggesting that the goddess was primarily a fertility deity. Astarte was also associated with love and procreation, and her cult included the practice of temple prostitution among her devotees.

In the Old Testament of the Bible, she appears as Ashtoreth, and *SOLOMON* had a temple built in her honour near Jerusalem. Indeed, the Israelites sometimes revered the goddess as the queen of heaven and wife of *YAHWEH*.

The goddess Asherat, or Ashera-of-the-Sea, tends to be viewed as identical with Astarte. She was called "Mother of the Gods" and was said to have had 70 children. According to texts dating from the 14th century BC, the supreme god *EL* took two women, generally believed to be Asherat and *ANAT*, as his consorts, and by them fathered *SHACHAR* and Shalim, "Dawn" and "Dusk", and many other deities.

It is still not certain whether Anat and Astarte were two separate goddesses or different aspects of the same goddess. Anat may have been the dark aspect of the goddess and Astarte the light, heavenly aspect. In one text, they are both described as the daughters of *NEITH*, an Egyptian mother goddess. Moreover, they were both known as "Lady of Heaven". Aphrodite is widely believed to have developed from Astarte.

ATAR, or "Fire", was said to be the son of the Iranian deity *AHURA MAZDA*, although fire worship probably existed long before the naming of the supreme being. According to the teachings of Zoroastrianism, fire was one of Ahura Mazda's seven creations. Atar was said to bring men comfort and wisdom, and to defend the world from evil. It represented the light of truth and the divine spark in humankind, which signified the presence of the supreme god.

The monstrous dragon *AZHI DAHAKA* sought to extinguish the divine fire in a bloody battle, which took place across land, sea and air. Eventually, Atar caught the dragon and chained it to a mountain.

ATEN was a sun god who came to pre-eminence in the 14th century BC under Amenhotep IV, a *PHARAOH* of the 18th dynasty. He was regarded as none other than the sun god *RA* himself. Amenhotep IV built temples to Aten close to those of the supreme god *AMON* and, to the disgust of Amon's priests, piled Aten's temples high with gifts. Four years into his reign, the pharaoh pronounced that the religion of Aten was the only official faith and that the god was to be worshipped as the exclusive creator of humankind. Worship of all other gods – especially Amon – was forbidden.

In an attempt to spread the religion of Aten throughout the empire, Amon's temples were closed and his images defaced. The pharaoh changed his name from Amenhotep, meaning "Amon is Satisfied", to Akhenaten, "Glory of Aten" or "He Who is Devoted to Aten", and relocated his capital from Thebes to a city known today as el-Armana, which he had built specifically to glorify Aten.

Aten is always depicted as an enormous red disc, from which rays of light emanate. The rays, ending in hands, were believed to extend the beauty of Aten to the ruler. When Akhenaten died, Amon and the other gods were reinstated, and Aten's rays were sliced through to prevent his beauty reaching Akhenaten.

ATEN, the sun-disc, was worshipped by the pharoah Akhenaten as the embodiment of the supreme force of light, and, during his reign, worship of all the other deities of the Egyptian pantheon was forbidden. His successor, Tutankhamun (below) restored the old gods. (CARVED WOOD, 14TH CENTURY BC.)

ATTAR was worshipped in southern Arabia in pre-Islamic times. A god of war, he was often referred to as "He who is Bold in Battle". One of his symbols was the spear-point, and the antelope was his sacred animal. He had power over Venus, the morning star, and was believed to provide humankind with water.

ATTIS was the consort of *CYBELE*, the great mother goddess of Phrygia in Asia Minor. A vegetation god, he was sometimes known as Papas, or "Father". One of the oldest stories concerning the birth of Attis tells how the hermaphrodite *AGDISTIS* fell asleep, whereupon the gods tied its genitals to a tree. Agdistis awoke with a start, and the severed genitals fell to the ground. An almond tree grew up on the spot, and in due course Nana, the daughter of the river god, became pregnant by one of its fruits. The girl eventually gave birth to Attis. Other legends say that the god was a foundling or the son of a king.

The best-known story of Attis is that in which his desperate love for Cybele drove him insane, leading him to castrate himself under a pine tree. Flowers and trees grew up from his blood. Although he died, the god was reborn and united with Cybele.

The cult of Cybele spread to Greece and Rome, and with it, that of Attis. Cybele was said to have fallen in love with Attis, who was regarded as a handsome young shepherd. She chose him as her priest and imposed a vow of chastity upon him. However, Attis fell in love with a river nymph, so Cybele caused him to suffer a fit of madness, during which he mutilated himself. When the god recovered, he was about to kill himself when Cybele changed him into a fir tree. In another version of the story, Attis was gored to death by a boar sent by Zeus.

Each spring, at the end of March, a five-day festival was held in honour of Attis. The first day was one of mourning. The god, represented by a sacred fir tree taken from the grove near Cybele's temple, was bound with bandages, decorated with ribbons and flowers, and carried through the streets. On the second day, Cybele's priests performed frenzied dances, and on the third day they castrated themselves, sprinkling the altar and effigy of Attis with their blood. The fourth day was that on which the resurrection of Attis was celebrated. The fifth day was one of rest. A ritual marriage between Cybele and Attis formed part of the ceremony, with Cybele's high priest taking the role of the god.

The Romans generally represented Attis as a shepherd, usually holding a shepherd's crook and sometimes carrying a sheep on his shoulders. He plays a pipe and wears a pointed cap on his head. The rays of the sun, or ears of corn, protrude from the cap, symbolizing his function as a god of regeneration and rebirth. (See also *DYING AND RISING GODS*)

***ATTIS** was a vegetation god in Phrygia in Asia Minor. His death and rebirth symbolized the natural cycle. In a Roman legend, Attis was gored to death by a boar sent by Zeus.* (MARBLE BUST, IMPERIAL ROME.)

AZHI DAHAKA, the monstrous dragon of ancient Iranian mythology, was said to have had three heads, six eyes and three pairs of fangs. He was sometimes regarded as a mythical king of Babylon,

B

Iran's enemy, or as the enemy of *YIMA*, the great king. Originally, Azhi Dahaka was believed to kill cattle and men. One story tells how the hero *FERIDUN* cut the creature open with his sword and was horrified to find lizards and toads pouring out of its insides.

In time, Azhi Dahaka came to be seen as the embodiment of falsehood and the servant of *ANGRA MAINYU*, the principle of darkness. *ATAR*, the fire god, went into battle against the monster and harried him through land, sea and air before finally catching him and chaining him to a mountain.

It was believed that at the end of time Azhi Dahaka would succeed in breaking free from his chains and ravage the earth again. Eventually, the hero *KERESASPA* would kill the monster. (See also *SERPENTS AND DRAGONS*)

THE BA AND KA were believed by the ancient Egyptians to be the soul and spirit, or vital essence, of a dead person. The Ba hovered over the deceased and was usually depicted as a bird with a human head. The Ka was said to appear to the deceased in the form of a blue phoenix and was believed to return to the tomb, where it ate food left by relatives and priests. So deeply entrenched was this belief that menus were sometimes inscribed on the walls of tombs.

***BAAL** was the name given by many Canaanite tribes to their chief gods. In the Bible his name is used as a synonym for "false god, and sacrifice to him is there condemned".* (ILLUSTRATION FROM MYTHS OF BABYLONIA AND ASSYRIA BY LEWIS SPENCE.)

BAAL, meaning "Lord" or "Owner", was the name given by many Canaanite tribes to their chief god. When the Israelites entered the land of Canaan, they took up the word and used it to describe any alien god – it is as a general term for a "false god" that the name Baal is used in the Bible. The most renowned Baal of Canaanite mythology was the rain and fertility god associated with the storm god, Hadad. He lived on a mountain in the north of the region and was sometimes referred to as "Lord of the North".

One story tells how this Baal defeated *YAM*, the sea deity. Yam asked the supreme god *EL* to crown him king. El agreed but warned him that first of all he would have to defeat Baal. Learning of the forthcoming battle, Baal equipped himself with magic weapons made by the gods, and as a result, he succeeded in killing Yam and scattering his remains. Baal then proclaimed himself king, built a sumptuous dwelling place on Mount Saphon and took control of several cities.

After this victory, Baal became so proud that he decided to challenge *MOT*, the god of death. He forced Mot to live in the barren wastelands and barred him from all fertile regions. In response, Mot challenged Baal to come to his underground dwelling and eat mud, the food of the dead. Baal took up the challenge and died.

All the gods mourned Baal's death. His wife, the ferocious *ANAT*, descended to the underworld to retrieve his corpse. However, she was unable to revive Baal and so appealed to Mot for help. When Mot refused to come to her aid, Anat burst into a frenzy and slaughtered him, whereupon Baal returned to life. Baal is thus seen as a dying and rising god. He is often depicted wielding a thunderbolt, or a flash of lightning. (See also *DYING AND RISING GODS*)

***BAAL** was said to have a voice like thunder, and that he watered the earth through a hole in the floor of his palace. In the Greco-Roman period, Baal became assimilated in the Palestine region with Zeus and Jupiter.* (GILDED BRONZE, SYRIA, C. 14-15TH CENTURY)

BASAMUM was worshipped in southern Arabia in pre-Islamic times. His name may come from the Arabic word for a balsam bush, suggesting that he was a god of healing. One ancient text tells how the god cured two wild goats.

BASTET was the local goddess of Bubastis, or "House of Bastet", the capital of a province of Lower Egypt. She was usually regarded as the daughter of the sun god *RA*, although she was sometimes said to be his sister and consort. Later, she became the wife of the creator god *PTAH*. According to some accounts, it was Bastet, rather than *NEPHTHYS*, who was the mother of the jackal-headed god *ANUBIS*.

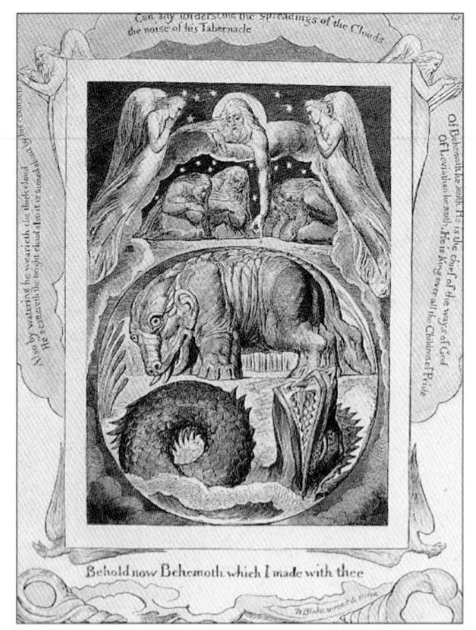

Originally a lioness goddess symbolizing both the warmth of the sun and the rage of the sun god's eye, from about 1000 BC Bastet came to be represented as a cat, or a cat-headed woman. However, in some stories she continued to possess the qualities of Sekhmet (see *HATHOR*), the lion-headed goddess. Usually a benevolent goddess, Bastet protected humanity from diseases and evil spirits. Most importantly, she was a goddess of fertility, sex and love, and enjoyed music and dancing. In the fourth century BC fertility festivals were held in her honour at her temple at Bubastis. Cats were venerated as Bastet's sacred animals, and their mummified bodies were buried at her sanctuaries. (See also *SACRED ANIMALS*)

BEHEMOTH was a terrifying monster of Hebrew mythology, the dry-land equivalent of the monstrous sea serpent *LEVIATHAN*. According to the Old Testament Book of Job, Behemoth was associated with the hippopotamus. The monster is sometimes said to have developed from *TIAMAT*, the fearsome Babylonian goddess.

***BASTET** (left) was usually portrayed as either a cat or a cat-headed woman. Originally a local goddess of Bubastis, her cult reached its height in the Late and Ptolemaic periods (c 660–30 BC) when animal cults became a major feature of popular religion. Bronze figurines and mummified cats were given as offerings.* (BRONZE, C. 5TH CENTURY BC.)

***BEHEMOTH** (left) and the sea monster Leviathan were used in the Book of Job as examples of the largest and strongest animals imaginable.* (HAND-TINTED ENGRAVING BY WILLIAM BLAKE, C. 1793.)

BEL see *ENLIL*.

BELILI see *TAMMUZ*.

***BORAK** (below) with a human head, the body of a winged horse and a peacock's tail, carries the prophet Muhammad to heaven, surrounded by winged peris.* (QAJAR LACQUERWORK, C. 1870.)

BORAK was a fabulous beast of Islamic mythology. Part human, part animal, the prophet Muhammad was said to have ridden on its back on the night of his ascension to heaven. The creature's name means "Lightning".

CORYBANTES see *KORYBANTES*.

CYBELE was the great mother and fertility goddess of Phrygian mythology. She probably originated as a mountain goddess and was sometimes referred to as the "Lady of Ida", a mountain in western Anatolia. She inhabited the wild and dangerous regions of the earth and ruled over the fiercest of wild animals. Cybele's origins have

CYBELE *(above) was the great mother of Phrygian mythology. She was associated with the earth and with a black stone – believed to be a meteorite – which was enshrined at Pergamum.* (2ND CENTURY AD.)

CYBELE*'s (right) priests, the Galli, celebrated rites in her honour which included music, convulsive dances, sacrifices and voluntary self-mutilation.* (ROMAN CARVING, 1ST–3RD CENTURY AD.)

sometimes been traced back as far as Çatal Höyük, a large Neolithic site in southern Anatolia. There, archaeologists unearthed a terracotta figure believed to be the mother goddess in the act of giving birth.

Cybele was primarily associated with the earth, and in particular with a black stone enshrined at Pergamum. Other cities where worship of the great mother was particularly fervent were Troy and Pessinus. In Phrygia, Cybele may originally have been known as *KUBABA*, or "Lady of the Cube". She is sometimes associated with an ancient goddess of that name who was worshipped at Carchemish in the Hittite empire. The shrines of both goddesses were situated in caves or near rocks.

The cult of Cybele eventually spread from Asia Minor to Greece. In the fifth century BC, a magnificent statue of the goddess flanked by lions was placed in her temple in Athens. In 204 BC, the black stone sacred to Cybele was brought from Phrygia to Rome. An oracle had foretold that if the "Phrygian Mother" were brought from Pergamum, she would aid the Romans in their war against the Carthaginians.

At Cybele's annual celebrations, held in spring, a chariot harnessed to lions would be drawn through the streets of Rome. According to the historian Lucretius (99–55 BC): "Borne from her sacred precinct in her car she drove a yoke of lions; her head they wreathed with a battlemented crown, because embattled on glorious heights she sustains towns; and dowered with this emblem even now the image of the divine mother is carried in awesome state through great countries. On her the diverse nations in the ancient rite of worship call as the Mother of Ida, and they give her Phrygian bands to bear her company, because from those lands first they say corn began to be produced throughout the whole world."

The public rites of Cybele were orgiastic and ecstatic. Her priests, the Galli or Galloi, would beat and castrate themselves in mad frenzies of passion, using whips decorated with knuckle bones. The celebrations were accompanied by the sacrifice of a bull or ram, during which the initiate, or high priest or priestess of Cybele, stood beneath a platform and was drenched in the blood of the sacrificed animal. Cybele's followers believed that her mysteries would lead them to be reborn after death in a new life.

Cybele's attributes are a mirror, a pomegranate and a key. The great myth attached to the goddess is that in which she takes vengeance on *ATTIS* for his infidelity and causes him to go mad, to castrate himself and to die. Eventually, however, she gives him back his life. According to another story, Cybele and Gordius, the king of Phrygia, had a son whom they called Midas. This was the Midas who, after wishing that everything he touched might turn to gold, found himself unable to eat or drink until the god Dionysus took pity on him.

D

THE DAEVAS were gods in the Indo-Aryan period of ancient Iran. The religious reformer *ZOROASTER* initially regarded them as unimportant, but he later came to view them as enemies of the true religion. Whereas the *DRUJS* were usually female, most daevas were male. *ANGRA MAINYU* or Ahriman, the principle of darkness, was said to rule over the demons. They specialized in trickery and deceit, and in putting obstacles in the way of all efforts to achieve good.

Many of the daevas stood in direct opposition to one of the *AMESA SPENTAS*, or "Holy Immortals". One demon would lie in wait on the Chinvat Bridge, which souls had to cross in order to reach *AHURA MAZDA*'s paradise. If the creature caught them, he would throw them into the depths below. Another demon attempted to persuade rulers to be tyrannical, and a third promoted pride and rebellion. Some demons brought about old age and senility, and others caused rage and devastation.

The great hero *RUSTEM* constantly fought demons. In one story, a demon called Arzang attacked, captured and blinded the king. Rustem finally managed to release the ruler and to restore his eyesight using the heart of a demon as medicine.

In Armenian mythology, the daevas were known as devs. The daevas continued to be revered as good spirits in India.

DAGAN, *the chief god of the Philistines, may have been a sea god and was represented with the tail of a fish.*

DANIEL *was preserved in the lions' den by an angel sent from Yahweh.* (MOSAIC, HOSIOS LOUKAS, GREECE, 11TH CENTURY.)

DAGAN was a god of corn and fertility who was worshipped in both Canaan and Mesopotamia. The deity was often regarded as the father of *BAAL*, the god of rain and fertility. Several kings of Akkad and Babylonia declared themselves to be "Sons of Dagan", including King Hammurabi and Ashurnasirpal II.

In the Old Testament, a god called Dagon is described as the chief god of the Philistines. Samson destroyed Dagon's temple at Gaza by pulling down its two main pillars. This Dagon may have been a sea god, and he was represented with the tail of a fish. However, there continues to be some dispute as to whether Dagan and Dagon are one and the same deity.

DAGON see *DAGAN*.

DANIEL appears in the Old Testament as a prisoner in the sixth century BC of the Babylonian king Nebuchadnezzar. In 597 BC, the king seized Jerusalem. A decade later, the city was attacked, and the Hebrews were taken to Babylon where they were held in captivity until the city fell. Daniel was one of these Hebrew exiles. He gained a reputation for interpreting dreams and visions, earning the title "Master of Magicians", and was made a provincial ruler. However, Nebuchadnezzar commanded all his subjects to worship an image of gold. Shadrach, Meschach and Abednego, Daniel's friends, refused to do so, insisting on remaining true to *YAHWEH*. The king threw the men into a fiery furnace but astonishingly, they remained unharmed.

Nebuchadnezzar had many troubling dreams and called on Daniel to interpret them for him. According to Daniel, the dreams meant that Nebuchadnezzar would be banished from Babylon. The prophecy came true, and in the king's absence, his son Belshazzar ruled the kingdom. One evening, during a magnificent feast that Belshazzar was holding for a thousand of his lords, mysterious writing appeared on the palace wall: "In the same hour came forth fingers of a man's hand and wrote over against the candlestick upon the plaister of the wall of the king's palace." Daniel took the message to mean that Babylon would be conquered by the Medes and Persians. In due course, Darius the Median did indeed take the kingdom from Belshazzar.

Members of the new court became envious of Daniel's position and powers. They devised a plot whereby the king was forced to have Daniel thrown into a den of lions. Darius sealed the entrance of the den with a stone, but Yahweh sent an angel to Daniel's aid, forcing the lions to close their mouths: "So Daniel was taken up out of the den, and no manner of hurt was found upon him, because he believed in his God."

THE DEVIL see *SATAN*.

THE DJINN, according to Arabic and Islamic belief, are usually ugly and evil demons with supernatural powers. In pre-Islamic belief, the djinn were nature spirits who were said to be capable of driving people mad. They roamed the wild and lonely desert areas and, though usually invisible, they were able to take on any shape, whether animal or human.

In Islamic lore, the djinn were modified. They were an intermediate creation, coming between humankind and the angels. Those that refused to believe in Islam became demons, whereas others became beautiful and good spirits.

King *SOLOMON* was said to have tamed numerous djinn and to have become their ruler with the help of his magic ring. He allegedly carried them on his back when he travelled and ordered them to build the Temple at Jerusalem, as well as beautiful gardens and palaces.

There were several kinds of djinn, each with different degrees of power. The ghouls were female spirits who lived in the wilderness and manifested themselves as animals. *IBLIS*, or *SATAN*, is often regarded as the chief djinnee.

Djinn are born from smokeless fire. They are often said to live with other supernatural beings in the Kaf, a mythical range of mountains that encircles the earth. (See also *ANGELS AND DJINN*)

THE DRUJS, according to ancient Iranian mythology, were the enemies of the *asha*, the universal law. The monstrous, demonic beings, usually female, made every effort to further the course of evil. The horrific dragon or snake *AZHI DAHAKA* was one of their number, as was Nasu, who was said to settle on dead bodies in the form of a fly with the intention of hastening their decay. The druj Jahi was a symbol of the evil within women. According to one tradition, *ANGRA MAINYU*, the principle or spirit of darkness, kissed Jahi and thus introduced the impurity of menstruation to women.

DUMUZI was the husband of *INANA*, the goddess of love and queen of heaven. He is the Sumerian equivalent of the Babylonian god *TAMMUZ*. In the Babylonian version of the goddess's journey to the underworld, *ISHTAR* descended into *ERESHKIGAL*'s kingdom in order to rescue Tammuz and awaken him from his sleep. However, in the Sumerian version of the myth, Dumuzi was seized by the demons of the underworld as a substitute for Inana on the goddess's own orders.

When Inana returned from the underworld to her city of Uruk, to find Dumuzi sitting happily on a throne rather than mourning her, she fastened the eye of death on him and elected that he should go to the underworld in her place. Dumuzi prayed to the sun god for help. The sun god turned Dumuzi into a snake and he escaped.

Dumuzi told his sister, Geshtinanna, about a dream in which he saw his own death, and Geshtinanna was overcome with grief. When the demons approached once more, Dumuzi changed into a gazelle. However, the demons found Dumuzi and again attacked him. This time, they succeed in dragging him away.

Dumuzi was mourned by Inana, his mother, and his sister Geshtinanna. Inana was so moved by Geshtinanna's grief that she eventually agreed that her husband need spend only half of each year in the underworld, with Geshtinanna taking his place for the other half.

EA, the Babylonian god of the earth, was tempted in a story reminiscent of that of Adam and Eve. (ILLUSTRATION FROM MYTHS OF BABYLONIA AND ASSYRIA BY DONALD A MACKENZIE.)

EA, or Enki, a Babylonian deity, was one of a trinity of creator gods that also included the sky god *ANU* and the wind god *ENLIL*. He corresponds to the Sumerian god Enki. *EA* lived in *APSU*, the primordial ocean that surrounded and supported the earth. He was the son of *ANSHAR* and Kishar, the male and female principles.

A god of the fresh waters, as well as of wisdom and magic, Ea had the power of an oracle and would advise and reason with human beings. When Apsu was plotting the destruction of the gods, Ea killed him, prompting *TIAMAT*'s fury. Later, when the god Enlil decided to destroy humanity, the wise Ea warned humankind of the conspiracy and advised Enlil to temper his fury. On earth, Ea lived in the city of Eridu, on the southern edge of Sumer. His home was the Ezuab or "House of the Apsu". Ea is usually represented as a goat with a fish's tail or as part human, part fish. His consort was Ninki, the "Lady of the Earth", or sometimes Damkina or Damgalnunna.

Ea was introduced into the Hittite pantheon by the Hurrians. In the story of the weather god *TESHUB*'s battle with *ULLIKUMMI*, Teshub seeks advice from Ea the wise. The gods are dismayed at Ullikummi's power, but Ea decides to visit Upelluri, on whose shoulder Ullikummi had been raised. Upelluri says, "When heaven and earth were built upon me I knew nothing of it, and when they came and cut heaven and earth asunder with a cutting tool, that also I knew not. Now something is hurting my right shoulder, but I know not who that god is." The god was Ullikummi, who was made of diorite stone. Ea used the ancient saw that had been used to separate heaven from earth to cut the stone creature's feet, thereby destroying Ullikummi's power.

EA was a Babylonian god who helped people survive by teaching them how to plough and till the land. With the sky god Anu and the wind god Enlil, he formed a trinity of creator gods. (BABYLONIAN SEAL.)

MYTHS OF THE FLOOD

A LIMITLESS OCEAN FEATURED IN MANY creation myths as the primeval state of the world. A flood of global proportions was also a common theme, in which an inundation was sent to wipe out sinful humankind and thus restore the world to its pristine original state, so that it could be repopulated by a nobler race. The Egyptians believed that their creator god, Ra, would one day tire of humanity and return the world to the watery abyss of Nun before beginning a new cycle of creation. Stories of overwhelming floods reflected the ambiguous nature of humanity's relationship with water, which was vital to life but also carried the threat of violence and devastation. The Tigris and Euphrates, the two rivers on which the civilizations of Mesopotamia depended, flooded unpredictably, and their fearsome nature is expressed in several versions of the flood myth, which was to find its way into the Hebraic tradition as the familiar story of Noah's ark.

ENLIL *(above), as Sumerian god of the air, controlled the terrifying forces of nature. Angered by the noise rising from overpopulated cities, he determined to destroy the inhabitants of the earth, and sent a flood so great that even the other gods were frightened. Warned by the water god, Ea, the wise man Utnapishtim weathered the cataclysm in his boat and was rewarded by Enlil with the gift of eternal life.*

(ILLUSTRATION BY E. WALLCOUSINS FROM MYTHS OF BABYLONIA AND ASSYRIA BY DONALD MACKENZIE.)

NOAH *(left) and his family were the only human survivors of the flood that covered the earth for 150 days before its level began to fall, and it deposited Noah's ark on Mount Ararat. Noah released a dove who failed to find dry land and came back to take refuge on the ark. Seven days later he released her again, and this time, though she was forced to return, she carried an olive branch as a sign that the flood was abating at last.*

(CATALAN BOOK ILLUSTRATION, C. AD 970.)

Noah *(above) released his dove a third time, seven days after her return carrying the olive branch. This time, she left the ark for good. Noah, looking out, saw dry land once more and was able to disembark. God promised him and his family that they were safe, and as a token of his covenant, he set a rainbow in the sky, which would appear when rainclouds threatened as reassurance that the flood would not return.* (The Dove Sent Forth from the Ark by Gustave Doré, 19th century.)

Noah *(above right) was given a precise specification for the ark by God, detailing the dimensions of the boat, its roof and door, the number of decks, the type of wood to use and how it should be waterproofed. Noah was already an extremely old man at the time of the flood and lived on for many more years after it – his longevity recalls the eternal life granted to the survivors in the Mesopotamian versions of the myth.* (Detail of the Verdun Altar, 1181.)

Utnapishtim's *(right) boat eventually came to rest on Mount Nisir and, as the water began to subside, he sent out a dove and a swallow. Both returned to the boat unable to find food or a place to perch. However, when a raven was released, it did not come back, and Utnapishtim concluded that it had found dry land. He offered a sacrifice on the summit of the mountain, which placated the gods.* (Illustration from Gilgamesh by Zabelle C Boyajian, 1924.)

EL, the creator god, sits on his throne and listens to the prayer of a supplicant. (RELIEF ON A STELE, SYRIA, 13TH CENTURY BC.)

EL, a Canaanite deity, was referred to as the "Father of the Gods". He caused the rivers to flow, thus making the land fertile, and made his home near the seashore. Sometimes referred to as "Creator of the Earth", he was also known as "Bull", or "Bull-El", to signify his strength and powers of fertility. His name is usually translated as "Mighty One" or "First One". In 1929, stories about El were found on clay tablets at Ras Shamra in Syria, the site of the ancient city of Ugarit. The tablets dated from the 14th century BC.

Although El was usually regarded as the consort of Asherat (see *ASTARTE*), one myth found at Ras Shamra tells how he had intercourse with two women, probably representing Asherat and *ANAT*. The women subsequently gave birth to the deities *SHACHAR*, "Dawn", and *SHALIM*, "Dusk". According to the story recorded on the clay tablets, El walked along the shore, then plunged into the waves. His hands reached out like the waves, and he made his wives fruitful. He kissed their lips, which tasted as sweet as grapes, and in the kiss, and the conception and the embrace, Dawn and Dusk were born. El went on to father many more deities. He was depicted as an old man, sitting on a throne and wearing bull's horns.

EL-'OZZA see *AL-UZZA*.

ENKI see *EA*.

ENLIL was originally worshipped in Sumer as "Lord of the Wind", the god of hurricanes who represented the power of nature. He was believed to have absolute power over humans and was represented among men by the earthly kings.

Long before humankind was created, Enlil was said to have supervised the gods in their task of digging out the beds of the Tigris and Euphrates rivers. In time, the gods became exhausted by their ceaseless toil and decided to rebel. Enlil was devastated, but the god Enki (see *EA*) came to his aid, suggesting that the goddess Nintur create humankind in order to take over the work from the gods. For hundreds of years, all went smoothly, but then the cities became so overpopulated that the clamour made by the men and women kept Enlil awake. Enlil decided to solve the problem by sending a plague down to earth. However, Enki warned the people of the impending disaster, and they made huge efforts to keep quiet.

In time, the men and women forgot Enlil's threat and reverted to their noisy ways. This time, Enlil threatened to send a drought down to earth. Once again, Enki warned the people and they became quiet. The next time that Enlil was disturbed by the people's clamour, the god threatened to instigate a famine, but again Enki warned humankind and they were quiet.

Finally, when the men and women again began to create a huge clamour, Enlil lost all patience and sent down a massive flood. However, Enki had advised a wise man to build a ship and to save himself and his family from the flood. In some versions of the myth, the wise man was called Atrahasis, in others, Ziusadra. For seven days and seven nights, the rains lashed down, and the world was submerged by a massive flood. When the waters finally subsided, only Atrahasis (or Ziusadra), his family and the animals on the boat remained alive. In another version of the flood myth, which forms part of the epic of *GILGAMESH*, the hero *UTNAPISHTIM* survives the flood with his family.

In earliest times, Enlil's consort was believed to be *NINHURSAGA*, the "Lady of the Great Mountain". Later, however, he was associated with the grain goddess, *NINLIL*.

The Babylonians often equated Enlil with the great god *MARDUK*, calling him Bel, or "Lord". He was also assimilated into the Hittite pantheon, by way of the Hurrians. There, he features in the myth of the monstrous being *ULLIKUMMI*. (See also *MYTHS OF THE FLOOD*)

ENLIL, Sumerian "Lord of the Wind", receives worshippers at his throne. Son of the sky god, Anu, he represented the power of nature and threatened to destroy humankind because the clamour they made kept him awake. (CYLINDER SEAL, MESOPOTAMIAN, 3RD MILLENNIUM BC.)

ENNUGI see *UTNAPISHTIM*.

ERESHKIGAL was the queen of the underworld in both Akkadian and Babylonian mythology. The underworld lay beneath the waters of *APSU*, the primordial ocean. It was a dry and dark realm, sometimes referred to as a mountain, sometimes as enemy territory. According to the epic of *GILGAMESH*, Ereshkigal, rather than having chosen her kingdom, was "given the underworld for her domain." Enthroned therein, she ate only clay and drank dirty water.

The goddess had an insatiable sexual appetite and never let compassion for others stand in the way of her desires. According to one story, when the war god Nergal entered the underworld, Ereshkigal

***EVE** was created by God, who placed her in paradise as a companion for Adam.*

(NUREMBERG BIBLE, 1483.)

copulated with him for six days and nights. None the less, when he left, she remained unsatisfied.

In order that no one should return to the land of the living, the underworld was guarded by seven walls. At each of its seven gates, people had to take off an item of clothing, each representing one of their earthly attributes. When they finally reached the centre, they found themselves naked and imprisoned forever in eternal darkness. According to one tradition, Ereshkigal was the sole ruler of the underworld until Nergal invaded her territory, posting two demons at each gate. In order to achieve peace, Ereshkigal agreed to marry Nergal and to give him authority over the underworld. Ereshkigal was the sister of the fertility goddess *ISHTAR*, the counterpart of the Sumerian goddess *INANA*.

ETANA was the 12th king of the city state of Kish after the flood. King Etana grew miserable because he had no children and appealed to the sun god *SHAMASH* for help. Shamash told Etana to go to a particular mountain. There, on the mountain, an eagle and a serpent had recently had a terrible quarrel. Each of the creatures had children but the eagle had eaten all the serpent's offspring. The serpent complained to Shamash, who told him to trap the eagle and leave him to die. Etana found the dying eagle and asked him for a special herb that would enable him to have a son. The eagle promised Etana that he would bring him the herb if he would cure him. For several months, Etana brought the eagle food and drink until finally the bird was fully recovered. Then, the eagle told Etana to sit on his back so that he could carry him up to the sky of *ANU*, the supreme god. The eagle flew up to the gods and continued flying upwards towards the dwelling place of *ISHTAR*, the fertility goddess. In some versions of the tale, Etana seems to succeed in his quest and is given the herb by Ishtar. In another version, Etana grows dizzy and begs the eagle to return to earth. However, the eagle's strength suddenly runs out, and the two of them fall to the ground with a mighty crash.

EVE was the first woman, according to the Hebrew creation story. She was said to have been formed from her husband *ADAM*'s rib. A serpent tempted Eve to eat the one fruit which God had forbidden the couple, and she persuaded Adam to join her. As a result, both Adam and Eve were expelled from paradise. Eve was seen as responsible for the Fall and for bringing death, sin and sorrow into the world.

Christians have often viewed Eve's sin as a sexual failing. However, the Fall also opened the way for growth and learning. Adam refers to Eve as Hawwah, which is usually translated as "Mother of All Living", or "She who gives Life". According to one tradition, Adam was buried in paradise and was promised resurrection, whereas Eve was buried with her son, Abel. (See also *SERPENTS AND DRAGONS*)

***EVE** bears the apple, traditionally the forbidden fruit that led to the Fall and expulsion from paradise.* (EVE BY LUCAS CRANACH THE ELDER, OIL ON WOOD, C. 1528.)

EYE see *HATHOR*.

FATIMA, the prophet Muhammad's daughter, is regarded by Isma'ilis as the "Mother of the Holy Imams". The Imams are the semi-divine leaders of Shi'ism, one of the two great forms of Islam of which the Isma'ilis form a subsect. Fatima is revered within esoteric Islam and is seen as symbolizing the "supra-celestial earth". She is considered to be the source of the Imams' wisdom because she is the "hidden tablet; upon which God has written."

FERIDUN, according to ancient Iranian mythology, was the hero destined to overthrow *ZOHAK*, the evil king sometimes regarded as the embodiment of the terrifying monster *AZHI DAHAKA*.

Zohak was warned in a dream that he would be deposed by someone called Feridun, and consequently ordered the massacre of all children. However, Feridun's mother, Firanak, saved her baby by hiding him in a garden, where he was suckled by a miraculous cow called Purmajeh. Firanak then hid the baby in Hindustan.

Throughout Feridun's childhood years, Zohak was obsessed with the thought that his destroyer was alive somewhere. Sure enough, Feridun grew up determined to overthrow the evil king.

One day, a man whose children had been killed by Zohak led a group of rebels to Feridun's palace. Feridun decided that the time was ripe for action. As he marched towards the king, an angel taught him magic and comforted him with tales of his future happiness. Zohak, learning of Feridun's approach, clad himself in armour. He attacked Feridun with his sword, whereupon Feridun smashed it with a club. However, an angel told Feridun not to kill the king but to chain him in a cave under a mountain. Feridun did as he was told and then succeeded to the throne. His reign lasted for several hundred years. (See also *SERPENTS AND DRAGONS*)

***FATIMA**, daughter of the prophet Muhammad, on her way to a Jewish wedding party with Muhammad, A'isha, Umm Salma and Umm al-Ayman, receives a gift of a green cloak brought by Gabriel from paradise.*

THE FRAVASHIS, according to the mythology of ancient Iran, were benevolent spirits or guardian angels. They helped *AHURA MAZDA* to create the world, and defended heaven from its enemies with their sharp spears while riding their fleet-footed steeds. They were believed to be the ancestral spirits of believers, a part of the human soul that Ahura Mazda had created before each individual's birth, and thus might be regarded as prototypes for living beings. Fravashi is usually translated as "She who is Chosen".

GABRIEL, or Jibril, is known as the spirit of truth or "Angel of Revelations" in Islamic tradition. He stands at the apex of the angelic host and is said to have dictated the Qur'an to Muhammad. Gabriel is also believed to stand at the north-east corner of the *KA'ABA*, Islam's most sacred shrine.

In the Bible, Gabriel appears as the messenger of *YAHWEH*. He visited the Old Testament patriarch *DANIEL* twice, to announce the return of the Hebrews from captivity in Babylon and to explain the diversity of nations. In the New Testament, it is the archangel Gabriel who brings Mary the tidings that she is to conceive Jesus. Gabriel is also the trumpeter who will sound the Last Judgment. According to Hebrew apocalyptic literature, Gabriel is an angel of retribution and death. (See also *ANGELS AND DJINN*)

GADD was the name given to a variety of beneficent deities in pre-Islamic northern Arabia. It is sometimes believed to refer merely to a personification of good luck.

GAYOMART was the primeval being of ancient Iranian mythology. His corpse, together with that of the primeval bull *GEUSH URVAN*, was said to have given rise to all life. According to tradition, Gayomart existed for 3,000 years as a spirit until, in the second great epoch, he was made into a physical being by *AHURA MAZDA*, the principle of

***GEB**, the Egyptian god of the earth, was the brother and consort of the sky goddess, Nut. (PAPYRUS.)*

GABRIEL, *angel of the Annunciation, tells Mary that she is to conceive Jesus. He is also believed to stand at the Ka'aba, Islam's most sacred shrine, containing the Black Stone.* (ICON, 12TH CENTURY.)

goodness. He was killed by *ANGRA MAINYU*, the principle of darkness. According to one myth, all the parts of the universe were created from his body; another tale tells how the seed of Gayomart was buried in the ground for 40 years, until it gave rise to the first human couple, *MASHYA AND MASHYOI*, as well as the seven metals. Gayomart's name is translated as "Mortal Life", or "Dying Life".

GEB, the Egyptian god of the earth, was the brother and consort of *NUT*, and the eldest son of *SHU* and Tefnut, the deities of air and moisture. Shu, or in some stories *RA*, was said to have separated Geb and Nut from a passionate embrace by violently pushing them apart so that Nut formed the sky and Geb the earth. Until then, there had not been sufficient space between the two bodies for Nut to give birth. Geb was said to grieve continuously for having been parted from his beloved Nut, and his distress was said to cause earthquakes.

He was usually regarded as a beneficent deity who provided humanity with crops for their fields, and who healed the sick. However, it was also feared that he might trap the dead within his body and thereby prevent them from entering the underworld. The god was usually depicted as a bearded man, often lying under the feet of Shu. He was sometimes coloured green, to indicate that vegetation was believed to grow from his body. Occasionally he was accompanied by a goose or portrayed as a bull.

Geb, the "Father of the Gods", and Nut were said to have begat *OSIRIS*, *ISIS*, *NEPHTHYS* and *SETH*. The kings of Egypt called themselves the "Heirs of Geb".

GEUSH URVAN, the primeval bull of ancient Iranian mythology, was created, along with the primeval man *GAYOMART*, by *AHURA MAZDA*, the essence of good. According to one tradition, Geush Urvan died, like Gayomart, at the hands of *ANGRA MAINYU*, the essence of darkness. Another tradition teaches that Geush Urvan was slain by *MITHRA*. All kinds of plants and animals were said to emerge from his corpse.

Widely believed to be the guardian of cattle, Geush Urvan's name means "Soul of the Cow". The sacrifice of a bull was an important part of Mithraic rituals.

GILGAMESH, the famous Mesopotamian hero, is believed to be based on a real person, who was most probably a Sumerian king. *The Epic of Gilgamesh*, a poem recording the hero's exploits, was transcribed on to tablets in the second millennium BC.

Gilgamesh was two-thirds god, one-third man. He was so active and such a womanizer that the inhabitants of Uruk, or Erech, the city where he lived, appealed to the gods for help. The deities responded by creating another man called Enkidu, or Eabani, who turned out to be a wild and savage being, even more troublesome than Gilgamesh. Eventually, it was Gilgamesh who helped the people of Uruk to hatch a plot whereby they succeeded in taming the wild being. Enkidu subsequently became Gilgamesh's friend and constant companion, and the two men lived a life of luxury together.

In time, however, Gilgamesh was instructed by the gods to leave his home in order to fight Khumbaba, or Huwawa, the horrible monster who lived some 20,000 marching hours away from Uruk at Cedar Mountain. Enkidu and Gilgamesh set off on their quest and, after entering the cedar forest, eventually found Khumbaba's home. Gilgamesh challenged the monster to battle and, after a fearsome struggle, the two men overcame him, although it was Enkidu's spear that struck the fatal blow.

GILGAMESH with a lion. Gilgamesh is the Mesopotamian hero of an epic poem, which describes his legendary adventures, taking him to death and back. (RELIEF FROM PALACE OF SARGON, KHORSABAD, 8TH CENTURY BC.)

Soon afterwards, the goddess *INANA* tried to seduce Gilgamesh. When the hero turned her down, she complained to the god An (see *ANU*) who was eventually persuaded to give Inana the bull of heaven to send against Gilgamesh. However, Enkidu caught the bull and Gilgamesh stabbed it to death. The gods, outraged that the bull had been killed, took their revenge by striking Enkidu down with illness. After a few days, he died.

Gilgamesh was devastated at the death of his friend, and became terrified at the thought of death. He decided to try and discover the secret of immortality and set out on a quest to find *UTNAPISHTIM*, the hero who, after surviving the flood, had been granted immortality by the gods. When he reached Mount Mashu, Gilgamesh was confronted by the scorpion men who guarded its gates. However, they recognized that he was in part divine and let him pass by them to proceed into the mountain.

At length, Gilgamesh came to a beautiful garden beside a sea and saw before him the tree of the gods, laden with amazing fruits, the ground covered with jewels. There, he met the goddess Siduri Sabitu, who tried to deter the hero from his quest. At Gilgamesh's insistence, the goddess eventually advised him to seek the help of Ushanabi, Utnapishtim's boatman. Ushanabi took Gilgamesh through the waters of death into the underworld, and at last, the hero reached Utnapishtim. Gilgamesh told him: "Because of my brother I am afraid of death; because of my brother I stray through the wilderness. His fate lies heavy upon me. How can I be silent, how can I rest? He is dust, and I shall die also and be laid in the earth for ever." The hero of the flood told Gilgamesh that death, like sleep, was necessary for humankind. To prove his point, he told Gilgamesh to try staying awake for six days and seven nights. Gilgamesh agreed, but fell fast asleep almost as soon as he had sat down.

Before Gilgamesh returned home, Utnapishtim showed him the plant of youth, which lay at the bottom of the ocean. Gilgamesh found the plant, but as he bent to pick it, it was stolen by a snake. The tale ends on a sad note, with the ghost of Enkidu telling Gilgamesh of the misery of life in the underworld. (See also *UNDERWORLDS; HEROES AND QUESTS*)

GUBABA see *KUBABA*.

GULA see *NINURTA*.

GULASES see *GULSES*.

THE GULSES, or Gulases, were Hittite goddesses whose name means either "Scribes", or "Female Determiners of Fate". The Gulses allotted the destinities of individual

GILGAMESH and his friend Enkidu fought bulls during their quest together, which culminated in the death of the monster Khumbaba. (AKKADIAN CYLINDER SEAL IMPRESSION, 3RD MILLENNIUM BC.)

men and women, dispensing good and evil as well as life and death. The Hurrians called them Hutena.

HADAD see *BAAL*.

THE HAFAZA, according to Islamic mythology, are a type of guardian spirit. They look after people, protecting them from *DJINN*, or demons. Everybody is said to be protected by four hafaza: two to watch over them during the day and two during the night. The hafaza record each individual's good and bad deeds. People are said to be most at risk from the djinn at sunset and at dawn since, at those times, the hafaza are changing guard.

HAHHIMAS, the disappearing god, according to one version of the Hittite myth of *TELEPINU*, was responsible for having caused the great devastation that afflicted the earth. The myth tells how "Hahhimas has paralysed the whole earth, he has dried up the waters, Hahhimas is mighty!" In response to this desperate state of affairs, the weather god *TARU* called on his brother, the wind, to breathe on the earth, thereby reinvigorating it. However, on his return, the wind simply reported that the whole earth was paralysed and that people were doing nothing but eating and drinking. Hahhimas then began to seize and paralyse the gods, including Telepinu. Hahhimas's name is sometimes translated as "Torpor".

HAN-UZZAI see *AL-UZZA*.

HANNAHANNA was the Hittite mother goddess and goddess of birth. Her name is usually translated as "Grandmother". She was served by the bee who eventually found the fertility god *TELEPINU* after he had disappeared from the world, leaving decay and death behind him. *TESHUB* protested at the bee being sent on the mission, saying, "The gods great and small have sought him but have not found him. Shall this bee now search and find him?" However, Hannahanna ignored Teshub's objections and told the bee to bring Telepinu home.

The bee searched the earth, and eventually found Telepinu asleep in a field. As directed by Hannahanna, the insect stung the god. Enraged, Telepinu embarked on a bout of destruction, killing humans and animals. The story may be influenced by the belief that honey has the power to expel evil spirits.

HAOMA, according to ancient Iranian mythology, was the lord of all medicinal plants. He was able to confer immortality on his followers and was sometimes said to be the son of *AHURA MAZDA*, the supreme god and principle of good. Equivalent to the Indian Soma, haoma was also a real herb from which an intoxicating drink could be made. The drink was believed to heighten spiritual awareness and also to confer immortality. It was used in sacrificial rituals, which were said to drive away evil spirits. The spirit of the great religious reformer *ZOROASTER* was said to be strengthened by drinking haoma.

HAOSHYANGHA, or Hoshang or Husheng, the son of Siyamek, was the first king, according to ancient Iranian mythology. Siyamek, the son of *MASHYA AND MASHYOI*, the first human couple, was killed by a demon. After killing the demon, Haoshyangha spread peace throughout his kingdom and then proceeded to spread justice throughout the world. He introduced all the arts of civilization to human beings. After extracting iron from a stone, he taught humankind how to make axes, saws and hoes. He then organized a system of irrigation, leading water from the rivers to the fields, and tamed wild animals so that they could be used to cultivate the land. He also taught people to make clothing from the skins of wild animals.

HAPI see *APIS*.

HARSIESIS see *HORUS*.

HAOMA was both a god of medicine and the name of a magical herb. Zoroaster was said to have drunk a fortifying potion made from haoma. (LIEBIG "CHROMO" CARD, 19TH CENTURY.)

HATHOR *(above), was depicted as a cow, or as a woman wearing a horned headdress with a solar disc.* (TEMPLE OF HUREMHEB, EGYPT.)

HATHOR *(left), daughter of the god Ra, in her usual form of a cow. She nourished the living with her milk and carried the dead to the underworld.* (TEMPLE OF HATSHEPSUT, EGYPT.)

HATHOR, the Egyptian sky goddess and daughter of the sun god, *RA*, was usually represented as a cow. The goddess of joy and love, dance and song, she looked after mothers and children. She nurtured the living and carried the dead to the underworld. There, she refreshed them with food and drink from the sycamore tree, in which it was believed she was incarnated. Royal coffins were made from sycamore trees, in the belief or hope that death was no more than a return to the womb.

The Eye of Ra was identified with Hathor. When Ra grew old, humankind began to plot against him. Hearing of this, the enraged god decided to send the divine Eye, the terrifying, burning power of the sun, to slaughter them. The Eye took the form of Hathor who, as the lioness Sekhmet, or the "Powerful One", threw herself at all the wicked men and women and killed them in a massive bloodbath. Eventually, Ra decided that enough carnage had been inflicted, and he called an end to the slaughter. Only by Ra's intervention was Sekhmet prevented from destroying humanity.

In order to put an end to Sekhmet's relentless slaughter, Ra drenched the battleground in thousands of jugs of beer mixed with pomegranate juice. The bloodthirsty Sekhmet drank the bright red potion, believing it was blood, and became so inebriated that she ceased her attack and was transformed back into the beautiful Hathor. In remembrance of the event, great jugs of beer and pomegranate juice were drunk annually on Hathor's feast day. (See also *SACRED ANIMALS*)

HATHOR, *as the goddess Sekhmet, is depicted in human form, with the head of a lioness surmounted by a sun disc, identifying her as the daughter of Ra.*

HAZZI was a mountain god worshipped by both the Hurrians and the Hittites. He formed part of the retinue of the weather god, *TARU*, and was invoked at Hittite state occasions as a god of oaths. Hazzi was also the home of the gods; it is thought to have been situated on Mount Sapon, near Ugarit.

HEBAT see *HEPAT*.

HEPAT, or Hebat or Hepit, the chief goddess of the Hurrians, was sometimes referred to as the "Queen of Heaven". The wife of the tempest god *TESHUB*, she was often granted almost equal status with her husband, and occasionally took precedence over him. She and Teshub produced a son, Sharruma, who was represented as a pair of human legs. When Hepat heard that *ULLIKUMMI* had forced Teshub to abdicate, she nearly fell off the roof of a tower in horror: "If she had made a single step she would have fallen from the roof, but her women held her and did not let her fall." Hepat was assimilated into the Hittite pantheon, where she was often equated with *ARINNA*, the sun goddess. She was depicted either sitting on a throne or standing on a lion, her sacred animal.

HEPIT see *HEPAT*.

HERARHTY see *HORUS*.

HORUS, in the story of *ISIS* and *OSIRIS*, is sometimes known as Harsiesis to distinguish him from the twenty or so other Horuses in the Egyptian pantheon. He was depicted as a falcon or with a falcon's head. He was born, after Osiris had retired to the underworld, on the island of Chemmis near Bhutto and was raised there in secret by Isis. Harsiesis eventually avenged Osiris's death at the hands of *SETH*, and reclaimed the throne. He ruled peacefully, and was worshipped throughout Egypt.

Horus was worshipped as the god of the sky. His eyes were said to be the sun and moon.

Herakhty, or "Horus of the Horizon", was a sun god who rose each morning on the eastern horizon. He was often identified with the sun god, *RA*, and was eventually absorbed by him, forming Ra-Herakhty.

HOSHANG see *HAOSHYANGHA*.

***HORUS** (above) was the son of Osiris and Isis, and a cosmic deity. He was depicted as a falcon or with a falcon's head. As the first ruler of all Egypt, he wore the double crown of the united kingdom.* (RELIEF OF THE TEMPLE OF SETI I IN HYPOSTYLE, 1303–1290 BC.)

***HORUS** (left) in battle. Raised in secret by his mother, Isis, he eventually avenged his father Osiris's death at the hands of Seth and reclaimed the throne.*

HOURIS, in Islamic mythology, were black-eyed women who provided dead men in paradise with sexual pleasure. Each man was said to be given 72 houris, whose virginity was eternally renewed.

HUBAL was a god worshipped in Arabia in pre-Islamic times. His image, made from red carnelian, still stands in the sacred *KA'ABA* in Mecca, Islam's holiest city. It is believed that the Black Stone of the Ka'aba might be connected with the god in some way. Hubal was particularly famed for his oracle.

HUPASIYAS was the lover of *INARAS*, the Hittite goddess whose duties seem to have been those of protecting gods and tradesmen. A mortal being, Hupasiyas bound the monstrous dragon or snake *ILLUYANKAS* with a rope after Inaras had trapped the creature at a feast. The weather god *TARU* then killed Illuyankas. Inaras rewarded Hupasiyas for his help by building him a house. She warned him that he must never look out of the windows of his new home in case he saw his mortal wife and children. When Hupasiyas disobeyed the goddess, she killed him.

HUSHEDAR, according to ancient Iranian mythology, is a saviour and a son of the prophet *ZOROASTER*. Hushedar would be succeeded every thousand years by other saviours, culminating in *SAOSHYANT*, who is expected to introduce the universal judgment of humankind.

Eventually, after a final conflict between good and evil, the universe will be made pure again, and humanity will dwell in perfection with *AHURA MAZDA*.

HUSHENG see *HAOSHYANGHA*.

HUTENA see *GULSES*.

IBLIS is the name for the devil in Islamic belief. He is a rebel against God and tempts humankind to evil. Originally, he was the angel Arazil. When *ALLAH* created the first man, *ADAM*, out of clay, Arazil refused to worship him.When Allah summoned the angels to praise his creation, Arazil refused to attend. As a result, Arazil was thrown out of paradise, and from then onwards he encouraged the *DJINN* to make war against Allah. Eventually, he brought about Adam and Eve's fall from grace by tempting them into sin.

On the Day of Judgment, Iblis and his hosts of evil spirits will be consigned to the fires of hell. It is disputed whether Iblis was an angel or a djinn since, though he behaved like a fallen angel, he was said to have been made from smokeless fire like a djinn.

SERPENTS AND DRAGONS

HUMAN FEARS OF POWERFUL, ungovernable forces were crystallized in visions of huge and terrifying monsters. Serpents and dragons were composite images of everything that was inhuman: scales, claws and wings, of fantastic, fearful strength and size. They might also exhibit the characteristics of other animals, such as the head of a lion and the talons of an eagle. Their hybrid appearance added to their monstrous nature. Many were sea creatures, embodying the malign power of unpredictable nature and the threat of chaos. The most dramatic myths concern human or immortal heroes who killed dragons that threatened the world. By destroying the monsters, heroes were able to restore order and preserve the safety of civilization. As emblems of chaos, serpents featured in creation stories such as the myth of the snake Apep, coiled in the primeval water, who fertilized the cosmic egg of the Egyptians. In time, snakes came to represent not just disorder, but evil.

THE SERPENT *(above) in the Garden of Eden is frequently portrayed with the face of Lilith, who in Hebrew legend was Adam's first wife. She considered herself his equal and left him – and Eden – rather than submit to him. She was often depicted as winged, with the body of a snake, and was said to be the temptress of Eve. She acquired the character of a wicked demon who killed new-born babies and was the enemy of men.* (ANONYMOUS ENGRAVING.)

EVE *(left), with her partner Adam, was free to eat the fruit of every tree in the Garden of Eden except one, the tree of the knowledge of good and evil. The serpent, more subtle than any other beast, persuaded Eve that this was the one fruit she desired and, having tasted it, Eve gave it to Adam to eat. According to the Old Testament of the Bible, their disobedience condemned humans to lives of toil, hardship and death. The serpent's punishment was to crawl on its belly and eat dust, and to be the enemy of humankind thereafter.* (ILLUSTRATION BY RICHARD RIEMERSCHMID.)

LEVIATHAN *(left), the great sea monster, was said to have existed from the fifth day of creation, and to represent the forces of chaos subordinated by Yahweh. According to later Hebrew traditions, Leviathan will be vanquished in a great final battle with the archangel Gabriel, and the banquet celebrating the eventual arrival of the Messiah will take place in a tent made from the monster's skin.* (LEVIATHAN BY ARTHUR RACKHAM, 1908.)

AARON'S ROD *(above), was turned into a serpent by Yahweh to help Moses and Aaron persuade the pharoah to allow the Israelites to leave Egypt. The pharaoh sent for all the sorcerers and magicians of Egypt, who responded by miraculously turning their own staffs into serpents as well, but they were all eaten by Aaron's.* (AND HE THREW DOWN HIS ROD. . ., BY QAJAR, MINIATURE, C. 1860–70.)

APEP *(left) the great serpent, lay in wait in the Egyptian underworld to ambush the sun god, who had to voyage through it each night ready to rise again. Night was a time of uncertainty and danger for the god, as it was for humans on earth. The return of the sun in the morning represented the triumph of life over death, symbolized by Ra-Herakhty, the falcon, vanquishing the serpent.* (SMALL LIMESTONE PYRAMID.)

MARDUK'S *(above) battle with Tiamat is part of the Babylonian creation myth. Tiamat was the primeval salt-water ocean, which had to be tamed to allow the universe to come into existence. Marduk subdued her and eventually split her in two to create the earth and sky. Her eyes became the sources of the rivers Tigris and Euphrates. Marduk went on to kill her son, Kingu, and mixed his blood with earth to create humankind.* (ILLUSTRATION FROM GILGAMESH BY ZABELLE C BOYAJIAN, 1924.)

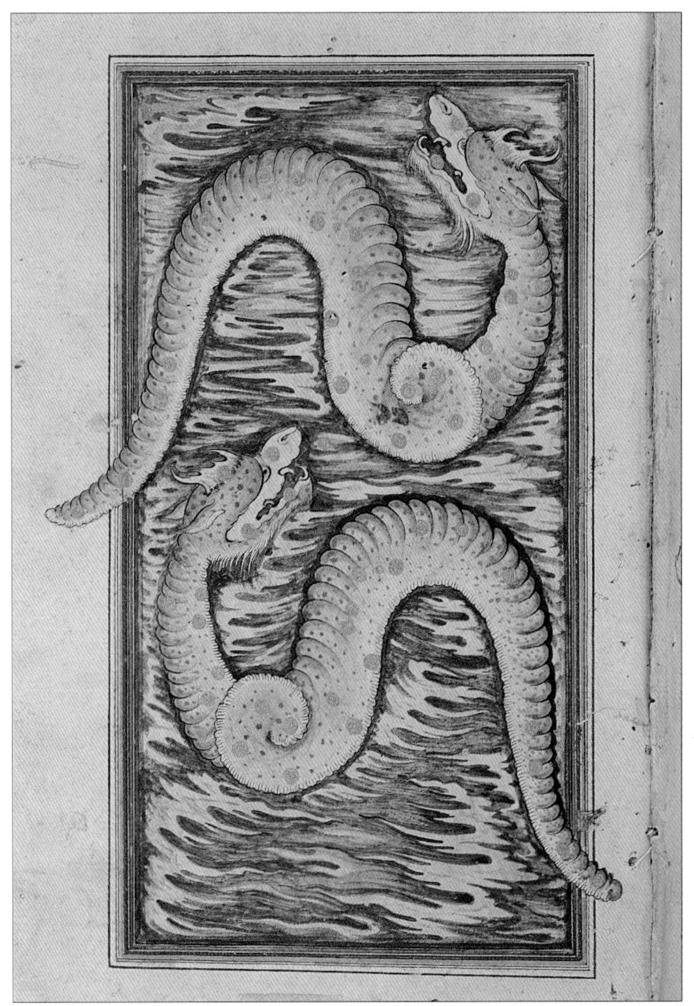

DRAGONS *(right) were appropriate emblems for the stars mapped by Arabic astronomers. These cosmic creatures engaged in battles far beyond human realms, such as the encounter between the Persian hero Feridun and the mighty dragon Azhi Dahaka. When Feridun stabbed the monster, snakes, toads and scorpions began to pour out, so instead of cutting him up, the hero imprisoned him in Mount Demavend.* (ILLUSTRATION FROM A DESCRIPTION OF THE FIXED STARS, 1629.)

IBRAHIM see *ABRAHAM*.

ILLUYANKAS was the monstrous snake or dragon of Hittite mythology. He waged war against the gods, particularly against the weather god, *TARU*. However, the monster was eventually slain by Taru, who was assisted in his assault by the goddess *INARAS* and her mortal lover, *HUPASIYAS*. In another version of the tale, Illuyankas seized the heart and eyes of the weather god. Taru responded by fathering a son whom he married to the daughter of Illuyankas, demanding the missing organs as a dowry payment. Taru then succeeded in slaying the monster.

The story of Illuyankas and Taru was assimilated into Canaanite mythology as the struggle of the gods against the *LEVIATHAN*. The Hittite monster was also the prototype for Typhon, the hundred-headed beast of Greek mythology. The tale of Taru's battle against Illuyankas was recited at an annual feast either of the New Year or of spring. The destruction of the monster was believed to signal the beginning of a new era.

IMHOTEP was a sage and scholar attached to the court of the ancient King Zoser, who ruled Egypt in the third millennium BC. A great architect, as well as an astronomer and scientist, Imhotep designed and oversaw the construction of the first pyramids. Until then, rulers had been buried in underground chambers. Imhotep's Step Pyramid at Saqqara was the first monumental stone building ever constructed. The sage was also credited with ending a seven-year famine by advising the king to make offerings to *KHNUM*, the god who controlled the flood waters of the Nile.

Admired during his lifetime, Imhotep gradually came to be celebrated as a god. According to some tales, he was the son of the great god *PTAH* and provided the high priest of Ptah with a son. The patron of scribes, he is usually depicted as a priest with a shaven head. He was also the patron of doctors. His name means "He Who Comes in Peace." (See also *GATEWAYS TO THE GODS*)

INANA, the goddess of love, fertility and war, queen of heaven and earth, was the most important goddess in the Sumerian pantheon. Her symbol was the reed bundle, and she was often portrayed with bright sunbeams radiating from her image. Inana's Babylonian equivalent was the goddess *ISHTAR*.

Like Ishtar, Inana descended to the underworld kingdom of *ERESHKIGAL*. At the gate, Inana explained why she had come: "Because of my sister Ereshkigal". Then, however, she claimed that she wanted to see the funeral of Gugalanna, the "Bull of Heaven".

INANA with Ea and Gilgamesh. She was the most important goddess in the Sumerian pantheon. (AKKADIAN CYLINDER SEAL, 3RD MILLENNIUM BC.)

At each of the gates of the underworld, Inana divested herself of one of her items of clothing, or earthly attributes, including her priestly office, her sexual powers and her royal powers. Finally, she was condemned to death and killed, becoming part of the underworld kingdom.

The goddess Ninshubur, Inana's handmaiden, mourned grievously for her queen and eventually appealed to the gods for help. Neither *ENLIL* nor Nanna (see *SIN*) would become involved. However, the god *EA* came to Inana's aid. From the dirt of his fingernails, he created two beings who, because they were sexless, were able to enter the land of infertility. These beings were mourners who eased the ceaseless pain of Ereshkigal, whose existence had been one of continuous rejection. In reward for thus soothing the ruler of the underworld, the beings asked that they be allowed to revive Inana. Ereshkigal agreed and the goddess was reborn.

Before leaving, Inana had to agree to find someone to take her place in the underworld. The goddess was escorted on her homeward journey by a group of horrific demons.

When she reached the world of the living, Inana found her handmaiden, Ninshubur, waiting for her by the gates of the underworld and her two sons waiting for her in their temples. All three were in mourning. However, she was aghast to discover that her husband *DUMUZI*, far from mourning her death, was thoroughly enjoying himself. Not only was he seated on his throne but he was also dressed in the splendid garments which she herself had given him. Furious with rage, Inana immediately appointed Dumuzi as her substitute in the underworld.

IMHOTEP, studying a papyrus. Probable architect of the famous Step Pyramid at Saqqara, and greatly admired during his lifetime, Imhotep gradually came to be celebrated as one of the gods.

Although Dumuzi attempted to hide, he was eventually dragged off by the demons who had accompanied Inana on her homeward journey. Geshtinanna, Dumuzi's sister, was so distraught that she offered to share Dumuzi's sentence with him. On the way to the underworld, Inana granted eternal life and death to both Dumuzi and Geshtinanna. For half of each year Inana and Dumuzi were together, while Geshtinanna took Dumuzi's place. When Dumuzi joined Inana, the milk flowed, the crops ripened and the fruit trees blossomed. During the barren months, however, Dumuzi had to return to the realm of Ereshkigal.

In ancient Sumer, a ceremony took place each year in which the king of each city would impersonate Dumuzi and the chief priestess would assume the role of Inana. The couple would take part in a marriage ritual, which was believed to ensure fertility and prosperity.

INANA *(left), often identified with Ishtar, the goddess of love and war, is shown here with Anubanini, king of the Lullubians.*

ISHTAR *(right), the Babylonian goddess of love and war, had countless lovers, both men and gods, but was fickle and cruel.* (ILLUSTRATION FROM LEWIS SPENCE'S MYTHS OF BABYLONIA AND ASSYRIA.)

INARAS features in Hittite mythology as the goddess who helped bring about the death of the monstrous dragon or serpent *ILLUYANKAS*. She is sometimes said to be the daughter of the weather god *TARU*. When Taru failed to overcome Illuyankas, Inaras devised a plot to bring about the monster's downfall. She prepared a marvellous feast, then asked a mortal, *HUPASIYAS*, to help her in her task. Hupasiyas agreed, on condition that she sleep with him.

Once she had carried out his request, Inaras invited the dragon, together with his offspring, to attend the banquet. When the monsters had eaten and drunk their fill, they found they were unable to squeeze back into their underground home. Hupasiyas then bound Illuyankas with a rope, and Taru killed him. Inaras built Hupasiyas a house in gratitude for his help. Then she said, "Farewell! I am now going out. Do not look out of the window; for if you look out, you will see your wife and children." When 20 days had passed, Hupasiyas threw open the window and saw his family. As soon as Inaras returned from her journey, Hupasiyas begged her to let him go home, whereupon the goddess killed him.

ISHTAR, the goddess of love and fertility, was a fearsome, often violent, deity, sometimes known as the "Lady of Battles". The Babylonian form of the Sumerian goddess *INANA*, she was the guardian spirit of life and the creator of wisdom. Her symbol was the eight-pointed star. Although she had countless lovers, she usually treated them cruelly.

On one momentous occasion, Ishtar descended to the underworld realm of her sister *ERESHKIGAL*. However, Ereshkigal cursed her sister, who subsequently died. As a result of Ishtar's death, the earth became infertile and neither birds nor beasts nor human beings mated. *EA*, the water god, eventually managed to save Ishtar by using his magic incantations, but Ereshkigal demanded she be given someone in her sister's stead. It was finally decided that *TAMMUZ*, her husband, should replace her for six months of each year.

Uruk or Erech, Ishtar's holy city, was called the town of the sacred courtesans, for prostitution formed part of her cult and she protected harlots, as well as alehouses. The personification of the planet Venus, Ishtar was sometimes believed to be the daughter of the moon god, *SIN*, sometimes of the sky god *ANU*. (See also *DYING AND RISING GODS; SACRED ANIMALS*)

ISHTAR *(left) became the principal goddess of the Babylonians and Assyrians. Like Inana, she was identified with Venus, the evening star.* (ALABASTER, 2800–2300 BC, SYRIA.)

ISHTAR *(right), in her violent form as "Lady of Battles", is shown heavily armed and mounted on a lion.*

ISIS, the Egyptian mother goddess, was the daughter of *GEB* and *NUT*, and the sister and consort of *OSIRIS*. She is usually depicted with huge, sheltering wings, and she is sometimes regarded as a personification of the throne. The hieroglyph for her name is the image of a throne, and her lap came to be seen as the throne of Egypt.

Isis helped Osiris to civilize Egypt by teaching women to grind corn as well as how to spin and weave. She also taught people how to cure illness and instituted the rite of marriage. When Osiris left Egypt on his world travels, Isis ruled the country wisely and well in his stead. Aspects of the myth of Isis occur in various Egyptian texts, and were assembled into a single narrative by Plutarch in the first century AD.

On hearing of Osiris's death at the hands of the evil god *SETH*, Isis was distraught. She cut off her hair, put on mourning clothes and set off in search of his body. A group of children told Isis they had seen the chest that enclosed Osiris's body floating down the Nile and out into the sea. It was eventually washed up underneath a beautiful tree on the shores of Byblos in the Lebanon. The tree immediately began to grow, so quickly that it had soon enclosed the coffin in its trunk. Hearing of the astonishing tree, the king of Byblos ordered it to be cut down and brought to his palace, where it was used to support the roof.

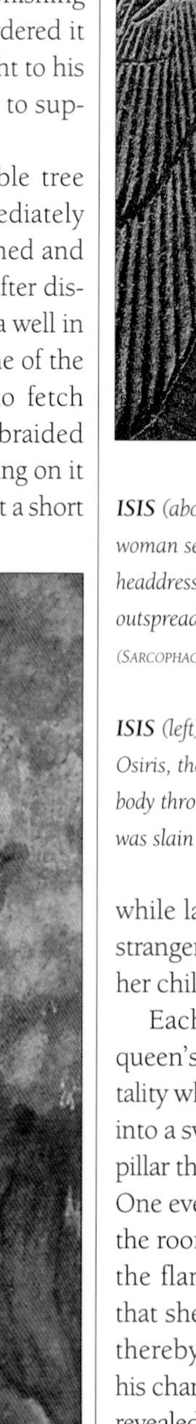

News of the remarkable tree rapidly spread. Isis immediately guessed what had happened and rushed to Byblos where, after disguising herself, she sat by a well in the city centre. When some of the queen's servants came to fetch water from the well, Isis braided their hair for them, breathing on it such beautiful perfume that a short while later the queen sent for the stranger and made her the nurse of her child.

ISIS (above) is usually depicted as a woman seated on a throne. She wears a headdress and huge wings which are outspread, protecting Egypt and its people. (SARCOPHAGUS OF RAMESES III, GRANITE.)

ISIS (left) was the sister and consort of Osiris, the murdered god. She sought his body throughout the land of Egypt when he was slain by the evil god Seth.

Each night, Isis placed the queen's child in the fire of immortality while she transformed herself into a swallow and flew around the pillar that enclosed Osiris's corpse. One evening, the queen came into the room and saw her son lying in the flames. She was so horrified that she let out a piercing scream, thereby causing her child to lose his chance of immortality. Isis then revealed her true identity and asked to be given the pillar.

Her wish was granted, and so at last she recovered Osiris's corpse. The goddess carried the body of Osiris back to Egypt where she hid it in a swamp. However, Seth discovered the body and cut it into 14 pieces, which he then scattered up and down the country. With the help of several other gods, Isis located all the pieces, except for the penis, which had been swallowed by a fish. According to one version of the story, Isis then reassembled the body and, using her healing and magical powers, restored Osiris to life. Before departing to the underworld, Osiris and Isis conceived a child, *HORUS*.

Isis became so famous throughout Egypt, and beyond, that in time she absorbed the qualities of almost all the other goddesses. She was a great mother goddess, a bird goddess, a goddess of the underworld who brought life to the dead and a goddess of the primeval waters. Her following spread beyond Egypt to Greece and throughout the Roman Empire. She was worshipped for more than 3,000 years, from before 3000 BC until well into Christian times. Her cult, and many of her images, passed directly on to the figure of the Virgin Mary.

ISKUR was a Hittite weather god who controlled the rain and thunderstorms. The "King of Heaven", he assisted the earthly king in battles and was represented sitting on two mountain gods or riding on a chariot drawn by bulls, his sacred animals. His attributes were a club and shafts of lightning, and his sacred number was ten.

JAHWEH see *YAHWEH*.

JAM see *YIMA*.

JAMM see *YAM*.

JEHOVAH see *YAHWEH*.

JEMSHID see *YIMA*.

JIBRIL see *GABRIEL*.

THE KA'ABA, or "Square House" is an oblong stone building, draped with black silk, which contains the sacred Black Stone of Islam. Situated within the mosque at Mecca, Islam's holiest city, the Ka'aba symbolizes the meeting of heaven and earth, and was an important shrine long before the time of the Prophet Muhammad (*c.* AD 570–632). It contained many images of gods and goddesses from the Arabian pantheon.

According to the Qur'an, the Ka'aba was rebuilt by *ABRAHAM* for the worship of the one true god – *ALLAH* – but the Meccans had enshrined a number of idols, the "Daughters of Allah", within it. Muhammad cleansed the Ka'aba of its idols and ordered that all prayers be directed to the structure. In pre-Islamic times, a four-month truce was called each year between the warring tribes of Arabia, and people from different tribes and towns would visit the shrine and circle round the structure.

Today, it is the sacred duty of all Muslim followers to try to make at least one pilgrimage to Mecca, specifically to the Ka'aba, in their lives. This pilgrimage is known as the hajj, and is one of the "Five Pillars of Islam". Its rites include seven circumambulations of the Ka'aba and, if possible, kissing the Black Stone.

Within Islam, the Black Stone is traditionally the place where Hagar conceived Ishmael, the ancestor of the Arabian people. Apocryphal stories abound as to its origins. One tale tells how it was once the most trustworthy of God's angels. God therefore placed the angel in the Garden of Eden, so that it might remind *ADAM* of his promise to God. However, with the Fall, Adam forgot his promise, and God turned the angel into a white pearl. The pearl rolled towards Adam and then miraculously turned back into the angel once more. The angel reminded Adam of his promise, whereupon Adam kissed it. God then turned the angel into the Black Stone, to symbolize a world into which evil has entered. Adam carried the Black Stone across the world until he reached Mecca. There, the angel Gabriel told Adam to build the Ka'aba and to place the Black Stone within the structure.

Another story tells how the Abyssinian general Abraha determined to destroy the Ka'aba but was unable to enter the city of Mecca because the elephant upon which he was riding refused to move. Eventually, the general's army was forced to retreat.

THE KA'ABA or "Square House" is an oblong stone building draped with black silk which contains the sacred Black Stone of Islam. (HAJJ CERTIFICATE, 1432.)

KAMRUSEPAS see *TELEPINU*.

KERESASPA, according to some traditions within Iranian mythology, was the hero who would finally kill the monstrous dragon *AZHI DAHAKA*. Keresaspa was renowned for numerous brave deeds, and it is also told how he once went into battle against the vast bird Kamak, whose huge wings had covered the sky and thus prevented the fertilizing rain from reaching earth. Another monster to die at the hands of Keresaspa was Gandarewa, a demon who lived in the water and constantly threatened to swallow all that was good in creation.

KERET, the king of Sidon, was said to be a son of *EL*, the supreme god of the Ugaritic pantheon. A legend describing Keret's exploits was contained in texts dating from the 14th century BC, which were discovered in 1929 at Ras Shamra in Syria, on the site of the ancient city of Ugarit.

Keret had been married to seven wives, but all of them had died, and the king was despairing of ever fathering an heir to the throne. At this point, El appeared and ordered Keret to lead his army into battle against Sidon's enemies. Keret was terrified. He locked himself away and burst into tears. However, in a dream he discovered that he was to father a son, and this encouraged him to undertake the campaign. Afterwards, Keret took a wife and promised that he would give the goddess Asherat (see *ASTARTE*) presents of silver and gold in thanks. El blessed the king and said that he would father eight sons.

The children were born in due course, but Keret failed to keep his vow to Asherat. He became seriously ill and vegetation withered throughout his kingdom. A ceremony was held in the palace of the rain and fertility god, *BAAL*. The rains appeared, and Keret recovered from his illness.

KHNUM, an Egyptian creator god, was said to have fashioned the world on his potter's wheel. His name means "Moulder". The god is frequently depicted as a ram-headed man sitting in front of a potter's wheel on which stands the being he has created. Khnum made the gods as well as people. He was also said to control the annual inundation of the river Nile.

In one story, the historical sage *IMHOTEP*, a minister and architect to King Zoser in the third millennium BC, was consulted by the ruler about the cause of a seven-year famine. The Nile was failing to rise high enough to irrigate the fields, and the people were starving. Imhotep told Zoser that he should make offerings to Khnum. The king did as he was advised, whereupon Khnum appeared to him in a dream and promised him that he would release the waters. That year, the kingdom enjoyed a splendid harvest. (See also *SACRED ANIMALS*)

KINGU was a demon of ancient Mesopotamia. He was either the son or husband of *TIAMAT*, the mother goddess and monster of chaos. Kingu sided with his mother in her tremendous battle against *MARDUK*, leading an army of ferocious monsters into battle. However, like Tiamat, Kingu was eventually slain by Marduk. According to one traditional story, Marduk mixed Kingu's blood with earth and used the clay to mould the first human beings. Kingu then went to live in the underworld kingdom of *ERESHKIGAL*, along with the other deities who had sided with Tiamat.

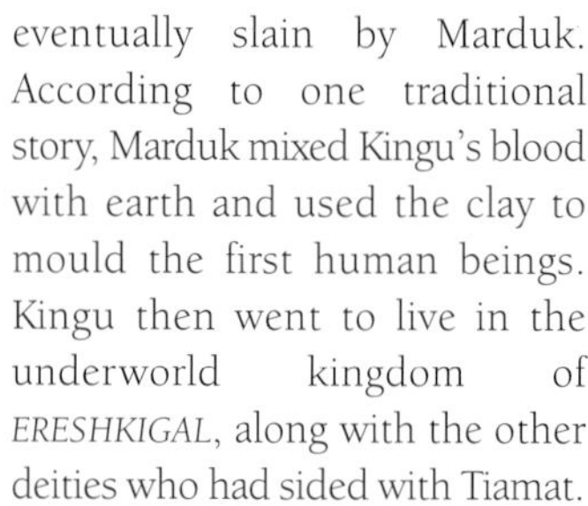

KHNUM *(far left), the creator god, was portrayed with a ram's head as a symbol of potency and virility.*

KHNUM *(left) was said to have made men and women on his potter's wheel, and was also responsible for the flooding of the Nile.*

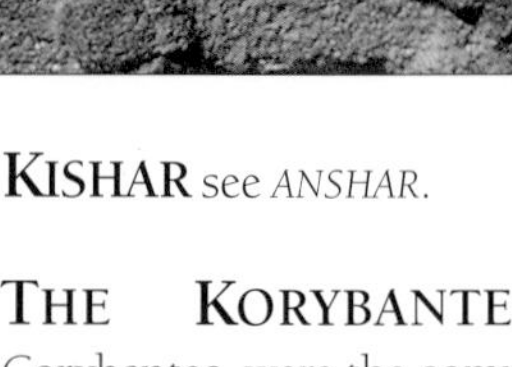

KISHAR see *ANSHAR*.

THE KORYBANTES, or Corybantes, were the companions of *CYBELE*, the great mother of Phrygian mythology. They performed frenzied dances, took part in orgiastic revelries and were believed to have the power both to induce and to heal madness.

According to one tradition, they were the offspring of the Greek god Zeus, who impregnated the earth by falling on it as rain. According to another story, they were the offspring of the Greek deities Thalia and Apollo.

KUBABA (left), at first a local goddess of Carchemish, later became the neo-Hittite mother goddess. (BASALT RELIEF, CARCHEMISH, SYRIA, 9TH CENTURY BC.)

KOTAR see *KOTHAR*.

KOTHAR, or Kotar, was the divine craftsman or blacksmith of Phoenician mythology. Lord of magic spells and incantations, he appears in myths dating from the 14th century BC discovered at Ras Shamra in Syria, the site of the ancient city of Ugarit. Kothar created a marvellous bow for the hero *AHAT*. It was made from twisted horns and shaped like a serpent. The servant of the supreme god *EL*, Kothar helped to build a palace for *BAAL*, the god of rain and fertility.

KUBABA was an ancient goddess of Carchemish in Asia Minor. As a local goddess, she had only a minor role to play in the mythology of the region. In due course, however, she became the chief goddess of the neo-Hittite kingdoms and took on the characteristics of a mother goddess, whose attributes included a mirror and a pomegranate. Her name, as well as some of her attributes, were taken over by the Phrygians for their mother goddess *CYBELE*, whose attributes also included a mirror and pomegranate. In Upper Mesopotamia she was known as Gubaba.

KUBABA holds a mirror, one of the attributes inherited from her by the Phrygian goddess Cybele. (BASALT RELIEF, CARCHEMISH, SYRIA, 9TH CENTURY BC.)

KUMARBI was the father of the gods in the mythology of the Hurrians, a people who lived in the mountainous regions south of the Caspian Sea and whose beliefs had a huge influence on those of the Hittites. Before acceding to the throne, Kumarbi had to depose *ANU*, to whom he had bowed down and ministered for nine years. At the end of the nine-year period, Kumarbi attacked Anu, who immediately flew up into the sky like a bird soaring to heaven. However, Kumarbi pulled Anu down by his feet and and bit off his penis. Anu told Kumarbi not to rejoice, for he had been impregnated by his sperm and would bear three terrible gods. These deities are believed to have been different aspects of the weather god *TESHUB*.

Kumarbi was eventually deposed by his son, Teshub. Kumarbi determined on revenge and, after seeking the help of the sea, proceeded to father another son. Known as *ULLIKUMMI*, he was made of diorite stone and was placed on the shoulders of the giant Upelluri, who lived in the middle of the sea. Teshub attacked Ullikummi, but he was unsuccessful in his onslaught and was forced to abdicate. Although the end of the myth is missing, it is widely agreed that Teshub eventually succeeded in defeating Kumarbi and regaining the throne.

KURUNTA was a Hittite god, generally believed to have been associated with the countryside. He appeared in a version of the myth of the disappearing god, *HAHHIMAS*, which describes the decline and death of all living things. The weather god *TARU* sought to prevent Kurunta from being beguiled by Hahhimas, who paralysed people into inaction, but even Kurunta, a "child of the open country", fell prey to him. Kurunta was depicted standing on a stag, his sacred animal, and holding a hare and a falcon. Models of stags have been found in tombs dating from the third millennium BC.

LEVIATHAN, the fearsome sea monster, was an expression of the chaos from which Yahweh protected humankind. (ILLUSTRATION BY GUSTAVE DORÉ FROM PARADISE LOST, 1866.)

LELWANI was originally a Hittite god of the underworld, referred to as "King". Over time, he seems to have developed into a female deity. She lived in the dark earth, and her shrines were connected with charnel houses and mausoleums.

LEVIATHAN was a ferocious monster of Phoenician mythology. His name means "Coiled". The figure of Leviathan drew on the Canaanite Lotan, a seven-headed monster killed by *ANAT*, as well as on the chaos monster *TIAMAT* of Mesopotamian mythology.

In the Old Testament, Leviathan is the chaos dragon who is overcome by *YAHWEH*. He is referred to in Isaiah as the "crooked serpent", and in the Book of Job, God says, "His heart is as firm as a stone; yea as hard as a piece of the nether millstone." The lashings of his tail "maketh the deep to boil like a pot . . . Upon earth there is not his like, who is made without fear. He beholdeth all high things: he is a king over all the children of pride."

In apocalyptic writings, as well as in Christianity, the devil is said to manifest himself as the serpent Leviathan. In the apocryphal Book of Enoch, he appears as a vast creature, which inhabits "the abyss over the fountains of the waters." Leviathan's jaws were sometimes regarded as the very gates of hell. (See also *SERPENTS AND DRAGONS*)

GATEWAYS TO THE GODS

THE EGYPTIANS BELIEVED THAT, on the death of the pharaoh, the sun god Ra would strengthen the rays of the sun to enable the king to ascend, as if he were climbing a heavenly staircase. The pyramid shape symbolized such a ramp, and the earliest pyramids were indeed designed in steps. Seen as a stylized mound, or hill, the pyramid also echoed the primeval hill which had risen out of the waters of Nun at the beginning of creation. The Mesopotamian equivalent of the pyramid was the ziggurat, a stepped structure that also rose skywards on a huge scale, with ramps and stairways connecting the levels and leading up to an altar at the top. The ancient builders of these colossal monuments saw the sun as an all-powerful creator and their ruler as a personification of the god. Their buildings, soaring skywards, connected them with the deity while glorifying his mortal embodiment on earth.

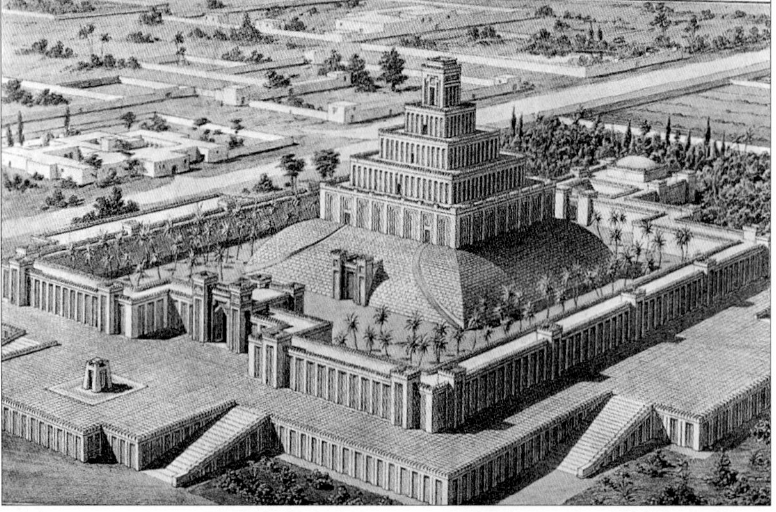

THE ZIGGURAT (above) of Ur was a temple dedicated to the Sumerian moon god Nanna, who measured time and brought fertility to the land. Built from rough, unbaked brick, it originally shone with a facing of glazed tiles. Long flights of steps connected the different levels and ultimately led to an altar at the very top: the ziggurat's function was to raise the worshippers closer to the sky deities.

ZIGGURATS (left) were built in most major Mesopotamian cities. They were huge, stepped pyramids, surmounted by a temple where offerings were made, to which it was thought that the deity would descend to communicate with his or her devotees. The temple of Marduk in Babylon, seven storeys high, was possibly the inspiration for the biblical story of the Tower of Babel. (OTTO GIRARD, A ZIGGURAT RECONSTRUCTED, *19TH CENTURY.*)

ANUBIS *(above) presided over mummification and funeral rites. Since the Egyptians regarded the afterlife as a continuation of their earthly existence, the correct preservation of the corpse was vital. Detailed incantations, designed as a guide to the underworld, accompanied the body, at first carved inside tombs, and later written on an illustrated papyrus scroll known as the* Book of the Dead. (THE BOOK OF THE DEAD OF KHENSUMOSE, *11TH–10TH CENTURY BC.*)

THE PYRAMIDS' *(below) vast size attested to the Egyptians' overriding concern with the continuation of life after death. Tens of thousands of men laboured for decades to construct them, under the direction of a single architect, who was given the title of "Overseer of All the King's Works". Most of the stone was quarried locally, and the huge blocks were hauled on sleds up ramps that rose higher and more steeply as the pyramid grew.*

THE TOWER OF BABEL *(above) was said to have been built on the plain of Shinar in Babylonia, according to the Bible, by the descendants of Noah, with the intention of reaching up to heaven. Yahweh, the god of the Israelites, disapproved of this product of human pride. He thwarted their plan by confusing their speech so that they no longer understood one another's instructions. The tower, and the planned city, were abandoned, and the people scattered.* (MEDIEVAL MANUSCRIPT REPRODUCED IN STRUTT'S ANTIQUITIES, 1773.)

THE PYRAMIDS *(above) of Giza were regarded by the Greeks as one of the Seven Wonders of the World, and are the only one of the seven to have survived virtually intact. Their awesome size and mysterious nature made it difficult to believe that they were the work of human hands. Imhotep, the architect of the first pyramid – and the first stone building in Egypt – achieved great renown by his feat: by the Late Period, 2,000 years after his death, he had become a god.* (ENGRAVING BY JACQUES PICART FROM THE SEVEN WONDERS OF THE WORLD, *17TH CENTURY.*)

M

LILITH is flanked by owls, her sacred animals. Created with Adam, she rejected his authority and consorted with demons. She wears a crown of lunar horns and a rainbow necklace. (TERRACOTTA.)

LILITH, according to Hebrew legend, was the first woman to be created. She was portrayed as part snake, part woman and wearing wings. *YAHWEH* blamed her for having tempted *EVE* to reveal the mysteries of the Garden of Eden to *ADAM*. In the Old Testament, she is the demon who disturbs the night. Her name means "Storm Goddess", or "She of the Night". The owl was her sacred creature.

According to Talmudic legend, Lilith was created at the same time as Adam. She refused to lie down beneath him, believing herself to be his equal, and flew away to the desert. There, she consorted with demons and became the mother of numerous other demons, at the rate of more than a hundred each day. God sent three angels to bring Lilith back from the desert, but she refused. The angels threatened to drown her, but she warned them that she had the power to kill children. Eventually she agreed not to harm children: "Whenever I shall see you or your names or your images on an amulet . . ." Lilith then wandered the world, looking for unprotected children who deserved to be punished because of the sins of their fathers. She killed them by smiling at them.

According to another tradition, Lilith desired to join the ranks of the cherubim, but God forced her to descend to the earth. When Lilith saw that Adam already had a partner, Eve, she attempted to return to the cherubim but instead found herself cast out into the desert. One Hebrew myth tells how Yahweh made Lilith, like Adam, from earth. However, instead of using clean earth, Yahweh made her from filth and sediments.

Lilith originated in Sumerian mythology as a goddess of desolation. She is also associated with the Babylonian demon Lilitu, who preyed upon men. (See also *SERPENTS AND DRAGONS*)

LILITU see *LILITH*.

LUCIFER see *SATAN*.

MAAT was the Egyptian goddess of truth, justice and harmony. A daughter of the sun god, *RA*, she ruled over the judgment of the dead in the throne room of *OSIRIS*. Each person, when they died, had to appear before the 42 judges of the dead and declare whether they were innocent or guilty of numerous crimes. The soul of the dead person would be weighed on a pair of scales against the goddess, represented by a single ostrich feather. The scales were held by the jackal-headed god, *ANUBIS*, and their verdict was recorded by Maat's consort, the moon god, *THOTH*. If the heart was weighed down by crimes, the terrifying female monster Ammut, part crocodile, part hippopotamus, part lion, would devour the dead person. If, however, the deceased had lived "with Maat in his heart", and was thus pure and virtuous, he became a spirit, and could live with the gods to fight against the serpent *APEP*.

Maat was depicted wearing on her head the feather that was said to be put in the scales of judgment. As the "Breath of Life", she was often pictured ministering to the *PHARAOHS* by holding the ankh, a symbol of life, to their noses. All human beings were intended to live "by Maat, in Maat and for Maat."

MAAT, *goddess of truth and justice, is depicted wearing a single ostrich feather, which is an ideogram of her name.* (TOMB OF HUREMHEB, EGYPT.)

THE MALA'IKA, according to Islamic belief, are angels. They are sometimes said to be made from light and are believed to be superior to ordinary humankind but inferior to the prophets. The four chief angels are Jibril or *GABRIEL*, the holy spirit; Mikha'il, the guardian of the Jews; Israfil, the angel who will sound the trumpet at the resurrection; and Arazil, the "Angel of Death". *IBLIS* is either regarded as the fallen arazil or as one of the *DJINN*.

MANAT, or Menat, was a goddess of pre-Islamic Arabia who was worshipped in the region between the holy cities Mecca and Medina. She was believed to be one of the three daughters of *ALLAH*, the supreme god, the others being *AL-UZZA* and *AL-LAT*. As a goddess of fate, Manat had control over human destiny.

MANDAH was the name given to a pre-Islamic group of Arabian gods who were concerned with irrigation as well as being protective deities.

MARDUK, the chief god of Babylon, was the oldest son of *EA*, the water god. Born in the waters of *APSU*, the primordial, fresh-water ocean, Marduk was originally regarded as a fertility or agricultural deity whose attribute was an agricultural implement with a triangular blade, called a "mar". However, he gained a reputation as a fearless warrior and was usually depicted armed for battle. His name means "Calf of the Sun God", and he was associated with the planet Jupiter. This most splendid of gods apparently had four eyes and four ears, and fire blazed forth when his lips moved.

In time, Marduk's reputation for bravery grew to such an extent that he was chosen by the gods to attack the terrifying monster *TIAMAT*. He was given a thunderbolt as a weapon and also equipped himself with his bow, spear and mace. After a ferocious battle, Marduk slaughtered Tiamat: "When Tiamat opened her mouth to consume him, he drove in the evil wind that she close not her lips. As the fierce winds charged her belly, Her body was distended and her mouth was wide open. He released the arrow, it tore her belly, It cut through her insides, splitting the heart. Having thus subdued her, he extinguished her life."

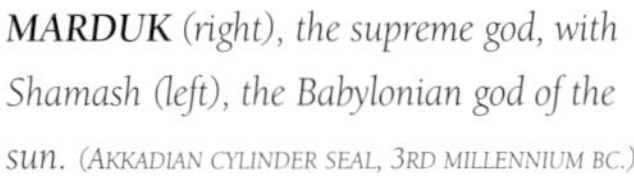

MARDUK *(right), the supreme god, with Shamash (left), the Babylonian god of the sun.* (AKKADIAN CYLINDER SEAL, 3RD MILLENNIUM BC.)

The great god cast down Tiamat's carcass, stood upon it and, after slicing her body in two, thrust one half upwards to form the vault of the heavens and pushed the other half down to form the floor of the deep. Thus, the earth and sky were created. Marduk then divided the year up into 12 months, made the constellations and appointed the sun and moon to their places in the sky. He then addressed his father saying "Blood I will mass and cause bones to be. I will establish a savage, 'man' shall be his name."

The gods tied up *KINGU*, who had sided with his mother, Tiamat, in the battle, and severed his blood vessels. Out of his blood, which they mixed with clay, they fashioned human beings.

Before agreeing to attack Tiamat, Marduk had successfully persuaded the gods that, if he rose to the challenge, he should be granted additional powers, including the ability to determine fates and the right to pardon or kill captives taken in battle. After killing the monster, he was awarded 50 titles, each of which corresponded to a powerful divine attribute. In this manner, Marduk came to absorb all the other gods and to symbolize total divinity. He even threatened *ANU*'s status as supreme god, taking from him the power of his dignity.

According to one tale, the evil genies were annoyed by the moon god, *SIN*, whose light revealed their wrongdoings for all to see. The genies, together with *SHAMASH*, *ISHTAR* and *ADAD*, devised a plot whereby they eventually succeeded in eclipsing Sin's light. However, Marduk, displaying no fear whatsoever, simply overcame the conspirators and put them to flight. (See also *SACRED ANIMALS; SERPENTS AND DRAGONS*)

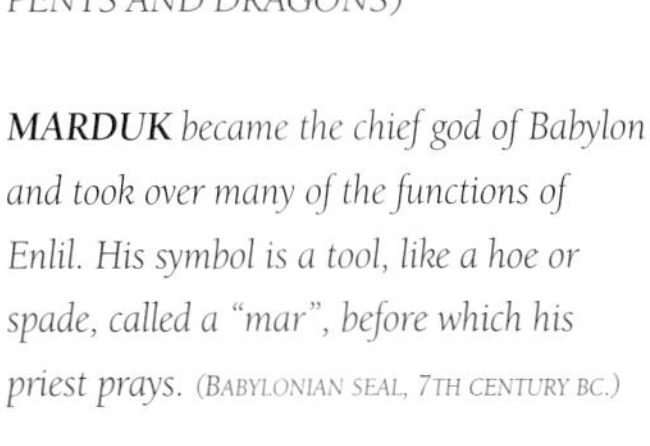

MARDUK *became the chief god of Babylon and took over many of the functions of Enlil. His symbol is a tool, like a hoe or spade, called a "mar", before which his priest prays.* (BABYLONIAN SEAL, 7TH CENTURY BC.)

MIN (left), the god of roads and travellers, wore upon his head a crown decorated with two upright plumes. (RELIEF, KARNAK.)

MASHYA AND MASHYOI were the first human couple of ancient Iranian mythology. In some traditions, they were said to have been born from the seed of *GAYOMART*, the primeval man, after it had lain in the soil for 40 years. Their first act was to walk, their second to eat. Then, however, they were sent a thought by a demon and, as a result, they became victims of *ANGRA MAINYU*, the principle of darkness. However, the good spirits continued to protect them. In time, Mashya and Mashyoi begat seven couples. One of these couples, Siyamek and Siyameki, became the parents of *HAOSHYANGHA* and of Fravak and Fravakain, who were said to be the ancestors of the 15 different peoples into which humankind was divided.

MEHUERET see *NEITH*.

MEN, a Phrygian moon god, was said to rule over both the underworld and the heavens. He was attributed with the good health of plants and animals and was referred to as Tyrannos or "Master".

MENAT see *MANAT*.

MIN, an ancient and popular Egyptian god, was always depicted with an erect phallus and with a flail raised in his right hand. On his head he wore a crown decorated with two tall, straight plumes. It is thought that Min may originally have been worshipped as a creator deity, but in classical times he was venerated as the god of roads and protector of those who travelled through the desert. His main cult centre was at Koptos, a centre for commercial travellers, and prayers were offered to the god before the travellers embarked on their expeditions. Min was also a god of fertility and growth, and a protector of crops. His main feast was known as the Feast of the Steps. Seated on his step, the god received the first sheaf of the harvest, which had been cut by the king.

MINUCHER, according to ancient Iranian mythology, was a descendant of *FERIDUN*, the great hero. When Feridun grew old he gave each of his three sons, Selm, Tur and Irej, a share of his kingdom. However, Selm and Tur plotted to take Irej's share from him. Irej was willing simply to give his brothers his part of the kingdom, and so he came before them unarmed. Without hearing what he had to say, Tur struck him over the head with a golden chair and then slashed him with his sword from head to foot until Irej's body was streaming with blood. Tur tore Irej's head from his body, filled his skull with musk and amber, and sent it to Feridun. The king, who was waiting for his youngest son to return home, was stricken with grief when he heard what had happened and sought revenge.

Eventually Irej's grandson *MINUCHER* attacked and killed Selm and Tur in a bloody and ferocious battle. Feridun then died, leaving the throne to Minucher.

MITHRA, known in Indian mythology as Mitra, was originally a god of contracts and friendship. In Iran he developed into the protector of truth. Before the time of *ZOROASTER*, the religious reformer, Mithra was often associated with *AHURA MAZDA*, the principle of good. Mithra was the light: he was believed to ride his golden chariot, the sun, across the sky, drawn by four white horses. He had 10,000 ears and eyes, possessed both strength and knowledge, and was renowned for his bravery in battle. The god was able to bless those who worshipped him with victory over their enemies as well as wisdom, but he showed no mercy to his foes. As a god of fertility, he caused the rain to fall and the plants to grow.

According to one tradition, Mithra, as the sun, formed a link between Ahura Mazda and *ANGRA MAINYU*, the principle of darkness. This supposition was built on the understanding that the sun marked the continual revolutions of light and dark. Under Zoroaster's reforms to Iranian religion, Mithra was ousted from power, and Ahura

***MITHRA** was a forerunner of the Graeco-Roman god Mithras, shown here. Mithra was worshipped in underground shrines, many of them decorated with a relief showing him slaying the bull Geush Urvan.* (MITHRAEUM OF SIDON, 4TH CENTURY AD.)

MOSES (left) was given the Ten Commandments on Mount Sinai. Here he presents them to the Hebrew people. (ILLUSTRATION BY H. PISAN.)

MOSES (right) loosens his sandal on Mount Horeb, or Sinai, obeying God's command from the burning bush. (MOSAIC, SAN VITALE, RAVENNA, ITALY.)

Mazda was given the position of supreme deity. Although, in the fourth century BC, Mithra returned as the focus of an extremely popular cult, Zoroastrians continued to give him no credence.

At his birth, Mithra was said to have emerged from a rock armed with a knife and a torch. He was worshipped in underground shrines, almost all of which were decorated with a relief showing him slaying the bull *GEUSH URVAN*, from whose corpse all plants and animals arose.

Regular sacrifices, particularly of bulls, were made to Mithra, in the belief that the fertility of nature would thereby be ensured. In the first century BC, when the Roman Empire expanded into western Asia, Mithra was assimilated into Graeco-Roman belief as the god Mithras.

MOLECH see *MOLOCH*.

MOLOCH, or Molech, was the name of an Ammonite god to whom human sacrifices were made. The Ammonites occupied the southern part of modern Jordan and were descended from Lot, who appears in the Old Testament as the nephew of the patriarch *ABRAHAM*. In the Second Book of Kings, Moloch is described as the "abomination of the children of Ammon."

Many Israelites are believed to have consecrated their children to Moloch by throwing them into the flames. It is sometimes argued that, rather than being the name of a god, Moloch refers simply to the sacrificial ritual. The children were burnt in a place called Tophet, in the valley of Hinnom, which had been built for the explicit purpose of sacrificial rituals.

The king was sometimes regarded as the son of Moloch, and the phrase "to the molech" may have meant "for the sake or life of the king" and referred to the sacrifice of a child conceived at a sacred marriage rite. Other research suggests that Moloch may have been the god Baal-Hammon who was worshipped at Tyre and Carthage.

MOSES was a great Hebrew prophet who is generally believed to have lived in the 13th century BC and who fulfilled many of the traditional functions of the mythic hero. He was the agent of God in delivering the tribes of Israel from their bondage in Egypt, and he presented them with the law establishing God's covenant with them. He is traditionally regarded as having written a portion of the Pentateuch, the first five books of the Bible.

During the period of the Israelites' exile in Egypt, Moses survived a decree to kill all male children by being hidden in the bulrushes. He was discovered there by an Egyptian princess and was brought up in the royal palace. Later, during a period in exile, Moses was grazing his flock when an angel of God appeared to him in a flame of fire, which issued from a bush. Speaking from the centre of the fire, the voice of God told Moses that he was called "I am that I am", which the Hebrews expressed by the four letters YHWH or JHWH, later pronounced as "*YAHWEH*".

In a later episode, recounted in the Book of Exodus, Moses led his people out of Egypt, and God drew back the Red Sea for them, so that they could walk across to freedom. On Mount Sinai, Moses received the Ten Commandments, written on tablets of stone, and the people of Israel made a pact, or covenant, with their new deity, Yahweh.

N

MOT, according to Phoenician mythology, was the god of death, drought and infertility. He ruled over the underworld and over the countryside when the ground lay dry. On one important occasion, *BAAL*, the god of rain, thunderstorms and fertility, challenged Mot to a contest, and banished death to the barren wastelands. In response, Mot challenged Baal to come to his underground home and eat mud, the food of the dead. Baal accepted the challenge but died as a result. The goddess *ANAT*, furious with grief, visited Mot to seek the release of her brother and consort. She carried off Baal's corpse and, when Mot refused to restore him to life, she killed Mot in a ritual slaughter: "With her sickle she cleaves him. With her flail she beats him. With fire she grills him. With her mill she grinds him. In the fields she scatters him, to consume his leaven, so that he no longer withholds his share [of the crop]." The supreme god *EL* learned in a dream that Baal was to come back to life: he saw the skies dripping with oil and streams running with honey.

The story of Mot and Baal provides a dramatic account of the agricultural cycle, its periods of dryness and death under the rule of Mot, alternating with the revival of the land's fertility when Baal was brought back to life. According to the Jewish historian Philo (*c.* 30 BC–AD 45), Mot was created at the beginning of time when the dark forces of chaos mingled with air. However, Mot was usually regarded as the son of *EL*.

NAMTAR see *RESHEF*.

NANNA see *SIN*.

NASR, an Arabian deity of pre-Islamic times, is mentioned in the Qur'an. He was one of the five idols who were erected by the descendants of Cain, the others being *WADD*, Sowa, Yaghut and Ya'uk. His name is translated as either "Vulture" or "Eagle".

NEBTHET see *NEPHTHYS*.

NEITH, the great mother of the Egyptians, was originally the local goddess of Sais, situated in the Nile delta of Lower Egypt. She was also a warrior goddess and a goddess of the home. As a goddess of war, who was believed to march into battle ahead of the soldiers, her symbol was a shield with crossed arrows. She was often said to be the mother of *SEBEK*, the crocodile god, and was also said to have created the terrible cosmic serpent *APEP* by spitting into *NUN*, the watery abyss.

Neith came to be regarded as the mother of all the gods, and in particular of *RA*, and was sometimes seen as the celestial cow, Mehueret, who gave birth to the sky before life began. Neith also became the protectress of the dead. She is sometimes depicted offering them food and drink on their arrival in the underworld.

***NEITH**, the Egyptian great mother, was envisaged as the great weaver who wove the world with her shuttle.* (TOMB OF RAMESES I.)

***NEKHBET**, the vulture goddess of Upper Egypt, protected the ruling pharaoh and suckled him and the royal children.* (TEMPLE OF HATSHEPSUT, EGYPT.)

NEKHBET was the vulture goddess of Upper Egypt. She was often depicted with her wings outspread, holding the symbols of eternity in her claws. Nekhbet was widely regarded as a mother goddess who looked after the ruling *PHARAOH*, along with *WADJET*, the cobra goddess of Lower Egypt.

NEPHTHYS, or Nebthet, the consort of the evil Egyptian god *SETH*, was a daughter of the earth god *GEB* and sky goddess, *NUT*. Her name means "Mistress of the House or Castle". The goddess was sometimes regarded as a symbol of the desert edge; often barren but occasionally, after a flood, fruitful.

Nephthys and Seth had no children of their own. However, according to one tradition Nephthys plied her brother *OSIRIS* with drink, seduced him and conceived a child. In some stories, the baby she gave birth to was *ANUBIS*, the jackal-headed god. When Seth murdered Osiris, Nephthys immediately abandoned her husband and helped her sister *ISIS* to embalm Osiris's corpse. The two goddesses then took the form of kites and hovered over the body, protecting it while it awaited burial. Nephthys thus came to be associated with the dead.

NEPHTHYS with her sister Isis. After the death of Osiris, Nephthys helped Isis prepare him for burial. The sisters are often portrayed protecting the bodies of the dead. (PAPYRUS, EGYPT. C. 1300 BC,)

NERGAL see *ERESHKIGAL*.

NINGAL see *SIN*.

NINGIRSU see *NINURTA*.

NINHURSAGA, the Sumerian goddess known as "Lady of the Great Mountain" or "Lady of the Stony Ground", was sometimes referred to as the mother of the gods, the great creative principle. As *NINLIL*, she was the wife of *ENLIL*, lord of the wind; and as Ninki, she was the wife of Enki (or *EA*), the god of water. Ninhursaga was said to nourish earthly kings with her milk, thereby making them divine. Many Mesopotamian rulers, including Nebuchadnezzar, called themselves her children.

The goddess was associated with birth; she was the power that gave shape to life in the womb and was the divine midwife of gods and mortals. However, she was also the stony ground that lies at the edges of the Arabian desert.

Enki and Ninki were believed to live together on the island of Dilmun, a paradise land sometimes thought to be present-day Bahrein. The divine couple had several children, and indeed, all the vegetation in the land was said to originate from their union. However, in time, Enki began to take a sexual interest in his daughters, whereupon Ninki fell into a terrifying rage. Retrieving Enki's semen from the body of Uttu, the spider goddess, she planted it in the ground. The seeds grew into eight plants. When Enki ate the plants, he was attacked by illness in eight parts of his body. Nobody but Ninki was able to cure him, which at length she did by placing him in her womb, from which he was reborn.

NINKI see *NINHURSAGA*.

NINLIL, the Sumerian grain goddess, was sometimes associated with the goddess *NINHURSAGA*. One day *ENLIL*, the god of the air, found Ninlil bathing in a canal near the city of Nippur and, unable to resist her beauty, raped her. In punishment, the gods banished Enlil from Nippur and sentenced him to death. Enlil departed for the land of the dead, but Ninlil followed him so that he should see her give birth to the son they had conceived. The child, when born, became the moon god, Nanna, or *SIN*. Enlil was overwhelmed with grief that his son would have to live with him in the land of the dead and tried to persuade Ninlil to have another child by him, who would act as Nanna's replacement while Nanna returned to the land of the living. Ninlil eventually agreed and in due course gave birth to three more children, thereby appeasing the underworld goddess *ERESHKIGAL* for the loss of Nanna.

NINURTA, or Ningirsu, was a Mesopotamian god of war. He was also associated with the irrigation of the land. Ninurta's warlike temperament prompted a vast army to rise up against him. All of nature joined in the battle, including the rocks and stones. Ninurta soon conquered his enemies. He rewarded those stones that had taken his side by giving them the power to shine and glitter, while those that had sided against him he left to be trodden underfoot.

In another story, Ninurta retrieved the tablets of destiny from the tempest bird, *ZU*. In some accounts, Ninurta is the son of *ENLIL* and *NINHURSAGA* and the husband of Gula, the goddess of healing. In early Sumerian tales, Ninurta took the form of Imdugud, the storm bird, but he gradually came to have human form. However, he was usually represented with wings, and when on the battlefield would still appear as a lion-headed storm bird.

***NOAH** cursed Ham's son Canaan because Ham had seen "the nakedness of his father", Noah. This may be a later attempt to explain Canaan's subjugation to the tribes of Israel.* (19TH CENTURY ENGRAVING.)

NOAH is the hero of the Old Testament story of the flood. According to the Book of Genesis, God saw that humankind had become wicked and declared, "I will destroy man whom I have created from the face of the earth; both man, and beast, and the creeping things, and the fowls of the air; for it repenteth me that I have made them." However, because Noah was a good and faithful man, God decided to save him, together with his family.

God instructed Noah to make an ark and to take into it two of every living thing. When the day of the flood arrived, water gushed from the ground, and the rain began to fall. For 40 days and 40 nights the torrent continued until

***NINURTA**, the Mesopotamian god of war, taking part in a New Year or creation ritual with the winged goddess, Ishtar, the water god, Ea, and the sun god, Shamash.* (AKKADIAN CYLINDER SEAL, C. 2400–2200 BC).

the entire earth was submerged. After some time had passed, Noah sent out a dove to see if the flood had abated but it returned to the ark. Eventually, another dove returned with an olive leaf in its mouth. God promised never again to flood the earth and offered the rainbow as a sign of good faith: "This is the token of the covenant which I make between me and you and every living creature that is with you, for perpetual generations: I do set my bow in the cloud."

Flood myths are found throughout the ancient world, from Greece to India. The story of a flood destroying earth appears in the epic of *GILGAMESH* as well as in the myth of the Sumerian water god Enki (see *EA*) and the hero Atrahasis, or Ziusadra.(See also *MYTHS OF THE FLOOD*)

***NOAH** was instructed by God to build an ark and take into it two of every living thing, to preserve them from the destruction of the flood.* (FRENCH BOOK ILLUSTRATION, C. 1260.)

UNDERWORLDS

THE MYTHOLOGY OF EVERY CULTURE included the idea that life in some way continued after death. The spirit might inhabit another physical body and live on earth again, or lead a perpetual existence in a murky netherworld. The concept of judgment invariably accompanied death and determined the future of the soul. A tribunal of gods or angels awaited the deceased to weigh up their conduct. The religion of the Egyptians was dominated by their funerary cult, but far from being obsessed with death itself, they saw it simply as a brief interruption. They aspired to an afterlife that was a continuation of their existence on earth in every respect, preserving their social status, family connections and even their physical possessions. Only for those who had failed to please the gods during their mortal lives, or who had not prepared themselves for their journey through the underworld with the proper rituals and incantations, was death really a termination.

OSIRIS *(right) was originally a deity of vegetation and agriculture, but the myth of his death became central to his cult and raised his status to that of a great god. The pharaoh, who was considered to be an incarnation of Ra the sun god while he was alive, became identified with Osiris on his death. Osiris was depicted wearing the crown of Egypt, and carrying the royal insignia of the crook and flail, but was tightly wrapped in mummy cloths. As lord of the underworld, he presided over the judgment of the dead on their arrival in his realm.* (WALL PAINTING FROM THE GRAVE OF SENNUTEM, 14TH CENTURY BC.)

MASHU *(right) was a magic mountain which formed the boundary of the Mesopotamian underworld, into which the sun set each night. When the hero Gilgamesh visited the underworld in search of the immortal Utnapishtim, he had to pass through the gates of Mashu, guarded by fearsome scorpion gods. After a journey in total darkness, he emerged into an enchanted garden of precious stones.* (ILLUSTRATION FROM GILGAMESH BY ZABELLE C BOYAJIAN, 1924.)

THE WEIGHING OF THE SOUL *(above) was a decisive moment in the Egyptian journey to the underworld. The deceased was brought by Anubis before a panel of judges and his heart, where thought and memory resided, was weighed on the scales. It had to balance exactly with the goddess of truth, Maat. If it failed, the spirit was destroyed: the terrible Ammut, with the head of a crocodile and the mane of a lion, crouched by the scales waiting to eat the condemned. The ibis-headed god Thoth declared the result.* (FROM THE BOOK OF THE DEAD OF HUNEFER, 13TH CENTURY BC.)

MUMMIFICATION *(left) was practised to preserve a corpse so that life could continue after death, and this was the domain of the mortuary god, Anubis. He took the form of a black dog or jackal – the very animal who might scavenge a body that was incorrectly buried. The heart was the only internal organ left in the body, and it was protected by a scarab beetle bearing a spell that would keep it from confessing any sins during interrogation before Anubis.* (WALL PAINTING FROM THE GRAVE OF SENNUTEM, 14TH CENTURY BC.)

O

NUN, according to Egyptian mythology, was the personification of the watery abyss that existed at the beginning of time and which contained the potential for all life.

According to one Egyptian creation myth, these formless, chaotic waters contained four pairs: Nun and Naunet, Kuk and Kauket, Huh and Hauhet, *AMON* and Amaunet. These pairs, known as the Ogdoad, symbolized the primeval waters. Eventually the four pairs formed an egg in the waters of Nun, and out of the egg burst a fabulous bird, or, according to some versions of the story, air. This bird was a manifestation of the creator god. According to one tradition, the sun god Atum rose from Nun in the form of a hill, a primeval mound, and gave birth to *SHU*, the god of air, and Tefnut, the goddess of moisture. Nun was depicted as a man standing in water, his arms raised to support the boat of the sun god. (See also *MYTHS OF THE FLOOD*)

NUSKU see *SIN*.

NUT, the Egyptian goddess of the sky, was the twin sister of the earth god, *GEB*. When, against *RA*'s wishes, she married her brother, Ra was so enraged that he commanded *SHU* to separate the couple. Shu pushed Nut upwards to form the sky and Geb down to form the earth. Ra was so angry with Nut that he decreed that she would be unable to bear children in any month of the year. However, the god *THOTH* took pity on her. He challenged the moon to a game of draughts, and, when he won, took as his prize enough of the moon's light to create five new days. On each of these days, Nut bore a child: *OSIRIS*, *SETH*, *ISIS*, *NEPHTHYS* and, according to some versions of the tale, *HORUS*.

Another myth tells how Nut helped Ra to distance himself from human beings when he became disillusioned with their ways. Taking the form of a cow, she raised the great god upwards on her back. However, the higher Nut rose, the dizzier she became, until she had to summon four gods to steady her legs. These gods became the pillars of the sky.

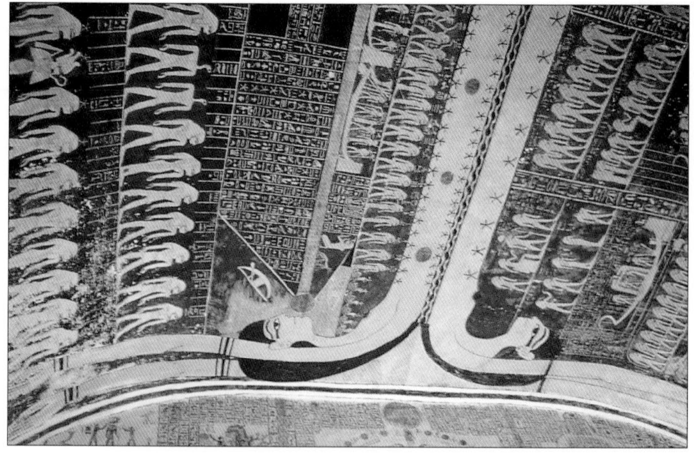

NUT, the Egyptian sky goddess, arches over the earth, formed by her consort, Geb. She balances on her outstretched fingers and toes, which touch the four cardinal points. (TOMB OF RAMESES VI.)

OG, according to Hebrew mythology, was one of the many giants who roamed the earth before the great flood that destroyed creation. Of these giants, Og alone survived the flood. According to one story, the flood waters reached no higher than Og's ankles, and so he remained unharmed by the deluge. Other stories tell how *NOAH* allowed Og to sit on the roof of his ark while Noah fed him oxen.

After the flood had subsided, Og fell in love with Sarah, the wife of *ABRAHAM*, and jealously plotted against the patriarch. The enmity between Og and Abraham continued down the years, and it culminated in a battle with *MOSES*. After the great prophet had led the Israelites out of Egypt into the land of Canaan, he was forced to engage in numerous battles against the local people. One of these battles was against Edrei, a city ruled by Og. When the giant spotted the approaching forces, he lifted a mountain high above his head and was about to drop it on Moses and his followers when *YAHWEH* caused the monstrous missile to drop on to Og's own shoulders. The giant

NUT was depicted on funerary amulets which were attached to a mummy for protection. At death, the pharoah was said to pass into the body of Nut. A scarab was placed over the heart to keep it silent during the judgment of the dead. (MUMMY ACCESSORIES, PTOLEMAIC PERIOD, C. 100 BC.)

struggled to throw off the mountain, but his teeth sank into it, and he was unable to see properly. Moses took an axe in his hands, leapt into the air and cut through the giant's ankles. Og crumpled, struck the ground and died. In the Old Testament Book of Deuteronomy, Og was said to be king of Bashan: "Behold, his bedstead was a bedstead of iron . . . nine cubits was the length thereof, and four cubits the breadth of it."

OGDOAD see *NUN*.

OHRMAZD see *AHURA MAZDA*.

OSIRIS, son of the Egyptian deities *GEB* and *NUT*, was originally a god of nature who symbolized the cycle of vegetation. In time, however, he became god of the dead. At his birth, he was proclaimed the "Universal Lord", and he grew into a tall and handsome deity. When his father retired, Osiris became king of Egypt and took his sister, *ISIS*, as his queen. He taught humankind how to make bread and wine, and oversaw the building of the first temples and statues to the gods. He also built towns, and laid down just and fair laws. Once Egypt was civilized, Osiris embarked on a great journey, civilizing each country to which he came. His success was largely due to the fact that everyone he encountered was immediately transfixed by his charisma.

When Osiris returned to Egypt many festivals were held in his honour. However, his younger brother, *SETH*, grew jealous of his popularity. He hatched a plan and invited Osiris to a feast, during which a superb coffin was carried in to them. Feigning innocence, Seth announced that the coffin belonged to whomsoever fitted it. Osiris entered into the joke and lay down in the coffin. Immediately, the lid was nailed down and the coffin thrown into the Nile. The coffin was eventually washed up on the shores of Byblos.

According to another version of the story, Seth killed Osiris after first transforming himself into a crocodile; yet another tale tells how Seth turned himself into a bull and trampled Osiris to death.

When Isis heard what had happened to her husband and brother, she was overcome with grief and began to search for his body. She eventually found it and brought it back to Egypt, where she hid it in a swamp. Seth found the body and cut it into 14 pieces. Undeterred, Isis remade Osiris's body and then performed a magic ritual whereby she restored Osiris to life. This was the first rite of embalmment. Osiris was by now so disillusioned with his brother that he decided to retire from life and to reign over the dead in the underworld. There, in the court of the underworld, he supervised the judgment of the dead.

Osiris was usually depicted as a bearded man wrapped in mummy bandages and holding a crook and a flail to symbolize his kingship. He symbolizes the regenerative powers of the natural world, as well as the threat posed by severe weather conditions to the well-being of humanity. (See also *UNDERWORLDS; DYING AND RISING GODS*)

***OSIRIS**, murdered by Seth and dying, gives his divine sperm, the source of life, to his consort, Isis.* (BASALT RELIEF FROM THE SARCOPHAGUS OF NES-SHUTFENE, SAQQARA, 4TH CENTURY BC.)

THE PHARAOHS' (top) treasure chambers were fabled for their unrivalled wealth of gold and magnificent artefacts, and many were rifled in antiquity. This is the treasure chamber of Rhampsinitus.

THE PHARAOH RAMESES II (above) defeated the Khetans in battle. The god-kings were often called to mediate in battle as well as between the gods and the people.

THE PHARAOH RAMESES II (above left) as a young man. Regarded as a divine monarch, the pharaoh was sometimes depicted worshipping his own image. (BAS-RELIEF, 13TH CENTURY BC.)

THE PHARAOH TUTANKHAMEN (right) had a fairly undistinguished reign. However, his tomb at Thebes survived intact throughout the centuries until it was opened in 1922. This golden mask from the inner tomb was amongst the most splendid of the many treasures discovered. (14TH CENTURY BC.)

PAPAS see *ATTIS*.

PHARAOHS ruled over Egypt from around 3100 BC, when the country became unified. In early times, the word pharaoh, meaning "Great House" or "Palace," was never used to refer to the king himself, but under the New Kingdom (*c*. 1570–1085 BC) the term could be applied directly to the king. Regarded as a divine monarch, the pharaoh was sometimes depicted worshipping his own image, thereby drawing attention to his divine status. He was given the titles of "Horus"; "The Two Ladies" (referring to *NEKHBET* and *WADJET*, the goddesses of Upper and Lower Egypt); "Horus of Gold"; "King of Upper and Lower Egypt and Lord of the Double Land"; and "Son of Ra and Lord of Diadems". Whenever there was a change of ruler, the queen was said to marry *RA* and to bear a son who became the new king. Pharaohs were often depicted suckling from a goddess to symbolize both their divinity and their relationship to the deity.

According to one papyrus, the wife of a high priest of Ra was made pregnant by the sun god. The ruling pharaoh, Khufu of the fourth dynasty, attempted to prevent the birth, but Ra sent several deities, led by *ISIS* and *NEPHTHYS*, to look after the woman. The deities delivered and named the children and, before leaving the house, hid three crowns. When the priest found the crowns he realized that his children would become kings.

The pharaoh was responsible for the economic and spiritual welfare of his people, and for the construction and upkeep of the temples. Priests were regarded merely as his representatives. After his death, the pharaoh was believed both to join Ra in his boat which sailed across the sky and to take up kingship in the underworld, as *OSIRIS*. (See also *GATEWAYS TO THE GODS*)

R

PTAH was the god of Memphis, the old capital in the north of Egypt where the *PHAROAHS* were crowned. His priests believed he created the world, although he probably originated as a fertility god. In the third millennium BC, he came to rank third in the divine hierarchy after *AMON* and *RA*.

Believed to be the inventor of the arts, Ptah designed and built secular buildings as well as overseeing the construction of temples, and he was said to have moulded the gods and kings out of metal. In one tradition, he created the world through the power of the word.

Ptah is usually depicted wearing a close-fitting linen wrap and skull cap, and holding the sceptre of dominion. Sometimes, however, he is shown as a twisted, frightening figure, in which guise he was believed to protect humanity from all kinds of evil.

When the power of Memphis declined, Ptah was often associated with other deities, including *OSIRIS*. His consort was the lioness goddess, Sekhmet (see *HATHOR*) and he was the father of Nefertum. The bull *APIS* was worshipped in a temple opposite his and was believed to be an incarnation of the god. (See also *SACRED ANIMALS*)

RA, the supreme manifestation of the sun god of Heliopolis, was a hugely important member of the Egyptian pantheon. He was said to have come into being on the primeval mound that rose out of *NUN* and to have proceeded to plan creation. Sometimes, however, he was depicted as a child rising out of a lotus flower. The Egyptians believed that each day the sun god was born. In the morning, after his bath and breakfast, he began his journey across the sky in his boat

***PTAH**, the creator god and patron of craftsmen, holds his sceptre of dominion, surmounted by the ankh, or symbol of life.*

(Statuette from the treasure of Tutankhamen, 14th century BC.)

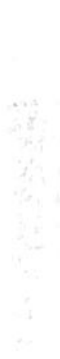

RA *(above), the supreme Egyptian sun god, with Aten, another sun god, to the left.* (WALL PAINTING FROM THE TOMB OF SENNEDJEM, THEBES, 13TH CENTURY BC.)

RA *(left), the supreme Egyptian manifestation of the sun god, is usually portrayed as a falcon-headed man wearing the disc of the sun on his head.* (GREAT TEMPLE, ABU SIMBEL.)

and would spend one of the hours of the day inspecting each of his 12 provinces. When the sun went down, Ra was believed to enter the underworld until the morning, when he was born again. All night long, the supreme god had to fight his enemy *APEP*, the terrible cosmic serpent of the underworld.

Ra gave birth to *SHU*, the god of air, and Tefnut, the goddess of moisture. According to one myth, the pair disappeared to explore the universe; when Ra finally found them, he was so relieved that he burst into tears. From his tears the first human beings were formed. Another tale tells how, when Ra was an old and dribbling man, the goddess *ISIS* determined to discover his secret name. She made a snake from earth moistened with the great god's spit and positioned the snake beside a path where the god liked to walk. In due course, the snake bit Ra, poisoning him and causing him such agony that he cried out in pain. Isis agreed to cure him only if he would reveal his name. Ra's suffering was such that he eventually agreed to disclose his secret. Isis promised not to pass on her knowledge to anyone but *HORUS* and, by speaking the god's true name, healed him.

The *PHARAOHS* called themselves "Sons of Ra", not only because he was held in great awe but also because he was said to have created order out of chaos. Ra was usually depicted as a falcon wearing a sun disc on his head. (See also *MYTHS OF THE FLOOD*)

DYING AND RISING GODS

STORIES OF BEAUTIFUL AND WELL-LOVED semi-divine youths who died tragically, or were seized by the grim ruler of the underworld but were then miraculously restored to life, echoed through many ancient cultures. Like the promise of a serene afterlife, they raised the possibility that death itself could be conquered. They underlined the regenerative powers of nature, suggesting the continuance of humanity in future generations and, above all, the annual rebirth of the natural world. Dying and rising gods were associated with vegetation, fertility and the harvest: their devotees worshipped them because they needed reassurance that when the summer drought came and food crops died away, they could rely on the resurgence of the next season's growth. Faith in the annual return of a force that could defy death and the powers of darkness gave them confidence that the following year would be fruitful. Fresh green shoots pushing up through the soil can be clearly identified with the eternal youth of these deities rising from the underworld.

ADONIS (above), the beautiful youth, was the lover of Venus, the Roman version of Astarte, goddess of the Phoenicians and Canaanites. He was gored to death by a boar while out hunting and descended to the underworld, but at Venus's entreaty was permitted to return to her for half of each year. On his annual departure from earth, an ecstatic mourning festival was held in the Phoenician city of Byblos, the centre of his cult. (VENUS AND ADONIS BY PYOTR SOLOKOV, CANVAS, 1782.)

WILD ANEMONES (left) forming a red carpet at the foot of Mount Lebanon after the winter rains were said to represent the blood of Tammuz, before his descent to the underworld signalled the beginning of a season of parched earth and withered vegetation. Tammuz, the Mesopotamian god of vegetation, was the consort of the fertility goddess Ishtar. He was consigned by her to spend half the year in the underworld, in recompense for her own release from death.

OSIRIS's *(right) death and the story of his grieving widow, Isis, contains elements common to other dying and rising myths. In some versions, Osiris was killed by Seth in the form of a bull or boar; in another he was encased in a coffin which became entwined in a living tree at Byblos, like the myrrh tree from which Adonis was born. Isis breathed new life into Osiris and conceived their son, Horus, but Seth dismembered his body and scattered the pieces, like grain being scattered in a field. Osiris crouches here on a pedestal, flanked by Isis and Horus.* (EGYPTIAN GOLD AND LAPIS LAZULI, 9TH CENTURY BC.)

BAAL *(left) was the son of the fertility god Dagan. He was armed with thunder (a mace) and lightning (a lance) for his epic battle with the sea god, Yam, who represented the forces of chaos and thus threatened nature. His victory spurred him to challenge the god of death, Mot, but he was killed. He was avenged by his sister and consort Anat, and Mot's defeat restored Baal to life so that fertility could return to the earth.* (SYRIAN LIMESTONE RELIEF, 17TH–13TH CENTURY BC.)

ATTIS *(right) was the consort of the Phrygian mother goddess, Cybele. In one version of his myth, he was gored by a wild boar, but according to the most famous story he is said to have castrated himself in a fit of madness brought on by the jealous Cybele. This theme was taken up by adherents of his cult, who mourned his death and celebrated his rebirth in frenzied and bloody rituals each spring.* (MARBLE BUST, IMPERIAL ROME.)

RA-HERARHTY see *HORUS*.

RASHNU was the personification of righteousness and a judge of the dead in ancient Iranian mythology. When people died, their good and bad deeds were weighed in golden scales in order to determine their fate. It took the judges three days and three nights to come to their decision, during which time the soul of the dead person would hover by its body, meditating on its life and anxiously awaiting the verdict. When the judgment had been made, the soul would be sent across the Chinvat, or Cinvat, Bridge, which led to *AHURA MAZDA*'s paradise. A beautiful lady would help the good souls across the bridge. Bad souls would find that the bridge was as narrow and sharp as the edge of a razor and would plunge downwards into the depths where demons waited to inflict every imaginable type of cruelty on them. But the stay in heaven or hell was only temporary, for not until the day of the resurrection will the whole person, body and soul, be judged.

RESEF see *RESHEF*.

RESHEF, or Resef, was the Phoenician god of lightning and plagues. He was referred to as "Lord of the Arrow", probably due to the manner in which he spread disease and sickness all about him. The god could also be invoked for healing. Reshef was sometimes regarded as the consort of the ferocious goddess *ANAT* and was the equivalent of the Mesopotamian plague god, Namtar. The Egyptians assimilated Reshef into their pantheon, where he was regarded as a god of war and depicted brandishing an axe.

***RESHEF**, the Phoenician god of plagues. From earliest times he was depicted as wielding an axe, or mace and shield, and wearing a tall, pointed headdress.* (BRONZE, CANAANITE, LATE BRONZE AGE OR EARLY IRON AGE.)

RUSTEM, the ancient Iranian hero, possessed a magnificent horse, Rakhsh, who was faithful and brave, and assisted him in his battles against dragons and demons. (ILLUSTRATION FROM SHAH-NAMEH MANUSCRIPT, 1486.)

RUDA, or "Gracious", was a pre-Islamic deity worshipped in northern Arabia. The deity sometimes appears in male form, sometimes female. Usually associated with the evening star, Ruda was sometimes known as Arsu.

RUSTEM, the hero of the 10th-century Iranian epic *Shah-Nameh*, was the son of *ZAL*, and a nobleman and adviser to the king. Whatever danger threatened the king's realm, Rustem always rode fearlessly into battle: he subdued countless earthly enemies, and fought and conquered demons. On one occasion, a demon surprised Rustem while he was asleep and threw him into the sea; none the less, the hero managed to escape.

Eventually the king, whom Rustem had looked after for countless years, became jealous of him. He ordered his men to dig deep ditches and to line their bases with sharp, upended spears and swords. The king then invited Rustem to go hunting on his land. Although Rustem's horse, Rakhsh, refused to enter the hunting ground, the hero spurred him onwards. Both horse and rider fell into a ditch and were pierced through and through. Rustem died, but before doing so, he shot the king dead with his bow and arrow. Rustem's bravery symbolized the battles between the Persians and the Turanians, Indians and Semites. (See also *HEROES AND QUESTS*)

SAHAR AND SALEM see *SHACHAR AND SHALIM*.

SANDA see *SANTAS*.

SANTAS was an ancient god of western Asia Minor. He was often associated with the mother goddess *KUBABA* and was sometimes referred to as "King". Santas sometimes appeared as the Babylonian god *MARDUK*, and he was assimilated into the Greek pantheon as the god Sandon.

SAOSHYANT is the name of the final saviour in Iranian mythology. His appearance will signal the arrival of the last days and the coming of Frashkart, the "final renewal". It is sometimes said that Saoshyant will be born of a virgin, who will become impregnated by the preserved seed of *ZOROASTER* while bathing in a lake. According to one tradition, the cycle of the world is made up of four ages, each lasting 3,000 years. The first 3,000 years were those of spiritual creation during which *AHURA MAZDA* brought the benign spirits and the *FRAVASHIS*, the guardian angels, into being. In the second 3,000 years, Ahura Mazda created the material world, *GAYOMART*, the primeval man, and *GEUSH URVAN* the primeval bull, although his work was hindered by *ANGRA MAINYU*, who introduced evil and destruction. In the third age, good and evil were locked in an intense struggle with one another and Angra Mainyu filled the world with evil spirits. At the beginning of the fourth and final period – the present age – the religious reformer Zoroaster appeared. This last age is that of Saoshyant, the saviour who will finally appear in order to renew the world and resurrect the dead.

A flood of molten metal will submerge and purify the whole planet, and Angra Mainyu will finally be destroyed. During the final renewal itself, the whole of humanity will be subjected to a burning torrent, which will cleanse them of all their evil ways and thus allow them to live with Ahura Mazda. Those who have lived blameless lives will experience the scalding torrent as no more than "warm milk". According to one tradition, Saoshyant will sacrifice a bull and mix its fat with the magical elixir, *HAOMA*, thereby creating a drink of immortality, which he will give to all humanity.

RUSTEM was surprised while sleeping by the demon Akwan, who tried to hurl him into the sea. Needless to say, the hero managed to escape. (ILLUSTRATION FROM SHAH-NAMEH, LITHOGRAPH.)

SATAN or Lucifer, the fallen angel, came to be seen as the ruler of hell. Here, with a triple face, he devours the traitor Judas Iscariot and two other sinners. (HAND-COLOURED WOODCUT, 1512.)

SATAN, whose name means the "Adversary", plays a minor role in the Old Testament as the opponent of humankind, ordered by *YAHWEH* to test humanity's faith. He is an angel in the kingdom of heaven and deals directly with Yahweh.

In the Book of Job, Yahweh instructs Satan to destroy Job's family and possessions and cover him with boils, with the intention of tempting him into cursing God. However, the patient Job declares: "What? Shall we receive good at the hand of God, and shall we not receive evil? In all this did not Job sin with his lips."

Satan came to be viewed by the Hebrews as the supreme evil being, under whom was ranged a hierarchy of demons. In opposition to the demons were the angels. Thus, the Hebrews came to see creation as a battle between the forces of good and evil, suggesting the influence of Persian thinking.

One tale relates how Satan, the devil and "prince of this world", rebelled against Yahweh and was hurled by an angel into the abyss. He is imagined in the form of a snake or a dragon. In Christianity, Satan became the embodiment of evil. He was pictured as a handsome man with horns, a pointed tail and cloven hoofs.

In the apocryphal Book of John the Evangelist, Jesus describes Satan's transformation: "My Father changed his appearance because of his pride, and the light was taken from him, and his face became unto a heated iron, and his face became wholly like that of a man: and he drew with his tail the third part of the angels of God and was cast out from the seat of God and the stewardship of the heavens." (See also *ANGELS AND DJINN*)

SEBEK, or Sobek, the Egyptian crocodile god, was represented either as the reptile itself or as a man with a crocodile's head. Sebek's following was greatest at Crocodilopolis, capital of the province of Fayum. A live crocodile called Petsuchos, said to be an incarnation of the god, was kept in a lake attached to Sebek's main sanctuary. Sebek's devotees sought the god's protection by drinking water from the pool and feeding the crocodile on delicacies. In the 13th dynasty, during the second millennium BC, many of the kings were called Sebekhotep, or "Sebek is Satisfied", and it is thought that many people regarded the god as the chief deity. According to some stories, the evil god *SETH* hid himself in Sebek's body to escape being punished for murdering *OSIRIS*.

Sebek was sometimes regarded as the son of *NEITH*, the great mother and warrior goddess, who was also credited with having given birth to the terrifying snake *APEP*. (See also *SACRED ANIMALS*)

SEKHMET see *HATHOR*.

SETH, an Egyptian god of storms and chaos, came to signify evil, although he was widely held in high esteem. The son of the earth god *GEB* and sky goddess *NUT*, he was rough and wild, with red hair and white skin.

Seth became so jealous of his gracious elder brother, *OSIRIS*, that he murdered him and appointed himself king of Egypt. However, unknown to Seth, Osiris and *ISIS* had conceived a child, *HORUS*. Isis nursed Horus in secret until he was old enough to avenge his father, and Osiris himself occasionally returned from the underworld to

SEBEK embodied the deadly power of the crocodile against its prey, and epitomized the military might of the pharoah. (RELIEF FROM TEMPLE OF SEBEK AND HORUS, KOM OMBO.)

SETH *(above), the slayer of Osiris, was not always considered evil. He was worshipped in prehistoric times, and again by the Ramessid pharaohs.*

SETH *(left), god of evil and the desert, with his wife Nephthys, the sister of Isis. He is depicted as a brutish animal, part pig, part ass.* (BASALT SCULPTURE.)

instruct his son in the art of war. When the right moment arrived, Horus went into battle against Seth and overcame him.

Before a divine tribunal, Seth declared that he was entitled to the throne of Egypt because he was the only deity strong and brave enough to protect *RA*. Although some of the gods sided with Seth, Isis persuaded them to change their minds. When Osiris was consulted in the underworld, he demanded to know why his son had not been allowed to take his rightful place on the throne and threatened to send demons to attack the gods. Ra finally agreed to Horus's claim.

According to one story, Seth went to live with Ra in the sky. Another version of the myth tells how Seth was condemned to carry Osiris on his shoulders for all eternity. Yet another tale relates how the goddess *NEITH* suggested that Seth should be given two foreign goddesses, *ANAT* and *ASTARTE*, as his wives, in order to console him for having lost the throne to Horus. A tale concerning Seth and Anat tells how the god came upon *HATHOR*, the cow goddess, when she was bathing in a river and raped her. Seth was immediately struck down with a terrible illness and his wife, Anat, appealed to Ra for help. Eventually Isis helped Anat cure Seth. The god symbolizes the harsh aspects of the natural world and was said to live in the arid desert.

SHACHAR AND SHALIM, or Shar and Shalim, "Dawn" and "Dusk", were the offspring of *EL*, the supreme god of the Phoenician pantheon. They were also known as Sahar and Salem. In ancient texts discovered at Ras Shamra in Syria, on the site of the city of Ugarit, the deities are described as having been conceived when El stretched out his hands like waves to the sea, making his two wives fruitful. The two wives are generally believed to be Ashera (see *ASTARTE*) and *ANAT*.

SHAMASH was the Babylonian sun god, able to expose injustice and falsehood with his searching rays. He was also the god of divination, and could be consulted through a soothsayer. He is shown here in his emanation as Mrn, chief deity of the city of Hatra. (PARTHIAN SCULPTURE, C. AD 150-200.)

SHAMASH was the Babylonian god of the sun, who saw all things and thus also came to be regarded as a god of justice and divination. Known to the Sumerians as Utu, his light uncovered every misdeed and enabled him to see into the future. Each morning, the scorpion men opened a gate in the vast mountain of Mashu and Shamash made his way out into the sky. Slowly, he climbed the mountain until he reached the high point of the sky; as evening approached, he rode his chariot towards another great mountain and disappeared through its gates. During the night, Shamash journeyed through the depths of the earth until he reached the first gate once more. The sun god's consort was Aya, who gave birth to Kittu, justice, and Misharu, law and righteousness. Shamash was depicted seated on a throne.

SHAR AND SHALIM see *SHACHAR AND SHALIM*.

SHAUSHKA was an important Hurrian deity who was identified with *ISHTAR*, the Babylonian goddess of love, fertility and war. Like Ishtar, she was depicted as a winged figure standing on a lion, and was attended by two women. The goddess seems to have had a dual nature.

SHU, the Egyptian god of air, was the male half of the first divine couple. His name is sometimes translated as "Emptiness", sometimes as "He Who Holds Up". Shu was created when the supreme god *RA*, as Ra-Atum, spat or sneezed him out of his mouth. His consort was Tefnut, goddess of moisture, who was created in the same fashion. Shu and Tefnut left Ra-Atum to explore *NUN*, the dark abyss that existed at the very beginning of time. Ra-Atum was distraught, thinking he had lost his children. When they returned, he wept tears of joy, from which the first human beings were formed.

Shu and Tefnut begat *GEB*, the earth, and *NUT*, the sky. Eventually, Shu separated his two children by pushing Nut upwards with his arms. He is often depicted as supporting the sky.

Shu succeeded Ra to the throne, but the followers of the terrifying snake *APEP* continually attacked him and, growing tired of the ceaseless conflict, Shu abdicated, leaving his son Geb to become king. After a terrible storm lasting more than a week, Shu took up residence in the sky. Sometimes, as son of the sun god, Ra, Shu is represented with the head of a lion.

SIN, the Sumerian-Babylonian moon god, was the father of *SHAMASH*, the sun god, *INANA* (or *ISHTAR*), the planet Venus, and Nusku, the god of fire. Sometimes known as Suen, or Nanna, he was conceived when the air god *ENLIL* raped the grain goddess *NINLIL* and was born in the underworld. Sin's consort was Ningal, or the "Great Lady". Sin was usually depicted as an old man with a blue beard, and he was called the "Shining Boat of Heaven". Every evening, he would climb into his crescent-shaped boat and sail across the skies. Sometimes, the crescent moon was regarded as the god's weapon and the full moon as his crown.

Sin was the enemy of the wicked, for his light revealed their evil ways. On one occasion, the utukku, or evil genies, hatched a plot against Sin and, with the help of Shamash, Ishtar, the goddess of love and fertility, and *ADAD*, the god of thunder, they eclipsed his light. However, the great god *MARDUK* waged war against the conspirators and gave Sin back his radiance.

Sin was also held to be wise and was believed to measure time with his waxing and waning. Moreover, by raising the marsh waters around the city of Ur, where his temple stood, he ensured the well-being of cattle by enabling them to enjoy an abundant supply of food. (See also *GATEWAYS TO THE GODS*)

SIYAMEK see *HAOSHYANGHA*.

SOBEK see *SEBEK*.

***SIN** (right) was the Babylonian moon god, whose symbol, the crescent moon, is depicted on this carved stone. The god was held in supreme regard in Mesopotamia. His chief cult centres were at Ur and Harran.* (KUDURRU, C. 1120 BC.)

***SHU** (below), supports a head-rest found in the tomb of Tutankhamen. The god of air, Shu was the father of the sky goddess, Nut, and was often depicted in this position, supporting the sky above his head.* (CARVED IVORY, 14TH CENTURY BC.)

T

SOLOMON's (left) wisdom and proverbs, led to this Old Testament king, the second son of David, becoming a legendary figure. It was said that he commanded djinn.

SOLOMON (right) reigned over Israel for 40 years. His great achievement was the building of the temple at Jerusalem. (BYZANTINE BOOK ILLUSTRATION, 11TH CENTURY.)

SOLOMON was the Old Testament king who ruled over Israel in the tenth century BC. He was noted for his great wisdom and for building *YAHWEH*'s marvellous temple at Jerusalem. Under the influence of his many foreign wives, Solomon also built shrines for other gods, thereby incurring Yahweh's wrath. Solomon's seal, a six-sided star, became an important symbol used as an amulet or talisman. According to Arabic mythology, the star and the real name of God were etched on King Solomon's magic ring, thereby enabling him to command armies of demons. (See also *ANGELS AND DJINN*)

SPENTA ARMAITI is one of the *AMESA SPENTAS*, or the "Holy Immortals", of ancient Iranian mythology. Like the other Amesa Spentas, she is believed to have originated before the religious reforms of *ZOROASTER* and to have been assimilated into the purified religion as an aspect of *AHURA MAZDA*, the supreme being. Spenta Armaiti was patroness of the earth, and symbolized submission and devotion. She was widely believed to be the spiritual mother of all human beings, and people were taught to say, "My mother is Spendarmat, Archangel of the Earth, and my father is Ohrmazd, the Lord Wisdom."

According to one tradition, she was the mother of *GAYOMART*, the primordial being. As Gayomart lay dying, his body separated into seven metals. Spenta Armaiti gathered together the gold and grew a plant from it. From this plant came the first human couple.

The name Spenta Armaiti is sometimes translated as "Wisdom" or "Devotion".

SRAOSHA was known as the "Ear" of *AHURA MAZDA*, the principle of good in ancient Iranian mythology. He was one of the *YAZATAS*, Zoroastrianism's "Beings Worthy of Worship". As the "Ear" of Ahura Mazda, he was the means by which those who worshipped the supreme being could gain access to him. During the night, Sraosha guarded the whole of creation from evil demons.

SUEN see *SIN*.

TAHMURAS, according to ancient Iranian mythology, was the son of *HAOSHYANGHA*, the first king. He taught people how to spin and weave, and how to train birds of prey. On one occasion, he succeeded in capturing *ANGRA MAINYU* and, after leaping on to his back, forced the evil being to carry him on a tour of the world. However, while Tahmuras was away on his travels, the *DAEVAS* began to create havoc, so Tahmuras had to return and take up arms against them.

The daevas gathered together a noisy army, which hid itself in thick black smoke. Undeterred by this, Tahmuras captured two-thirds of the aggressors with the help of his magic arts and struck down the remainder with his massive club. The daevas pleaded for mercy and promised Tahmuras that if he spared their lives, they would teach him a marvellous secret. Tahmuras relented and, in return, the daevas taught him how to write and made him extremely wise and learned.

TAMMUZ, the Babylonian god of vegetation and the harvest, was a dying and rising god. Relatively low in standing among the gods, he was nevertheless extremely popular with the people and had a widespread following. His marriage to *ISHTAR*, the lustful goddess of love and fertility, led to his death: just as corn is cut down suddenly at the height of its splendour, so Tammuz was forced to retire to the underworld. Ishtar was devastated at his loss and underwent a period of wailing and lamentation. Each year after the harvest, those who worshipped Ishtar and Tammuz took part in a mourning ritual.

Ishtar eventually sought out Tammuz in the underworld and managed to secure his release, on condition that he return to the underworld for half of each year. Tammuz returned to the land of the living and took up his position at the gate of the sky god, *ANU*. It was there that the wise man *ADAPA* encountered him, when Adapa was summoned before Anu for demonstrating too much power. Adapa flattered Tammuz, who rewarded him by interceding on his behalf.

Tammuz's sister was Belili. In Sumerian myth, he was known as *DUMUZI*, the consort of *INANA*. (See also *DYING AND RISING GODS*)

TAMMUZ (below) was sought after his death by the goddess Ishtar, who followed him to the underworld. (ILLUSTRATION FROM GILGAMESH BY ZABELLE C. BOYAJIAN, 1924.)

СОЛОМѠН

HEROES AND QUESTS

MYTHS ABOUT MORTAL HEROES HAVE AN immediacy that comes from their recognizable human characteristics. Though the great heroes performed astonishing acts of bravery and achieved feats that were far beyond the capability of any real man, their adventures took place on earth and, in some ways, they behaved as other men did – falling in love, falling asleep, making friends, making mistakes – so that those who listened to their stories could identify with them as they could not with remote gods and goddesses. These men feared death and could not avoid it, hard as they tried. A perilous journey was usually central to the hero's story. There were many thrilling adventures on the way, with twists and turns that diverted him from his path, and selfless deeds such as killing monsters that frustrated him in his quest but saved the day for ordinary folk.

GILGAMESH (above), king of Uruk, or Erech, was the hero of a number of Sumerian stories that were combined and written down by Babylonian scribes in about 2000 BC. Gilgamesh was said to be two-thirds god and one-third man because his mother was the goddess Ninsun. From her he derived his great strength. Despite his heroic stature, he began his reign as a tyrannical king, whose people were eventually driven to call on the gods for help in subduing him. (ASSYRIAN CYLINDER SEAL IMPRESSION, 1350–1000 BC.)

ENKIDU (above left) was a wild man sent by the gods to deal with Gilgamesh, in answer to his people's prayers. He was, however, even more unruly than the king. Gilgamesh conceived a plan to civilize Enkidu. As a test of strength, they fought in a great wrestling match, but neither could outdo the other, and the two became friends. Their adventures together included the killing of fierce bulls and the fire-breathing demon Humbaba. (AKKADIAN CYLINDER SEAL IMPRESSION, C. 2300 BC.)

GILGAMESH (left) resisted the seductive advances of the goddess Ishtar. Incensed, she sent the bull of heaven to avenge her honour, but with Enkidu's help, Gilgamesh managed to stab the bull. The gods were outraged and decided that Enkidu must pay for his part in the exploit. Within a few days, he had fallen ill and died. The loss of his friend instilled the fear of death in Gilgamesh and he embarked on a quest to find eternal life. (ILLUSTRATION BY E. WALLCOUSINS FROM MYTHS OF BABYLONIA AND ASSYRIA BY DONALD MACKENZIE.)

USHANABI (above), the ferryman, was the only man who knew how to cross the treacherous waters of death safely. He guided Gilgamesh over them on his way to reach the old man Utnapishtim, the sole survivor of the great flood, who had been granted immortality by the gods. Gilgamesh hoped that Utnapishtim would be able to tell him the secret of eternal life. (ILLUSTRATION FROM GILGAMESH BY ZABELLE C BOYAJIAN, 1924.)

UTNAPISHTIM (above) reluctantly told Gilgamesh of a plant growing at the bottom of the sea which had the power to give him eternal youth. Gilgamesh found the plant, but as he bent to pick it, a serpent smelt it and stole it. In this way, snakes acquired the ability to stay young forever by simply shedding their ageing skin. Gilgamesh was forced to understand that his death was inevitable and returned to his kingdom. (ILLUSTRATION FROM GILGAMESH BY ZABELLE C BOYAJIAN, 1924.)

RUSTEM (left), alone of all men, dared to fight the great White Demon in order to free the king, who had been inspired by the evil Angra Mainyu to try to usurp the throne of the ruler of Mazinderan. Rustem found the demon sleeping in his mountain lair, woke him and wrestled with him until "blood and sweat ran down in rivers from their bodies." Rustem was victorious and cut off the demon's head. (ILLUSTRATION FROM SHAH-NAMEH, LITHOGRAPH.)

RUSTEM (above), the Iranian hero, was born in a mysterious fashion, as a result of the incantations of a wizard and with the help of the magical feathers of the Simurgh bird. He was as tall as eight normal men and was famed for his strength and prowess in battle. One of his exploits in his youth was the killing of a rogue white elephant with a blow from an ox-headed mace. (ILLUSTRATION FROM SHAH-NAMEH BY SHIRAZ, C. 1545.)

RUSTEM (left) searched the country for a horse and eventually caught one that had in fact been set aside for him from birth. Rakhsh was as magnificent and brave as the hero himself, with the strength of an elephant and the speed of a racing camel. On one occasion, when Rustem was sleeping and unarmed, his horse saved his life by killing a lion before it could attack him. (ILLUSTRATION FROM SHAH-NAMEH BY INJU SHIRAZ, 1341.)

TARU, the Hittite weather god, was the father of *TELEPINU*. Like many other myths originating in West Asia, those featuring Taru are concerned with the annual cycle of vegetation. The tales relate his battles against a terrible monster, the giant serpent or dragon *ILLUYANKAS*. When Taru overcame the monster, vegetation flourished, but when he was vanquished all plant life withered and died.

According to one tale, Illuyankas managed to defeat the weather god. However, the goddess *INARAS* then hatched a plot whereby she managed to trap the terrible monster. The goddess prepared an enormous banquet and invited Illuyankas and his numerous offspring to come and join her in feasting.

When they had eaten their fill, the monsters discovered that they were too fat to fit through the tunnel that led to their underground home. The hero *HUPASIYAS*, Inaras's human consort, then tied the monsters up with a rope, whereupon Taru, assisted by the other gods, overcame them.

According to another version of the myth, the serpent overcame Taru, and seized his heart and eyes. Taru then fathered a son whom he married to the daughter of Illuyankas. The son asked for his father's missing organs as a dowry payment and returned them to Taru. The weather god then slew Illuyankas in a terrifying sea battle. He also killed his son, probably in revenge for his having sided with the monster during the battle.

TEFNUT see *SHU*.

TELEPINU was a Hittite god of agriculture who controlled the fertility of plants and animals. His father, *TARU*, the weather god, said of him: "This son of mine is mighty; he harrows and ploughs, he irrigates the fields and makes the crops grow."

On one famous occasion, which has become known as the "myth of the disappearing god", Telepinu suddenly vanished; his haste was such that he put his boots on the wrong feet. Immediately, all life on earth began to wither and die. Even the gods began to starve. Fire was extinguished, animals perished, the trees lost their leaves, and the fields became dry and parched. "Barley and emmer wheat throve no more, oxen, sheep and humans ceased to conceive, and those who were pregnant could not bear." The sun threw an enormous feast for the gods, but his guests were unable to eat their fill or quench their thirst. Finally Taru explained that his son was angry and had disappeared, taking all good things with him.

TESHUB (above) god of the tempest and head of the Hittite pantheon, bears an axe and a three-pronged lightning fork. He was also a god of battle and overcame Kumarbi, the father of the gods. Kumarbi's son Ullikummi fought to take control of Teshub's city, but without success.

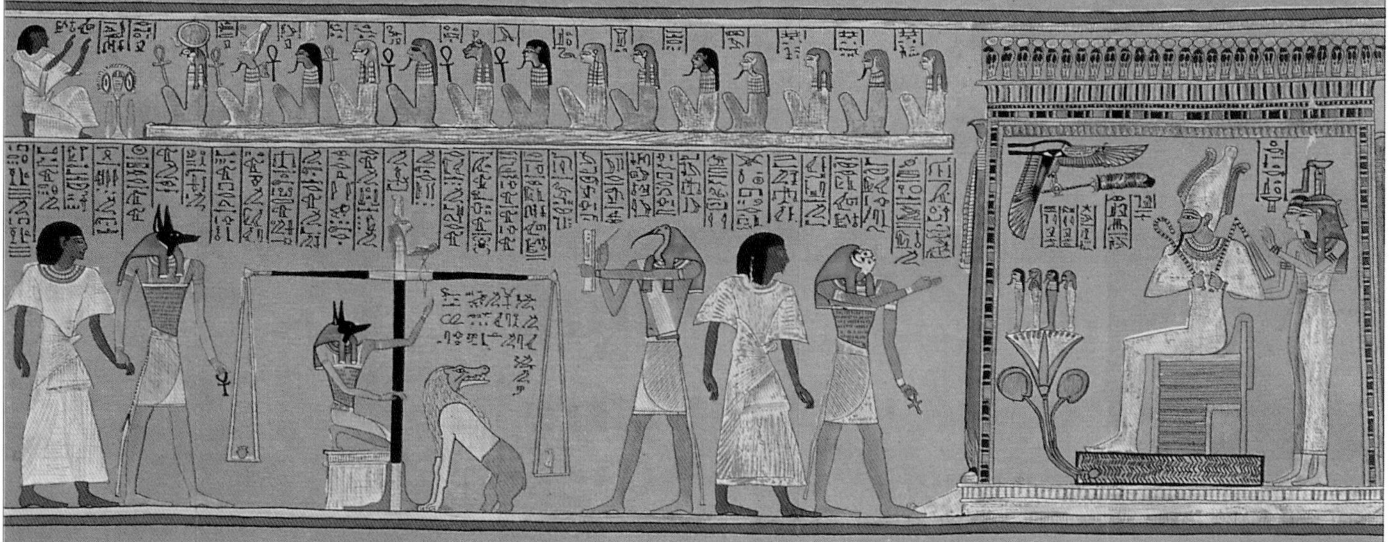

THOTH (below), the Egyptian moon god and vizier of Osiris, records the result of the weighing of a heart. As Osiris' sacred scribe, he was associated with secret knowledge and helped at the burial of Osiris. (FROM THE BOOK OF THE DEAD OF HUNEFER, C. 1310 BC.)

All the gods, both great and small, proceeded to search for Telepinu. The sun sent out the eagle saying, "Go, search the high mountains, search the hollow valleys, search the dark-blue waters." However, although the eagle explored the entire country, he failed to find the missing god. Then, the weather god asked the mother goddess, *HANNAHANNA*, for advice. Hannahanna told the weather god to go himself and look for Telepinu, but Taru soon gave up and sat down to rest. Then Hannahanna suggested sending a bee to look for the god. Although the weather god objected, the goddess ignored him and told the bee to find the Telepinu, sting him on his hands and feet to wake him up, and then bring him back home.

At length, the bee found Telepinu asleep in a field. When the bee stung him, the god fell into such a frenzy that he proceeded to cause yet more devastation, killing human beings, oxen and sheep in his wake.

Eventually, the goddess Kamrusepas managed to calm him down using her magic spells: "She stilled his anger, she stilled his wrath, she stilled his rage, she stilled his fury." Telepinu flew home on the back of an eagle, and life returned to normal: "He released the embers of the hearth, he released the sheep in the fold, he released the oxen in the stall. The mother attended to her child, the ewe attended to her lamb, the cow attended to her calf."

TESHUB was a god of the tempest who was worshipped throughout western Asia. He is believed to have originated among the Hurrians, although the chief myth concerning his activities has been passed down by the Hittites. In the Hittite mythological texts, it is recorded how the fearsome god Teshub overcame *KUMARBI*, the father of the gods. Kumarbi fathered a son, *ULLIKUMMI*, who was made of diorite stone and grew to a huge size on the back of the giant, Upelluri. In order to view the vast creature, Teshub climbed to the summit of a high mountain. On seeing the monster, the terrified weather god persuaded the other deities to join him in launching an attack. However, their assault proved unsuccessful. Ullikummi succeeded in advancing as far as the gates of Teshub's city, whereupon he forced the god to abdicate his throne.

Teshub sought advice from the wise god *EA* who, after pondering a while, unearthed the ancient saw with which heaven and earth had been divided, and used the tool to sever the diorite stone at its feet. As a result, Ullikummi's power quickly faded, whereupon the gods decided to renew their attack on him. Although the end of the myth is missing, it is generally believed that Teshub eventually regained his kingdom and throne.

Teshub was the husband of *HEPAT*, who was often given almost equal standing with her husband, and sometimes took precedence over him. Teshub's attributes were an axe and lightning flashes, and he was sometimes depicted as a bearded figure, holding a club, with his feet resting on mountain deities. His chariot was drawn by two bulls.

THOTH, the Egyptian moon god, presided over scribes and knowledge, and was "Lord of the Sacred Words". He was sometimes said to be the sun god *RA*'s eldest son, although, according to one tradition, he sprang from the head of the evil god, *SETH*.

Thoth is usually regarded as the vizier of *OSIRIS*, god of vegetation and the dead, as well as his sacred scribe. Because he was associated with secret knowledge, Thoth was able to help at the burial of Osiris. He also helped to look after *HORUS* when *ISIS* was bringing him up.

Eventually, Thoth succeeded Horus to the throne of Egypt and reigned peacefully over the land for more than 3,000 years. Afterwards, he took his place in the sky as the moon.

According to one story, he was ordered by Ra to light up the sky at night. There, he was slowly devoured by monsters who were, however, repeatedly forced to disgorge him bit by bit. Thoth was usually depicted as an ibis or as a baboon. It was said that Thoth wrote a book of magic, known as the *Book of Thoth*, which lies buried in a tomb near Memphis. The spells within the book were said to give the user power over the gods. Thoth was also said to record the verdict of the judgment of the dead in the underworld. (See also *SACRED ANIMALS*)

THOTH, god of the moon, writing and knowledge, with a scribe. Thoth was often depicted as a baboon, one of his sacred animals. (BRONZE, ARMARNA, C. 1340 BC.)

TIAMAT embodied the raw energy of the ocean. In the Babylonian creation story, she was split in two by Marduk to form the sky and the ocean floor. Her eyes became the sources of the great rivers Tigris (left) and Euphrates, on which the lives of the Mesopotamians depended.

TIAMAT, according to Mesopotamian mythology, was the turbulent, salt-water ocean that existed at the beginning of time. The universal primeval mother, she was depicted as a monstrous female dragon and was believed to embody the forces of chaos. The waters of Tiamat mingled with the fresh-water primordial ocean, *APSU*, and, in doing so, initiated the creation of the gods.

In time, Apsu grew tired of the clamour of the gods and began to plot their destruction. Tiamat at first refused to take part in Apsu's plan, but when the water god *EA* captured both Apsu and Mummu, the waves, Tiamat was spurred into action. After giving birth to an army of monsters, "sharp of tooth and merciless of fang", she marched against Ea and the other gods.

For some time, all attempts to subdue Tiamat failed until finally *MARDUK*, Ea's son, was chosen to confront her. Tiamat opened her jaws to swallow Marduk, but the god threw a raging storm into her mouth so that she was unable to close it. Marduk then caught Tiamat in a net and, after piercing her with an arrow, tore her innards apart. After slaughtering Tiamat's army of monsters, Marduk split Tiamat's skull and slashed her body in two. From one half of her body, he made the vault of the heavens, from the other half, the floor of the ocean. Then Marduk pierced Tiamat's eyes to form the sources of the rivers Tigris and Euphrates and bent her tail up into the sky to make the Milky Way. (See also *SERPENTS AND DRAGONS*)

TISHTRYA, or Tistriyn, was the name given by the ancient Iranians to the dog star. He was regarded as the god of water, whether that of the clouds, lakes, rivers or seas. Tishtrya also provided the seeds of useful plants. It was said that he helped *AHURA MAZDA*, the principle of goodness, in his struggle against every evil.

TISTRIYN see *TISHTRYA*.

ULLIKUMMI was the son of *KUMARBI*, originally an ancient Anatolian deity who was later introduced into Hittite mythology. The myth of Ullikummi concerns Kumarbi's attempt to wreak vengeance on his first son, *TESHUB*, who had overthrown him.

Kumarbi nursed the thought of creating an evil being and eventually slept with a vast stone, which subsequently gave birth to a son, Ullikummi. The boy was made of diorite stone, and in order that he might grow up in safety the deities placed him on the shoulders of the giant Upelluri in the middle of the sea. The child rapidly grew bigger and bigger until the water reached no higher than his middle, at which point the sun god noticed him and immediately told Teshub of the impending threat. Teshub wept

TIAMAT was the personification of the primeval ocean who, with Apsu, initiated the creation of the gods. Depicted as a mighty dragon, she eventually marched against Ea and the other gods. Only Marduk, Ea's son, stood against her and overcame her. (ILLUSTRATION BY EVELYN PAUL.)

with fear but, after being comforted by his sister, resolved to attack the monstrous being. However, though Teshub summoned the thunder and rain to help him, he was unable to defeat the creature.

Before long, Ullikummi had reached the gates of Teshub's city and forced the weather god to abdicate. Distraught, Teshub sought help from the wise god *EA*, who retrieved a saw that had originally been used to separate heaven from earth. Ea sliced through Ullikummi's ankles, and the monster's power faded. The gods then renewed their attack on Ullikummi, and Teshub regained the throne.

UTNAPISHTIM, according to one version of the Mesopotamian flood myth, was the wise man who alone survived the flood. The gods *ANU*, *ENLIL*, *NINURTA* and Ennugi decided to destroy humankind, having grown tired of their ways. However, *EA*, the water god, warned Utnapishtim of the conspiracy, and told him to build a boat and in it store the seeds of all life. Utnapishtim built a huge vessel 120 cubits high and loaded it with his family, his cattle and numerous other animals and birds.

On the evening that he finished his work, a filthy rain began to fall, and everyone on earth was stricken with terror. For six days and six nights, the deluge continued until, at daybreak on the seventh day, it suddenly ceased and all that was left of humanity was a vast heap of thick mud.

Utnapishtim, whose marvellous boat had come to the rest on the summit of Mount Nisir, cried out in grief. He let loose one bird after another from his boat, but they all returned, having found nowhere they could alight. However, when at last Utnapishtim released a raven, it failed to return, signifying that it must have found dry land.

In gratitude to the gods, Utnapishtim placed offerings to them on the summit of the mountain. Enlil, however, was furious to see that a human being had escaped the wrath of the gods. Ea eventually managed to calm Enlil down, whereupon Enlil took Utnapishtim and his wife by the hand and said that from now on they would be immortal, like the gods themselves.

Some time after these events, the hero *GILGAMESH*, a descendent of Utnapishtim, sought out the immortal in the hope of learning the secret of eternal life from him. Utnapishtim refused to disclose the secret, but nonetheless directed Gilgamesh to the bottom of the sea to find the plant of rejuvenation. Unfortunately, on Gilgamesh's journey home, it was stolen from him by a serpent when the hero stopped to bathe and rest. (See also *MYTHS OF THE FLOOD; HEROES AND QUESTS*)

UTTUKU see *SIN*.

UTU see *SHAMASH*.

***UTNAPISHTIM** was told by Ea to build a boat and take every kind of living thing aboard. The gods were about to punish the wicked city of Shurripak with a deluge, but Ea wished Utnapishtim to survive.*
(ILLUSTRATION FROM GILGAMESH BY ZABELLE C BOYAJIAN, 1924.)

W

VOHU MANO was one of the *AMESA SPENTAS*, or "Holy Immortals", of ancient Iranian mythology. These divine beings were believed to people the universe and to look after humanity. They are thought to have been worshipped before the time of the religious reformer *ZOROASTER*. Although Zoroaster denounced the old gods, he continued to venerate the Amesa Spentas as aspects of *AHURA MAZDA*, the one true spirit set in opposition to *ANGRA MAINYU*, the spirit of darkness. It was said that when Zoroaster was about 30 years old, Vohu Mano transported his spirit to Ahura Mazda, thereby bringing about his spiritual enlightenment. Vohu Mano ("Good Thought" or "Spirit of Good") reigned over useful animals and was often represented by the cow.

WADD was a moon god worshipped in certain parts of southern Arabia from the fifth to second centuries BC. His name means "Love" or "Friendship", and his sacred animal was the snake. Wadd is referred to in the Qur'an as a pagan divinity, one of five idols erected by the descendants of Cain.

***VOHU MANU**, the "Good Thought", was one of the Amesa Spentas of Iranian mythology. He personified the wisdom of Ahura Mazda, portrayed here presenting the crown of the kingdom of Persia to Ardechir I.* (ROCK CARVING, EARLY 3RD CENTURY BC.)

YAHWEH's followers avoided pronouncing the four Hebrew letters that made up his name, considering it too sacred to be pronounced aloud.

WADJET was the cobra goddess of Lower Egypt. She was usually represented as a cobra about to strike, although she sometimes appeared as a lioness. In the myth that relates how *ISIS* brought up her child *HORUS* in secret, Wadjet appears as the young god's nurse. Both Wadjet and *NEKHBET* were believed to protect the *PHARAOH*. (See also *SACRED ANIMALS*)

YAHWEH, or Jahweh, was regarded by the tribes of Israel as the creator of all things and the judge of all nations. He probably originated as a mountain god and was identified with *EL*, the supreme deity of the Canaanite pantheon. Yahweh intervened in earthly affairs, often through his prophets. He demanded that his followers should worship no other deity and was a jealous god. Though he dealt severely with anyone who strayed from his teachings, he was a god of righteousness and ultimately merciful. No physical likeness was ever attributed to him.

The Third Commandment decrees, "Thou shalt not take the name of the Lord thy God in vain", so his followers avoided pronouncing the four Hebrew letters, YHWH or JHWH, which made up his name. The letters are supposed to represent the identity of God and are usually interpreted as meaning "I am that I am". From the 13th century, Yahweh was sometimes known in English as Jehovah. (See also *SERPENTS AND DRAGONS*; *ANGELS AND DJINN*)

YAM, or Yamm, or Jamm, was the Phoenician god of the sea and water in general. One of his titles was "Ruler River". According to one myth, Yam asked the supreme god, *EL*, to grant him power over the other gods. El agreed but warned him that he must first conquer *BAAL*.

The fertility god equipped himself with magical weapons made by the smith gods and went into battle. He succeeded in killing Yam, proceeded to scatter his remains and then crowned himself king. The myth symbolizes the chaotic forces of nature being overcome by its civilizing aspect, which ensures the fertility of the crops.

Another tale tells how Yam was compensated for his defeat by being given the goddess *ASTARTE* as his bride. Yam was sometimes referred to as a dragon or serpent, or as the sea monster, *LEVIATHAN*.

YAMM see *YAM*.

THE YAZATAS, or "Beings Worthy of Worship", were the protective spirits of Zoroastrianism. Most of them were ancient Iranian gods who were incorporated into *ZOROASTER*'s reformed religion as helpers of the supreme being, *AHURA MAZDA*. Some of the Yazatas corresponded to the stars and planets, others to the elements, while many embodied abstract concepts. Sometimes, the celestial Yazatas were said to be led by Ahura Mazda and the terrestrial Yazatas by Zoroaster. They included in their number *RASHNU* and *SRAOSHA*.

YAM, the Phoenician sea god, represented the turbulence of nature. He was defeated by the fertility god, Baal. In some versions of his myth he married the goddess Astarte, though she is more often described as the consort of Baal himself. (GILDED BRONZE, 19TH–18TH CENTURY BC.)

ANGELS AND DJINN

ANGELS ARE INTERMEDIARIES BETWEEN heaven and earth, sent to bring messages to humankind – their name comes from the Greek word for "messenger". The Hebrew patriarch Jacob had a vision of angels on foot, ascending and descending a ladder which stood on the earth and reached up to heaven. Later concepts of heaven were of a more remote realm, from which winged angels flew down to earth. Angels are mentioned frequently in the Bible, praising Yahweh or appearing to humans bearing announcements or instructions from him. Islamic angels are also winged messengers; another of their tasks is to record the good and bad deeds of men, and they examine the faith of the dead on their first night in the grave. Djinn are less predictable. Originally nature spirits, they are a disruptive influence on humankind, capable of causing madness. A sinful man risks being turned into a djinnee (a lesser djinn) after his death.

THE PROTECTIVE SPIRITS *(above) of ancient Iranian mythology were portrayed as winged creatures, and it was perhaps this imagery that influenced the development of the idea of angels' wings. Protective, sheltering wings were an important symbol of the beneficence of Ahura Mazda, the supreme god of the Iranians, and are used to represent him.* (PERSIAN MINIATURE, C. 1370–80.)

THE DJINN *(above) were ugly and evil supernatural beings in pre-Islamic times, the fiery spirits of wild, desolate places who exercised their malign powers under a cloak of invisibility or by changing their shape at will. Their name means "furious" or "possessed". Though they were capable of redemption under Islam, those who refused to acknowledge Allah became demons.* (SYRIAN RELIEF SCULPTURE, 9TH CENTURY BC.)

THE ANGELS *(left), who were created before human beings, objected to Allah's plan to populate the earth, on the grounds that humanity would rebel against him. However, when Allah created Adam as the first prophet and taught him the names of all things, all the angels agreed to bow down before him. The single exception was Iblis, the devil, who considered that as he was born of fire he was superior to a being made of earth.* (OTTOMAN MINIATURE, 1558.)

LUCIFER *(above left), arriving in hell with Beelzebub, entered a new and dreadful domain, where he plotted his revenge as the adversary of humankind. Early Christian tradition, based on a passage of Isaiah and the words of Jesus – "I beheld Satan falling as lightning from heaven" – held that Satan had originated as an angel who had been thrown out of heaven because he was too proud to acknowledge the supremacy of Yahweh.* (ILLUSTRATION TO MILTON'S PARADISE LOST BY JOHN MARTIN, 1827.)

THE ARCHANGEL GABRIEL *(below) sits on the left hand of Yahweh and, in Hebrew literature, guards the left side of humans while they sleep. As a warrior, he will fight the last great battle with Leviathan, the symbol of chaos, at the end of time. According to Christian tradition it was Gabriel who was sent to announce the births of John the Baptist and Jesus. In Islam, he is Jibril, the angel of revelations.* (ARCHANGEL GABRIEL, BYZANTINE SERBIAN ICON, 14TH CENTURY.)

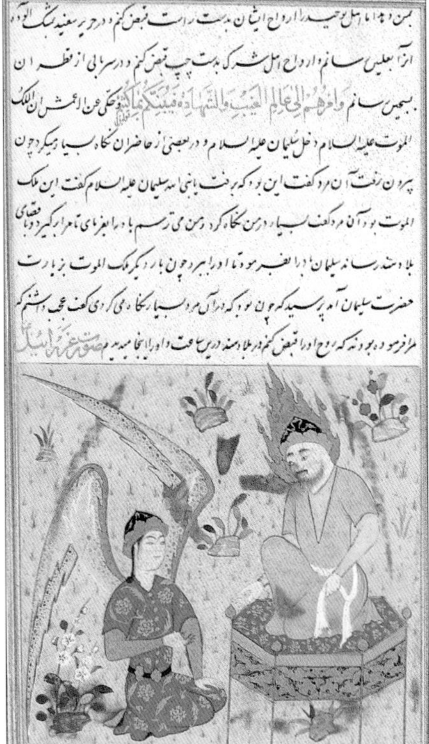

SOLOMON *(left), the son of David, was king of Israel for 40 years in the tenth century BC. His wisdom was legendary, and his reign prodigiously successful: his wealth and knowledge, together with his interest in the various religious practices of his many wives, led to his being credited with supernatural powers. He was said to converse with spirits such as peri and djinn, and the six-pointed star called Solomon's Seal was a powerful talisman.* (KING SOLOMON AND A PERI BY QAZWIN, C. 1570.)

THE TEMPLE *(above) in Jerusalem was the outstanding achievement of Solomon's long reign. It was built using a labour force of 180,000 men, but its scale and splendour prompted the legend that Solomon's magic powers gave him command over an army of djinn who had carried out the work. When the temple was completed, it was dedicated in a ceremony lasting 14 days, during which 22,000 oxen and 120,000 sheep were sacrificed.* (ILLUSTRATION FROM CALMET'S DICTIONARY OF THE HOLY BIBLE, 1732.)

MUHAMMAD *(above) travelled as a young man to Syria, where he met Christians, Jews and others who believed in a single god. He became convinced that they were right. When he was about 40 he retreated to a cave on Mount Hira to wrestle with his beliefs alone. There, he was visited by the angel Jibril, who insisted that Muhammad should "recite" his beliefs, in other words, that he should preach the truth about Allah.* (ILLUSTRATION FROM AN UNDATED MINIATURE.)

Z

YIMA, or Jam, or Jemshid, according to ancient Iranian mythology, was a great king. He was usually regarded as the son of *TAHMURAS*, one of the civilizing heroes, although according to some traditions the boy was born in a pillar of fire when a bolt of lightning struck the earth.

Yima governed the land wisely and justly, earning the title of the "Good Shepherd". As a priest, he was pious; as a warrior, he was strong; and as a herdsman, he was rich in cattle. He lived in a time known as the Golden Age, when death did not exist.

Because nobody died, Yima had to enlarge the earth three times, with the aid of his magic instruments. However, it came to pass that Mahrkusha, an evil demon, sent terrible floods followed by scorching summers down to earth, with the intention of annihilating all living creatures, both human beings and animals. Seeing what was about to happen, *AHURA MAZDA*, the principle of good, decided that the noble and upright Yima should be saved. He told him to build an underground dwelling place and to take into it every variety of man and beast. The fabulous chamber should also contain running water and trees, flowers and fruits. No diseased, wicked, ill-natured or deformed creature should be allowed entrance. Yima asked how he was to make this chamber, and Ahura Mazda replied that he should mould the earth with his hands and feet, as potters do. After the disaster, Yima emerged unscathed.

A later tradition claims that Yima eventually fell victim to the evil monster *AZHI DAHAKA*, who sawed him in two. It seems that he deserved this fate because he had committed the sin of pride.

ZAL, a hero of ancient Iranian mythology, was the son of Sam, a descendant of *FERIDUN*. Zal was born with white hair. Horrified by his strange appearance, his father ordered him to be left to die on the slope of a mountain. However, Simurgh, a noble vulture, rescued the baby and carried him to her nest on the peak of Mount Elburz. Simurgh was a mythical bird, said to be so old that she had seen the world destroyed three times, and had thus acquired great wisdom.

Zal grew up to become an extraordinarily beautiful young man. Sam, by now consumed with guilt for having abandoned his son, went in search of the child. He reached the home of Simurgh and entreated the vulture to return the young man to him. The bird agreed, and Sam blessed his son and called him Zal.

Zal had many adventures. On one occasion, he visited Kabul, which lay in his father's land of Hindustan. While staying with Mihrab, one of his father's servants, he learnt that his host had a beautiful daughter, Rudabeh. Without even having seen the young woman, Zal fell in love with her and she, hearing of Zal, fell in love with him. They arranged to meet in secret in a palace, which Rudabeh had filled with beautiful flowers and strewn with jewels. Rudabeh stood on a high terrace and looked down on Zal. Then, let-

ZAL was rejected as a baby by his father Sam, and exposed on a mountain. He was rescued by a fabulous bird called Simurgh, who raised him in her nest. (MINIATURE, MID 15TH CENTURY.)

ting down her beautiful hair, she told Zal to climb up it to her. Zal refused to do anything that might harm Rudabeh and instead climbed up a rope, which he managed to throw on to the terrace.

Although the young couple were deeply in love, they had to overcome the fact that Rudabeh's family were old enemies of Sam's employer, King *MINUCHER*. At length, Sam agreed to let Zal marry Rudabeh, particularly since astrologers had said that the couple would give birth to a great hero. That hero proved to be *RUSTEM*.

ZARATHUSTRA see *ZOROASTER*.

ZOHAK, according to ancient Iranian mythology, was the son of a desert king. He was persuaded by *ANGRA MAINYU*, the principle of darkness, to kill his father and seize the throne. Angra Mainyu then took up residence in Zohak's castle as his cook and persuaded the new king to introduce meat to his diet. Zohak was so pleased with his new cuisine that he promised Angra Mainyu a gift of his choosing. Angra Mainyu asked that he might kiss Zohak's shoulders, and rest his face and eyes there. After kissing the king, Angra Mainyu disappeared. Suddenly, a snake appeared from each of Zohak's shoulders. His courtiers tried to destroy them, but each time the snakes were sliced off, they grew again.

Disguised as a doctor, Angra Mainyu returned and told Zohak that he should feed the snakes each day with human brains. In this way, Zohak himself became a demon and ruled over the world for a thousand years, during which time evil reigned supreme. Finally, one night Zohak had a terrifying dream; when his advisers interpreted it for him, they said that it signified that he would be overthrown by a man called *FERIDUN*. Zohak ordered all children to be put to death, but the baby Feridun survived. When Feridun grew up he succeeded in killing Zohak and taking over the reins of power.

ZAL was carried by Simurgh to the highest peaks of Mount Elburz, where he grew up without his father's knowledge. Eventually, Sam was prompted by a dream to seek his son in the mountains, and the two were reconciled.

ZOROASTER, or Zarathustra, was a great religious reformer of ancient Iran. He was thought to have lived in the north-east of the country, some time in the sixth or fifth centuries BC, but scholars now believe that he lived much earlier, around 1200 BC. The compelling figure of Zoroaster gave rise to many myths. It was said that his birth was foretold from the beginning of time. The moment he was born, he burst out laughing and the whole universe rejoiced with him.

Although the evil demons, the *DRUJS*, tried to destroy the child, he was protected by *AHURA MAZDA*, the principle of good. When he reached the age of 30, Zoroaster was given numerous revelations from the *AMESA SPENTAS*, or "Holy Immortals". Once armed with these spiritual insights, Zoroaster was able to resist the temptations of *ANGRA MAINYU*, or Ahriman, the principle of darkness.

Zoroaster denounced the worship of numerous gods, which until then had been prevalent in Iran, and instead preached a purified faith, focused on the struggle between good and evil, or Ahura Mazda and Angra Mainyu. His faith was a type of monotheism, although it inclined to dualism.

It was said that on one occasion, Zoroaster visited the court of a king and performed numerous miracles, including curing the king's favourite horse, before finally winning him over to his religion. The king then waged war against numerous neighbouring kings in an attempt to convert them. According to tradition, Zoroaster was murdered at the age of 77 while at his prayers.

***ZOROASTER** was traditionally said to have had a miraculous birth. According to legend, his mother, Dughdova, who was a virgin, conceived after she had been visited by a shaft of light. Though evil forces repeatedly tried to destroy the baby, he was protected by Ahura Mazda.* (LIEBIG "CHROMO" CARD, 19TH CENTURY.)

ZOROASTER's *teaching was embraced by the Achamenian rulers of Iran, who built this square tower facing the royal rock tombs at Naqsh-i-Rustam near their capital, Persepolis. Known as the Ka'bah-i-Zardusht, it may have been used as a fire temple; fire was a Zoroastrian symbol of purity and wisdom.*

ZU was the demonic tempest bird of Mesopotamian mythology who lived in the underworld and stole the tablets of fate from *ENLIL*, "Lord of the Wind". The tablets gave whoever possessed them control of the universe. The supreme god *ANU* promised sovereignty over the gods to whoever recovered the tablets. Although the fragmentary nature of the surviving text makes the outcome difficult to establish for certain, it seems that the god *MARDUK* succeeded in regaining the tablets, although in some versions of the tale Zu is overcome by *NINURTA*, Enlil's son.

ZURVAN AKARANA came to prominence in Iranian mythology as the transcendent being who gave rise to *AHURA MAZDA*, the principle of good or light, and *ANGRA MAINYU*, or Ahriman, the principle of evil or darkness.

The religious reformer *ZOROASTER* had taught that Ahura Mazda was the one true god, who was set in eternal opposition to Angra Mainyu. This dualism, which became sharper as time passed, presented a problem: if Ahura Mazda was all-powerful, then he must have created evil. The concept of Zurvan Akarana, or "Infinite Time", managed to circumvent this intellectual dilemma.

ZOROASTER *was a priest, prophet and thinker who made huge innovations in religious thought. He preached a purified faith that focused on the struggle between light and darkness, or Ahura Mazda and Angra Mainyu.* (SYRIAN MURAL.)

It is probable that Zurvan Akarana originated as an important god of early Iranian mythology. However, in the centuries following *ZOROASTER*, devotees of the religious movement known as Zurvanism came to regard him as the primal and eternal being, beyond good and evil, who formed Ahura Mazda and Angra Mainyu in order that they should both struggle to dominate creation.

According to one tradition, Zurvan Akarana promised authority to the firstborn, leading Angra Mainyu to tear his way out of the womb. As a result, evil reigned for several thousand years. It was also said that Zurvan Akarana conceived his two offspring at the very moment when he began to doubt that he would ever give birth. In consequence, Ahura Mazda embodied his wisdom and Angra Mainyu his doubt.

THE MYTHS OF SOUTH AND CENTRAL ASIA

INTRODUCTION

THE IMMENSE INDIAN subcontinent encompasses an astonishing diversity of geographical regions. In the north lie the rugged Himalayan mountains, further south the vast agricultural plains of the river Ganges; there are high plateaux and low-lying coastal regions, vast rainforests and deserts. The climate is extreme, with scorching heat followed by drenching monsoons. This tremendously varied and unpredictable land has given rise to a rich mythology, many of whose deities have spread elsewhere, for example to Tibet and Sri Lanka, the other countries that are under consideration here.

A significant feature of Indian belief is the desire to transcend the chaos and unpredictability of the world in order to find the truth, nirvana (spiritual ecstasy) or enlightenment. From the earliest times, evidence suggests that people believed that they might achieve this goal through the practice of meditation. For example, modern excavations have uncovered evidence that the people of the Indus Valley civilization, which flourished around the middle of the third millennium BC in the region of modern Pakistan, worshipped a deity associated with meditation.

In the second millennium BC, the remarkable Indus Valley civilization collapsed under the constant incursions of the Aryan invaders, a group of Bronze Age tribes. The Aryans, or

GAUTAMA BUDDHA, *the founder of Buddhism, attained enlightenment after many incarnations as a bodhisattva, or "buddha-to-be", setting an example for all Buddhists to follow.* (GANDHARA-STYLE RELIEF, 3RD CENTURY BC.)

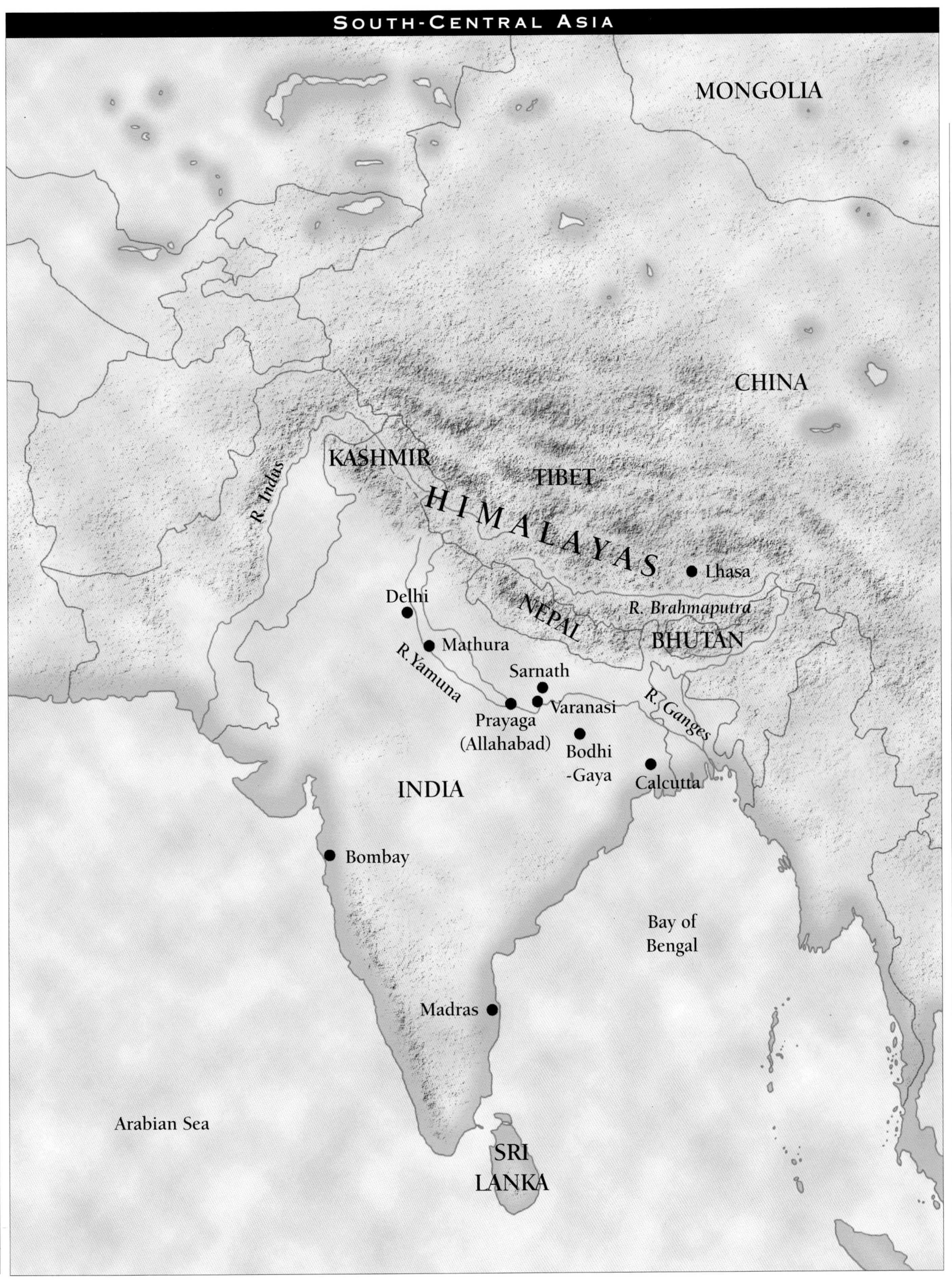
South-Central Asia
MONGOLIA
CHINA
KASHMIR
TIBET
R. Indus
HIMALAYAS
Lhasa
NEPAL
R. Brahmaputra
BHUTAN
Delhi
Mathura
R. Yamuna
Sarnath
Varanasi
R. Ganges
Prayaga
(Allahabad)
Bodhi
-Gaya
Calcutta
INDIA
Bombay
Bay of
Bengal
Madras
Arabian Sea
SRI
LANKA

"Noble Folk", believed in many gods, spirits and demons. Among their most important deities were Indra, a weather and warrior god; Varuna, a maintainer of order and morality; Agni, a fire god; Surya, a sun god; and Yama, king of the dead.

Many of the gods of the Aryan invaders are venerated in India to this day. None the less, some of the beliefs attributed to the people of the Indus Valley civilization were to resurface. For example, the great Hindu god Shiva is believed to have taken on some of the characteristics of the Indus Valley civilization's fertility god. Indeed, this ancient figure is sometimes known as "proto-Shiva". The god also demonstrates something of the continuity of Indian belief, the willingness of the people to adopt and assimilate deities into their own world-view. In the *Rig Veda*, a collection of sacred hymns composed between the 14th and tenth centuries BC, Shiva is only a minor deity known as Rudra. However, he later rose to become one of the three major gods of Hinduism, the belief system that developed from India's earlier religious traditions and prevails. Shiva also embodies the implicit contradictions of Hindu belief: that genesis cannot take place without previous destruction and that the ordered cosmos can only evolve from an initial state of chaos. Thus, though Shiva is known as the "Destroyer", his name means "Auspicious"; he is an ascetic (denying physical pleasures), but he is also extremely wild and has a huge sexual appetite.

Whereas the Aryans believed that after death they would either ascend to the heavens or descend to the underworld, by the time of the *Upanishads*, sacred teachings composed between the eighth and fifth centuries BC, the human condition had come to be seen as one in which people were trapped within a relentless cycle of birth and death. The goal was to transcend the cycle and achieve liberation. It may be that such ideas, totally absent from the teachings of the Aryan invaders, had their roots in the beliefs of the Indus Valley civilization.

Followers of Buddhism and Jainism, two religions which arose in India in the sixth century BC, were also dedicated to the use of

MANDALAS *symbolize the universe as a circle. Though often found in paintings, for ritual purposes they are drawn in rice or coloured powder on consecrated ground. The dance called mandala-nrtya, performed in a circle, is based on Krishna's dance with the gopis and symbolizes the constant presence of the god.* (DETAIL OF MANDALA OF BODHISATTVA AMOGHAPASA, GOUACHE, NEPAL, 1860.)

SHIVA *as Nataraja, "Lord of the Dance", represents creation and destruction in balance. He is supported by the bull, Nandi.* (STONE CARVING, 12-13TH CENTURY.)

meditative techniques as a means of release from the cycle of death and rebirth. For Jains, the path to liberation demanded that stringent austerities, including self-mortifications, be practised, while Buddhists emphasized the inward struggle. Although both Buddhism and Jainism deny the existence of a creator god, they have a rich mythology. Jainism focuses on the tirthankaras, the great teachers who show the way to achieve liberation. Buddhism, on the other hand, gave rise to the cult of buddhas and bodhisattvas ("buddhas-to-be"), who helped people along the path to enlightenment.

Veneration of the numerous buddhas and bodhisattvas smoothed the way for the assimilation of Buddhism by people used to deity worship. Moreover, the adoption of many deities from Hinduism, as well as other religions, helped Buddhism to spread and flourish. At the same time, such a policy produced a vast and often bewildering pantheon.

In the third century BC, Mahinda, a close relative of the great Indian emperor Ashoka, introduced Buddhism to Sri Lanka. The king of Sri Lanka was converted, and Buddhism became the country's dominant religion, remaining so to this day. In the seventh century AD, Buddhist missionaries travelled from India to Tibet. Although the new beliefs faced resistance from followers of the indigenous Bon religion, by the 12th century, Buddhism was firmly entrenched.

The Bon religion was characterized by a belief in the existence of two creator deities, the principles of good and evil, as well as a host of lesser gods and goddesses, and shared some similarities with shamanism. Buddhist teachers adopted many of the old shamanistic rites, attempting to contact the spirit world, and would often take the role of oracles or divine soothsayers for those Bon deities that had been brought into the new religion. This assimilation produced a very individual form of Buddhism, sometimes known as Lamaism, from the title, "Lama", given to Tibetan Buddhist religious masters or gurus. In time, Lamaism spread to Nepal, Mongolia and Bhutan.

VISHNU *was seen as the protector of the world. His first incarnation, or avatar, was as the fish, Matsya.* (WOODCUT BY BERNARD PICART, 18TH CENTURY.)

Within India, Buddhism was largely reabsorbed into Hinduism; the Buddha himself was said to have come into being as the ninth incarnation of the great Hindu god Vishnu. This continual absorption and assimilation of different beliefs is perhaps the dominant characteristic of Indian religion. Certainly, it is what has helped give rise to such a rich and varied mythology.

A

THE ADIBUDDHA, or "Primordial Buddha", rose to prominence in the 11th century as a result of an attempt to transform Mahayana, or "Great Vehicle" Buddhism, into a monotheistic religion, inspired by a sentence within a Buddhist text, which claimed that there was a self-emanating buddha who existed long before anything else. In Nepal, the Adibuddha came to be seen as infinite, omniscient and the supreme creator. It was said that he emanated from the mystic syllable "Om" and gave rise to the five *DHYANIBUDDHAS*, or "Great Buddhas of Wisdom".

In Tantric Buddhism, Vajradhara is identified with the Adibuddha, and is portrayed holding a bell and a thunderbolt. In Nepal and Tibet, the Adibuddha is usually shown wearing robes and the ornaments of a *BODHISATTVA*. His *SHAKTI*, or female energy, is Adidharma.

THE ADIBUDDHA or "Primordial Buddha", in the posture of Yab-Yum ("Father-Mother") with his shakti. (BRASS AND COPPER, TIBET, 16TH CENTURY.)

ADITI, a Hindu mother goddess, is regarded as the personification of the earth, and her bosom as its navel. Her name means "Infinity" or "Free from Bounds". She is symbolized by the immortal cow and is said to embody unlimited light, consciousness and unity.

Aditi is usually said to be the mother of the great god *VISHNU*, and she appears in the Veda, the "sacred knowledge" of the Hindus, as the consort of *BRAHMA* or *KASYAPA*. *DAKSHA*, the son of Brahma, is said to have been born of Aditi, and Aditi to have been born of him. The goddess is also the mother of the *ADITYAS*, the deities who protect the world from chaos and ignorance. She rules over the divine ordering of the world and is said to be able to free all those who believe in her from sickness and sin. Whereas Aditi corresponds to the universal and divine in humankind, her sister, Diti, corresponds to all that is individual, human and divided.

THE ADITYAS are the offspring of *ADITI*, the Hindu mother goddess. They are usually said to number seven or eight deities, including *MITRA* and *VARUNA*. However, in later times, there were sometimes said to be 12 Adityas, each of whom was associated with the sun as the source of life, and each connected with a month of the year.

The Adityas are believed to offer salvation from all ills. Martanda, the eighth son of Aditi, is sometimes regarded as the divine ancestor of human beings.

THE ADIBUDDHA, in Tibetan Buddhism, is the personification of pure sunyata, or emptiness, combined with wisdom. All buddhas are aspects of his nature. (TIBETAN PAINTING.)

AGASTYA was a great Hindu sage who was said to have been conceived when the beautiful Urvasi, one of the *APSARAS*, slept with both *MITRA* (or sometimes *SURYA*) and *VARUNA*. Agastya caused any obstacle that stood in the way of the well-being of the universe to disappear. When a range of mountains threatened to grow so high that it hid the light of the sun, Agastya begged it to shrink back down in order to let him pass, and to stay that size until he returned. The sage then tricked the mountain range by returning home along another route. On another occasion, Agastya helped the hero *RAMA*, an *AVATAR* of the great god *VISHNU*. When Rama went into battle against *RAVANA*, the king of *LANKA*, he shot off each of the demon's ten heads with his arrows. However, the hero found that as soon as one head was removed, another sprang up in its place. Rama finally produced a miraculous weapon which had been given to him by Agastya. The weapon's point was made of sunlight and fire, and it weighed as much as the mountains *MERU* and

AGNI *(left) spouts flames and carries a torch or flaming spear.* (FRENCH, 19TH CENTURY.)

AGNI *(right), as the god of sacrificial fire, is a mediator between gods and humankind.* (BRONZE, ORISSA, 11-12TH CENTURY.)

Mandara put together. The arrow struck Ravana, killed him, and then magically returned to Rama.

AGNI, or "Fire", is one of the chief deities of the *Rig Veda*, the sacred hymns of Hinduism. He is both the protective god of the hearth and the god of the sacrificial fire. In the latter role, he mediates between deities and human beings by taking sacrifices to the gods. Agni appears in the sky as lightning and is regarded as both cruel and kind: although he dispels darkness, he devoured his parents as soon as he was born and consumes the bodies on the cremation pyre. He is referred to as the son of heaven and earth, and is usually said to have emerged either from the sun or from lightning. Other sources regard him as the son of ADITI and KASYAPA, and he is sometimes said to have been born from stone or from the rubbing together of two pieces of wood.

One of the guardian deities of the world, Agni can grant immortality and purify people of their sins after death. He looked after the monkey god HANUMAN when the demon king of LANKA, RAVANA, set light to his tail. The god is portrayed as red in colour, with two or three heads, several arms, a long beard and clothes of flames. He is sometimes shown riding in a chariot drawn by horses but is also said to ride a ram or a goat.

AIRAVATA, *the great white elephant, carries Indra into combat with Krishna, who is mounted on Garuda. Krishna was to overcome Indra.* (WATERCOLOUR, C. 1590.)

AIRAVATA, according to Hindu mythology, was the great white elephant ridden by INDRA, the king of the gods. One myth tells how the goddess PARVATI invited all the gods to a great party held to celebrate the birth of her son, GANESHA. Sani, the planet Saturn, at first refused the invitation, but Parvati insisted that he accept. When Sani looked at Ganesha, the child's head was reduced to ashes. VISHNU, the preserver of the universe, went in search of another head for Ganesha, and returned with that of the elephant Airavata.

AKSOBHYA, one of the five *DHYANIBUDDHAS*, or "Great Buddhas of Wisdom", rules over the eastern paradise Abhirati. His name means "Immovable", and he is said to subjugate the passions and enjoy mirror-like wisdom. Long ago, when Aksobhya was a monk, he vowed before the buddha who then ruled over Abhirati that he would never experience anger or repulsion. After endlessly striving to achieve this goal, he finally became a buddha and took up rulership over Abhirati. Anyone who is reborn in Abhirati will never fall into lower levels of consciousness, so all believers seek, like Aksobhya, to conquer passion.

In Tibet, Aksobhya is represented as *GAUTAMA BUDDHA*. He is usually depicted as blue in colour, and he is sometimes shown supported by a blue elephant. His main attribute is the thunderbolt and he is associated with the element. His *SHAKTI*, or corresponding female energy, is Locana. Aksobhya emanates the *BODHISATTVA MANJUSHRI*, the patron of the kings of Tibet. (See also *DHYANIBUDDHAS*)

***AKSOBHYA** (above), whose name means "Immovable", rules over the eastern paradise Abrihati, a land without evil, ugliness or suffering.* (BRASS AND SILVER, TIBET, 13TH CENTURY.)

AMITABHA is one of the five *DHYANIBUDDHAS*, and one of the most important buddhas of Mahayana or "Great Vehicle" Buddhism. His name means "Boundless Light" or "He Whose Splendour is Immeasurable".

Amitabha rules over the western paradise, a state of consciousness known as Sukhavati. Everyone who believes in the buddha is promised entry to Sukhavati, where they are reborn. Amitabha is thus a type of saviour who assures people of a life after death: individuals are able to achieve liberation through calling on his name, rather than having to endure countless rebirths.

AMITABHA *(above) seated on a lotus flower, emits rays of golden light.*

AMITABHA *(left), who gave up his throne to become the monk Dharmakara, is shown here with a begging bowl. He achieved enlightenment and rules over the western paradise, Sukhavati.* (GILT BRONZE, TIBET.)

In a previous existence, Amitabha was a king who, after encountering the Buddhist teaching, gave up his throne to become the monk Dharmakara. The buddha is thus sometimes depicted with a shaven head. Dharmakara took 48 vows in which he promised to help all those who attempted to tread the path towards enlightenment. Through meditation, the monk eventually fulfilled his vows and became the buddha Amitabha.

His element is water, and he is associated with the twilight and life in the beyond. He is usually shown as red in colour, sitting on a lotus blossom; sometimes, however, he is depicted riding a pair of peacocks.

Although he originated in India, Amitabha achieved his greatest popularity in China and Japan, where he is known as Amida, the buddha who inspired the "Pure Land" school of Buddhism. In the eighth century, the Indian monk *PADMASAMBHAVA* introduced Amitabha's cult to Tibet, where it also gained a wide following. In both Tibet and Nepal, Amitabha is often depicted in Yab-Yum, the posture of embrace, with his *SHAKTI*, or corresponding female energy, Pandara. (See also *DHYANIBUDDHAS*)

AMOGHASIDDHI is one of the five *DHYANIBUDDHAS*. He presides over the paradise of the north, and his name means "He Whose Accomplishment is Not in Vain". Amoghasiddhi is sometimes identified with *GAUTAMA BUDDHA* and is normally coloured green. In Tibet, he is sometimes shown in Yab-Yum, the posture of embrace, with his *SHAKTI*, or corresponding female energy, Aryatara. The buddha sometimes sits on a throne decorated with garudas, eagle-like mythological birds. He may hold a sword in one hand and make the gesture of "Fear not" with the other. Amoghasiddhi's element is the earth and he is associated with the future buddha *MAITREYA*. (See also *DHYANIBUDDHAS*)

AMOGHASIDDHI *(above) one of the five Dhyanibuddhas, makes his characteristic mudra, or gesture, of fearlessness with his right hand.* (BRONZE ENGRAVED WITH SILVER, 14TH CENTURY, TIBET.)

AMRITA is the elixir of immortality that features in the popular Indian myth of the churning of the ocean. The tale tells how, when the authority of the old gods was weakened, the *ASURAS*, or demons, began to threaten to usurp their power. The great god *VISHNU*, the preserver of the universe, suggested that the gods revitalize themselves by drinking the miraculous elixir Amrita, which they would have to produce by churning the celestial ocean. However, Vishnu said that they would need the assistance of the demons to accomplish the task.

In accordance with his instructions, the gods uprooted Mount Mandara and placed it in the middle of the ocean. Using the snake Vasuki as a churning rope, they whirled the mountain around and around until eventually it bored downwards into the earth, forcing the gods to turn to Vishnu once again for help. In his incarnation as the turtle *KURMA*, Vishnu took the mountain on to his back and the churning began again, this time more smoothly. However, the snake Vasuki began to suffer terribly and eventually poured forth venom, which threatened to engulf the whole of creation. *SHIVA* then came to the rescue. He succeeded in swallowing the poison, although it burned his throat, leaving a blue mark on his neck.

In due course, the ocean turned to milk and then to butter. By now the gods were growing tired, but they persisted in their efforts until at long last the water gave rise to the sacred cow Surabhi. After Surabhi came Varuni, goddess of wine; Parijati, the tree of paradise; the sun, the moon and *LAKSHMI*, goddess of wealth and good fortune. Finally, the divine doctor *DHANVANTARI* appeared holding the precious drink Amrita.

According to one version of the tale, the evil demon Rahu snatched the Amrita and began to drink it. Quickly, Vishnu chopped off Rahu's head in order to prevent the elixir from spreading throughout the demon's body. None the less, Rahu's ghastly head remained immortal. According to another version of the myth, the drink penetrated throughout Rahu's body, whereupon Vishnu cut the demon into little pieces and set them among the stars. Yet another tale tells how the demons ran off with the sacred drink, whereupon Vishnu transformed himself into a beautiful woman, beguiled the demons and then succeeded in snatching the elixir back from them. The gods at last drank the Amrita and, having regained their power, drove the demons away.

AMRITA (left), nectar of the gods and the elixir of immortality, is held by the buddha Amitayus, sitting in meditation with the vase in his lap. (BRONZE, TIBET, 10TH CENTURY.)

AMRITA (right) came into being when the gods stirred up the oceans using the snake Vasuki as a churning rope.

ANANGA see *KAMA*.

ANANTA see *NAGAS*.

ANIRUDDHA, in Hindu mythology, is an epithet of Vahara, the third *AVATAR* of *VISHNU*. A *DAITYA* princess, Usha, fell in love with him and, assisted by her magical powers, brought him to her chambers. Hearing what had happened, Bana, the princess's father, sent his men to capture Aniruddha. The hero killed his assailants, whereupon Bana used his powers to kidnap the young man. When *KRISHNA*, his brother *BALARAMA* and his son, *PRADYUMNA* discovered what had happened, they determined to rescue Aniruddha. A tremendous battle ensued. *SHIVA*, the destroyer, and the god of war, *KARTTIKEYA*, both sided with Bana but, despite their help, Bana lost the battle. After acknowledging that Krishna was the supreme god, Shiva persuaded him to spare Bana's life. Aniruddha then returned home with the princess.

THE APSARAS, according to Hindu mythology, are heavenly nymphs who were originally associated with water and later with the countryside. According to the great epic, the *Ramayana*, their origin can be traced to the churning of the ocean (see *AMRITA*). When the Apsaras emerged from the water, neither the gods nor the *ASURAS* wanted to marry them, so they belonged to everyone and were known as the "Daughters of Joy".

The Apsaras are charming and beautiful dancers, and are said to be fond of games of chance. However, according to one tradition, they can also cause madness. They are sometimes said to live in fig trees and banana plants.

One myth tells how when King Pururavas was out hunting one day, he heard cries for help and discovered that two Apsaras were being carried off by demons. The king rescued the Apsaras and, struck by their beauty, begged one of them, Urvasi, to become his lover. Urvasi agreed on condition that she was never forced to see the king's naked body.

After living together for a while, Urvasi discovered she was pregnant. By this time, however, the *GANDHARVAS*, the friends of the Apsaras, missed Urvasi and hatched a plot, which would enable her to return to them. Urvasi possessed two pet lambs,

which she kept by her bed at night. One evening, the Gandharvas approached Urvasi and Pururavas as they lay sleeping, and stole one of the lambs. Urvasi loudly protested that she was shocked that anyone had managed to steal her lamb when "a man and a hero" lay next to her. The Gandharvas then took Urvasi's second lamb, whereupon she made the same comment. This time, Pururavas leapt out of bed, unable to bear the suggestion that he was not a man, and went to catch the thieves. The Gandharvas then lit up the sky with flashes of lightning so that Urvasi saw the naked body of her husband. At once, as she had sworn, she disappeared.

Pururavas set off in pursuit of Urvasi and eventually found her as one of a flock of swans, swimming on a lake with other Apsaras. He begged Urvasi to return to him, but she refused. Eventually she promised him that he could spend the last night of the year with her, in order that he might see his son.

On the last night of the year, the Gandharvas took Pururavas to a golden palace and brought Urvasi to him. Urvasi told him that, the following morning, the Gandharvas would grant him a wish. When Pururavas asked Urvasi what she thought he should ask for, she told him that he should seek to become a Gandharva.

The next morning, Pururavas did as Urvasi had advised. The Gandharvas gave him some sacred fire in a dish and said he must return home and offer up sacrifices. Back at home, Pururavas neglected the fire for a moment and it disappeared. One tree grew where he had left the fire, and another where he had left the dish. The Gandharvas told him that he should make another fire by rubbing together two pieces of wood, one from each tree. Having made the fire, Pururavas cast his offerings into it and achieved his wish to become a Gandharva. He lived with Urvasi ever after.

Another Apsara, Shakuntala, the mother of King Bharata, was said to live in the hermitage of a *RISHI*, or seer. King Dushyanta fell in love with her and asked her to marry him, then gave her a ring and returned home. Shakuntala, dreaming of her love, forgot to look after one of the hermitage's guests. In punishment, the guest told her that unless she journeyed to find Dushyanta and showed him her ring, the king would fall out of love with her. On her way to find the king, Shakuntala lost the ring in a lake, where it was swallowed by a fish. The fish was later caught and sold to the king who then remembered the Apsara and sent for her to come and live with him.

THE APSARAS, *or "Daughters of Joy", are invoked at weddings to bring good fortune. They are dancers in Indra's heaven.* (ANGKOR WAT, CAMBODIA, 12TH CENTURY.)

ARJUNA, the Hindu hero, was the son of the great god *INDRA* and Kunti, the wife of Pandu. Although Kunti was married to Pandu, he was under a curse and could not father children. Kunti conceived Arjuna and the other *PANDAVA* heroes after worshipping a variety of different gods.

ARJUNA is best known for his role in the *Bhagavad Gita* or "Song of the Lord", part of the Hindu epic, the *Mahabharata*. While waiting for the start of the great battle of Kurukshetra, Arjuna was troubled by the thought of the bloodshed and suffering that would ensue, especially since his opponents, the Kauravas, were his relatives. *KRISHNA*, the eighth *AVATAR* of the great god *VISHNU*, disguised himself as Arjuna's charioteer, and offered the hero comfort and spiritual teaching. He then urged Arjuna to do his duty as a kshatriya, or member of the warrior caste. Arjuna, overwhelmed with awe and devotion, was filled with renewed resolution. On another occasion, Arjuna and Krishna helped the fire god *AGNI* recover his power by burning down a huge forest.

ARUNA see *GARUDA*.

ASANGA see *MAITREYA*.

THE ASURAS, according to early Indian mythology, were beings who possessed supernatural or divine power. They were power-seeking and dangerous, and were opposed to the gods, or *DEVAS*. They are sometimes misleadingly described as demons, though they were not necessarily evil.

According to later Hindu texts, the creator being *PRAJAPATI* was the ancestor of both the devas and the asuras. The devas chose to follow truth, and the asuras chose to follow falsehood. At first, the asuras became rich through telling lies,

ARJUNA (left) the archer, a Pandava prince, rides into the battle of Kurukshetra against the Kauravas, which ended with the total destruction of both armies.

ARJUNA (above) and Krishna, the eighth avatar of the great god Vishnu, sound their transcendental conch shells. Krishna is disguised as Arjuna's charioteer.

but eventually they were destroyed. Occasionally, the devas were obliged to join forces with the asuras – as, for instance, during the churning of the ocean, when the gods sought to obtain *AMRITA*, the elixir of immortality.

One famous asura, Jalamdhara, was the product of the union of *GANGA*, the goddess of the river Ganges, with the ocean. There came a time when the power of the war god *INDRA* rose to equal that of *SHIVA*. Feeling threatened, Shiva manifested a towering form of anger and ordered it to wed the goddess Ganga to the ocean. The asura Jalamdhara was produced from their union, and *BRAHMA* bestowed upon him the ability to conquer the gods. Jalamdhara performed countless miracles in his youth before marrying Vrinda, the daughter of a nymph. He then gathered together an army of asuras and declared war on the gods.

A tremendous battle ensued and the great asura even succeeded in overcoming *VISHNU*, although the goddess *LAKSHMI* persuaded Jalamdhara to spare his life. Eventually, Jalamdhara succeeded in driving the devas from heaven.

The devas sought help from Brahma, who directed them to Shiva. He advised the devas to combine their powers and to make a fabulous weapon, whereupon the

***ARJUNA**, having broken a vow he had made to his brothers, had to endure 14 years' exile. During this time, he journeyed to the river Ganges, where he became the lover of the river goddess Ganga. She gave him the power to become invisible in water.* (PAINTING BY WARWICK GOBLE.)

devas forged a huge and dazzling disc, so bright that no-one could look at it.

Meanwhile, Jalamdhara tried to seduce Shiva's wife, *PARVATI*, although the goddess managed to escape him. Vishnu then disguised himself as Jalamdhara and succeeded in seducing Vrinda. When Vrinda realized what had happened, she died of grief.

Jalamdhara was furious. He resurrected his dead asuras and summoned them to battle once more. Shiva threw the marvellous disc at Jalamdhara, cutting off his head. However, the asura simply grew a new head in the old one's place each time Shiva beheaded him. Eventually, Shiva summoned the wives of the gods. Taking the form of monstrous ogres, the goddesses drank all the asuras' blood, whereupon the gods won the battle and regained their kingdom.

The Hindu epic the *Mahabharata* tells how Brahma granted three *DAITYAS* – asuras descended from Diti – permission to establish three cities: one of gold in heaven, one of silver in the air and one of iron on earth. The three brothers ruled over them for many years. Countless asuras flocked to the cities where they were provided with their every desire. Eventually, Shiva burned the three cities to the ground, together with all the asuras, and threw them into the depths of the ocean.

***THE ASURAS**, outwitted by Vishnu, chose to hold the head end of the serpent Vasuki during the churning of the ocean, and were nearly suffocated by the creature's hot breath.* (KANGRA MINIATURE, 18TH CENTURY.)

THE ASVINS, or "Horse Drivers", according to Hindu mythology, are golden-coloured twins who drive a three-wheeled golden chariot drawn by horses or birds. Known individually as Nasatya and Dasra, they bring divine bliss to humankind, and symbolize strength and energy. The offspring of the sun and the cloud goddess Saranyu, the Asvins are both married to daughters of the light. Each morning, they make a path through the clouds for the dawn goddess *USHAS* and scatter the dew with their whips.

In the *Rig Veda*, the ancient Hindu hymns, the Asvins often intervene with the gods on behalf of humankind. They also guard the *RISHIS*, or seers, from drowning in the sea of ignorance. The doctors of the gods, they are friends of the sick and unfortunate. They heal the blind and the lame, and rejuvenate the aged. They are chiefly associated with the war god *INDRA* and prepare the equipment of the warrior gods.

Although they are kind and beautiful, the gods originally forbade the Asvins entry to heaven. However, the rishi Syavana eventually came to their aid. Despite being well advanced in years, Syavana had a beautiful young wife, Sukanya. One day, the twins saw her bathing in a river and, after flattering her, tried to persuade her to leave her husband for one of them. Sukanya refused, whereupon the twins said that they would make Syavana young and beautiful again and that Sukanya should then choose from among the three of them. Syavana agreed and, after bathing in the river, the three men emerged, all looking young and handsome. Sukanya took a long time to come to a decision, but finally chose to stay with her husband. Syavana was delighted: not only had he kept his wife, but he had regained his youth and beauty. In gratitude, he persuaded Indra to allow the Asvins into heaven.

Mythical Mountains

The vast mountain range of the Himalayas inspired awe in all those who beheld it. Its peaks appeared to reach up out of the human world to touch the realms of the gods, and the range was regarded as sacred by both Tibetans and Hindus as a transitional domain between the human and the heavenly worlds. Mount Meru, the mythical axis of the cosmos, lay at its centre. One legend credited the mighty god Indra with the formation of the mountains: it was said that they had been a herd of flying elephants who had displeased him. He punished them by cutting off their wings. All the gods were thought to make sacrifices on the mountains, but Shiva was particularly associated with them. Mount Kailasa was his mythological paradise and, as an ascetic, his deep meditation on this mountain ensured the continued existence of the world.

__Parvati__ (above right) was the daughter of the god Himavat, king of the Himalayas, who was a deified personification of the mountains. Parvati's name means "Daughter of the Mountain" and she was an aspect of the mother goddess, Devi. She became the consort of the great god Shiva, who had his home on Mount Kailasa. Another daughter of Himavat was Ganga, the deity of the sacred river whose source is in the Himalayas and was said to flow through Shiva's hair. (Shiva and Parvati with Skanda, bronze, 10–11th century.)

__Meru__ was supported on the hood of the coiled primeval cobra, Vasuki, who created earthquakes when he yawned and will consume the whole world with his fiery breath at the end of the present age. Both Hindus and Buddhists acknowledge the mountain's sacred status, and its shape is symbolized in conical objects of worship and meditation called yantras, on which the material world is depicted at the outer edge, and the absolute and eternal at the centre. (Nepalese yantra.)

MERU (left) was the mythical mountain at the centre of the cosmos, the navel of the world, and was sacred to both Hindus and Buddhists. All the spheres of existence, from Brahma's heavenly city of gold at its summit, to the seven nether worlds at its foot, centred on the mountain, and the sacred river Ganges sprang from it. Its slopes glittered with precious stones and were clothed with trees laden with delectable fruits. It was surrounded by a vast lake and ringed with golden peaks. (MURAL PAINTING, WAT KO KEO SUTTHARAM, THAILAND.)

THE GODS (below) assembled on Mount Meru in search of the elixir of immortality, Amrita, which had been lost with other precious treasures in a catastrophic flood. Vishnu's solution was to churn the cosmic ocean until the treasures emerged. The gods uprooted Mount Mandara and set it on the back of the tortoise Kurma. The gods, with the help of the asuras, coiled the world serpent Vasuki around the mountain like a rope and each took an end. (THE CHURNING OF THE MILKY OCEAN, BASOHLI, C. 1700.)

MOUNT MANDARA (right), as it was spun, churned the cosmic ocean until it turned to milk, and then to butter. Eventually, the precious things it contained began to emerge: the sacred cow, Surabhi; the sun; the moon; Lakshmi, the goddess of good fortune; and, finally, the physician of the gods, Dhanvantari, holding the precious Amrita. The demon Rahu got hold of the elixir, but Vishnu rescued it by chopping off Rahu's head. The gods drank the Amrita to regain their power, and restored Mount Mandara to its proper place. (KANGRA MINIATURE, 18TH CENTURY.)

AVALOKITESHVARA is the most popular *BODHISATTVA* or "buddha-to-be" of Mahayana or "Great Vehicle" Buddhism. His name is translated as "Lord of Compassionate Sight" or "Lord Who Looks From On High". The Bodhisattva of the present age, Avalokiteshvara is said to have emanated from the great buddha *AMITABHA*. Although his residence is in Amitabha's paradise, he remains in this world in order to attend to the salvation of humans and animals. He is usually represented as a handsome man, with several heads and arms.

According to one myth, when Avalokiteshvara was looking down on the suffering in the world, his head burst open in pain. Amitabha put the pieces back together as nine new heads. Then, because Avalokiteshvara wanted to help all creatures, he grew 1,000 arms, and in the palm of each hand was an eye: "From his eyes were derived the sun and the moon, from his forehead, Mahesvara, from his shoulders, *BRAHMA* and other gods, from his heart, Narayana, from his thighs, *SARASVATI*, from his mouth, the winds, from his feet, the earth, from his belly, *VARUNA*."

Avalokiteshvara helps everyone who asks for his assistance. He visits hell to take cooling drinks to those suffering the heat of the damned, and he preaches the Buddhist law to beings incarnated as insects or worms. He is also said to protect people from natural disasters and to bless children. Moreover, the bodhisattva is said to have converted the female ogres of Sri Lanka and to have been given the task of converting Tibet to Buddhism.

In Tibet, his name is sPyan-ras-gzigs or *CHENREZIG*. In China, Avalokiteshvara developed into the goddess Kuan Yin, or Guanyin, and in Japan into the god, or sometimes goddess, Kwannon. (See also *BODHISATTVAS*)

AVALOKITESHVARA *(left) is also known as Padmapani, or "Lotus-bearer", and holds a pink lotus blossom in his hand. In eastern religions, the lotus signifies non-attachment, freedom from ignorance, and the path to enlightenment.*

AVALOKITESHVARA *(above) the bodhisattva of universal compassion, is an emanation of the meditation of the Dhyanibuddha Anitabha, and therefore wears an effigy of the great buddha in his headdress.* (BRONZE, 14TH CENTURY.)

THE AVATARS of *VISHNU* are his incarnations on earth in order to help humankind in moments of great crisis. It is generally accepted that Vishnu has ten avatars, although their number varies, and their identities are also flexible. Usually, the incarnations are said to consist of Matsya, *KURMA*, Varaha, *NARASIMHA*, Vamana, Parashurama, *RAMA*, *KRISHNA*, *GAUTAMA BUDDHA* and Kalkin.

Matsya, the first avatar, appeared as a fish who protected *MANU*, the first man, during the great deluge. The second avatar, Kurma the tortoise, supported Mount Mandara on his back during the churning of the ocean. Varaha, the boar, rescued the earth. The story tells how the earth, lost beneath floods, had been captured by a demon, whereupon Vishnu, as the boar Varaha, plunged into the waters and traced the earth by its smell. He killed the demon who had captured the earth and raised it out of the ocean on his tusks. Vishnu as Varaha is depicted as a giant with a boar's head, carrying the goddess of the earth.

The fourth avatar was Narasimha, who killed the powerful demon Hiranyakashipu, an incarnation of *RAVANA*. The demon had persuaded *BRAHMA* to give him the power to dethrone the storm god, *INDRA*, and to send the sky gods into exile. The demon then proclaimed himself king of the universe. Hiranyakashipu's son, Prahlada, was, however, a devotee of Vishnu. This so enraged Hiranyakashipu that he tortured the young man in an effort to dissuade him from his worship. Prahlada remained unswayed. Hiranyakashipu then ordered Prahlada to be put to death, but nothing could harm the young man. Eventually, Hiranyakashipu flew into such a rage that he struck a pillar, saying that if Vishnu was so important and omnipresent, why was he not right there, within the pillar? Immediately, the pillar collapsed, and Vishnu emerged in the form of Narasimha, a man with a lion's head. Narasimha immediately seized Hiranyakashipu and tore him to pieces, whereupon Prahlada succeeded his father to the throne.

Vamana, a dwarf, was the fifth avatar who came to save the world from the demon Bali. The sixth avatar was Parashurama. When his mother had impure thoughts, Parashurama decapitated her at his father's command. However, when his father granted him a wish, Parashurama asked that his mother be brought back to life. Later, when King Kartavirya insulted his father, Parashurama destroyed the whole kshatriya, or warrior, caste to which the king belonged. He then ordered the brahmans to sleep with the widows of the kshatriya men, in order to produce a new and purer warrior caste.

Rama, the warrior, is the seventh avatar of Vishnu, and the god, Krishna, is the eighth. Vishnu was said to assume his ninth avatar, the Buddha, in order to mislead the sinful so that they would receive their just deserts. Kalkin, the final avatar, has yet to come. He will appear at the end of the present age, or Kali *YUGA*, to establish a new era. It is thought that he will take the form of a warrior on a white horse, or a man with a horse's head. Kalkin will put an end to the wicked, and everything will be reabsorbed into the "Absolute" until creation begins again. (See also *THE AVATARS OF VISHNU*)

***THE AVATARS** surround this picture of the god Vishnu. Taking the form of various animals, the avatars appeared on earth to help humankind during times of crisis.*

(JAIPUR, RAJASTHAN, 18TH CENTURY.)

B

BALARAMA was the elder brother of *KRISHNA*, the eighth *AVATAR* of *VISHNU*, and was himself regarded as a partial avatar of the great Hindu "Preserver of the Universe". When the evil King Kamsa heard of Krishna's amazing exploits, he determined to kill him. He announced a wrestling match, challenging all the local young men to try their strength against the champions of his court. Krishna and Balarama, eager to take up the challenge, immediately made their way to the city where the contest was to take place. However, when it was their turn to fight, King Kamsa released a wild elephant into the ring. The elephant charged towards the two young men, but Krishna simply leapt on to its back, put his arms round its neck and squeezed it to death. King Kamsa then sent his two strongest champions into the ring, but Krishna broke the neck of the first and Balarama crushed the other so hard that his heart burst.

Krishna later killed King Kamsa, but Balarama was killed in a drunken brawl involving Krishna's kinsmen, the Yadavas.

***BALARAMA** holding a horn, with his younger brother Krishna, playing the flute. The brothers overcame the champions of the court of the evil King Kamsa.* (PAINTING BY BECHERAM DAS PANDEC, 1865.)

BALI see *VISHNU*.

***BODHISATTVAS** are living symbols of compassion. They choose to delay the moment of entering nirvana in order to help others along the path to enlightenment.* (STONE, 2ND–4TH CENTURY.)

BANA see *ANIRUDDHA*.

BANDARA was the title that was originally given to important officials within the Singhalese kingdom of Sri Lanka. In time, however, the term came to be used for a group of gods who were considered superior to the lesser deities, or *YAKSHAS*. For example, the god *DADIMUNDA*, treasurer to the supreme god *UPULVAN* and protector of Buddhism, is held to be a Bandara. Very often, a principal local god will be known simply as Bandara.

BCAN see *BTSAN*.

THE BDUD were the heavenly spirits of the indigenous Bon religion of Tibet. However, within Tibetan Buddhism, the bDud came to be seen as devils. They were said to be black and to live in a castle.

BEG-TSE, a *DHARMAPALA*, or "Protector of the Teaching", is a mythical warrior who is regarded as a symbol of the conversion of the Mongols to Tibetan Buddhism. He

BEG-TSE *(above), flanked by dakini, supernatural beings who are said to devour humans. He stands in his characteristic warlike pose, with one foot on a horse and the other on a man.*

wears armour and carries a garland of human heads. In Lamaism, he is a god of war. According to tradition, in the 17th century, Beg-tse sided with the Mongolian warriors and led an army of animals against the Dalai Lama. However, the Dalai Lama assumed the form of the *BODHISATTVA AVALOKITESHVARA* and converted Beg-tse to Buddhism.

BHAGIRATHA, according to Hindu mythology, was the sage who persuaded *BRAHMA* and *SHIVA* to send the sacred river Ganges down to earth from heaven. The earth had become littered with the ashes of the dead, and Bhagiratha realized that the waters of the Ganges would wash them away and liberate the spirits of those who had been cremated. In order to prevent a disastrous flood, the great god Shiva allowed the river to fall on to his head. For several years, the river meandered around the god's tangled locks, until at last Shiva divided it into seven streams and allowed it to flow safely out over the world.

BODHISATTVAS are "enlightenment beings" who are destined to become buddhas. They put off the moment when they will enter nirvana and escape the cycle of death and rebirth, in order that they may help others along the long path to enlightenment. Bodhisattvas are thus living symbols of compassion.

According to Mahayana, or "Great Vehicle" Buddhism, human beings are sometimes able to enter paradise by means of a bodhisattva's merits and spiritual power rather than through their own, provided that they call on the bodhisattva in faith.

Bodhisattvas are usually shown robed as princes, wearing five-leaved crowns. *AVALOKITESHVARA* and *MANJUSHRI* are two of the best known bodhisattvas. (See also *BODHISATTVAS)*

BHAGIRATHA *(below) endured rigorous austerities to induce the gods to allow the sacred river Ganges to flow down to earth, to carry away the ashes of his ancestors so that their spirits might be freed.* (ROCK CARVING AT MAMALLAPURAM, INDIA, 7TH CENTURY.)

BRAHMA, according to Hindu mythology, was the creator and director of the universe. He was the father of gods and humans alike, and in classical Indian thought, he forms a trinity with *VISHNU* and *SHIVA*. The three gods are collectively known as the Trimurti. Vishnu and Shiva represent opposing forces and Brahma, the all-inclusive deity, represents their balancing force.

Brahma was also the personalized form of Brahman. Originally, this term referred to the sacred power inherent within a sacrifice, but it came to refer to the power, known as the "Absolute", which lay behind all creation.

While the god Brahma meditated, he produced all the material elements of the universe and the concepts that enabled human beings to understand them. In each day of Brahma's existence, the universe is created, and in each night, it is reabsorbed. Within each of these cycles, there are four successive ages, or *YUGAS*, beginning with the Krita Yuga, or golden age, and ending with the Kali Yuga, the present age of conflict and despair.

According to one myth, Brahma produced the beautiful goddess Satarupa from his own body. She was so lovely that he was unable to stop staring at her, and whenever she moved aside to avoid his gaze, he sprouted a new head in order that he might continue looking at her. Eventually, Brahma overcame her shyness and persuaded Satarupa to marry him, and they retired to a secret place for 100 divine years, at the end of which *MANU*, the first man, was born.

BRAHMA, *the creator of the universe. His attributes include a vessel containing water from the sacred Ganges river. He is attended by Hamsa, a goose or swan.*

Another creation myth describes how, in the beginning, the universe was shrouded in darkness. Eventually, a seed floating in the cosmic ocean gave rise to a beautiful, shining egg. According to the sacred texts known as the *Laws of Manu,* "In this egg the blessed one remained a whole year, then of himself, by the effort of his thought only, he divided the egg into two." From the two halves, he made heaven, the celestial sphere, and earth, the material sphere. Between the two halves of the egg he placed the air, the eight cardinal points and the eternal abodes of the waters. "From himself he drew the Spirit, including in itself being and not-being, and from the Spirit, he drew the feeling of self which is conscious of personality and is master." The egg finally revealed Brahma the god, who divided himself into two people, a male and a female. In due course, these two beings gave rise to the whole of the rest of creation. Another version of the myth describes how Brahma

Brahma is often shown with four heads and four hands in which he holds the four Vedas, the holy scriptures of ancient India. His other attributes include a vessel containing water from the Ganges and a garland of roses. He rides on Hamsa, a goose or swan. Brahma's wife is the beautiful *SARASVATI*, the goddess of learning and patroness of arts, sciences and speech.

THE BTSAN, or bCan, are Tibetan demons who live in the air and appear before human beings as fierce hunters who ride their red steeds over the mountains. Anyone who finds themselves alone in wild and deserted places may be killed by the arrows of the bTsan.

CANDI see *DURGA*.

CANDRA see *CUNDA*.

CHAKRA SAMVARA see *SAMVARA*.

***BRAHMA** (above) produced a beautiful young woman from his own body. Each time she moved to avoid his gaze, he sprouted a new head so that he might continue looking at her.* (STONE, CHOLA PERIOD, 11TH CENTURY.)

***BRAHMA** (right) receives an offering in the presence of a sacred fire. In one of his left hands he holds the Vedas, the collections of sacred writings that form the basis of Hindu belief and religious practice.*

came forth from the egg as the primeval being known as *PURUSHA*. This creature had 1,000 thighs, 1,000 feet, 1,000 arms, 1,000 eyes, 1,000 faces and 1,000 heads. In order that the universe might come into being, he offered himself as a sacrifice. The gods and the brahman caste came from his mouth, the seasons came from his armpits, earth came from his feet and the sun emerged from his eyes.

Brahma was also sometimes known as Narayana, or "He Who Comes From the Waters". In this guise, he was regarded as lying on a leaf, floating on the primeval waters sucking his toe – a symbol of eternity.

Brahma's following was probably at its height in the early centuries of the first millennium AD, when he seems to have been the focus of a cult. Usually, however, he was regarded as less important than Vishnu and Shiva, the other two great gods. Today, there is only one temple dedicated to him in the whole of India.

Brahma's fall from supremacy is accounted for in a myth concerning the origins of Shiva. According to the tale, Brahma and Vishnu were arguing over which of them was the most powerful. At the height of their quarrel a huge lingam, the phallic-shaped symbol of Shiva, arose from the cosmic ocean, crowned with a flame. When Brahma and Vishnu examined the lingam, it burst open. Deep within it the gods found the ultimate creator deity, Shiva, and they had to admit his supremacy.

CHENREZIG, or sPyan-rasgzigs, means "Looking with Clear Eyes" and he is the Tibetan form of *AVALOKITESHVARA*, the *BODHISATTVA* of compassion. He is believed to be the protector of Tibet and, according to tradition, is the founding father of the Tibetan people.

One tale tells how the Buddha *AMITABHA* saw the suffering of human beings and created Chenrezig out of his compassion for them. The bodhisattva is said to have appeared on a small island in the middle of Lhasa and, on seeing the immense suffering of all the creatures who surrounded him, to have vowed that he would never leave the world until every one attained peace.

The innumerable creatures all begged to be given bodies. Chenrezig did as they requested and, in order that they might achieve spiritual liberation, he preached the Buddhist teachings to them. However, more and more creatures kept appearing. Eventually, Chenrezig despaired of ever being able to help everybody. He begged Amitabha to allow him to break his vow and, in despair, his body broke into countless pieces.

Amitabha felt sorry for Chenrezig and re-created him, giving him even greater power. The bodhisattva now had numerous heads, 1,000 arms and an eye in the palm of each hand. Chenrezig still felt daunted by the task that lay ahead of him and began to weep at the thought. From one of his tears, the goddess *TARA* was born, and together, they proceeded to help everyone attain liberation.

Tibetans traditionally regard their original ancestors as Avalokiteshvara in the form of a monkey and the goddess Tara (sGrol-ma) in the form of a rock ogress. One story tells how the monkey journeyed to the Himalayas in order to engage in a prolonged and undisturbed period of meditation. When he arrived at his destination, he was soon spotted by a rock ogress. Although the ogress attempted to seduce the monkey, none of her charms succeeded in persuading him to break his vow of chastity. The ogress became so frustrated and angry that it seemed that she might be about to destroy the world, whereupon the monkey finally gave in to her entreaties. The couple eventually produced six children. From these children, the entire population of Tibet arose.

King Songtsen Gampo (AD 620–49), who was responsible for the introduction of Buddhism to Tibet, is traditionally said to have been an incarnation of Chenrezig. The Dalai Lama is also regarded as an incarnation of the bodhisattva.

***CHENREZIG**, the bodhisattva, is the protector of Tibet and is believed to be incarnated in its spiritual leaders.*

CUNDA, or Candra, or Cundi, is a *BODHISATTVA*, regarded either as a female form of *AVALOKITESHVARA* or as an emanation of Vajrasattva or *VAIROCANA*, whose image she sometimes bears on her crown. She is said to have given birth to 700,000 buddhas and is therefore sometimes referred to as "Mother of the Buddhas".

Cunda may have developed from the Hindu goddess of the dawn, *USHAS*. She has one face, numerous arms and is coloured

white, like the autumn moon, or green. She rides upon the back of a prostrate man. The bodhisattva is kindly but threatening and possesses numerous weapons, including a thunderbolt, sword, bow, arrow, axe and trident. However, two of her hands are held in the gestures of teaching and charity. Although she helps the good, she is terrifying to the wicked. According to one Tibetan tale, she helped a warrior to destroy a wicked queen, who took a different king to her bed each night and killed him. (See also *BODHISATTVAS*)

CUNDI see *CUNDA*.

DADIMUNDA, or Devata Bandara, is one of the most popular gods of the Singhalese people of Sri Lanka. Originally, he looked after temples, but later he became treasurer to the supreme god *UPULVAN*.

Dadimunda finally emerged as the protector of Buddhism in Sri Lanka. He is said to ride on an elephant, attended by numerous *YAKSHAS*, or lesser deities.

THE DAITYAS, according to Hindu mythology, are giant *ASURAS* who oppose the gods. They are the offspring of Diti, the sister of *ADITI* and one of the wives of the sage *KASYAPA* who fathered *GARUDA*.

HAYAGRIVA is a famous daitya who appears in both Hindu and Buddhist mythology. On one occasion, he attacked *BRAHMA* and stole from him the four books that make up the Veda, the "sacred knowledge" of the Hindus. *VISHNU*, reincarnated as the *AVATAR* Matsya the fish, managed to kill Hayagriva and retrieve the sacred texts. In Tibetan Buddhism, Hayagriva was a lord of wrath, the leader of the terrifying gods known as Drag-shed (see *DHARMAPALAS*.)

Another daitya, Prahlada, was renowned for his devotion to Vishnu. According to one tradition, Prahlada was raised by Vishnu in order that one day he might become king of the daityas. Prahlada's father, the demon king Hiranyakashipu and avatar of *RAVANA*, was furious that his son worshipped Vishnu, but eventually Vishnu, as the avatar *NARASIMHA*, killed Hiranyakashipu.

The Hindu epic, the *Mahabharata*, tells how three daitya brothers asked Brahma to grant them invulnerability. Brahma said it was impossible to do so, whereupon the brothers asked that they might establish three cities and return to them after 1,000 years. Brahma agreed. He told the great asura Maya to build the cities: one of gold in heaven, one of silver in the air and one of iron on earth. The three brothers then ruled over their realms, populated by countless asuras, for many years, until, eventually, *SHIVA* burned the three cities, together with all the asuras, and threw them into the ocean.

***THE DAITYAS**, with the other asuras, were persuaded by the gods to help them obtain Amrita. The daityas wanted to drink the elixir, but the gods offered them wine instead. When the daityas were all drunk, the gods made off with the Amrita.* (Illustration to the Mahabharata.)

***THE DAITYAS** fought the gods for possession of Amrita, which the gods needed to restore their superior power. Here, it is carried by Brahma, in the midst of the battle.* (Illustration to the Mahabharata.)

BODHISATTVAS

Bodhisattvas are future Buddhas. They have such compassion for humanity that they take a vow to attain enlightenment, not just for their personal liberation but to show others the path they have found. In Mahayana Buddhism, this means that, even though they have reached the threshold of nirvana, they delay their own freedom and resolve to stay in the world to help others. For them, their own achievement of nirvana is not their only goal. They perceive further stages of enlightenment to be attained on the route to becoming a buddha. Celestial bodhisattvas, such as Manjushri and Avalokiteshvara, are very near to becoming buddhas themselves, and they act as mediators between the buddhas and mortals. They are not monks, but lay figures who are often portrayed as princes, wearing elaborate jewellery and a five-leaved crown. The bodhisattva Maitreya is the buddha of the future, a benevolent character who will arrive on earth in about 30,000 years, when the Buddhism of the present age has expired.

PADMAPANI *(left), the "Lotus Bearer", is an aspect of Avalokiteshvara, depicted holding a lotus blossom. The lotus is a religious symbol in both Hinduism and Buddhism; in the latter it represents those who have conquered ignorance and achieved enlightenment. Padmapani is associated with the colours red and white, and wears an image of the buddha Amitabha on his crown, since Avalokiteshvara is Amitabha's attendant.* (BODHISATTVA PADMAPANI, KHARA KHOTO, 13TH CENTURY.)

AVALOKITESHVARA *(above), "The Lord Who Looks Down", is greatly revered in Mahayana Buddhism as the embodiment of compassion. He is sometimes depicted with as many as a thousand arms, all of which he uses to help humanity. The bodhisattva's compassion is so great that he even enters the realms of hell to alleviate the sufferings he finds there. In Tibet, where he is known as Chenrezig, the successive Dalai Lamas are regarded as incarnations of the bodhisattva.* (TIBETAN STATUE, 14TH CENTURY.)

A MANDALA *(left) has Avalokiteshvara at its centre. He is shown with many heads because he was so distraught by his vision of the sufferings on earth that his head split open with pain. In the mandala, a symbolic representation of the universe, the four walls and four open gateways are taken to include within them the whole external world, at the centre of which sits the bodhisattva in the position of lord of the world.* (TIBETAN PAINTING.)

MANJUSHRI *(above), the great bodhisattva, personifies wisdom and learning. The sword he wields in his right hand is used to cut through the veil of ignorance. In his left hand he carries a lotus blossom, holding a scroll which contains the "Perfection of Wisdom": these writings describe the ideal of the bodhisattva as the highest aspiration of religious life, and the emptiness of phenomena which characterizes Mahayana Buddhism.* (CHINESE, 15TH CENTURY.)

CUNDA *(left) is a female bodhisattva, sometimes called the "Mother of the Buddhas". She is said to be kindly to the good but terrifying to the wicked: she is portrayed with as many as 16 arms, each of which holds a threatening weapon, but for a worshipper who knows how to regard her, her hands are in the positions of teaching and charity.* (RELIEF FROM CENTRAL INDIA, 10TH CENTURY.)

VAJRAPANI *(left), the indigo bodhisattva, is one of the most important wrathful deities. Vajrapani is the destroyer of evil. His fierce demeanour represents the attitude needed to turn hatred against itself and transcend it. He is armed with a Vajra, or thunderbolt, which is the weapon of the Hindu gods Indra and Karttikeya. Vajrapani is also said to be the embodiment of skilful actions.* (TIBETAN PAINTING.)

THE DAKINI, according to traditional Buddhist belief, are supernatural beings, or low-ranking goddesses. They fly through the air and are said to eat human beings. The dakini have magical powers and are able to initiate novices into the secret wisdom of the Tantra, a series of ritual texts dealing with the attainment of enlightenment. They can also help Yogis who wish to further their spiritual progress since they are able to concentrate the powers that the Yogi releases.

The dakini are usually shown dancing and appear as young naked women, as horrible monsters, or with the heads of lions or birds and the faces of horses or dogs. They also feature in Hindu mythology, as witch attendants on the goddess *KALI*.

In Tibetan Buddhism, dakinis are known as khadromas, female beings who move in celestial space. Their nakedness symbolizes their knowledge of perfect truth. The khadromas are said to live in Urgyen, a mythical realm that is also regarded as the birthplace of *PADMASAMBHAVA*, one of the founders of Tibetan Buddhism. In Tibet, eight goddesses, represented as beautiful young women, are sometimes included within the group of dakinis. They are known as the "Eight Mothers" and are thought to have developed from Tibetan shamanism.

DAKSHA, according to Hindu mythology, is the lord of cattle and the son of the mother goddess *ADITI*. He chose Sati, one of his 60 beautiful daughters, to be the wife of the great god, *SHIVA*. One tale tells how Daksha prepared an important sacrifice to which he invited all the gods, including *INDRA*. However, he failed to invite Shiva. Sati was outraged at this slight to her husband but decided that, even if her husband were not invited, she herself would attend the ceremony. Shiva was highly impressed by his wife's loyalty. However, he told her that Daksha was sure to insult him and that she must be strong and not respond to his insults.

When Sati arrived at her father's house, Daksha immediately began to insult Shiva, scorning his wild dancing and his appearance. Sati, finally overwhelmed with fury, denounced her father in front of all the gods. Then, since she had broken her promise to Shiva, she threw herself on to the sacrificial fire and was burnt to death.

Shiva was so angry and distraught at this turn of events that he sent one of his emanations, a terrifying demon, to kill everyone who had attended the ceremony. At length, the great god *VISHNU*, the preserver of the universe, persuaded Shiva to bring the guests back to life. Daksha finally acknowledged that Shiva was indeed a great god, and as a sign that he recognized his own stupidity he adopted the head of a goat. Shiva entered into a deep and prolonged meditation and awaited the time when Sati would be reincarnated as *PARVATI*.

In another version of the myth, Daksha's head was torn off, and Sati was brought back to life after the massacre. The goddess begged Shiva to restore her father to life. The great god agreed but, because nobody could find Daksha's head, he was given that of a ram.

THE DANAVAS are half-divine, half-demonic beings of Hindu mythology who were banished by the war god, *INDRA*, to live in the ocean. The monster Bali, whom it is said that *VISHNU* overcame in his incarnation as Vamana the dwarf, was a danava. The danavas were *ASURAS*, and although they are often described as "demons", they were not totally evil.

Vishnu, for example, recognized that Bali had shown himself to be capable of honourable behaviour and so rewarded him by making him king of the underworld.

DASRA see *ASVINS*.

DEVADATTA was a cousin of *GAUTAMA BUDDHA*. He became a member of the Buddhist community but grew jealous of Gautama and planned to murder him. First of all, he sent a group of assassins to murder the great teacher. However, the men were so impressed by the Buddha that they repented their evil intentions and became his followers. Then, Devadatta tried to crush Gautama by rolling an enormous boulder on

DHANVANTARI features in the ancient Indian myth of the churning of the ocean. It was he who appeared bearing *AMRITA*, the elixir of immortality, from the milk ocean. Dhanvantari was also known as Sudapani, or "One Who Bears Nectar in His Hands". The master of universal knowledge, he came to be regarded as the physician of the gods. He is the guardian deity of hospitals which are usually in the vicinity of a sanctuary of *VISHNU*.

top of him. However, the boulder stopped before it reached its target. Finally, he sent a wild elephant to gore the Buddha to death. The elephant was, however, tamed by the Buddha's kindness. When he died, Devadatta was condemned to lengthy sufferings in hell.

DEVAKI see *KRISHNA*.

***DEVI** (above), the great Hindu goddess, is the subject of an attempted seduction by her husband Shiva. On the right, he praises her for having resisted temptation.* (SANDSTONE, CAMBODIA, 13TH CENTURY.)

***DEVI** (left) is honoured by the Hindu gods, Shiva, Vishnu, Brahma, Ganesha and Indra.* (ILLUSTRATION BY J. HIGGINBOTHAM, 1864.)

THE DEVAS are the divine beings of the Veda, the ancient sacred teachings of India. The devas were regarded as immortal, and their chief attribute was their power, which enabled them to help human beings.

They later came to be regarded as those gods who are less important than great gods such as *ISHNU* and *SHIVA*. Although they inhabit a realm higher than that of human beings, they are still mortal. Among these Hindu devas are groups such as the *ADITYAS*, the rudras and the vasus.

In Buddhism, the devas are divine beings who live in the celestial heavens but are none the less subject to the ongoing cycle of death and rebirth. Most of the Buddhist devas originated in the Indian pantheon. They have long, pleasurable lives, and promote and protect Buddhism.

DEVATA BANDARA see *DADIMUNDA*.

DEVI is an aspect of the "Great Goddess" in Hindu mythology. It is the name by which the god *SHIVA*'s wife is sometimes known and is also the name given to female Hindu deities in general. Devi, as Shiva's *SHAKTI*, or consort, is both a benevolent and a fearsome deity, and is regarded as a major goddess within Hinduism.

She is a complex figure, taking many different forms, including those of *DURGA*, *KALI*, *PARVATI* and Sati. Sometimes, she also takes the form of goddesses who are independent of Shiva. Her main attributes are the conch, hook, prayer wheel and trident. (See also *THE MOTHER GODDESS*)

***DEVADATTA**, the Buddha's cousin and his rival from childhood, hatched a plot to murder him, but his hired assassins were all stricken with remorse as soon as the Buddha touched the wall behind which they were hidden.*

***THE DAKINI** include eight Tibetan goddesses, of which images such as this one were used in rites of exorcism which drew on shamanistic practices.* (CARVED HUMAN BONE, TIBET, 18TH CENTURY.)

DHARMAPALAS are "Protectors of the Dharma", or teaching. In Buddhism, particularly in Tibetan belief, they are regarded as ferocious divine beings who protect the faithful from the evil demons and bad influences which might thwart their spiritual progress. As such, the Dharmapalas are similar to the *GUARDIAN KINGS*. In Tibet, the Dharmapalas are worshipped either individually or in groups of eight, when they are known as the "Eight Terrible Ones" or Drag-shed. The eight are usually said to be *KALADEVI* (Lha-mo), *BRAHMA* (Tsangs-pa), *BEG-TSE*, *YAMA*, Kuvera (Vaishravana), *HAYAGRIVA*, *MAHAKALA* or Mahalka ("Great Black One") and *YAMANTAKA*. Vaishravana is also one of the Guardian or Celestial Kings.

In Tibet, the Dharmapalas are usually shown frowning, with tangled hair surmounted by a crown of five skulls. Most of them are in Yab-Yum, the posture of embrace, with their *SHAKTI*.

Some of the Dharmapalas were also Lokapalas (Guardian Kings) who existed in pre-Buddhist times as members of the Bon pantheon. *PADMASAMBHAVA*, one of the founders of Tibetan Buddhism, assimilated some of these ancient deities and transformed them into deities who protected the Buddhist law. However, some of the Lokapalas were adopted from the Hindu religion.

THE DHYANIBUDDHAS, or five "Great Buddhas of Wisdom", are the five meditating buddhas who, according to some traditions, are said to have arisen from the primeval buddha, *ADIBUDDHA*. They are sometimes referred to as Tathagatas ("Perfected Ones"), Transcendent Buddhas, or Jinas.

***DHARMAPALAS** with ferocious frowns decorate these ceremonial weapons. They wear jewellery of writhing snakes and each have a third eye in its forehead.* (NEPALESE RITUAL AXES, 18–19TH CENTURY.)

G

DURGA, *mounted on a lion, in combat with Mahisha, the terrible buffalo demon who threatened the power of the gods.* (PAINTING BY BIKANER, RAJPUT SCHOOL, 1750.)

The term Jina means "Conqueror", and refers to someone who has succeeded in overcoming the cycle of rebirth and suffering.

The Dhyanibuddhas are *VAIROCANA* or Mahavairocana, *AKSOBHYA*, *RATNASAMBHAVA*, *AMITABHA* and *AMOGHASIDDHI*. They are sometimes regarded as symbols of the various aspects of enlightened consciousness. On the other hand, they are sometimes believed to represent the body of the Dharma or teaching. Whereas followers of the non-Mahayana schools of Buddhism tend to venerate *GAUTAMA BUDDHA*, Mahayana Buddhists make any one of the five Dhyanibuddhas their chief object of worship. Occasionally, Gautama Buddha replaces Amoghasiddhi as one of the Dhyanibuddhas and sometimes *KSHITIGARBHA* is considered one of their number. (See also *DHYANIBUDDHAS*)

DIPANKARA, or the "Lighter of Lamps", was a Buddha of a past age whom Shakyamuni, or *GAUTAMA BUDDHA*, met in a previous life when he was the sage Sumedha. After having honoured Dipankara, Sumedha determined that he would become a Buddha himself. He became a *BODHISATTVA*, or "buddha-to-be", and passed through countless lives before entering the *TUSHITA* heaven prior to his final birth, to Queen *MAYA*. Dipankara recognized that Sumedha would become Gautama Buddha, and proclaimed his glorious future.

DITI see *ADITI*.

THE DMU were supernatural beings of the indigenous Bon religion of Tibet. They are said to have lived in heaven.

DRAG-SHED see *DHARMAPALAS*.

DURGA is the great Hindu mother goddess whose name means "She Who is Difficult to Approach", or "Inaccessible". She is an aspect of the *SHAKTI* of *SHIVA*, and can be terrifying and ferociously protective. She is usually depicted with a beautiful face and with eight or ten arms, in which she carries various weapons given to her by the gods.

Other goddesses are often identified with her, including Candi, who protects against wild animals, and Shitala, who protects against smallpox. She also manifests herself as the bloodthirsty *KALI*.

Durga is said to have been born fully formed, ready to do battle against demons. When the terrible buffalo demon Mahisha threatened the power of the gods, not even *VISHNU* nor Shiva dared stand against him. However, Durga rose to the occasion. The demon changed first into a buffalo, then into a lion, whereupon Durga sliced off his head. Mahisha then turned into an elephant, but the goddess cut off his trunk. Although he hurled mountains at her, Durga overcame the monster, crushing him and killing him with her spear (See also *THE MOTHER GODDESS*).

DUSHYANTA see *APSARAS*.

THE GANDHARVAS are a class of Hindu demigods who are said to inhabit the heaven of the war god *INDRA* along with the *APSARAS*. They are part human, part horse and, as nature spirits, are associated with the fertility of the earth. The gandharvas guard the *SOMA*, the sacred drink that conveys divine powers. Some of them appear at Indra's court as divine musicians and singers. According to the *Rig Veda*, the ancient hymns composed by Vedic Aryans who came to India from central Asia, at the beginning of existence a gandharva united with an apsara to produce the first pair of human beings, *YAMA* and Yami.

DURGA *is a slayer of demons who threaten the order of creation. She killed Mahisha, who was invulnerable to man and beast.* (ILLUSTRATION BY J. HIGGINBOTHAM, 1864.)

GANESHA is the Hindu god of wisdom and literature, and the son of *PARVATI*, the wife of the great god *SHIVA*. He is portrayed with the head of an elephant and a pot belly, a symbol both of his greed and his ability to dispense success. He has four arms but only one tusk. An extremely popular deity, he is invoked at the outset of new undertakings. He is regarded as the patron of business, and business-people hold ceremonies in his honour. He was traditionally the first scribe of the great Hindu epic, the *Mahabharata*. He was said to have been so keen to write it down that he tore off one of his tusks to use as a pen.

One myth tells how, when Shiva was away from home, Parvati grew bored and lonely. She decided to make herself a baby and created Ganesha, either from the rubbings of her own body, from dew and dust, or from clay. She later ordered the child to stand guard outside the entrance to her rooms. When Shiva returned home and tried to see his wife, Ganesha, not realizing who he was, barred his entrance, whereupon Shiva knocked his head off. Parvati was distraught and demanded that her son be brought back to life. The first head Shiva could find was that of an elephant. Parvati was delighted. Ganesha subsequently looked after the ganas, Shiva's attendants.

According to another myth, Parvati invited the god Sani, the planet Saturn, to visit her son. However, she had forgotten how dangerous the god could be and when he looked at Ganesha, the child's head burst into flames. *BRAHMA* told Parvati to repair her child with whatever she could find, which turned out to be the head of the elephant, *AIRAVATA*.

GANESHA's *(above) mount, the rat, was originally a demon, who was vanquished and transformed by the elephant-headed god.* (STONE, 11TH CENTURY.)

GANESHA *(below), patron of literature, with Sarasvati, goddess of learning and the arts, mounted on a peacock and holding a lute.* (ILLUSTRATION BY J. HIGGINBOTHAM, 1864.)

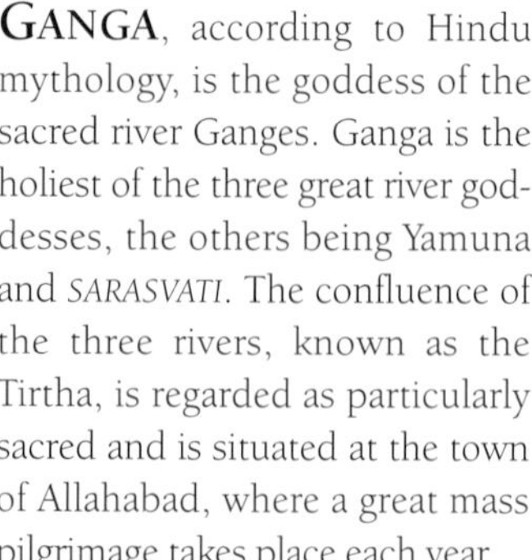

GANGA, according to Hindu mythology, is the goddess of the sacred river Ganges. Ganga is the holiest of the three great river goddesses, the others being Yamuna and *SARASVATI*. The confluence of the three rivers, known as the Tirtha, is regarded as particularly sacred and is situated at the town of Allahabad, where a great mass pilgrimage takes place each year.

Ganga is said to have emerged from one of *VISHNU*'s toes. Until her descent, she was believed to live in the sky, but when the earth became filled with the ashes of the dead, the sage *BHAGIRATHA* prayed that the gods might allow her purifying waters to come down to earth. The gods agreed. However, the descent of the great river threatened to engulf and destroy the entire earth, so *SHIVA* allowed it to land on his head as he sat meditating on Mount Kailasa. After spending several years in Shiva's hair, the river separated into seven different streams and flowed down over the earth.

GANGA *(right) the personification of the sacred river Ganges, is usually depicted holding a waterpot and a lotus in her hands.* (STONE, BENGAL, 12TH CENTURY.)

According to one myth, Ganga nourished the semen of Shiva in her waters, eventually producing the warrior god Skanda, also known as *KARTTIKEYA*. The tale tells how Shiva offered up six of his seeds to the fire god *AGNI*, who gave them to Ganga for safekeeping. Swaha, the daughter of a sage, visited the river on six successive nights and was impregnated by the seeds, eventually giving birth to Karttikeya. The child had six heads, and six or 12 arms and legs.

Another myth tells how *INDRA*'s power was beginning to threaten that of Shiva, whereupon a form of anger manifested itself before Shiva and asked that it might serve him. Shiva told the form to submerge itself in the Ganges and to marry the goddess to the ocean. A son called Jalamdhara, an *ASURA*, resulted from the union, and *BRAHMA* gave the asura the power to conquer the gods. (See also *SACRED RIVERS*)

GARUDA, according to Hindu mythology, was the prince of birds and the son of the sage *KASYAPA*. According to one account of Garuda's birth, Kasyapa had two beautiful wives, Kadru and Vinata. The sage promised to provide both wives with heirs. Kadru chose to give birth to 1,000 splendid serpents, whereas Vinata asked for only two sons. However, Vinata requested that her sons' strength and prowess should surpass that of Kadru's offspring.

Eventually, Kadru laid 1,000 eggs and Vinata laid two. After 500 years, 1,000 serpents emerged from Kadru's eggs. However, Vinata's two sons failed to appear. Impatient, Vinata broke open one of her eggs to find an embryo with only the upper half developed. The embryo became Aruna, the red glow of dawn. Aruna cursed his mother and ascended into the sky, where he remains to this day. Another 500 years passed and Vinata's remaining egg finally broke open to reveal Garuda.

***GARUDA**, half human, half eagle, was the chosen mount of Vishnu, who rides him with his consort, Lakshmi, seated on a lotus flower.* (PAINTING, BUNDI, C. 1770.)

Another tale tells how, in order to free herself from a curse, Vinata was forced to acquire *AMRITA*, the elixir of immortality and to give it to her nephews, the 1,000 serpents. Vinata asked Garuda to seize the drink from the gods and, after a mighty struggle, he succeeded in doing so. He put the drink down in front of the serpents, but said that they must purify themselves before drinking it. While they were busy performing their ablutions, *INDRA* retrieved the Amrita, as had been previously arranged with Garuda.

Garuda was a devotee of *VISHNU*, the preserver of the universe, and he was chosen by the god to be his mount. He appeared whenever summoned by Vishnu's thought, and fought with him against demons and demonic serpents. Garuda is depicted with the head, wings and claws of an eagle. In Buddhism, garudas are divine bird-like creatures.

GAURI see *PARVATI*.

GAUTAMA BUDDHA (left) has an urna, or symbolic circle of hair, between his eyebrows, derived from Indian images of Shiva's third eye: it indicates spiritual vision. (GILT-COPPER, NEPAL.)

GAUTAMA BUDDHA (right), having decided to renounce the world, cuts off his hair. (TIBET, 18TH CENTURY.)

GAUTAMA BUDDHA was the founding master of Buddhism and is regarded as the most perfect of holy men, rather than as a deity. By most accounts, he was born in the sixth century BC into the kshatriya, or warrior, caste at Kapilavastu, just inside the border of what is now Nepal. Gautama was the Buddha's family name; his given name was Siddhartha. In later legend he was known as Shakyamuni, or the sage of the Shakya clan. Gautama is venerated by all Buddhists, although for the "Pure Land" sect of Japanese and Chinese Buddhism, the Buddha *AMITABHA*, or Amida, has supreme importance.

The story of Gautama's life has become a legend. According to tradition, while in one of the Buddhist heavens, Gautama realized that the time had come for him to descend to earth. The spirit of the Buddha appeared in a dream to Queen *MAYA*: a small, snow-white elephant floating on a raincloud, a symbol of fertility, seemed to circle around the queen three times and then enter her womb. At that moment, all around the world, musical instruments played, trees and flowers bloomed and lakes were suddenly covered with lotus blossoms. Astrologers forecast that Queen Maya and the Buddha's father, the local ruler King Suddhodana, would have a son who would become either a universal emperor or a buddha.

When the boy was born, he immediately began to walk, and a lotus sprang from the place where his foot first touched the ground. The child took seven steps in the directions of the seven cardinal points, and thus symbolically took possession of the world. Soon after his birth, his mother died of joy.

When Gautama was 12 years old, a wise man predicted that, if he were to witness old age, sickness or death, or to see a recluse, he would leave the palace in order to become an ascetic, one who shuns physical pleasures. In fear of the prophesy, the king surrounded his son with luxury and had high walls built around his palaces.

When Gautama reached the age of 16, he was married to Princess Yasodhara and 12 years later, their son *RAHULA* was born. At about this time, Gautama's curiosity about the outside world was aroused and he decided to set out to explore the land outside the palace grounds. The king immediately ordered that every sign of suffering and sadness should be removed from his son's path. However, on the first day of his excursion, Gautama saw a wrinkled old man; on the second day, he saw someone suffering from an incurable disease, as well as a funeral procession; and on another day, he came across a wandering ascetic. Gautama finally decided to leave home and become an ascetic. His father was devastated and provided even more amusements for the prince. However, nothing would deter the young man.

After six years of asceticism, Gautama realized that he was no nearer enlightenment than he had been while living his former life of luxury. Deciding that he must free himself from desire, he set off for the town of Bodh Gaya; as he journeyed, light radiated from his body, attracting peacocks and kingfishers. When Gautama reached Bodh Gaya, he sat down beneath the branches of a sacred tree, whereupon the earth shook six times.

While Gautama was meditating, he was tested by the demon *MARA*, the Buddhist equivalent of Satan. First, he was subjected to fear, then enticed with pleasure. However, Gautama remained unmoved. Eventually he became aware of the "Four Noble Truths" that became the basis of his teaching: that life is full of suffering, that suffering depends on certain conditions such as craving, that these conditions can be removed, and that the way to make suffering cease is to practise the eightfold path: right view, right thought, right speech, right action, right livelihood, right effort, right mindfulness and right concentration or contemplation.

Gautama had reached a state of perfection and at that moment attained complete spiritual insight. The earth swayed, breezes blew, flowers rained down from heaven, the gods rejoiced and all living things were happy. Seven weeks later, he preached his first sermon at Sarnath, on the outskirts of the holy city of Benares.

Gautama preached for more than 40 years, during which time he performed many miracles and converted all who heard him, including his father, his son, his first cousin Ananda, his wife and his adoptive mother,

GAUTAMA BUDDHA (left), seated in the witness attitude, is assailed by the powers of evil, led by the demon Mara. Demons in threatening human and animal shapes seek to terrify him, and Mara's daughters try to seduce him. (MURAL, AJANTA, BERAR.)

MAHAPRAJ-APATI GAUTAMI. He even ascended into heaven, where he converted his mother, Queen Maya, before climbing back down to earth on a ladder, accompanied by the gods. At the age of 80, Gautama entered nirvana, the ultimate state of spiritual bliss, near his birthplace. (See also *THE AVATARS OF VISHNU; THE LIFE OF THE BUDDHA*)

GESAR was a mythical king who inspired the greatest epic of Tibetan Buddhism. Tales of his exploits began to arise in the 11th century, at the time when Buddhism was beginning to infiltrate Tibet and threaten the indigenous Bon religion. The legends describe King Gesar's battle against the ancient beliefs and are said to be several times the length of the Bible.

Gesar, whose name means "Lotus Temple", was said to have been born in the kingdom of Ling in eastern Tibet. He is regarded as the embodiment of the *BODHISATTVA AVALOKITESHVARA*, as well as of *PADMASAMBHAVA*, one of the founders of Tibetan Buddhism. His warriors are said to be incarnations of the Mahasiddhas, great ascetics.

Although the stories about Gesar are influenced above all by Buddhism, traces of the Bon religion can also be found in the tales that tell of mountain deities and spirits of places. Travelling singers transmitted the early versions of the epic, whereas the later tales were said to arise from Tibetan monks.

The story of Gesar tells how an old woman died cursing all religions. Her final wish was that in a future life she and her three sons might rule over all Buddhist lands and wreak their revenge on the Buddhist teaching. The gods, hearing that the woman and her sons were threatening to return to the world as horrifying monsters, decided to send one of their number, Gesar, down to earth in order to do battle against them.

Gesar was reluctant to assume human form and so, before agreeing to descend to earth, he drew up several conditions that he set before the gods, believing that they would be impossible to fulfil. He demanded that his father should be a god and his mother a snake; that he should be given an immortal horse, which could fly through the sky and speak all languages; that he should be supplied with a magical bow and arrow and strong companions; that he should be given a beautiful wife, for whom everybody would be willing to fight; and a clever uncle, who would be able to assist him with battle plans. He also insisted that the gods should protect and help him at all times. To Gesar's distress, the gods agreed to all his demands, so he was forced to descend to earth.

The earthly Gesar was conceived when a god descended in the form of a rainbow and gave Gongmo – a *NAGA* who had transformed herself into a beautiful young girl – a drink of water from a holy vase. Gongmo became pregnant, and in due course, Gesar emerged from his mother as a globe of golden light, which eventually broke open to reveal a baby. According to some versions of the tale, the baby had three eyes, whereupon his horrified mother immediately plucked one out.

Having been warned that he would be overthrown by Gesar, the ruling king tried to kill the child almost as soon as he was born, but, despite his every effort, the boy remained unharmed. However, Gesar and his mother were forced into exile. At the age of 15, Gesar entered a horse race, and on winning it, was made King of Ling and given the former king's daughter as his wife. King Gesar then fought and conquered several demons and converted several countries to Buddhism.

He finally returned to heaven, although in the knowledge that he would have to return to earth one day. Gesar came to be regarded as a warrior god and god of wealth; his consort was a *DAKINI*.

TIRTHANKARAS

JAINISM IS AN INDIAN RELIGION and philosophy which offers an austere path to enlightenment. Much of its mythology was inherited from Hinduism, including huge numbers of gods, and ideas on the structure of the universe, but Jains differ from Hindus in that they do not believe in the idea of creation, considering that time is cyclic. Jain ascetics attempt to conduct their lives following five vows: to injure no living thing (because everything has a soul); to speak the truth; to take only what is given; to be chaste; and to achieve detachment from places, people and things. Their examples in following this discipline are 24 tirthankaras, or "spiritual teachers", who have appeared in the present cycle of time. A *tirtha* is a ford or crossing-place, or a sacred place, person or path which enables believers to cross over into liberation from an endless round of rebirth: for Jains, the tirthankaras were the builders of the ford.

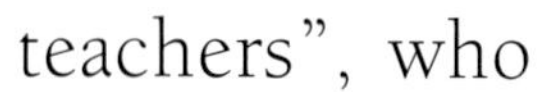

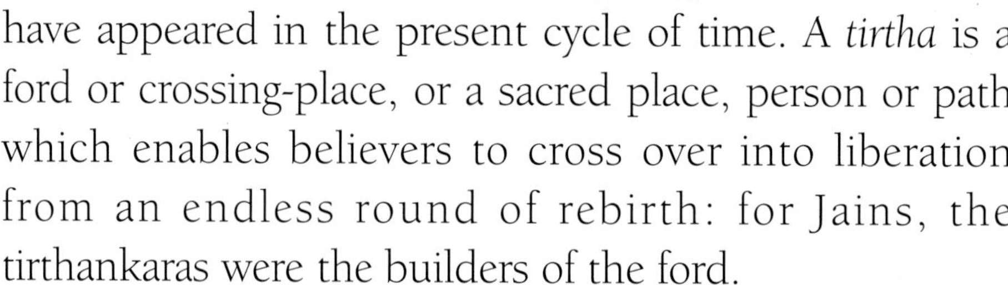

RISHABHA *(left) also called Adinatha, was the first tirthankara of the present cycle. He lived for an extremely long time, and was credited by Jains with the establishment of the caste system, the monarchy and the rule of law. He also organized the cultivation of the land, the pursuit of the arts, and taught humankind the 72 sciences, including arithmetic and writing. In Hindu mythology, he was a minor avatar of Vishnu. He is represented by the bull motif and is usually shown naked in a standing yoga posture.* (TIRTHANKARA, *SRI ADINATH TEMPLE, KHAJURAHO, INDIA.*)

MAHAVIRA *(above), the twenty-fourth tirthankara, was a contemporary of Gautama Buddha. At the age of 30, he renounced family life and embarked on life as a wandering ascetic. He endured 12 years of fasting, silence and meditation to achieve enlightenment, then spent the next 30 years preaching throughout northern India. He and his followers went about naked to indicate their conquest of passion, and he and other tirthankaras are traditionally portrayed with downcast eyes, dead to the world.* (HEAD OF A TIRTHANKARA, *STONE, 10TH CENTURY.*)

THE TIRTHANKARAS *(above) were all considered to have come from the kshatriya, or warrior caste, and were not deities but human teachers who had achieved enlightenment. Worship of their images focuses on their teaching and achievements rather than on themselves. They are all depicted as identical, except for an animal or other symbol which identifies each one, such as the boar that is associated with Vimala (top) and the goat that distinguishes Kunthu (bottom).* (DETAIL FROM THE TWENTY-FOUR JAIN TIRTHANKARAS, BUNDI, C. 1720.)

PARSHVA *(left) was the twenty-third tirthankara, born to Vama, queen of Benares, in the ninth century* BC. *He spent 70 years as a wandering ascetic before attaining nirvana when he died at the age of 100 on Mount Sammeda. His symbol was the snake, and he was often depicted under a canopy of cobras. He systematized the Jain religion, dividing its adherents into monks, nuns, and male and female laity, and giving his chief disciples responsibility for the Jain community.* (TIRTHANKARA PARSHVANATHA, ORISSA, 11TH CENTURY.)

GNOD-SBYIN see *YAKSHAS*.

THE GNYAN are Tibetan spirits who live in trees and stones. They send plagues, diseases and death down on humankind.

GREAT BUDDHAS OF WISDOM see *DHYANIBUDDHAS*.

GRI-GUM, according to Tibetan belief, was a king who, unlike the rulers who preceded him, cut the magic rope that connected him to heaven. The first human ruler was said to have come down from the sky, landing on top of a mountain. At the end of his reign, he returned to heaven by means of a magic rope. The six kings who followed him did the same. However, Gri-gum, the eighth king, failed to return to heaven. During a duel, the air became so filled with soot that, unable to see while waving his sword around, he severed the magic rope. He was then killed by his opponent.

GSHEN-LHA-OD-DKAR, in the Tibetan Bon religion, was the "God of White Light" from whom all other gods emanated. When nothing else existed, two lights emerged; one was black and the other was white. A rainbow then appeared and gave rise to hardness, fluidity, heat, motion and space. These phenomena merged with one another and formed a gigantic egg. From that egg, the black light produced sickness, disease, pain and countless demons, whereas the white light produced joy, prosperity and numerous gods. The gods and demons together gave rise to all kinds of creatures. These beings inhabit the mountains, trees and lakes of the land.

THE GUARDIAN KINGS (below) who guard the four quarters of the world. Acolytes of the bodhisattva Avalokiteshvara, they are said to have assisted at the birth of Gautama Buddha.

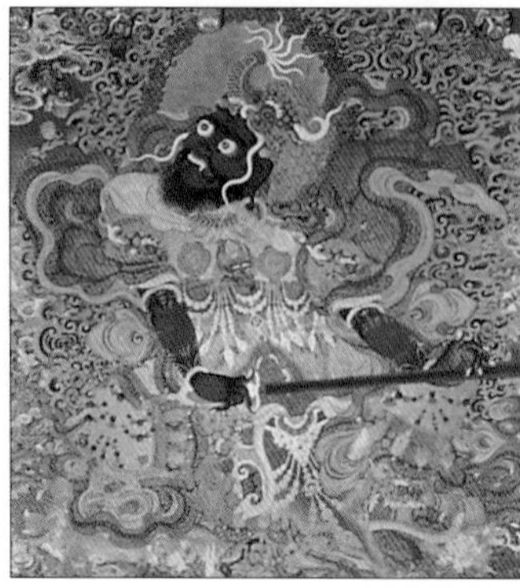

GSHEN-RAB, or Shenrab Miwo, is traditionally said to have been the founder of the later or purified form of the Bon religion of Tibet, which came into being after the introduction of Buddhism to the country. He is said to have come from a mystic land known as Zhang Zhung, and he came to be regarded as identical to *GAUTAMA BUDDHA*. Some scholars have also identified him with Laozi, the founder of Daoism. He is represented seated on a lotus.

THE GUARDIAN KINGS, according to Buddhist belief, guard the four quarters of the world and protect the Buddhist law. They are said to live on the mythical Mount *MERU*, at the gates of the paradise of *INDRA*, the protector of Buddhism. The Guardian Kings are acolytes of the *BODHISATTVA AVALOKITESHVARA*.

Originally, they were regarded as benevolent, but they developed into menacing warriors. They are usually shown wearing armour and helmets or crowns. The kings are said to have assisted at the birth of *GAUTAMA BUDDHA* and to have held up the hooves of his horse when he left the palace of his father for the outside world. In Indian art, they are usually shown riding elephants, whereas in Tantrism they are often shown trampling demons.

The chief Guardian King is Vaishravana, the guardian of the north and of winter. His name means "He Who is Knowing", and he is lord of the *YAKSHAS*, divine beings who protect and serve their ruler.

The guardian of the south, Virudhaka or the "Powerful One", fights ignorance and protects the root of goodness in human beings. He rules over the summer, and, in Tibet, he is often shown with a helmet made from an elephant's head. The guardian of the east, Dhritarashtra, or "He Who Maintains the Kingdom of the Law", presides over the spring and maintains the state. The guardian of the west, Virupaksha, or "He Who Sees All" presides over the autumn. Virupaksha is usually represented standing on a rock or on demons, and wearing armour.

In Hinduism, the guardians are known as Lokapalas. Vaishravana is worshipped as Kuvera, a god of wealth who guards his buried treasure. Kuvera became the king of

HANUMAN *(above) wrestles with the demons of Ravana as he strives to find Rama's wife, Sita.* (TERRACOTTA, 5TH CENTURY.)

HANUMAN *(left), the Hindu monkey god, was well known for his extraordinary agility, which enabled him to escape from the demon Ravana.* (JAIPUR, 17TH CENTURY.)

LANKA and drove a magnificent chariot, which the demon king *RAVANA* used in battle in the Hindu epic, the *Ramayana*.

HANUMAN is the monkey god of Hindu mythology. He is regarded as the patron of learning and is the son of *VAYU*, god of the winds. According to one myth, Hanuman once tried to snatch the sun from the sky, thinking it was something to eat. To prevent the catastrophe, the war god *INDRA* threw his thunderbolt at the monkey, smashing his jaw.

In the great Hindu epic the *Ramayana*, Hanuman is the minister of the monkey king Sugriva and the loyal companion of *RAMA*, the famous *AVATAR* or incarnation of *VISHNU*, the preserver of the universe. Hanuman assisted Rama when the hero was locked in battle with the demon king *RAVANA*, who had run off with Rama's wife, *SITA*. It was Hanuman who discovered Sita's whereabouts, on the island of *LANKA*, Ravana's kingdom.

Hanuman's extraordinary agility enabled him to leap across the waters to the island like an arrow. However, in mid-flight, a sister of the demon king caught Hanuman's shadow and managed to pull the monkey beneath the waters, where another demon tried to swallow him. Hanuman succeeded in escaping by stretching out so that the demon had to open her jaws, then contracting, so that he was able to leap from her mouth.

Hanuman finally found Sita in a grove of trees. Each day, Ravana threatened the goddess with torture and death if she refused to marry him, but Sita insisted on remaining faithful to Rama. Although Hanuman offered to carry her away, Sita refused to touch any man but her husband. As Hanuman left to tell Rama that he had found Sita, Ravana and his demons set his tail on fire. However, the fire failed to hurt the monkey god, who instead caused vast destruction on the island by swishing his tail from side to side, setting light to countless buildings.

Back in India, Hanuman encouraged an army of monkeys to build a bridge across the sea from India to Lanka, thereby enabling Rama and his troops to approach and attack the demon king. Rama rewarded Hanuman for his help by giving him the gift of eternal life.

Hanuman was said to be as large as a mountain, with yellow skin, a red face and a tremendously long tail. His roar was like thunder, and he flew through the clouds with a great rushing sound.

HAYAGRIVA is one of Tibetan Buddhism's *DHARMAPALAS*, or "Protectors of the Teaching". He is the lord of wrath, the leader of the terrifying gods known as Drag-shed. His name means "Horse's Neck", and he is small, with a pot belly and a horse's head. In Buddhism, Hayagriva is regarded as an emanation of either the buddha *AMITABHA* or the buddha *AKSOBHYA* and as the terrifying aspect of the *BODHISATTVA AVALOKITESHVARA*.

In a Hindu myth, Hayagriva was one of the *DAITYAS*, giant *ASURAS* who opposed the gods. He stole the Veda, the sacred knowledge of Hinduism, when it fell from *BRAHMA*'s mouth. *VISHNU*, reincarnated as the *AVATAR* Matsya the fish, managed to kill Hayagriva and retrieve the sacred texts.

Hayagriva is also regarded as an avatar of the god Vishnu, who is said to have taken on this form in order to retrieve the Veda, after it had been stolen from the gods by two daityas.

HERUKA is a Buddhist deity, an emanation of the buddha *AKSOBHYA*. In Tibet he is regarded as one of the protective deities, or *ISHTADEVATAS*. Heruka is usually depicted with three eyes, wild hair and bared teeth. His body is smeared with ashes, and he holds a severed human head in his hand. The deity sits or dances on a corpse and is sometimes shown with his female partner, Prajna, with whom he creates nirvana (spiritual bliss). Heruka confers buddhahood and protects the world from evil.

The herukas as a group are terrifying energies who are usually portrayed with haloes of flame. They dance with their huge and terrifying consorts. The herukas exist in the head region, and meditators who achieve their level are believed to be capable of reaching a realm of the ultimate reality.

HAYAGRIVA, *the leader of the terrifying gods known as Drag-shed, wreathed with his enemies' heads.* (BRONZE, TIBET.)

I

HEVAJRA is a *YIDAM*, or tutelary god, worshipped in Mongolia, Cambodia, Thailand and Tibet. He is usually represented with four legs and eight heads; his body is blue, and his heads are different colours. He is sometimes shown alone, but often in Yab-Yum, the posture of embrace, with his *SHAKTI* or corresponding female energy.

HIMAVAT see *PARVATI*.

HIRANYAKASHIPU see *AVATARS* and *RAVANA*.

INDRA, one of the chief deities of Indian mythology, is a god of storms and war. He appears in the *Rig Veda* – the ancient hymns forming part of the Veda, the sacred knowledge of Hinduism – as the king of the gods. Indra is red or gold in colour, and is large, fierce and warlike. In his right hand he carries a thunderbolt, which he uses either to slay his enemies or to revive those killed in battle. He is said to ride through the heavens in a chariot, often said to be the sun. In later times, he was frequently depicted on the elephant, *AIRAVATA*.

Indra was born from heaven and earth, which he separated for ever. He challenged the old order and became the leading deity, a less remote figure than the Vedic god, *VARUNA*. Indra was best known as a destroyer of demons, who led the gods against the *ASURAS*. He fought and destroyed the serpent *VRITRA* with a pillar of foam and, in doing so, gave form to chaos, liberating the waters, generating life and causing the sun to rise.

On another occasion, Indra set free some cows which had been stolen from the gods. This myth is interpreted as symbolizing how Indra released the sacred force, or light of the world. Indra was also worshipped as the god who provided rain. As the bringer of light and water, he absorbed many of Varuna's functions, becoming a fertility god and a god of creation.

***HEVAJRA** is the Buddhist equivalent of the Hindu god Shiva Nataraja. He is shown in Yab-Yum with his shakti, Nairamata, who stands on two corpses.* (TANTRIC BRONZE.)

A vast drinker with a huge belly, Indra was also associated with *SOMA*, an intoxicating drink used in religious rituals. It was from Soma that the god was said to derive his special powers. After drinking it, he became so large that he filled both heaven and earth.

Indra's importance gradually declined. Although he remained a terrifying god of thunder, he came to be regarded as a divine earthly monarch who reigned in Swarga, a luxurious heaven situated on the sacred Mount *MERU*.

According to one myth, it was Indra, rather than *VISHNU*'s *AVATAR* Vamana, who fought the demon Bali. While Indra was attacking a host of demons led by Jalamdhara, Bali fell, and a stream of jewels poured from his mouth. Indra was so amazed that he struck open the demon's body with one of his thunderbolts. The different parts of Bali's body then gave rise to the seeds of precious stones. Diamonds were produced from his

INDRA *(above) is a weather and fertility god, and a leading Hindu deity. He is shown wielding a vajra, or thunderbolt, and is seated on his mount, the elephant Airavata.* (11TH CENTURY.)

bones, sapphires from his eyes, rubies from his blood, emeralds from his marrow, crystal from his flesh, coral from his tongue and pearls from his teeth.

In a story from the Hindu epic, the *Ramayana*, Indra seduced Ahalya, the wife of the great sage Gautama. One day, when he knew that the sage was away from his home, Indra disguised himself, visited Gautama's wife and pressed her to become his lover. Despite his disguise, Ahalya immediately recognized Indra and, because she was curious about the chief god, she agreed. Afterwards, as Indra was leaving, he met Gautama returning. Realizing what had happened, the sage caused the god's testicles to fall off. Gautama then cursed Ahalya, condemning her to lie on ashes and eat only air until *RAMA* visited her. The gods later replaced Indra's testicles with those of a ram. (See also *MYTHICAL MOUNTAINS*)

ISHTADEVATAS are protective Buddhist deities or sacred beings who are especially common in Tibet. Ishtadevata means "Beloved (or Desired) Divinity".

Each individual who decides to enter the path of Bhakti yoga – that of loving submission to a deity – chooses their own ishtadevata. Alternatively, the individual's guru may choose the ishtadevata, since the guru will be able to discern which aspect of the divine will be most useful to the disciple.

JALAMDHARA see *THE ASURAS* and *GANGA*.

JINAS see *DHYANIBUDDHAS*.

KADAVUL see *KATAVUL*.

KADRU see *GARUDA*.

KALADEVI, known in Tibet as Lha-mo, is the only female *DHARMAPALA*, or protector of the Buddhist law. She is said to have been created by the other deities and provided with weapons, in order that she might defend Tantrism, a tradition of gaining enlightenment through ritual practices. Kaladevi rides a mule whose reins are made from poisonous snakes and whose back is covered with the skin of a *YAKSHA*. According to one myth, the skin is that of Kaladevi's son, whom she is said to have devoured. Kaladevi has three protruding eyes, ten arms and, like all Dharmapalas, wears a crown and garland of skulls. She is sometimes said to be the wife of a yaksha king of Sri Lanka and is occasionally depicted walking on a lake of blood along with two other female beings. A terrifying and bloodthirsty goddess, she is often regarded as a consort of *YAMA*, god of the dead. She helps those who earnestly seek her protection.

KALADEVI, *a bloodthirsty goddess who is the only female Dharmapala, or protector of the Buddhist teaching.* (BRONZE AND ENAMEL, TIBET, 18TH CENTURY.)

KALI, dancing on the god Shiva in a frenzy of blood lust. Eventually she realized what she was doing, and the world became safe once more. (INDIAN PAINTING, 18TH CENTURY.)

KALI, the "Black One", is the terrifying aspect of the great mother goddess and *SHAKTI* of *SHIVA*. The personification of death and destruction, she is said to spring from the forehead of *DURGA*, another aspect of the goddess, when she becomes angry. Kali is usually depicted with blood-red eyes, four arms and with her tongue lolling out of her mouth in search of blood. She is naked, but for a girdle of severed heads or hands, a necklace of skulls and a tiger skin.

Like Shiva, Kali has a third eye in her forehead. In one hand she holds a weapon, in another the severed head of a giant, while her remaining two hands, in contrast, are raised in blessing. Her devotees regard her as a loving mother goddess who can destroy death as well as demons.

One myth tells how a monster, Raktabija, was destroying the world. Each time he was wounded, 1,000 demons sprang from each drop of his blood. The gods asked Kali to destroy the monster and, as she set about killing the demons, she drank their blood before it reached the ground, so that they were unable to multiply. When only the original monster remained, Kali gulped him down in one mouthful.

In celebration of her victory, she began to dance. As her movements became more and more frenzied, all creation began to shake, and the whole of existence was threatened with destruction. The gods begged Shiva to stop the goddess from dancing, but even the great god was unable to calm her. Eventually, Shiva threw himself on the ground in front of the goddess, whereupon she began to dance on his body. Finally, Kali realized what she was doing and stopped dancing.

The city of Calcutta is called after the goddess: its name means "Kali Ghat" or "Kali's Steps". Each day, animals are sacrificed to her, and it is believed that human sacrifices were made to her in the past. (See also *THE MOTHER GODDESS*)

KAMA, in the form of Kamadeva, is the god of love. Often depicted as a young man riding on a parrot, he bears a bow and arrows made of sugar cane and decorated with flowers. (ILLUSTRATION BY J. HIGGINBOTHAM.)

KALKIN see *AVATARS*.

KAMA, according to the ancient sacred teachings of India, is either sexual desire or the impulse towards good. However, Kama is sometimes regarded as a deity. Described as the first being to be born, he is superior to gods and humanity and, as a symbol of original desire, he is said to have brought about the created world.

In the form of Kamadeva, he is the god of love. He is sometimes regarded as the son of Dharma, god of justice and Shraddha, goddess of faith. Elsewhere he is described as the son of *LAKSHMI*, or as having arisen from the heart of *BRAHMA*. His consort is Rati, or "Voluptuousness", the goddess of sexual passion. Kama is said to rule over the *APSARAS*, the heavenly nymphs.

According to one myth, the goddess *PARVATI* grew bored because her consort, the great god *SHIVA*, was deep in meditation on Mount Kailasa. Parvati persuaded Kama to come to her aid. Kama was loathe to intervene, but Parvati insisted, whereupon Kama prepared to fire his arrow at Shiva's heart in order to remind him of his duties to his wife. The god Mahesvara saw what was about to happen; since it was

KARTTIKEYA, *the Hindu warrior god, is named after the Kirttikah, or Pleiades.* (SANDSTONE, PUNJAB, 6TH CENTURY.)

necessary for Shiva to finish his meditation in order for the cycles of creation to run their course, he struck Kama with a thunderbolt. Later, however, he brought Kama back to life. In another version of the myth, Shiva struck Kama with a flash of his third eye and burned him to ashes. As a result, Kama was sometimes called Ananga, or "Bodiless".

KAMSA see *KRISHNA*.

KARTTIKEYA, also known as Skanda, is a warrior god who campaigns against demons. The deity is sometimes said to have been raised by the stars of the Pleiades, or Kirttikah. He is sometimes also regarded as a god of fertility.

In the great Hindu epics the *Mahabharata* and the *Ramayana*, Karttikeya is described as the son of *SHIVA*. He is said to have been conceived when Shiva offered his seeds to the fire god *AGNI*, who gave them for safekeeping to the river goddess *GANGA*. Eventually, a child with six heads, and six or 12 arms, was born.

Alternatively, Shiva is said to have directed the fire of his third eye at a lake. Six children emerged and were brought up by the wives of the *RISHIS*, or seers. One day, *PARVATI* hugged the children so tightly that they were squeezed together into one child, although the six heads remained.

KASYAPA was an ancient Indian sage whose name means "Tortoise". According to the sacred Hindu *Atharva Veda*, "Kasyapa, the self-born, emerged from Time". One of his wives, Kadru, gave birth to 1,000 serpents, while the other, Vinata, gave birth to *GARUDA*, the bird chosen by the great god Vishnu to be his mount. Kasyapa is sometimes said to have fathered the *ADITYAS* by *ADITI* and the demonic *DAITYAS* by her sister, Diti. He is described in the Hindu epics, the *Mahabharata* and the *Ramayana*, as the son of *BRAHMA* and the father of Vivasvat, or the sun, who in turn was the father of *MANU*, the first man, from whom all human beings are descended.

In Buddhism, Kasyapa is one of the six Manushi, or "human", buddhas. He is the immediate predecessor to *GAUTAMA BUDDHA*. He is often shown seated on a lion, and is coloured yellow or gold because he represents the light of the sun and the moon.

KATARAGAMA DEVIYO is one of the four great gods of Sri Lanka. He is the equivalent of the Indian god *KARTTIKEYA* and the southern Indian Tamil god, *MURUKAN*. Originally, Kataragama Deviyo was called Ceyon, or "God with the Red-coloured Body".

KATAVUL, or Kadavul, is the name for the supreme personal being of the Tamils of southern India and Sri Lanka. The source of all existence, his name means "He Who Is". He is the judge of humankind, rewarding or punishing people according to their deeds during life.

KATUKILAL see *KORRAWI*.

KHADROMAS see *DAKINI*.

KHYUNG-GAI MGO-CAN was an ancient Tibetan god who may have been connected with the sun. He was said to have had the head of a bird.

KORRAWI is the Tamil goddess of battle and victory. She also takes the form of Katukilal, a goddess of the woods. The mother of *MURUKAN*, her temples are guarded by demons and spirits.

KARTTIKEYA *is sometimes shown riding a peacock, holding a bow in one hand and an arrow in the other.*

THE AVATARS OF VISHNU

THE GREAT GOD VISHNU WAS SEEN as the protector of the world, having measured out the universe in three giant strides and established it as the home of both gods and humanity. He was a benevolent deity, and his consort Shri, or Lakshmi, was the beautiful goddess of good fortune. In token of his willing involvement with the human race, he descended to earth and became incarnate at times when the world of mortals was threatened by evil. His incarnations, or avatars, follow an evolutionary pattern, from fish and reptile, through animals and the dwarf Vamana, to men and finally to the future creator, Kalkin. The number was traditionally fixed at ten, although the individual avatars varied slightly in different texts. The Buddha was assimilated into the series much later than the others, while the seventh and eighth avatars, Rama and Krishna, are important heroes of Hindu mythology.

MATSYA *(above), the fish, was Vishnu's first incarnation. It was rescued by Manu from being eaten by a larger fish. Manu looked after it while it grew, then released it to the ocean. In return, the fish warned Manu of a catastrophic flood. It helped him build a boat on which he could save seeds and animals to repopulate the world, and towed the boat to safety.* (ILLUSTRATION FROM DEVOTIONAL TEXT, 17TH CENTURY.)

KURMA *(left), the tortoise, supported Mount Mandara on his back during the churning of the cosmic ocean. As the gods had uprooted the mountain and turned it upside down for this task, the peak drilled into the earth when the churning began. Vishnu, in his second incarnation as Kurma, dived underneath it and twisted with the mountain, acting as a paddle to speed up the operation. The milk ocean turned to butter and tossed up Amrita, the elixir of immortality.* (ILLUSTRATION BY J. HIGGINBOTHAM, 1864.)

VARAHA *(right) was the rescuer of the earth. The demon Hiranyaksha tossed the earth into the cosmic ocean, but in his third avatar, as Varaha the boar, Vishnu plunged into the ocean and killed the demon. He then found the earth in the form of a beautiful woman, whom he carried back up to the surface on his tusks.* (BRONZE, GURJARA PRATIHARA, 10TH CENTURY.)

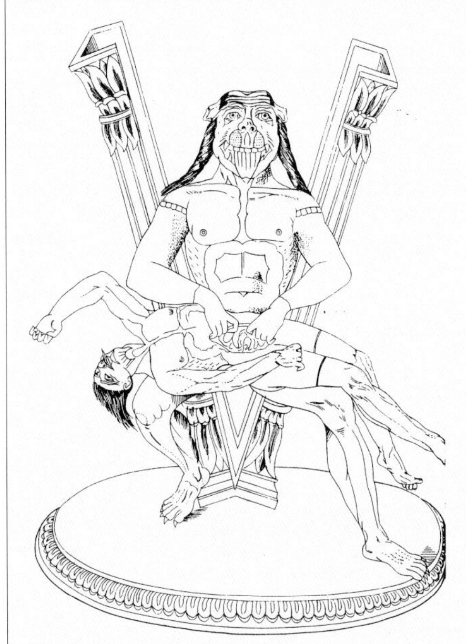

Narasimha *(above) was the fourth avatar. Hiranyakashipu the demon, the twin brother of Hiranyaksha, dethroned the god Indra and proclaimed himself king of the universe. He was enraged by his son's veneration of Vishnu and condemned him to death, but failed to kill him. In his anger, the demon struck a pillar demanding to know why Vishnu did not show himself. The pillar split open, and Vishnu was incarnated as the man-lion Narasimha, who disembowelled Hiranyakashipu.* (Illustration by J. Higginbotham, 1864.)

Vamana *(above), the dwarf, rescued the universe from the demon Bali, who had assumed power over it. To release it from his grasp, Vishnu assumed the form of a dwarf for his fifth incarnation. He requested from Bali as much territory as he could cover in three strides. Bali easily granted this apparently trivial request, and Vishnu, transformed into the giant, Trivikrama, covered the underworld, the earth and the heavens in three vast strides.* (Illustration by J. Higginbotham, 1864.)

Parashurama *(above), although he was born a brahman, was destined to lead the life of a warrior. He was armed with a celebrated axe that had been given to him by Shiva. In revenge for insulting his father, he wiped out all the male members of the warrior caste and ordered their widows to sleep with brahmans to produce a new and purer caste of warriors. He was Vishnu's sixth avatar.* (Parashurama killing Arjuna Kartavirya by Chamba or Bilaspur, c. 1750–60.)

Rama *(left) was Vishnu's seventh avatar, assumed at the gods' request to destroy Ravana, the evil ruler of Lanka (the island of Sri Lanka). Rama, son of the king of Ayodhya, won his wife, Sita, by bending and breaking Shiva's unbendable bow. He was banished by his stepmother for 14 years to the forest, where Sita was abducted by Ravana. After many adventures, Rama killed Ravana, won Sita back, returned to his kingdom and reigned for 1,000 years.* (Illustration to the Ramayana by Mir Kalan, c. 1750–60.)

Gautama Buddha *(left), Vishnu's ninth incarnation, was not identified until the third or fourth century* AD. *In the earliest accounts of it, Vishnu was said to have assumed this avatar in order to convert demons to Buddhist beliefs, with the intention of weakening them in their war against the gods, or to mislead sinful mortals so that they would receive their just punishment. Later, a more positive reason was suggested: Vishnu was said to want to abolish animal sacrifices.*

Krishna *(above), the god and the eighth avatar, was hidden at birth because of a prophecy that his mother's eighth child would kill the evil King Kamsa. Krishna was brought up in obscurity among a community of cowherds. After killing a succession of demons, including Vatsasura, who came in the guise of a calf, Krishna killed Kamsa. He assisted the hero Arjuna in the great battle of Kurukshetra, disguised as his charioteer.* (Illustration to the Bhagavata Purana by Mankot, c. 1730–40.)

Kalkin *(above) is Vishnu's tenth and final avatar, and is still to come: he will appear at the end of the present age, the Kali Yuga, which began in 3102*BC *and will last 432,000 years. In its final years, humanity will face a breakdown of civilization and a loss of spiritual and moral values. The divine incarnation of Kalkin, riding a white horse, will be needed to wipe out the wickedness of the world and establish a new era.* (Stone carving on Prasanna Chennakeshava Temple, Somnathpur.)

KRISHNA, according to Hindu mythology, is an *AVATAR* of *VISHNU*, the preserver of the universe. He is traditionally referred to as the only complete avatar. A divine hero, Krishna is said to have been miraculously born in the town of Mathura in northern India. The gods wanted to destroy the evil oppressor King Kamsa, and so Vishnu decided to be born as the eighth son of the king's sister Devaki. According to one story, Vishnu plucked out two of his hairs, one black, one white. The black hair became Krishna and the white hair *BALARAMA*, Krishna's older brother. Krishna's name means the "Dark One".

King Kamsa learned that he was to be assassinated by one of his nephews, so he imprisoned Devaki and her husband Vasudev and killed each of their sons as they were born. When Devaki gave birth to Krishna, Vishnu told the couple to exchange their baby for the daughter of some cowherds who lived on the other side of the river Yamuna. The doors of the prison miraculously opened, and Vasudev carried the baby to the river. As soon as the child's toe touched the waters, they parted, allowing the father and son to pass through safely. Vasudev left the baby with the cowherds Yashoda and Nanda. However, King Kamsa discovered what had happened and sent a demon disguised as a nurse to look after the infant. Krishna sucked at the demon's breast until he drained her life away.

Krishna was a playful child, teasing the cows, laughing at his elders and stealing butter and sweets. He also displayed signs of his divine origins by, among other pranks, uprooting two trees at once; on another occasion, his adopted mother, Yashoda, was amazed to see the whole universe when she looked down his throat. Once, when the cowherds were about to worship the great god *INDRA*, Krishna told them that instead they should worship Mount Govardhana and their herds. The mountain, he explained, provided their herds with food and the cows themselves gave them milk to drink. Krishna then declared that he himself was the mountain. Indra was furious and sent down torrents of rain. However, Krishna lifted Mount Govardhana and held it above the storms for seven days and seven nights. Indra was so amazed that he came down from the heavens and asked Krishna to befriend his son, the hero *ARJUNA*.

One of the most popular myths concerning Krishna is that of his youthful dalliances with the gopis, the female cowgirls, and in particular with a girl called *RADHA* with whom the young hero fell passionately in love. Once, when the cowgirls were bathing in the river Yamuna, Krishna stole their clothes, then hid in a tree. He refused to return their garments to them until they came out, one by one, their hands clasped in prayer. Because all the cowgirls wanted to hold Krishna's hands when they danced, he multiplied his hands countless times. The sound of

KRISHNA *(left) is said to have taught the science of Bhakti yoga to the sun god, Surga, who instructed Manu, father of humankind.*

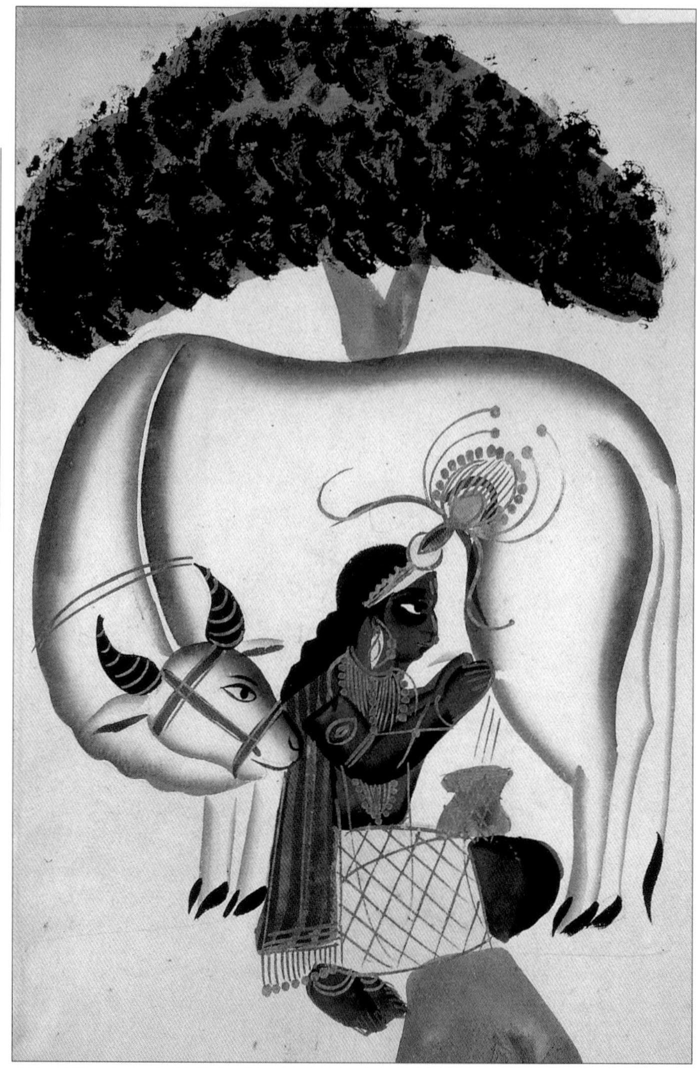

KRISHNA *(above), an avatar of Vishnu, spent his childhood as the adopted son of cowherds.* (Kalighat painting, c. 1860.)

Krishna's flute, calling the cowgirls out to dance in the moonlight, is believed to symbolize the voice of the supreme lord calling all who hear him to divine pleasures.

As Krishna grew older, he began to rid the neighbourhood of monsters and demons. Eventually, King Kamsa heard of his exploits and determined to kill him. However, Krishna not only succeeded in killing Kamsa but also went on to destroy numerous other oppressive kings as well as demons.

The most important battle he participated in was that of Kurukshetra. On the eve of the battle, Krishna, disguised as a charioteer, is said to have preached to the hero Arjuna the *Bhagavad Gita*, or "Song of the Lord", which forms part of the great Hindu epic, the *Mahabharata*. The war ended in the destruction of both armies, with only the merest handful of survivors on each side. Krishna died shortly afterwards. He was sitting in the forest, meditating, when a huntsman mistook him for a deer and shot an arrow, which struck him on his left heel, his only vulnerable spot. Krishna told the huntsman not to grieve or be afraid, and then ascended into the sky in a beacon of light.

Krishna is believed to embody divine beauty, joy and love, using his charm, playfulness and compassion to draw his devotees into the embrace of the supreme lord. (See also *THE AVATARS OF VISHNU*)

KSHITIGARBHA, who is a *BODHISATTVA*, or "buddha-to-be", is said to look after the six paths taken by souls after they have been judged. These paths are the destinies of humankind, *ASURAS*, demons, gods, animals and the damned. Patient and persevering, he consoles those who live in hell, seeking to lighten the burdens that they have brought upon themselves by evil actions when alive.

Kshitigarbha came to be regarded as the protector of all travellers. In India, he had only a small following, but he attracted many devotees both in China and Japan. According to one Chinese myth, he was a young Indian boy of the brahman caste who was so upset by how his late mother was suffering in hell that he determined to save all the other inhabitants of hell from such a terrible fate. Kshitigarbha's name means "He Who Encompasses the Earth". In China, he is known as Dizang Wang, and in Japan as Jizo-Bosatsu.

KUNTI see *ARJUNA*.

KUN-TU-BZAN-PO, according to the Bon religion of Tibet, created the world from a lump of mud, and living beings from an egg.

KURMA, the tortoise, was the second incarnation, or *AVATAR*, of the Hindu god *VISHNU*, the preserver of the universe. During the churning of the ocean, Kurma supported Mount Mandara on his back in order to prevent the mountain from boring a hole in the earth. The gods were thus able to obtain *AMRITA*, the elixir of immortality, to restore their power. (See also *THE AVATARS OF VISHNU*)

KRISHNA *visiting Radha, a young gopi, or cowgirl, with whom he fell passionately in love. His name means "Dark One" and he is often depicted as dark-skinned.*

(ILLUSTRATION TO RASAMANJARI BY BHANUDETTA, BASOHLI, C. 1865.)

L

KURUKULLA is a Buddhist goddess who emanates from *AMITABHA*. She is said to be able to cast spells on men and women in order to ensure that they serve her. In Tibet, she became a goddess of riches. Her main attributes are a red lotus, a bow and an arrow. She is often represented as reddish in colour, seated in a cave and with four arms. Her two upper arms are held in a threatening posture, while the two lower arms offer comfort.

KUVERA see *GUARDIAN KINGS*.

LAKSHMANA, according to Hindu myth, was the son of King Dasaratha and Sumitra and the half-brother of *RAMA*, an incarnation of the great god *VISHNU*. When Rama was exiled from his late father's kingdom, Lakshmana accompanied him on his travels. While the two brothers were living in the wilderness, Surpanaka, one of the demon king *RAVANA*'s sisters fell in love with Rama. He sent the woman to Lakshmana who in turn sent her back to Rama. The demoness, seeking revenge for being thus insulted, attacked Rama's wife *SITA*, but to no avail. Rama then asked Lakshmana to disfigure the seductress, which he did by cutting off her nose and ears. The demoness demanded that Ravana avenge her, and it was during this great battle that the demon king succeeded in abducting Sita.

LAKSHMI, or Shri, according to the Veda, the sacred knowledge of the Hindus, was alleged to have been many deities, including the consort of *VARUNA* or *SURYA*. However, she is best known as the beautiful consort or *SHAKTI* (female power) of the great Hindu god *VISHNU*. The goddess of wealth and good fortune, Lakshmi is usually depicted as a beautiful golden woman sitting on a lotus flower, the symbol of the womb, immortality and spiritual purity. During the Hindu celebration of Diwali, the festival of lights, thousands of lanterns are lit and fireworks exploded in order to please the goddess. People gamble and feast, while the goddess is said to wander from house to house looking for somewhere to rest, and blessing with prosperity all houses that are well lit.

Lakshmi was said to have been born several times. For example, when Vishnu was incarnated as *RAMA*, Lakshmi was born as *SITA*.

Everyone wants to possess Lakshmi, but she insists that no one can keep her for long. She immediately leaves anyone who puts her on their head, which is what the demons do whenever they manage to catch hold of her. In early myths, Lakshmi was sometimes associated with *INDRA*, the war god. However, even Indra had to divide her into four parts in order to keep hold of her for any length of time. Lakshmi's presence is believed to bring fertility. According to one tale, when the goddess sat down next to Indra, he began to pour down rain so that the crops flourished. Another myth tells how Lakshmi was born by her own will in a beautiful field, which had been cut open by a plough.

Lakshmi appears in the famous myth of the churning of the ocean. Using the snake Vasuki as a rope to turn Mount Mandara, the gods churned the cosmic ocean for 100 years. Eventually the ocean turned to milk and gave rise not only to *AMRITA*, the elixir of immortality, but also to the "Fourteen Precious Things", including the beautiful goddess Lakshmi, who rose seated on a lotus flower. The heavenly musicians and great sages began to sing Lakshmi's praises; the sacred rivers asked her to bathe in their

***LAKSHMANA** and Rama wandering in search of Rama's abducted wife, Sita.* (ILLUSTRATION TO THE RAMAYANA, KANGRA, 1780.)

***LAKSHMI** (far left), laden with flowers, is a beautiful golden woman. Her presence is believed to bring fertility, and ancient Indian rulers would perform a marriage ritual in which they took Lakshmi as their bride to secure wealth and fertility.*

***LAKSHMI** (left) sat on Vishnu's lap and refused to look at the demons who wanted to own her as goddess of prosperity when she emerged from the cosmic ocean.* (ILLUSTRATION BY J. HIGGINBOTHAM, 1864.)

LANKA was the site of the battle between Rama and Ravana, the demon king. Ravana's horde of demons was eventually defeated by Rama's army of monkeys, assembled by Hanuman. (ILLUSTRATION TO THE RAMAYANA, RAJASTHAN, EARLY 19TH CENTURY.)

waters; the sea of milk offered her a crown of immortal flowers; and the sacred elephants who hold up the world poured the holy water of the Ganges over her.

LANKA was the old name given to Ceylon, now Sri Lanka. It was also the name of its capital. The walls of Lanka are said to have been made from gold by Vishvakarma, a creator deity and the architect of the gods. Originally, Lanka was intended as a home for Kuvera, god of riches, but the demon king *RAVANA* later captured it and took it as his own.

According to one tale, *VAYU*, a god of the winds, was responsible for creating the island. Narada, a sage, or *RISHI*, challenged Vayu to break off the summit of Mount *MERU*, the world mountain. *GARUDA*, the mythical bird, normally protected the mountain, but one day, in the bird's absence, Vayu succeeded in breaking off the summit. He immediately threw the summit into the depths of the ocean, where it remained as the island of Lanka.

THE LHA-DRE are gods, or supernatural beings, of the indigenous Bon religion of Tibet. When Buddhism entered Tibet, the Buddhist teachers assigned to the Lha-Dre the role of protectors of the new faith, thereby assimilating them into the Buddhist pantheon, where they are regarded as "Deities of the World" rather than the symbolic deities of Buddhism.

LHA-MO see *KALADEVI*.

LOKAPALAS see *DHARMAPALAS* and *GUARDIAN KINGS*.

THE LU are supernatural beings of the indigenous Bon religion of Tibet, who were assimilated into Buddhism as protectors of the faith. They live in lakes and rivers, and require regular placation.

MAHAKALA, or Mahalka, is known in Tibet as Mgon-po. The destructive form of the god *SHIVA*, he is one of the *DHARMAPALAS* of Tibetan Buddhism, and a *YIDAM*, a tutelary god of Tibet. He is known as the "Great Black One", and has three eyes. He is covered with a tiger or elephant skin and holds a noose made from snakes.

His function, like that of all Dharmapalas, is to destroy all known enemies of the Buddhist teaching. Mahakala's most important duties are to pacify, enrich, magnetize and destroy. In the 17th century, he was accepted as the tutelary god of Mongolia, then under Tibetan influence.

LANKA (left) burns as Hanuman, the monkey god of Hindu mythology, leaps across the water to safety.

MAHALKA see *MAHAKALA*.

MAHAMAYA see *MAYA*.

MAHAPRAJAPATI GAUTAMI was the stepmother and aunt of *GAUTAMA BUDDHA*. She raised him after his mother, Queen *MAYA*, died of joy a few days after his miraculous birth. The devotion of Mahaprajapati became legendary. After the death of her husband, Mahaprajapati persuaded the Buddha to allow her to found a Buddhist order of nuns.

MAHAKALA is a destructive aspect of the god Shiva. Threatening and armed with a sword, he is known as the "Great Black One". (TIBETAN, 19TH CENTURY.)

MAITREYA *(above) will appear far in the future, when India becomes an earthly paradise.* (TIBETAN BRONZE, 11TH CENTURY.)

MAITREYA *(right), the buddha of the future, and the last earthly buddha.*

MAITREYA is the buddha of the future and the last earthly buddha. Regarded as the embodiment of love, his name means the "Benevolent" or "Friendly One". Maitreya is currently a *BODHISATTVA* dwelling in the *TUSHITA* or "Joyful" Heaven. In due course, *GAUTAMA BUDDHA* will enthrone him as his successor. Maitreya is expected to appear at the end of the present Buddhist age, in around 30,000 years' time.

Maitreya is often depicted as one of a triad with Gautama and the bodhisattva *AVALOKITESHVARA*. In non-Mahayana, or "Great Vehicle" Buddhism, the term *bodhisattva* usually refers either to Maitreya or to the historical Gautama Buddha, prior to his spiritual enlightenment.

The cult of Maitreya is very widespread in Tibetan Buddhism. According to one Tibetan tale, Asanga, a learned sage who founded the Yogachara school of Mahayana Buddhism, received his teaching directly from Maitreya. The Yogachara school teaches that everything consists of "mind only" and puts particular emphasis on the practice of yoga.

Asanga spent many years meditating on the future buddha. He eventually began to feel that his efforts to attain wisdom were fruitless and started to feel frustrated. One day, Asanga noticed that the wings of birds had worn a groove in a rock against which they always brushed when landing. The sage then heard the drip of water on a stone and saw that the drip had cut a deep passage through the rock. These two observations caused him to renew his determination to attain wisdom. However, though he continued to meditate, and though he continued to invoke Maitreya, he still got nowhere.

Some time later, while he was searching for food, Asanga met a man who was rubbing an iron bar with a piece of cotton. When Asanga asked the man what he was doing, the man replied that he was making a needle. Once again, Asanga determined to continue his pursuit of wisdom.

Many years passed, and still Asanga had failed to achieve his goal. Finally, he decided to leave his cave for good. As he was making his return to the outside world, Asanga met a dog who was suffering excruciating pain from a wound infested with worms. Although Asanga felt great compassion for the animal, he knew that if he removed the worms, they would die for want of food. Eventually, he decided that he would pick off the worms and allow them to eat his own flesh. However, he then worried that he might crush the worms, and so he decided to lick them off the dog instead.

Just as his tongue brushed against the worms, the dog disappeared and in its place stood Maitreya. Asanga asked Maitreya why he had failed to appear to him during his many years of meditation, whereupon the future buddha replied that only in this act of pure compassion had Asanga's vision been cleansed, although he had been with the sage throughout his many years of meditation.

Maitreya then told Asanga to carry him on his back into the city so that everyone might see him. Asanga did as instructed, but

MANJUSHRI, enthroned and surrounded by deities, is flanked by two lotus blossoms, on which rest a sword of wisdom and the Prajnaparamita-sutra, a holy text that advocates the ideal of the bodhisattva. (TIBETAN PAINTING.)

nobody saw Maitreya because their vision was so clouded. Maitreya then took Asanga to the Tushita heaven, where he was able to gain the spiritual insight which he had sought for so many years.

MANJUSHRI is the *BODHISATTVA* of wisdom and one of the most important members of the Buddhist pantheon. His name means "He Who is Noble and Gentle", and his *SHAKTI*, or female energy, is *SARASVATI*. Manjushri is usually depicted with two lotus blossoms, on which rest his attributes, a sword of wisdom and a sacred text. He dispels ignorance, bestows eloquence and is a symbol of the enlightenment that can be reached through learning. He is said to be the father and mother of the bodhisattvas, as well as their spiritual friend.

In Tibetan Buddhism, certain great saints and scholars are regarded as incarnations of Manjushri. The Tibetans often depict Manjushri with several heads and arms. In Nepal, he is believed to have introduced civilized life, and his festival is celebrated on the first day of the year. According to legend, Manjushri originally came from China. In Japan he is known as Monju-Bosatzu. (See also *BODHISATTVAS*)

MANU, according to Hindu mythology, was the first man and the precursor of humankind. One myth tells how Manu was the son of *BRAHMA* and a young woman whom the god had produced from his own body. According to another tradition, Manu was the son of the sun god *SURYA*. Manu was saved from a cataclysmic flood by Matsya, an *AVATAR* or incarnation of the great god *VISHNU*, the preserver of the universe.

One day, Manu was washing in the river when he found a tiny fish, Matsya, which begged the sage to protect it. Manu took the fish home, where it grew bigger and bigger until eventually it asked to be taken to the sea. Before the fish swam away, it warned Manu that there would be a huge flood, which would engulf the earth, and it advised the sage to save himself by building a huge boat. Manu did as the fish advised, taking on board the boat all kinds of creatures and seeds of plants.

Almost before he had finished his task, the rains began to fall heavily and soon the whole world was flooded. The waters grew rough and threatened to capsize Manu's craft. However, Matsya appeared again, this time as a gigantic fish, and towed the boat safely through the waters. The fish then told Manu to fasten the boat to the summit of a mountain, which still remained above the water, and to wait for the floods to subside. Before leaving, the fish confessed to Manu that he was in fact Vishnu.

In gratitude to the god, Manu made a sacrifice of milk and melted butter. After a year, the offering turned into a beautiful woman who revealed that she was his daughter, Ida. The couple proceeded to engender the human race.

MANJUSHRI, seated on a lotus-moon throne, wields his sword of wisdom, poised to strike down ignorance.

MARA is the evil demon of Buddhist belief who tempted *GAUTAMA BUDDHA* as he sat meditating under the sacred tree at Bodh Gaya. Mara's name means "Death". He realized that if Gautama achieved enlightenment, his own power would be destroyed, and he therefore sent his three beautiful daughters to tempt the sage. Although Mara's daughters sang and danced and tried every trick they knew to beguile him, Gautama remained unmoved. Eventually, they admitted defeat.

Mara then sent an army of terrifying devils to threaten Gautama. Some of the creatures had 1,000 eyes, others were horrifically deformed; they drank blood and ate snakes. However, as soon as they came near to the sacred tree, they found that their arms were bound to their sides. Finally, Mara himself attacked Gautama with his fearsome weapon, a disc which could slice mountains in two. None the less, when the disc reached Gautama, it was transformed into a garland of flowers. At last, the demon realized that he was beaten.

MARA (below) sent his three beautiful daughters to tempt Gautama and tried in every way to threaten the sage as he sat meditating under the sacred tree at Bodh Gaya. (TIBETAN PAINTING, 18TH CENTURY.)

MAYA (above) gave birth to Gautama Buddha while holding on to the branch of a tree. He is also shown taking seven symbolic steps. (TIBETAN PAINTING, 18TH CENTURY.)

THE MARUTS are a group of either 27 or 60 storm gods, usually said to be the sons of the goddess Prisni and *RUDRA*, an ancient Vedic deity who later came to be identified with *SHIVA*. The Maruts accompanied the war god *INDRA* and were armed with lightning arrows and thunderbolts. According to the *Rig Veda*, the ancient collection of sacred hymns, they wore golden helmets and breastplates, and used their axes to split the clouds so that rain could fall. They were widely regarded as clouds, capable of shaking mountains and destroying forests.

According to a later tradition, the Maruts were born from the broken womb of the goddess Diti, after Indra hurled a thunderbolt at her to prevent her from giving birth to too powerful a son. The goddess had intended to remain pregnant for a century before giving birth to a son who would threaten Indra.

MATSYA see *MANU*.

MAYA, or Queen Mahamaya, was the mother of *GAUTAMA BUDDHA*. According to Buddhist tradition, she possessed all the qualities required of a woman destined to bear a buddha. She was not passionate, she drank no alcohol and she observed the precepts of a lay Buddhist. On the day she conceived Gautama, she is said to have had a dream in which a small white elephant, carrying a white lotus in its trunk, entered her right side. In due course, Maya gave birth to Gautama from her side as she stood holding on to a tree. She suffered no pain. Seven days later, she died of joy and joined the gods.

Maya, or "Miraculous Power", was a term used in Hinduism to describe the power of the Vedic gods. Later, Maya was regarded as the illusion of reality which we perceive, which will be dispelled when the universal reality of Brahman or the "Absolute" is understood. (See also *THE LIFE OF THE BUDDHA*)

***MAYA** (above) dreams of a small white elephant and conceives Gautama Buddha, who is seen arriving for reincarnation, riding on the elephant.*

MERU is a mythical world mountain, also known as Sumeru. According to ancient Indian beliefs, both Buddhist and Hindu, it is situated at the centre of the universe and is the dwelling place of the gods. In Hindu tradition, the sacred Ganges flows from the summit of Mount Meru, and *BRAHMA*'s magnificent golden city is situated at its peak. Beneath the mountain lie seven lower worlds, in the lowest of which lives the snake Vasuki, who bears Mount Meru and all the worlds on his coils and destroys them at the end of each *YUGA*.

In Buddhist belief, Meru is surrounded by seas and worlds, beneath which lie the hells. The realms of the gods and the Buddha-fields are situated above the mountain. According to one Tibetan myth, in the very beginning, there was nothing but emptiness. Eventually, a wind began to stir, caused by the karma of the inhabitants of a previous universe. After many ages, the winds grew stronger, and rain began to fall. Many years later, the primeval or cosmic ocean arose, and the winds began to move the waters of the ocean, churning them until they gave rise to the cosmic mountain Meru, or Rirap Lhunpo. In due course, Meru became the abode of the gods and semi-divine beings.

Meru is made of precious stones; its slopes are covered with trees and fruits. Around the mountain lies a vast lake, and around the lake lies a ring of golden mountains. Altogether, there are seven rings of mountains and seven lakes. The final lake is Chi Gyatso, within which lie the four worlds. Each world is like an island and has its own unique inhabitants. Our own world is called Czambu Ling. At first, Czambu Ling was inhabited by gods from Mount Meru. Everyone was happy, there was no illness or pain.

However, it so happened that one day, one of the gods noticed a creamy substance lying on the surface of the earth. The cream tasted delicious, and soon all the other gods began to eat it. The more the gods ate, the less powerful they became. Eventually, the light the gods had radiated was extinguished, the world became dark and the gods became human beings. When the creamy food ran out, the people began to eat fruit. Each individual had his own plant, and each day the plant would produce just one piece of fruit, which was just enough to satisfy one person's hunger.

One day, a man noticed that his plant had produced two pieces of fruit. He ate both pieces and, when the next day his plant produced no fruit, he stole some from his neighbour's plant. In this way, theft and greed were introduced to the world. (See also *MYTHICAL MOUNTAINS*)

MGON-PO see *MAHAKALA*.

MITRA, according to Vedic mythology, was a god of light. He was one of the *ADITYAS*, and was closely associated with *VARUNA*, the supreme Vedic deity. Sometimes regarded as twins, Mitra and Varuna maintained universal order and justice and were said to embody the power that formed the essence of the kshatriya, or warrior caste. A good-natured deity, Mitra has particular responsibility for friendships and contracts. He is believed to direct human beings towards the light and to enable them to live happily with one another. In Iran, his parallel is the god Mithra.

MURUKAN, or the "Youthful One", was a deity of the Dravidians of southern India. He is sometimes known as Ceyon, or the "Red One". He is an important figure in present-day Tamil religion. Murukan is usually represented riding an elephant or a peacock, and he carries a spear and a garland of flowers. He is sometimes identified with *KARTTIKEYA*, the Hindu warrior god. His equivalent in Sri Lanka is *KATARAGAMA DEVIYO*.

***MERU** (right), the golden mountain, is the centre of the world in both Hindu and Buddhist mythology.* (MURAL PAINTING, WAT KO KEO SUTTHARAM, THAILAND.)

SACRED RIVERS

THE GREAT RIVER GANGES, which rises in the Himalayas and flows across north-east India, is sacred to Hindus, who believe that bathing in her water will enable them to reach Indra's heaven, Svarga, on Mount Meru. They also revere the holy city of Prayaga (now Allahabad), where the Ganges is joined by her two tributaries, the Yamuna and the subterranean Sarasvati. This is a place of pilgrimage so sacred that a tiny piece of its soil is believed to be capable of wiping away sin. Each of these great rivers was deified as a goddess, of which the most holy was Ganga, daughter of the mountain god Himavat and an aspect of the great mother goddess, Devi. She was said to have emerged from the toe of Vishnu, and to have descended from heaven to cleanse the earth of the accumulated ashes of the dead. The ashes of the faithful are still committed to her care.

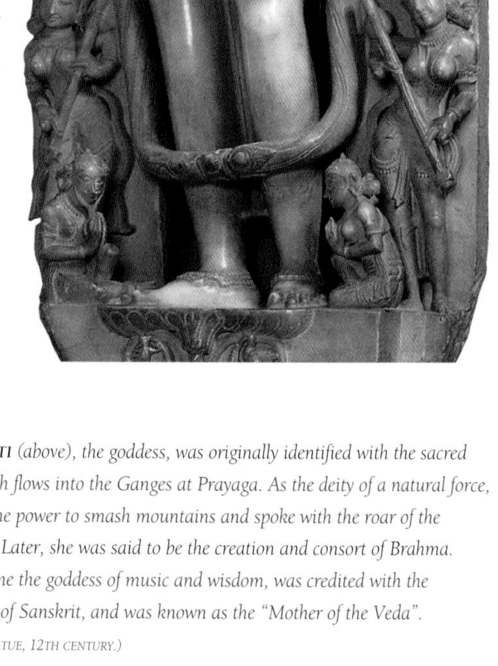

SARASVATI (above), the goddess, was originally identified with the sacred river which flows into the Ganges at Prayaga. As the deity of a natural force, she had the power to smash mountains and spoke with the roar of the waterfall. Later, she was said to be the creation and consort of Brahma. She became the goddess of music and wisdom, was credited with the invention of Sanskrit, and was known as the "Mother of the Veda". (MARBLE STATUE, 12TH CENTURY.)

VARANASI (left), the city on the west bank of the Ganges, is a holy place for Hindus. They believe that to die here, or to have their ashes committed to the river, will release their souls from the cycle of rebirth and death. The dead are cremated on the "burning" ghats (the stone steps that run down to the water), and their ashes are given to the Ganges to be carried down to the sea.

YAMUNA *(left), the river goddess, was the daughter of the sun god Surya and his wife Sanjna, and was also sometimes said to be the sister of Yama, the Vedic god of death. As a river goddess, she was thought to bring fertility and good harvests, and was therefore identified with prosperity. The river Yamuna, a tributary of the Ganges, parted miraculously to allow Krishna's father, Vasudev, to carry him to safety as a baby.* (STONE CARVING, 9TH CENTURY.)

GANGA'S *(above) fall from heaven was cushioned by the matted hair of Shiva, sitting on Mount Kailasa. It separated the river into seven different streams so that it would not engulf the earth. Ganga was believed to flow through the underworld too, linking all three worlds. She was seen as a symbol of purity and was portrayed as a beautiful woman, the consort of Vishnu and Shiva, and also of a mortal king, Shantanu.* (ILLUSTRATION BY WARWICK GOBLE.)

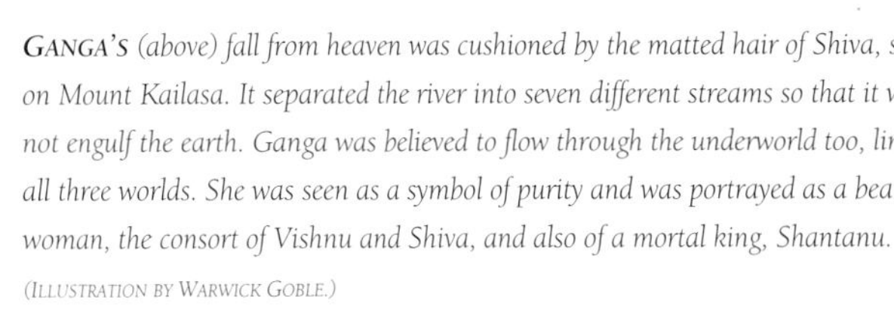

THE YAMUNA *(left) is one of the seven great rivers of India – the others are the Ganges, Sarasvati, Godavari, Narmada, Sindhu and Kaveri – that are particularly revered, though Hindus hold all water to be sacred. On the bank of the Yamuna lies the ancient city of Mathura, the mythical birthplace of Krishna, which is also a place of pilgrimage for Buddhists and Jains.*

P

NAGAS, according to Hindu belief, are semi-divine but powerful serpents who guard the treasures of the earth. They are often associated with fertility but can occasionally prove dangerous. Whereas some nagas are depicted with several heads, others are represented as human beings. The naga Vasuki was used as a rope in the myth of the churning of the ocean and was afterwards worn by *SHIVA* as a girdle that had the power to dispel demons. When the great god *VISHNU* is resting, he sleeps on the naga known as Sesha, or Ananta. Seshas's hoods shade the god, but his yawns cause earthquakes.

In Buddhist belief, the nagas are often regarded as water deities who guard Buddhist texts. One story tells how the nagas took the Buddhist philosopher Nagarjuna to their realm, where he rediscovered the *Prajnaparamita-sutra* of Mahayana Buddhism. The *GAUTAMA BUDDHA* is said to have given the text to the nagas for safekeeping until a time when humans were ready to receive it. Another story tells how the naga king Elapatra disguised himself as a man to listen to the Buddha preach.

Naga kings are depicted in representations of Gautama Buddha's birth. One such king, Mucilinda, is said to have sheltered the meditating Buddha during a great storm by surrounding him with the coils of his body and forming an awning with his hood. The naga kings are said to control rainfall and to look after rivers, lakes and seas. They protect against fires caused by lightning. In spring, the nagas climb to the heavens, whereas in winter they live deep in the earth.

NAGAS are semi-divine but powerful serpents who guard the treasures of the earth. (ALAMPUR, 7TH–8TH CENTURY.)

NANDA see *KRISHNA*.

NANDI, or Nandin, is the milk-white bull who is an animal form of *SHIVA*, the great Hindu god. As well as being Shiva's chosen mount, Nandi is a member of his retinue and represents the great god's virility and fertility.

When Shiva took the form of Nataraja, Nandi provided the music for his wild dancing. In the *Puranas*, Hindu scriptures dating from the fifth century AD, Nandi is invoked as a divinity. He is the son of Surabhi, the divine cow who arose from the churning of the ocean, and *KASYAPA*, the sage.

Nandi looks after all four-legged creatures and stands guard at the four corners of the world. A sculpture of the bull is usually situated at the entrance of temples dedicated to Shiva.

NANDI's statue stands at the entrance of many temples dedicated to Shiva, and devotees customarily touch the bull's testicles as they enter the shrine. Nandi is Shiva's principal attendant.

NANDIN see *NANDI*.

NANG-LHA is one of the supernatural beings of the indigenous Bon religion of Tibet. He was assimilated into the Buddhist pantheon as a protector of the religion. Nang-Lha looks after the house and is usually shown with the head of a pig and the body of a human being.

NARASIMHA was the fourth incarnation, or *AVATAR*, of the great Hindu god *VISHNU*, preserver of the universe. A man-lion, he overcame the king Hiranyakashipu, an incarnation of *RAVANA*. See also *THE AVATARS OF VISHNU*)

NARAYANA see *BRAHMA*.

NASATYA see *ASVINS*.

NATARAJA see *SHIVA*.

NATHA is one of the four principal gods of Sri Lanka. His name means "Master". He was identified with the *BODHISATTVA*, or "buddha-to-be", *AVALOKITESHVARA*, and was also sometimes regarded as *MAITREYA*, the future Buddha. The Buddhist goddess *TARA* is said to be his consort.

NILARANTHA see *SHIVA*.

PADMASAMBHAVA was one of the founders of Tibetan Buddhism. His followers worship him as the

NARASIMHA *was a man-lion, the fourth avatar of the Hindu god Vishnu. He overcame the demon king Hiranyakashipu.* (CARVING, HALEBIDU, KARNATAKA.)

"second Buddha". A contemporary of the Tibetan king Trisong Detsen (AD 755–97), Padmasambhava was allegedly born in the mythical land of Urgyen, believed to be situated in north-west Kashmir. He is said to have been created by the buddha *AMITABHA* and to have appeared, aged eight years old, in a lotus blossom, thereby earning his name, which means "He Who is Born from the Lotus".

After murdering a king's minister, Padmasambhava was condemned to live in the charnel grounds. However, while there, he mastered all the learned disciplines of his time, in particular the teachings of the Tantras, and achieved great spiritual power through conversing with the *DAKINI*, the female "Sky-goers". At that time, the ancient Bon religion still flourished in Tibet. King Trisong Detsen decided that he wanted to introduce Buddhism to the country, and so sent messengers to India, instructing them to find the most learned men in order that they might teach his people. The messengers advised the king to send for Padmasambhava.

Padmasambhava arrived in Tibet and imparted the Buddhist teachings to 25 main students, as well as to the king. Some accounts say that he stayed for a few months, others that he was in Tibet for 50 years. He transformed many demons into *DHARMAPALAS*, or "Protectors of the Teaching", founded the "Inconceivable" temple with the help of local spirits, and composed the "Hidden Treasures". The treasures, known as Gter-ma, are religious instructions, which are said to have been hidden away in order to be revealed sometime in the future when the world needs a fresh revelation.

PADMASAMBHAVA *was worshipped as the "second Buddha" and instrumental in introducing Buddhism to Tibet.* (PAINTING, TANKA LAMA SCHOOL, 19TH CENTURY.)

One story tells how the king eventually grew worried that his people showed greater reverence for Padmasambhava than for himself. In order to demonstrate his supreme authority, he summoned all his courtiers to watch Padmasambhava bow down before him. However, as Padmasambhava raised his arms as if to prostrate himself before the king, flames sprang from his fingertips, setting the ruler's clothes on fire. Immediately, the king tore off his ceremonial scarf, already smouldering, and threw himself at Padmasambhava's feet in submission. He later gave Padmasambhava the scarf as a token of his humility, establishing the tradition of giving scarves as a sign of respect.

Before leaving Tibet, the sage promised to return every month on the tenth day of the waxing moon in order to bless anyone who called out his name. According to legend, he travelled to Bhutan, where he continued his religious teaching. Padmasambhava is said to have lived for more than 1,000 years.

PADMASAMBHAVA *in his eight forms. He built the first Tibetan Buddhist monastery, at Samyé, where previous attempts had been foiled by demons, who tore down the buildings as soon as they were erected.*

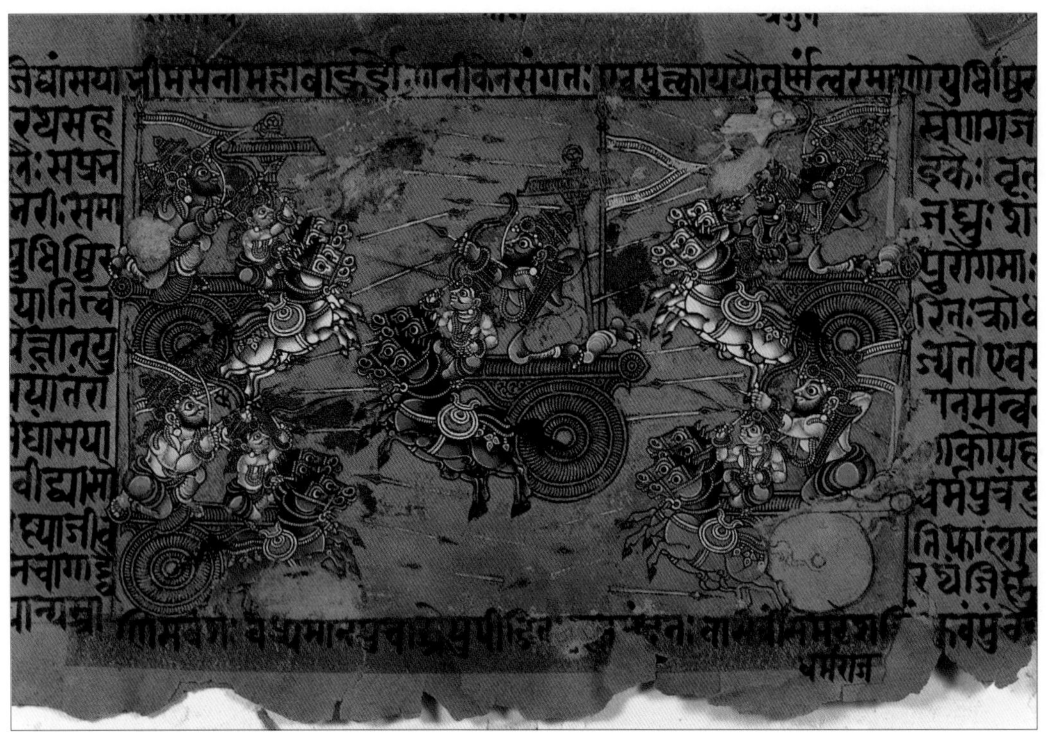

***THE PANDAVAS** were descended from King Pandu. Two of their number, Bhima and Arjuna, fought against Drona, the leader of the Kauravas.* (ILLUSTRATION TO THE MAHABHARATA, INDIA, C. 1542.)

THE PANDAVAS were the descendants of King Pandu. The five Pandava princes fought the Kauravas in the famous battle of Kurukshetra, which is described in the Hindu epic, the *Mahabharata*.

On the eve of the battle, *ARJUNA*, one of the five brothers, received spiritual instruction from *KRISHNA*, an *AVATAR* of the great god *VISHNU*, who disguised himself as Arjuna's charioteer. Krishna's teaching forms the *Bhagavad Gita* or "Song of the Lord".

PARASHURAMA see *AVATARS*.

PARVATI is an aspect of the divine mother of Hindu mythology, the consort of the great god *SHIVA*. She is the graceful aspect of the *SHAKTI* of Shiva. Parvati's name means "Daughter of the Mountains"; her father was Himavat, king of the mountains, and she was the mother of the elephant god *GANESHA*, whom she is sometimes said to have created from the rubbings of her own body. According to one myth, Shiva produced six children without Parvati's assistance. The goddess became extremely fond of her husband's offspring and one day hugged them so tightly that they merged into one child, although the six heads remained. The boy grew up to become the warrior god *KARTTIKEYA*, or Skanda. According to another story, when Parvati first saw Karttikeya, she felt such maternal love for him that milk flowed from her breasts.

Another tale tells how Shiva criticized Parvati's dark skin, whereupon the goddess retired to the forest in shame and became an ascetic. However, *BRAHMA* was so impressed by Parvati's austerities that he transformed her into Gauri, the golden-skinned goddess. In some versions of the story, Parvati's dark skin became the goddess *KALI*.

Shiva once turned Parvati into a fisherwoman to punish her disobedience. On another occasion, Parvati crept up behind Shiva and put her fingers over his eyes. Darkness enveloped the world, and so Shiva made a third eye appear in the middle of his forehead. (See also *MYTHICAL MOUNTAINS*; *THE MOTHER GODDESS*)

PATTINI is the most important Singhalese goddess. She is said to look after marriages and to keep epidemics at bay. According to one myth, she was born from a mango, which had been struck by a divine arrow. Another myth tells how she introduced the cultivation of rice into Sri Lanka.

THE PEY, according to the Tamils of southern India and Sri Lanka, are demons who drink the blood of the dead and of wounded warriors, and bring misery and bad luck to the living. They are wild creatures with tangled hair.

PRADYUMNA, according to Hindu mythology, was the son of *KRISHNA*, the eighth *AVATAR* of *VISHNU*, and his wife Rukmuni. He is sometimes said to have been a reincarnation of *KAMA*, god of desire. When he was six days old, Pradyumna was kidnapped by a demon, Shambhara, who threw him into the sea. The infant was swallowed by a fish, which was later caught and brought to Shambhara's home. Pradyumna

***PARVATI** (right), mother of the elephant-headed god Ganesha, with Shiva, who is shown with the goddess Ganga in his hair.* (ILLUSTRATION BY J. HIGGINBOTHAM, 1864.)

PARVATI *with her husband, Shiva, and children Karttikeya and Ganesha, in their home on Mount Kailasa, attended by Nandi, the bull.* (MINIATURE, 18TH CENTURY.)

emerged from the fish, and Mayadevi, the mistress of the house, looked after him. The sage Narada, lord of the *GANDHARVAS*, told her who the child was. When Pradyumna became a young man, Mayadevi fell in love with him and told him the truth about his origins. Pradyumna then killed Shambhara and fled with Mayadevi to Krishna's palace.

PRAHLADA see *AVATARS*.

PRAJAPATI, according to Hindu mythology, is the lord or master of created beings. In the Hindu epic, the *Mahabharata*, he is the protector of the sexual organ. By his own powers, he produced numerous children including a daughter, *USHAS*, or "Dawn".

On one occasion, Prajapati attempted to commit incest with Ushas, whereupon she transformed herself into a gazelle or deer. Prajapati then took the form of a stag, whose seed gave rise to the first humans. In other versions of the myth, Prajapati succeeded in mating with Ushas when she appeared in numerous different animal forms. The couple thereby gave rise to all living creatures. Another myth tells how Prajapati rose weeping from the primordial waters. The tears that fell into the water became the earth, whereas those that the god wiped away became the sky and the air. Prajapati then created night and day, the seasons, death, and people to relieve his loneliness.

The name Prajapati sometimes refers to a variety of gods, including *INDRA*, *SOMA*, *SHIVA*, *GARUDA*, *KRISHNA* and *MANU*. It is also the name given to ten sages from whom humanity is said to be descended, and to seven *RISHIS*, or seers. *BRAHMA* is sometimes attributed with myths that later became associated with Prajapati.

PRAJNA see *HERUKA*.

PRAJNAPARAMITA, according to Buddhist belief, is the deification of the *Prajnaparamita-sutra*, a sacred text in which *GAUTAMA BUDDHA* is said to have set out his teachings. According to tradition, the Buddha gave the text to the *NAGAS* until the time was ripe for it to be revealed to the faithful. The sutra is said to have been "restored" by the Buddhist philosopher Nagarjuna.

Prajnaparamita is thus regarded as an incarnation of the divine word. Her name means "Perfection of Insight" or "Wisdom that Reaches the Other Shore". In Tibet, the goddess is usually depicted coloured white or yellow, holding a lotus flower in one hand and the sacred text in the other.

PRITHIVI, a Vedic earth goddess, is sometimes said to be the mother of *USHAS*, the dawn, *AGNI*, the god of fire, and *INDRA*, the great war god. She is also the consort of Dyaus, the sky father of the Vedic religion. When giving birth to Indra, numerous portents warned the goddess that this particular son was destined to supplant the old order. As a result, she hid the child away. Prithivi is usually depicted in the form of a cow.

PURURAVAS see *APSARAS*.

PURUSHA was the primordial man or cosmic giant of Indian mythology. According to the ancient sacred hymns known as the *Rig Veda*, Purusha was three-quarters immortal and one-quarter mortal. From his mortal quarter, he released his wife, Viraj, and he was then born from her as a universal spirit. Purusha assumed the form of a giant with 1,000 thighs, 1,000 feet, 1,000 arms, 1,000 eyes, 1,000 faces and 1,000 heads.

In order that the world might be created, he offered himself up to be sacrificed. His head became the heavens, his navel, the atmosphere and his feet, the earth. The seasons came from his armpits, the earth from his feet, the sun from his eyes, and the moon from his mind. The gods and people of the brahman caste came from his mouth, and the wind was born from his breath. His arms became the kshatriyas, or warrior caste; his thighs became the vaishyas, or the traders and farmers; and his feet became the shudras, or servant class.

In the *Brahmanas* and the *Upanishads*, religious texts composed after the *Rig Veda*, Purusha was regarded as *PRAJAPATI*, the lord of created beings. His name is also used to denote the spiritual core of a person; in Buddhist texts, it is sometimes applied to the Buddha.

***RADHA** (above) and Krishna walking by the Yamuna river in the moonlight, having exchanged clothes.* (Illustration to the Bhagavata Purana, Kangra, c. 1820.)

***PURUSHA** (left) was the primal being of Indian mythology. He was sacrificed to create all living things.*

RADHA, according to Hindu mythology, was the favourite gopi, or cowgirl, of *KRISHNA*, the eighth *AVATAR* of the great god *VISHNU*. She lived in Vrindavan, the village in northern India where Krishna was brought up. Radha is sometimes regarded as Krishna's wife, sometimes as his lover. According to one tale, she was married to Ayanagosha, a cowherd. When Ayanagosha heard of Radha's adultery, he went in search of the couple. However, Krishna assumed the form of a goddess, and they thereby escaped Ayanagosha's

***RADHA** (left) has her toenails painted by her lover, Krishna.* (KANGRA, C. 1820.)

wrath. According to another tradition, Radha is an incarnation of *LAKSHMI*, the goddess of good fortune and wife of Vishnu. The goddess took the form of Radha in order that she might not be separated from her husband.

Radha's love for Krishna is seen as a symbol of the interplay between the individual soul and the divine. When Radha is apart from Krishna, she longs for his return, and Krishna likewise pines for Radha. Devotees of Krishna regard the human feeling of love and surrender as a means of achieving knowledge of and union with the divine.

***RADHA** (right) listens to her lover, Krishna, (left), entertaining her with his flute as she attends to her toilette.* (MINIATURE, 18TH CENTURY.)

RAHU see *AMRITA*.

RAHULA, whose name means "Fetter", was the son of *GAUTAMA BUDDHA* and the princess Yasodhara. He is usually said to have been born shortly before Gautama left his family to seek enlightenment, although he is sometimes said to have been born on the day of his father's enlightenment. According to the former version of the myth, Gautama crept into his wife's rooms to kiss her goodbye but, seeing her asleep with Rahula in her arms, feared he might wake them and so left them sleeping.

Rahula entered a Buddhist community at the age of seven and is regarded as the guardian of novices. He is one of the ten great disciples of the Buddha and was said to be "first in esoteric practices and in desire for instruction in the Law". He died before the Buddha. He is sometimes represented holding a fly whisk (swatter) and a scroll of scriptures, and is often accompanied by a deer or a disciple.

RAKSHASAS, according to Hindu belief, are semi-divine, usually evil-natured, spirits. They are able to assume any shape they choose. Whereas they tend to be good-natured and faithful towards one another, with outsiders they can be gluttonous, lustful and violent. They live in a magnificent city, designed by Vishvakarma, the architect of the gods. Harmless beings, such as the *YAKSHAS*, are rakshasas, as are numerous enemies of the gods, including demons who live in cemeteries and harass human beings.

According to one tradition, the rakshasas emerged from *BRAHMA*'s foot, whereas another tradition tells how they are descendants of *KASYAPA*, the great *RISHI*, or sage. In some texts, the rakshasas are described as the original inhabitants of India who were subjugated by the Aryans.

THE MOTHER GODDESS

DEVI, OR MAHADEVI ("THE GREAT GODDESS"), is a composite figure who includes various aspects of the female deity in a series of contrasting incarnations. In the earliest Indian cultures, the mother goddess was Shakti, the source of all energy in the universe, the creative force who brought fertility to the earth. Some of her manifestations were associated with natural forces, such as Ushas, the dawn, and Ganga, the river. Later she was subsumed in the patriarchal Hindu creation myth as the consort of Shiva. In this role she continued to appear in a variety of incarnations. Some were benign, such as Sati and Parvati, both of whom were loving and caring, but others were terrifying, such as the warrior goddesses Durga and Kali. Although she lost her autonomy in her new role as consort, she was still the creative force. While Shiva embodied potency, Shakti was the energy needed to release his power.

KALI (above), the "Black One", was the most terrifying aspect of the goddess Devi. She was portrayed as a black-skinned hag with pendulous breasts and a necklace of skulls or severed heads. Like Shiva, she had an all-seeing third eye in her forehead. Her male victims, made impotent without the goddess's activating energy, had no way of resisting her attack. (THE GODDESS BEHEADING A MAN, BUNDI, C. 1650.)

UMA (right) was an early form of the goddess Parvati, the shakti of Shiva. Uma was the consort of Chandrashekhara, an aspect of Shiva who was also called Umapati ("Uma's spouse"). She was the daughter of Himavat, the king of the Himalayas. In her fierce aspect as Uma Maheshvara, she fought with demons. (KHMER STATUE, 11TH CENTURY.)

PARVATI *(above right), the wife of Shiva (above left), was a reincarnation of his first wife, Sati, who had immolated herself in shame when Shiva was not invited to her father Daksha's sacrifice. Shiva showed no interest in Parvati at first, objecting to her dark skin, but she won his love by enduring austerities. She became the personification of the loving wife and mother, domesticating Shiva, and they led an idyllic family life with their children Karttikeya (above centre) and Ganesha.* (BRONZE SOMASKANDA GROUP, 16TH CENTURY.)

DURGA *(left) the invincible warrior goddess, fought demons that threatened the world. She was the embodiment of the anger of the gods, whether of Shiva and Vishnu, or of Parvati. When Durga herself was angry, Kali emerged from her forehead. Durga fought the demon Mahisha in an epic battle, in which he transformed himself into a buffalo, a lion, an armed man and an elephant. Finally, Durga cut off Mahisha's head.* (DURGA SLAYS MAHISHASURA, MANDI, C. 1750–60.)

KALI *(right) set out to kill demons but could become so intoxicated with blood that she threatened the world as well. She vanquished the demon Raktabija, who was reproduced with every drop of his blood that touched the ground, by catching the drops in her huge mouth before they fell, and then sucking the demon dry. Inflamed by her feast, she began to dance wildly, and when Shiva tried to stop her, she danced on his body, nearly destroying the cosmos.* (ILLUSTRATION BY J. HIGGINBOTHAM, 1864.)

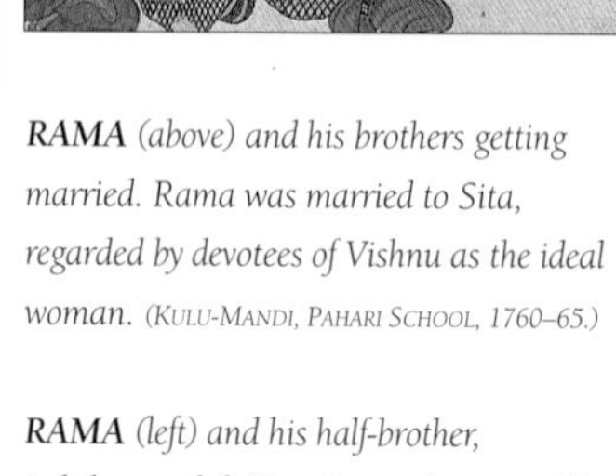

RAMA *(above) and his brothers getting married. Rama was married to Sita, regarded by devotees of Vishnu as the ideal woman.* (KULU-MANDI, PAHARI SCHOOL, 1760–65.)

RAMA *(left) and his half-brother, Lakshmana left Sita alone to hunt a golden deer planted in the forest by Ravana. Meanwhile, the demon captured Sita.* (MUGHAL PAINTING, EARLY 17TH CENTURY.)

RAMA was an *AVATAR*, or incarnation, of *VISHNU*, the great Hindu deity known as the preserver of the universe. He is said to have been sent down to earth in order to overcome the powers of darkness as embodied by the evil demon *RAVANA*, king of *LANKA*. His life and exploits are immortalized in the Hindu epic, the *Ramayana*.

Rama probably originated as a folk hero and only gradually came to be regarded as an avatar of Vishnu. He was courageous and peace-loving, dutiful and virtuous. Devotees of Vishnu regard him as the ideal man and they regard his wife, *SITA*, as the ideal woman: chaste, faithful and devout.

Rama was said to be the son of King Dasaratha of Ayodhya. On his father's death, his stepmother Sumitra cheated him out of his inheritance and banished him into exile in the forest for 14 years. Although Rama advised his wife to stay in the palace, away from the hardships of forest life, Sita insisted on accompanying her husband: "With you it is heaven, away from you hell," she said. Once in the forest, Rama protected the sages who had their hermitages there. When Rama failed to respond to the advances of a horrible female demon, Surpanaka, she persuaded her brother, Ravana, to kidnap Sita. Ravana succeeded in abducting Sita and carried her off to the island of Lanka. Rama, mad with grief, went in search of his wife and succeeded in overcoming numerous demons, often with the help of the monkey god *HANUMAN*.

In order to reach Sita, Rama had to take his army across the sea. He asked the ocean for help and, when none was forthcoming, became so enraged that he shot his arrows at the waters in an attempt to dry them up. Nothing happened. Rama then fired an arrow tipped with a charm given to him by *BRAHMA*. Immediately, the sky grew dark, and all living creatures trembled with fear. Finally, the ocean spoke and explained that, though he was unable to halt the movements of his waters, he would support a bridge over which Rama's soldiers could cross. Soon, Hanuman's army of monkeys had built a bridge and the troops began to cross over to Lanka. Immediately, Rama and Ravana entered into a fearsome battle. Rama's army appeared to be winning when Ravana approached to attack Rama in person. Rama destroyed the demon's ten heads one after another, but new ones kept growing in their place. Finally, Rama fired an arrow which the sage *AGASTYA* had given to him. The arrow killed Ravana, then returned to Rama. The battle was won.

Despite Sita's innocence, she repulsed Rama, since her reputation had been stained by her long stay with Ravana. Sita despaired and threw herself on to a funeral pyre. *AGNI*, the fire god, rescued her from the flames. In another version of the story, Sita remained unharmed by the flames, thus publicly proving her innocence.

Rama regained his kingdom and ruled over it with wisdom, fairness and tenderness for 1,000 years. He finally returned to heaven where he was reunited with Vishnu. The

RAMA *(far left) spurned the advances of the sister of the demon Ravana. In revenge, she persuaded Ravana to kidnap Rama's wife Sita.* (ILLUSTRATION BY WARWICK GOBLE.)

RAMA *(left) gives his ring to Hanuman for the monkey god to send to Sita. Hanuman is the courageous and ever-loyal supporter of Rama.* (ILLUSTRATION BY WARWICK GOBLE.)

victory of Rama over Ravana continues to be celebrated annually in India at the festival of Dussehra. In northern India, his name refers to the supreme god. His attributes are a bow and arrows. (See also *THE AVATARS OF VISHNU*)

RATI see *KAMA*.

RATNASAMBHAVA is one of the *DHYANIBUDDHAS*, "Great Buddhas of Wisdom". He is the "Source of Secret Things" and "He Who is Born of the Jewel". In Tibet he is often shown embracing Mamaki, his *SHAKTI*. His element is fire, his heavenly quarter the south, and he is yellow in colour. His carriage is drawn by a pair of lions or a horse.

RATNASAMBHAVA's *element is fire, and he represents the branch of the cosmos conerned with sensation.* (TIBETAN BRONZE, WITH SILVER AND COPPER, 15TH CENTURY.)

RAVANA was the demon king of *LANKA* whom *RAMA*, an *AVATAR* of the great god *VISHNU*, was sent down to earth to vanquish. He had ten heads and was said to be indestructible. In the Hindu epic, the *Ramayana*, he is portrayed as the embodiment of evil. According to one tradition, a high-ranking member of Vishnu's heaven committed a sin and was given the choice of two means to clear his name: he could either descend to earth and live out seven incarnations as a friend of Vishnu or three incarnations as the enemy of the god. The offender chose the latter option, believing that he would thereby return to heaven more quickly.

Ravana's first incarnation was as the demon king Hiranyakashipu. Such was his power that he dethroned the mighty god *INDRA* and shut the gods out of heaven. He proclaimed himself king of the universe and ordered everyone to worship him. However, his son Prahlada persisted in worshipping Vishnu; try as he might, the demon king was unable to sway him from his vocation. Hiranyakashipu determined to kill Prahlada, but Vishnu protected him. Eventually, Vishnu destroyed the demon and Prahlada became king.

Ravana's second incarnation was as the enemy of Rama, another avatar of Vishnu. Ravana abducted Vishnu's wife, *SITA*, and took her away to the island of Lanka. Helped by the monkey god *HANUMAN*, Rama found her there and made war against the demon, eventually killing him. On the eve of the great battle in which he was slain, the demon admitted that he had only kidnapped Sita in order that he might be killed and so go on to live out his third incarnation as a demon, after which he would be able to return to heaven.

In his third incarnation, Ravana appeared as the demon Sisupala. The son of a king, he had three eyes and four arms. Although his parents were horrified at the sight of him, they were reassured by a voice which told them that, until the time of his death, Sisupala would be both famous and fortunate. The voice also announced that his mother would be able to recognize whoever it was that would eventually kill the boy: when the child sat on his knee, his third eye and extra arms would disappear.

The king and queen travelled from kingdom to kingdom, placing their son on the knee of each ruler, but nothing happened. When they returned home the young prince *KRISHNA*, the eighth avatar of Vishnu, visited the palace. As soon as Sisupala sat on Krishna's knee, his third eye vanished, and his extra two arms fell off. The queen then begged Krishna to forgive her child should he ever offend him. Krishna agreed that he would.

Years later, Sisupala attended a great sacrifice along with numerous important kings. Krishna was also present. The celebration was hosted by King Yudhishthira, who decided that the first homage should be paid to Krishna. Sisupala was outraged, saying that many of the guests present were more important than Krishna. Sisupala appealed to *BRAHMA* for advice, who simply said that Krishna himself should settle the dispute. Sisupala was furious and insulted Brahma, who proceeded to tell the guests the story of Sisupala and the predictions made about him at his birth. Sisupala became increasingly angry and, drawing his sword, continued to insult Brahma. Krishna's flaming disc then rose into the air, shot towards Sisupala and cut him in two. Sisupala's soul appeared as leaping fire and, moving towards Krishna, was absorbed into the hero's feet.

RAVANA *(above left), the demon king of Lanka, is conquered by Rama, who rides away in triumph with his wife Sita.*

RAVANA *(above right) with Hanuman, the monkey god. When Ravana abducted Rama's wife Sita, Hanuman leapt across the waters to the island of Lanka to discover where Ravana had hidden her.* (ILLUSTRATIONS BY J. HIGGINBOTHAM, 1864.)

S

RIRAP LHUNPO see *MERU*.

RISHIS are usually regarded as the seers and great sages of Hinduism, but the term is also applied to saints and inspired poets. The Veda, the sacred knowledge of the Hindus, was said to have been revealed to the seven great rishis who preserved and transmitted it. The identity of these seven great rishis varies. According to the *Shatapatha Brahmana*, a commentary on the Veda, they were *GAUTAMA*, Bharadvaja, Vishvamitra, Janmadagni, Vasishtha, *KASYAPA* and Atri. The seven great rishis were sometimes regarded as holy beings who were identified with the seven stars of the Great Bear.

RUDRA appears in the *Rig Veda*, the great collection of ancient Indian hymns. His name means "Howler" or the "Red One". A god of storms and the dead, he was sometimes associated with the destructive aspect of the fire god *AGNI*. According to one myth, he emerged from the forehead of *BRAHMA* when the god became angry. Rudra fired his arrows of disease at gods, men and animals, but he also brought health and performed good deeds.

When *PRAJAPATI* committed incest with *USHAS*, the dawn, Rudra was about to shoot him when Prajapati promised to make him lord of animals. In this role, Rudra was represented in the form of a bull. He gradually came to be seen as an increasingly dark god who developed into the destructive aspect of *SHIVA*. He is often regarded as the father of the *MARUTS*, companions of *INDRA*.

SAMANTABHADRA, enthroned on a lotus, is mounted on his six-tusked white elephant, which also stands on lotus flowers. (EMEI, SICHUAN, CHINA.)

THE SA-DAG are the supernatural "Lords of the Soil" of the indigenous Bon religion of Tibet. They were assimilated into the Buddhist pantheon as protectors of the religion and are propitiated before any building work or farming is carried out.

SAMANTABHADRA is an emanation of the *DHYANIBUDDHA VAIROCANA*, and represents the Buddhist law and compassion. He is one of the most important *BODHISATTVAS* of Mahayana, or "Great Vehicle" Buddhism, and is worshipped as the protector of all those who teach the dharma, or law. Samantabhadra is often depicted together with *GAUTAMA BUDDHA* and *MANJUSHRI*, bodhisattva of wisdom. He is shown riding on a white elephant with six tusks, a symbol of the ability of wisdom to overcome all obstructions to enlightenment, including the six senses.

SAMVARA, or Chakra Samvara, is a god of initiation in Tantrism, a tradition that uses ritual practices as a path to enlightenment. One of the *YIDAMS* or tutelary gods of Tibet, he is depicted with 12 arms and four or five heads. He is associated with the buddha *AKSOBHYA*. In China, he is believed to be incarnated in the chief Tibetan Buddhist priest in Beijing. His *SHAKTI*, or corresponding female energy, is *VAJRAVARAHI*.

SANI see *AIRAVATA*.

SANJNA see *SURYA*.

SARASVATI is one of the three sacred rivers mentioned in the *Rig Veda*, a collection of ancient Hindu hymns. The Sarasvati is believed to flow underground to join the other two sacred rivers, the Ganges and the Yamuna, at Allahabad, a town in northern India where mass pilgrimages occur each year.

SAMVARA (above) in the posture of Yab-Yum with his shakti, wears a garland of heads and a crown of skulls. (BRASS AND COPPER, KASHMIR, 9TH CENTURY.)

Sarasvati means "Watery"; as the river, she gives fertility and wisdom to the earth. In later times, Sarasvati became the wife and the creation of *BRAHMA*, the creator of the universe.

Sometimes identified with Vak, the goddess of eloquence, Sarasvati was herself the goddess of language, art and learning. She was sometimes called the "Mother of the Veda", the sacred texts of Hinduism, and was also credited with having invented the Sanskrit alphabet. Offerings are made to her by schoolchildren before classes.

Beautiful but temperamental, she was sometimes depicted with four arms and was represented riding on a swan or peacock, or sitting on a lotus. In some branches of

__SARASVATI__ (right) with Brahma. Sarasvati was the creation and the wife of Brahma, the creator of the universe. (CHAPRA ILLUSTRATION, BIHAR, 1802.)

Buddhism, Sarasvati is the goddess of instruction and a companion of the *BODHISATTVA MANJUSHRI*. (See also *SACRED RIVERS*)

SATI see *DAKSHA*.

SESHA see *NAGAS*.

SHAKTI means "Force", "Power" or "Energy". In Buddhism, shaktis, who are female, embody the active energy of the male deities with whom they are often shown in a sexual embrace known as Yab-Yum. The five main shaktis correspond to the five male *DHYANIBUDDHAS*, or the "Great Buddhas of Wisdom": Vajradharisvari corresponds to *VAIROCANA*, Locana corresponds to *AKSOBHYA*, Mamaki corresponds to *RATNASAMBHAVA*, Pandara corresponds to *AMITABHA* and Tara to *AMOGHASIDDHI*. When in Yab-Yum, these shaktis may hold a cup made from a skull.

In Hinduism, Shakti is regarded as the creative force of *SHIVA* and is worshipped under many names, including *PARVATI*, Uma, *DURGA* and *KALI*. Shaktism is an aspect of Tantrism. Shaktas worship Shakti and revere her as the life-force and the energy that maintains the universe. As a means towards experiencing the supreme reality, Shaktas use sexual practices, including those shown in the *Kamasutra*, the manual of erotic art. However, in some sects, these practices are meditated upon rather than actually performed.

__SARASVATI__, one of the three sacred rivers mentioned in the Rig Veda, was also a beautiful but temperamental goddess, sometimes depicted with four arms and sitting on a lotus.

SHAKUNTALA see *APSARAS*.

SHAMBHALA, according to Tibetan Buddhist mythology, is a mythical kingdom generally said to lie to the north-east of India, although it is also believed to be located in China and at the North Pole. It is claimed that the saviour of the world will appear from Shambhala when war and destruction threaten civilization. The Kalachakra teachings, a complex system of meditation, are also said to have arisen in Shambhala. According to tradition, a mythical king Suchandra ruled over Shambhala and received the Kalachakra teachings from the Buddha in his 80th year. The king wrote the teachings down and passed them on through six further kings and 25 "Proclaimers". At the time of the 25th teacher, Rigden Pema Karpo, a golden age will dawn and Shambhala will become a universal kingdom.

SHENRAB MIWO see *GSHEN-RAB*.

SHITALA see *DURGA*.

SHIVA, sitting on a lotus throne and ringed by a circle of flames, sustains the world with his meditation. (PAINTING, C. 1890.)

SHIVA is one of the principal Hindu deities who, together with *VISHNU* and *BRAHMA*, forms the Trimurti, or triad of great gods. He is believed to have developed from *RUDRA*, a minor deity who appears in the *Rig Veda*, the collection of ancient Hindu hymns dating from between 1500 and 900 BC. It seems that the god grew in stature after absorbing some of the characteristics of an ancient fertility god sometimes referred to as "proto-Shiva". Representations of this god, sitting in the position of a yogi and associated with animals and plants, have been ascribed to the Indus Valley culture, which dates from before 1500 BC.

Shiva can be kind and protective, but he is also terrifying and is found in such places as battlefields and cremation grounds. He is often shown decorated with a string of skulls. Although he is a god of creation, he is also the god of time and thus the great destroyer. He is a fertility god, but he is also an ascetic who has conquered his desires and lives on Mount Kailasa in the high Himalayas, deep in the meditation which keeps the world in existence.

Although Shiva brings death, he also conquers death as well as disease and is invoked to cure sickness. He is sometimes depicted as half-male, half-female. The conflicting qualities and attributes found within the god are intended to symbolize a deity within whom all opposites are reconciled. Even Shiva's name, which means "Auspicious", is intended to reconcile and propitiate the dark aspect of his character, which caused him to be known as the "Destroyer".

As Nataraja, Shiva is the "Lord of the Dance", and is often depicted as such. He dances out the creation of the world, but when he grows tired he relapses into inactivity and the universe becomes chaotic. Destruction thus follows the period of creation. One myth about Shiva as Nataraja concerns the 10,000 *RISHIS*, or sages. Shiva visited the rishis in order to persuade them to become his devotees. The rishis responded by cursing Shiva and, when this had no effect, they sent a fearsome tiger to devour him. The great god simply removed the skin of the tiger with his fingernail and draped it around his neck like a shawl. The rishis then sent a snake to attack Shiva, who merely hung it around his neck as a garland. Finally, the rishis sent an evil dwarf armed with a club to attack the god, but Shiva responded by placing his foot on the dwarf's back and beginning to dance. The rishis watched the performance in wonder. Even the heavens opened so that the gods were able to look down at the astounding dance. Eventually, the rishis were no longer able to resist the dancing Shiva and threw themselves at his feet.

Shiva's principal symbolic representation is the lingam, a phallic shaped stone. One myth tells how the god visited a pine forest where some sages were meditating. The sages, not recognizing Shiva, suspected him of trying to seduce their wives and caused him to lose his phallus. Immediately, the world grew dark, and the sages lost their virility. Eventually, they made offerings to Shiva, and the world returned to normal.

Shiva is often shown with four arms and with a third eye, the eye of inner vision, in the middle of his forehead. He frequently has a serpent as a necklace, one around his waist and others wrapped around his arms. He may also be depicted smeared with ashes as a symbol of his asceticism. His throat is often coloured blue, and he is sometimes

SHIVA, as Nataraja, the "Lord of the Dance", orders the universe with his dance, with one foot on the back of the dwarf who personifies ignorance. (BRONZE, C. AD 846.)

known as Nilakantha, or "Blue Throat", due to the important part he played in the myth of the churning of the ocean.

According to this popular tale, the great snake Vasuki was used as a rope with which to turn Mount Mandara and so churn the seas in order to produce *AMRITA*, the elixir of immortality. However, the snake became so exhausted that he eventually spewed out venom, which threatened to destroy all existence. Shiva came to the rescue by swallowing the poison, which stained his throat.

Shiva is the father of the elephant god *GANEṢHA* and the warrior god *KARTTIKEYA*. His mount is the bull *NANDI*. His consort or *SHAKTI* (female power) is called *PARVATI* in her gentle aspect.

SHIVA *with the wives of the rishis, whose husbands feared he was trying to seduce them: an episode from the* Puranas. *(PAHARI SCHOOL, 1710–25.)*

Her other aspects are called Uma, the gracious; Bhairavi, the terrible; Ambika, the generatrix; Sati, the good wife; Gauri, the brilliant; *KALI*, the black; and *DURGA*, the inaccessible.

One myth tells how Shiva gained his third eye as a result of a prank played by Parvati. While Shiva was meditating on Mount Kailasa, Parvati crept up behind him and covered his eyes with her hands. Immediately, the sun grew pale, and every living being trembled with fear. Suddenly, a burning eye appeared on Shiva's forehead, banishing the darkness. Flames shot out from the eye and set light to the whole of the Himalayas. Parvati was devastated and, in due course, Shiva was moved by her distress to restore the mountains to their former glory.

SHIVA, *as Nataraja, dances holding a drum, symbolizing the rhythm of creation, and a flame, symbolizing destruction.*

According to another myth, when Shiva was deep in meditation on Mount Kailasa, Parvati grew bored. She persuaded *KAMA*, god of desire, to come to her aid. Kama was loathe to intervene, but Parvati insisted, whereupon Kama prepared to fire his arrow at Shiva's heart in order to remind him of his duties to his wife. The god Mahesvara saw what was about to happen; since it was necessary for Shiva to finish his meditation in order for the cycles of creation to run their course, he struck Kama down with a thunderbolt. Later, however, Mahesvara brought Kama back to life.

In another version of the myth, Shiva destroyed Kama with a flash of his third eye. Parvati retired from life, having become tired of Shiva's lack of interest in her. One day she was visited by a young man who, while praising her for her asceticism, tried to persuade her to give it up. Parvati grew angry, and eventually the man revealed himself to be none other than Shiva.

The god promised his wife that he would demonstrate his love to her, but Parvati demanded that he should first return Kama to his wife. Shiva did as she requested, and the couple then retired into the mountains. The intensity of their love-making shook the whole world.

DHYANIBUDDHAS

FIVE GREAT MYSTIC BUDDHAS appear together in the "Mandala of the Five Jinas", and are therefore known collectively as Dhyanibuddhas, or "Meditation Buddhas". They are said to have arisen from the Adibuddha, or "Primeval Buddha". Jinas, or spiritual conquerors, are those who have overcome the perpetual cycle of rebirth and human suffering. As subjects for meditation, they each represent a different aspect of the enlightened consciousness.

Mandala is the Sanskrit word for a circle: a mandala is both a symbolic picture of the universe and an aid to meditation, helping the onlooker to achieve different states of mind. For ritual purposes, the mandala is traced on the ground using coloured powders which are brushed away afterwards. It may also be a picture or a three-dimensional object, such as a sculpture or even a building. Mandalas can also be visualized during meditation – they do not have to exist physically.

AMITABHA reigns in the western paradise of Sukhavati, or "Pure Land". Once a king, the buddha renounced his throne and vowed to create a realm which combined all the perfections of existing lands. As its ruler, he devoted himself to good deeds and eventually became a buddha. Sitting on his lotus, his aura is bigger than a billion worlds and he has 84,000 marks of his virtues. Rebirth in Pure Land leads to the attainment of nirvana without difficulty. (TIBETAN PAINTING.)

AMOGHASIDDHI *(right) rules the paradise of the north, seated on a throne flanked by a pair of garudas, or mythical birds with human heads, on which he travels. He is coloured green, and his hand is traditionally raised in a posture meaning "Fear not". His emblem is the Vajra, the thunderbolt, an indestructible weapon, as hard as a diamond.* (TIBETAN PAINTING, 15TH CENTURY.)

AKSOBHYA *(above), the "Immovable", was a monk who took an oath that he would never again feel anger or revulsion. His adherence to his vow eventually resulted in his attainment of enlightenment. He is the buddha of the eastern paradise, Abhirati, where the virtuous are reborn into a land without evil or suffering and where they can quickly achieve nirvana. He touches the earth with his hand to symbolize his enlightenment.* (LOTUS MANDALA WITH AKSOBHYA, 12TH CENTURY.)

VAIROCANA *(left) is the oldest of the Dhyanibuddhas. His name means "Coming from the Sun", and he was at one time identified with the Adibuddha. He is often depicted clasping his hands in the gesture of supreme wisdom. The great monument of Borobodur, in Java, is itself a mandala, designed in concentric circles and squares with four open entrances. A long series of stone reliefs depicting the Buddha's life story is designed to aid meditation.* (RELIEF OF BUDDHA MAHAVAIROCANA AT BOROBODUR, JAVA, 9TH CENTURY.)

THE MANDALA *(left) has a fixed, symbolic format. It has an outer ring of flames, protecting the area within, and burning away the impurities of the onlooker. A ring of Vajras indicates the indestructability of enlightenment, and lotus petals show the nature of the Pure Land. Within the circles is a palace, with four walls and four open gates, symbolizing the whole world. At the centre sits a presiding deity, with whom the meditator attempts to identify.* (SAMVARA MANDALA, TIBET.)

SITA (left) and Lakshmana, Rama's half-brother, watch the monkey god Hanuman worshipping Rama.

SITA (right) finds Rama among the lotus blooms. (PAINTING BY WARWICK GOBLE.)

SHRI see *LAKSHMI*.

SISUPALA see *RAVANA*.

SITA appears in the Veda, the sacred knowledge of the Hindus, as a goddess who rules over agriculture and vegetation and is the wife of the war god *INDRA*. However, according to the Hindu epic, the *Ramayana*, she is the wife of *RAMA*, an *AVATAR* of the great god *VISHNU*, and the daughter of King Janaka.

Rama won Sita as his wife after proving his worth by stringing a miraculous bow, which the god *SHIVA* had given to the king. *RAVANA*, the demon king of *LANKA*, later abducted Sita and took her to his kingdom.

According to one version of the myth, when Rama finally reclaimed his wife, he suspected her of having committed adultery with the demon. Sita proved her innocence and was immediately swallowed by the earth, her mother. Shortly afterwards, Rama drowned. In another version of the traditional tale, Sita demonstrated her innocence by throwing herself on to a funeral pyre, which left her unscathed. The goddess is believed to embody all the virtues of an ideal wife: chaste and devout.

SITA before Rama – her husband and an incarnation of Vishnu. Lakshmana waves a fan. (ILLUSTRATION BY J. HIGGINBOTHAM, 1864.)

SKANDA see *KARTTIKEYA*.

SOMA, according to Hindu mythology, is the vital life force in all living beings. A plant, as well as the state of ecstasy induced by the sacred drink extracted from the plant, it played a central role in Vedic sacrificial rituals.

Soma was regarded as a deity, and one entire book of the ten that comprise the *Rig Veda*, the sacred Hindu hymns, is devoted to his glory. After swallowing the juice, the war god *INDRA* grew so vast that he filled heaven and earth. It was said to be the power of Soma that enabled Indra to overcome the monstrous snake *VRITRA* and to make the sun rise. In due course, Soma developed into the moon god. The source of water, he was associated with fertility and the powers of creation.

Sometimes regarded as the father of the gods, Soma was married to the daughters of *DAKSHA*, a lord of creation. One myth tells how Daksha believed that Soma was showing one of his daughters preference over the others, and so sentenced the moon to death by consumption. However, Daksha's other daughters intervened, causing Soma's punishment to be only periodic rather than eternal. According to another traditional myth, the waxing and waning of the moon is due to the gods' gradual consumption of the Soma it contains. Soma is the equivalent of the ancient Iranian Haoma. Soma can appear as either a bull or a bird.

SUDAPANI see *DHANVANTARI*.

SUMERU see *MERU*.

SURABHI see *AMRITA*.

SURYA, the sun god, was one of the most important deities in the Veda, the sacred knowledge of the Hindus. His father was either the sky god Dyaus or the warrior god *INDRA*.

Sometimes, however, Surya is said to form a trinity with Indra and the fire god *AGNI*, who are regarded as his brothers. His mother is *ADITI*, the mother goddess. According to the *Rig Veda*, the sacred Hindu hymns, Aditi had eight sons known as the *ADITYAS*. She threw one of her offspring, the sun, away from her, possibly because she did not want to be associated with its burning heat. Another myth tells how Surya arose from the eye of a great giant, *PURUSHA*.

Surya has golden hair and golden arms, although sometimes he is represented as dark red in colour. His chariot is drawn by a team of horses and he holds a lotus flower in his hands. His symbol is the swastika, which was widely used throughout the ancient world as a symbol of the sun.

Surya's scorching heat was so intense that his wife Sanjna became exhausted and left him. Before abandoning the god, she persuaded her handmaid to take her place. Surya went in search of Sanjna and found her in the forest in the form of a mare. The god transformed himself into a horse, and the couple produced the warrior Revanta and the two *ASVINS*. The Asvins are golden youths who act as messengers of the dawn.

Eventually, Sanjna's father cut off some of Surya's brightness so that Sanjna was able to bear his heat. Surya's shavings fell to earth, where they were made into weapons for the gods.

In the *Brahmapuranas*, sacred writings dating from the fourth century AD, Surya is attributed with 12 "splendours" and given 12 names of distinct deities including *INDRA*, *VISHNU*, *VARUNA* and *MITRA*. Surya himself is said to be "the supreme spirit who, by means of these splendours, permeates the universe and radiates as far as the secret soul of men."

SURYA *(left), the sun god in Hindu mythology.* (LIMESTONE VOTIVE IMAGE FROM THE SUN TEMPLE AT KONARAK, ORISSA, 11TH CENTURY.)

SURYA *(below), the Hindu sun god, drives his chariot across the sky.* (ILLUSTRATION BY J. HIGGINBOTHAM, 1864.)

T

TAKSHAKA, according to Hindu mythology, was king of the *NAGAS*, the semi-divine serpents. He ruled over a glorious city in the underworld. One myth tells how King Parikchit, when out hunting, mistakenly insulted a hermit who had taken a vow of silence. The hermit's son cursed the king, saying that within a week the snake Takshaka would burn and kill him with his poison. The king decided to protect himself by building a palace on top of a column in the middle of a lake. Takshaka transformed an army of serpents into monks and sent them to the king with gifts. Among the gifts, the king found a strange insect. He was so relieved that Takshaka had spared him that he boasted to his courtiers that, having no fear of death, he dared to put the insect on his neck. Immediately, the insect turned into Takshaka. The serpent bound the king in his massive coils and uttered a tremendous roar, whereupon the king's courtiers burst into tears and fled. Meanwhile, Takshaka rose high into the air, king Parikchit fell down dead, and his palace burst into flames.

According to another tale, Takshaka coveted some beautiful jewels, which belonged to the queen, wife of King Parikchit's son. The queen decided to give the jewels to the wife of a tutor and asked Utanka, one of the tutor's students, to take them to her. On the journey, Utanka stopped to wash. Immediately, a beggar stole the jewels and ran off with them. Utanka pursued the beggar, but when he finally caught hold of him, the man turned into the serpent Takshaka, slid into a hole in the ground, and hid in his palace.

The god *INDRA* saw Utanka's distress and sent a thunderbolt down to earth. The bolt split the ground open, allowing Utanka to continue pursuing the thief. Beneath the earth, Utanka discovered a glorious kingdom filled with beautiful palaces and temples. He chanted a hymn of praise to the nagas, but the snakes remained unmoved. Utanka then began to praise Indra. Flattered, Indra again offered to help the student, whose horse burst into flames and engulfed the nagas' kingdom in smoke. Terrified, Takshaka returned the jewels to Utanka. At long last, riding Indra's horse, Utanka arrived at the appointed place to deliver the jewels to his tutor's wife.

TARA *(above) as the Green Tara, is regarded as the saviour of Tibet, and holds the blue lotus of compassion in each hand.* (MONGOLIA, 19TH CENTURY.)

TARA is one of Tibetan Buddhism's most popular deities. Her name means both "She Who Delivers" and "Star". She is regarded as an emanation of the *BODHISATTVA AVALOKITESHVARA* and is said to have been born from a lotus floating in one of his tears in order to help him in his work. According to another account, Tara was born in a beam of blue light

TARA *(left), in her white form, is the symbol of transcendent knowledge.*

TARA *(right), the patron goddess of Tibet, has 21 forms, including that of the Green Tara, who embodies the feminine aspect of compassion.*

which shone from one of Avalokiteshvara's eyes. She embodies the feminine aspect of compassion and incorporates the essence of the goddess. As a result, her name is sometimes applied to other female deities.

The earliest representations of the goddess date from the sixth century AD, when Tara came to be regarded as the *SHAKTI*, or sometimes the wife, of Avalokiteshvara. In Tibet, where her cult spread widely in the 11th century, it was said that the goddess was reincarnated in every virtuous woman. Since then she has been worshipped widely as a personal deity. There are 21 different forms of Tara, each of which has its own colour, posture and attributes, and they all can appear to be either peaceful or wrathful.

The most common forms are Green Tara and White Tara. In Tibet, the White Tara is often said to be a form of the Green Tara. She is believed to be a form of *SARASVATI*, the wife of *BRAHMA*. The Green Tara, said to be the original Tara, holds a blue lotus in each hand to signify her compassion. The consorts of the seventh-century Tibetan king Songtsen Gampo are said to have been embodiments of these two Taras. When red, yellow or blue, Tara is said to be in a menacing mood, whereas when green or white she is said to be gentle and loving. Tibetan Buddhists believe that their ancestors are Avalokiteshvara in the form of a monkey and Tara (sGrol-ma) in the form of a rock ogress.

TATHAGATAS see *THE DHYANI-BUDDHAS*.

THE TIRTHANKARAS are the ancient "Ford-makers" of Jainism, who taught the Jain doctrine. These leaders, through their own ascetic observances, succeeded in finding a way of escaping the continual round of death and rebirth, and were thus able to show others the path to enlightenment.

According to Jain belief, there are ten regions of the universe, in each of which 24 tirthankaras appear in each of the three ages – past, present and future. Since Jains do not believe in a creator god, their mythology concentrates on the figures of these tirthankaras, who have become objects of worship. Tirthankaras are usually depicted naked, each with his own characteristic colour and posture, but otherwise identical.

In the current age, the first tirthankara was Rishabha, who is usually said to be the founder of Jainism. At his birth, the great warrior god *INDRA* appeared in order to welcome the child into the world. Rishabha taught human beings how to cultivate the land, how to ply different trades and how to execute the arts. He also organized people into three castes. He then left worldly affairs and became a monk. After meditating for six months, Rishabha achieved enlightenment and finally entered nirvana. 21 tirthankaras followed Rishabha, ending with Neminatha, a cousin of *KRISHNA*.

The twenty-third tirthankara, Parshva, appeared 84,000 years after Neminatha's death. Before being born, Parshva lived in heaven as the god Indra. In order to descend to earth, he entered the womb of Queen Vama. As a child, Parshva disdained worldly life and finally withdrew to live in the forest as a recluse. Eventually, he learned how to achieve liberation from the world and from then onwards he passed on his knowledge to his followers. When he died, at the age of 100, his soul entered nirvana. His death occurred 246 years before the birth of Mahavira, the twenty-fourth Tirthankara.

Mahavira, or the "Great Hero" was also known as Vardhamana. One night, he entered the womb of Devananda, the wife of a brahman. That same night, Devananda saw 14 apparitions, all of favourable omen – an elephant, a bull, a lion, the goddess Shri, or *LAKSHMI*, a garland, the moon, the sun, a standard, a vase, a lake of lotuses, the ocean, a heavenly dwelling, a heap of jewels and a flame.

Devananda's husband was delighted by this omen, as he felt sure it meant that he would father a wise and learned son. However, the king of the gods decided that he would prefer Trisala, the wife of Siddhartha, a kshatriya (member of the warrior caste) to bear the child, and so the embryo was transferred. Trisala also witnessed 14 splendid apparitions before the birth.

***THE TIRTHANKARA** Malli, the nineteenth, was a woman according to one Jain tradition. Tirthankaras are portrayed with downcast eyes, to indicate their detachment.* (CHAUHAN SCULPTURE, 11TH CENTURY.)

When Mahavira was born, the gods rejoiced and the demons threw gifts. As a youth, Mahavira married Yasoda, but at the age of 30, he gave away his wealth and withdrew from the world. After 12 years of austerity, he achieved enlightenment. When Mahavira died, his soul ascended to nirvana. Jainism still requires its followers to practise austerity for at least 12 years. (See also *TIRTHANKARAS*)

V

TRANSCENDENT BUDDHAS see *DHYANIBUDDHAS*.

TUSHITA is the Buddhist heaven inhabited by contented or joyful gods. It is home to all the buddhas who need to be born on earth only once more, and is thus the abode of *MAITREYA*, the future buddha. Before his final incarnation, *GAUTAMA BUDDHA* lived in the Tushita heaven as a *BODHISATTVA*. From there, he descended to earth to enter the right side of Queen *MAYA*, his mother. In the Tushita heaven, one day corresponds to 400 years of human life.

UPULVAN is the highest of the four great gods in the Singhalese pantheon. His name means the "Water-lily Coloured One". He is said to have been the only god who remained faithful to *GAUTAMA BUDDHA* during his battle with the demon *MARA*.

URVASI see *APSARAS*.

USHA see *ANIRUDDHA*.

USHAS, the dawn, is the daughter of *PRITHIVI*, the earth goddess of Hindu mythology. Her father is usually said to be the sky god Dyaus and her lover *SURYA*, the sun god. Sometimes, however, the fire god *AGNI* is regarded as her lover, and she herself is said to be the mother of the sun. According to another tradition, Ushas was the daughter of *PRAJAPATI*, the lord or master of created beings. When the god attempted to commit incest with her, Ushas turned into a deer in order to escape his advances.

Ushas is the bringer of life in all its richness. She drives away the dark but is the source of aging. She herself is born each morning, yet because she exists for ever, she is regarded as old. It is said that through the light provided by Ushas, human beings can find their way towards the truth. Each morning, like a good housewife, she wakes all living beings and directs them towards their work. The gods implore her to leave the wicked asleep and wake only the good. In the *Rig Veda*, the ancient sacred hymns, Ushas is depicted as a bride dressed in rose-coloured garments and a golden veil. She is sometimes described as a dancing girl, covered with jewels, or as a beautiful young woman who is stepping out of her bath. The goddess drives a carriage pulled by rosy-hued cows or horses, who represent the morning clouds.

VAIROCANA is the principal of the five Dhyanibuddhas, or "Great Buddhas of Wisdom". (TIBET, 15TH CENTURY.)

VAIROCANA, according to Hindu mythology, was an *ASURA*, the son of Prahlada, who became king of the *DAITYAS*. He was the father of Bali, who was overcome by *VISHNU* in his incarnation as a dwarf.

One account tells how, together with *INDRA*, Vairocana attempted to discover Atman, or the "Self". The gods sent Indra and Vairocana to ask *PRAJAPATI* to help them in their quest, whereupon Prajapati told them, "That which is reflected in the eye, that is the Self." Vairocana and Indra then asked whether that which was reflected in the water was the Self. Prajapati confirmed their suspicion and told them to look at themselves in the water. He added that they should let him know if there was anything they failed to understand. Vairocana decided that he now knew the Self, and returned to the asuras. Indra looked at himself in the water but was troubled by numerous questions which he put to Prajapati. Eventually, Indra achieved absolute certainty about the Self and became fully enlightened.

Vairocana appears in Buddhist teaching as the principal of the five *DHYANIBUDDHAS*, or the "Great Buddhas of Wisdom". He is said to be the personification of the "Absolute" and is sometimes regarded as a type of *ADIBUDDHA*, or primordial Buddha. In Tibet, the snow lion is regarded as Vairocana's mount. His colour is white, and he is often shown holding a disc. Vairocana is sometimes said to have introduced humankind to the Yogacara school of Mahayana, or "Great Vehicle" Buddhism, which teaches that everything is "mind only" and that the disciple's aim is to achieve mystical union with the divine. (See also *DHYANIBUDDHAS*)

VAISHRAVANA see *GUARDIAN KINGS*.

THE VAJRA, or Vajrakila, is a deified spike, sometimes known as a "Thunderbolt Sceptre", which is believed to embody a powerful god and is said to be capable of dispelling evil forces. It is mainly employed by Tantric Buddhists in Tibet. The Vajra originated in India, where the thunderbolt sceptre is the favourite weapon of *INDRA*.

VAJRAVARAHI is regarded as an important Buddhist deity in both Tibet and Nepal. Her name means "Diamond Sow", and she is represented with the head of a pig. Her attributes are a thunderbolt, a skull and a club.

VAMANA see *AVATARS*.

VARAHA see *AVATARS*.

VARUNA appears in the *Rig Veda*, an ancient collection of sacred Hindu hymns, as a sky god. He symbolized the heavens and lived in his palace high above the realm in which *INDRA* operated. In one sense, then, he was more important than Indra, but because he was more remote, the part he played was of less consequence. He could see everything going on in the world and surveyed the affairs of human beings, reading their secret thoughts and sending his messengers out to oversee their activities. Varuna was omnipresent and knew both the past and the future. Above all, he was concerned with the moral order. He presided over oaths and he initiated and sustained the *rta* or order, which was believed to govern both nature and society, and which human beings had to obey. Those who failed to follow the *rta* would be bound with Varuna's noose. However, the god had a reputation for gentleness and could undo sin easily. Varuna was sometimes said to have created the sun; at other times, the sun was said to be his eye. Later, he came to be seen as lord of the night and as the god of water, ruler of the rivers and seas. The wind was his breath, and the stars his eyes. He was linked with the moon, and presided over the care of *SOMA*, the sacred drink. He also shared with *YAMA*, the first person who died, the title of "King of the Dead". Sometimes regarded as one of the *ADITYAS* and the twin brother of *MITRA*, Varuna is also known as "King of the Snakes".

VARUNA (left) was represented riding a sea monster and holding the noose he used to bind the disobedient. (STONE, 8TH CENTURY.)

THE VAJRA, or "Thunderbolt Sceptre", is carried by the god Indra, the Hindu god of weather, mounted on Airavata.

VASUDEV see *KRISHNA*.

VASUKI see *NAGAS*.

VAYU appears in the *Veda*. He is god of the winds and sometimes shares a chariot with *INDRA*. He is said to have been born from the breath of *PURUSHA*, the original being or world giant.

According to one myth, Vayu was responsible for creating the island of *LANKA*, now known as Sri Lanka. Narada, a sage or *RISHI*, challenged Vayu, who was known for his unstable temper, to break off the summit of Mount *MERU*. *GARUDA*, the mythical bird, protected the mountain, but one day, in the bird's absence, Vayu succeeded in his efforts. He immediately threw the mountain peak into the sea where it became the island of Lanka.

THE LIFE OF THE BUDDHA

BEFORE HE ACHIEVED enlightenment, the Buddha had lived through a long series of existences as a bodhisattva, striving to be generous and moral, to shun possessions and to gain insight. He was eventually reborn in the Tushita heaven, the domain of those who need be born only once more, where he prepared for his final miraculous birth as Siddharta Gautama. King Snddhodana, his father, had been told in a prophecy that if his son were to be king, he must be prevented from seeing the miseries of life. So, Siddharta enjoyed a splendid and carefree life in three palaces, surrounded by guards to stop him from looking out. He married Yasodhara and had a son, Rahula. But at about the age of 30, he ventured out of his palaces and encountered the "Four Sights": old age, disease, death and an ascetic looking for a way to transcend suffering. Siddharta resolved to do the same and left his royal existence behind.

QUEEN MAYA *(above), the Buddha's mother, dreamed on the night of his conception that an elephant laid a lotus blossom in her womb while the whole of nature shook with joy. At his birth, the Buddha emerged from his mother's side while she rested by a tree in a garden. He began to walk immediately, and lotus flowers sprang up each time his feet touched the ground. With seven symbolic steps, one in each of the cardinal directions, he took possession of the world and declared that there would be no more rebirth for him.* (SCENES FROM BUDDHA'S LIFE BY MULGANDHA VIGARA.)

GAUTAMA BUDDHA *(left), having left behind his early life of absolute luxury, endured six years of strict austerities which reduced him to little more than a skeleton. Eventually, however, he realized that this way of life would do nothing to end human suffering and that he needed to achieve a middle way. On the bank of the river Nairanjana, a woman called Sujata mistook him for a god and made him an offering of rice milk, which he accepted. Knowing now that his enlightenment was near, he divided the milk into 49 mouthfuls, one for each day he would spend in contemplation, striving to see things as they really are.* (FROM A PAINTING BY ABANINDRO NATH TAGORE.)

GAUTAMA BUDDHA (left) spent the 45 years following his enlightenment wandering and preaching the truths he had learnt. He taught everywhere he went, talking to everyone from kings to beggars, and lived by begging himself. He converted all those he met and performed many miracles, and his following increased in number. A community of Buddhist monks, the Sangha, grew up. (THE BUDDHA BEING OFFERED HERBS, TIBETAN, 18TH CENTURY.)

ANANDA (below), the Buddha's first cousin and devoted attendant, was one of his disciples who attained enlightenment in his presence. Ananda recited the Buddha's teachings at the first Buddhist council. He could explain all 60,000 words and was known as the "Treasurer of the Teachings". He was also responsible for encouraging women to join the Sangha, and established an order of nuns. (BURMESE SHRINE.)

GAUTAMA BUDDHA (above) sat under the Bodhi tree in Bodh Gaya for 49 days, and achieved enlightenment when his knowledge was crystallized into the "Four Noble Truths": that life is full of suffering, that suffering depends on craving, that suffering can be ended, that the way to end it is to follow the eightfold path: right view, right thought, right speech, right action, right livelihood, right effort, right mindfulness and right concentration. His initial response was to remain where he was, but he was persuaded by the god Brahma to preach the truth he had discovered to his growing band of disciples.

THE VIDYARAJAS are Buddhism's semi-divine kings of mystical knowledge. They symbolize the power which the five *DHYANIBUDDHAS*, "Great Buddhas of Wisdom", exert over the passions and forces of evil. They are sometimes regarded as wrathful emanations of the Dhyanibuddhas, or as the energy which the adept assumes on meeting obstacles.

In India and the Hindu pantheon, the Vidyarajas are represented by the Bhairavas, the "Terrifying Ones", and the Krodharajas, or "Kings of Wrath", who eat flesh. The five great Vidyarajas correspond to the five Dhyanibuddhas, while other Vidyarajas correspond to the *BODHISATTVAS*. Acalanatha corresponds to the Dhyanibuddha *VAIROCANA*, Trailokyavijaya corresponds to *AKSOBHYA*, Kundali corresponds to *RATNASAMBHAVA*, *YAMANTAKA* corresponds to *AMITABHA*, and Vajrayaksa or Vajrapani corresponds to *AMOGHASIDDHI*.

VINATA see *GARUDA*.

VISHNU is one of the most important gods of Hinduism and the most widely worshipped. Together with *SHIVA* and *BRAHMA*, he belongs to the triad of great gods known as the Trimurti. The preserver of the world, Vishnu is majestic and at times terrifying. On the whole, however, he is a benevolent deity and far less frightening than Shiva. Vishnu's devotees, the Vaishnavas, regard him as the supreme god: one of his many epithets is the "Highest God". Brahman, the Hindu concept of the "Absolute" or supreme reality, is sometimes depicted as Vishnu.

According to one myth, a lotus flower emerged from Vishnu's navel on the end of a long stalk held by *VAYU*, the vital force and god of the winds. Seated in the centre of the flower was Brahma, who subsequently proceeded with the act of creation.

VISHNU sits enthroned on the coils of the world snake Ananta or Sesha, on which he sleeps during the intervals between Brahma's successive creations. He holds a shell, mace, disc and lotus. (IVORY STATUETTE.)

Vishnu's main function is to ensure the triumph of good over evil. In the *Rig Veda*, the ancient sacred hymns of Hinduism, Vishnu appears as only a minor deity. He seems to have originated as a solar god, and in his manifestation as the sun, he was said to be able to traverse the cosmos in only three steps, an act probably intended to symbolize the god measuring out the universe, making it habitable for gods and humans. Later, Vishnu began to be associated with other figures, including a fish and a dwarf. This association developed into the concept of Vishnu's incarnations, known as *AVATARS*, or "descents". Vishnu appears in these different guises in order to combat demons and to restore divine order when the cosmos is threatened. The most important of Vishnu's avatars are the hero, *RAMA*, and the god, *KRISHNA*. Within Hinduism, *GAUTAMA BUDDHA* also came to be regarded as one of the great god's incarnations.

In his incarnation as the fish Matsya, Vishnu saved *MANU*, the first man, from a great flood. The tale tells how Manu found a tiny fish, which begged him to rescue it from the other fish, which were trying to eat it. Manu took the fish home and kept it in a pot. Soon the fish grew too big for the pot, so Manu put it into a pond. Matsya then grew too big for the pond, so Manu took it to the ocean.

As Manu released the fish into the waters, Matsya turned and warned him that there was to be a great flood, which would drown the whole world. He advised Manu to save himself by building a boat. The floods arrived and Manu took shelter in his boat. Fierce waves and winds attacked the boat, and Matsya again appeared, this time as a gigantic fish. Matsya towed the boat behind him for several years until he reached Mount Hemavat, the summit of which remained above the waters. Manu moored the boat to the mountain and awaited the end of the flood. Matsya then announced that he was in fact Vishnu and that he had saved Manu so that he could repopulate the world.

In his incarnation as the dwarf Vamana, Vishnu saved the world from the demon Bali. He persuaded Bali to give him as much land as he could cover in three strides. As soon as Bali granted his request, Vishnu was transformed into a giant. In two strides, he crossed the universe, which he returned to the gods. He then turned to the demon and insisted that he be allowed to take a third step, as promised. Bali offered Vishnu his head to stand upon and, in recognition of this honourable behaviour, Vishnu gave the demon the underworld to rule as his kingdom.

In the intervals between Brahma's successive creations, Vishnu is believed to lie asleep on the cosmic waters, on top of the many-headed world snake Ananta or Sesha. During his sleep, he slowly develops into another avatar, who will appear in the impending cycle of creation.

Vishnu is usually depicted as a beautiful young man, blue in colour and with four arms. His attributes include the club, associated with the power of knowledge; a conch shell, associated with the origins of existence; a wheel, associated with the powers of creation and destruction; and the lotus, which is associated with the sun and with the tree of life that springs from Vishnu's navel. His mount is the mythical bird *GARUDA*.

The god is also identified with the cosmic pillar, the centre of the universe which was believed to support the heavens. His consort is *LAKSHMI*, the goddess of wealth and good fortune. (See also *THE AVATARS OF VISHNU*)

VISHVAKARMA see *LANKA*.

VIVASVAT see *YAMA*.

VRINDA see *ASURAS*.

VRITRA was the fearsome serpent of Hindu mythology whom the great god *INDRA* destroyed. He embodied the dark and unproductive forces of nature, and deprived humanity of the light of knowledge. A powerful Brahman called Tvashtri was determined to overthrow Indra. He fathered a son, Trisiras, whom he strengthened with his own powers. The son had three heads; he read the Veda with his first head, he fed himself with the second head and he used his third head for surveying the world. He was exceedingly pious, and Indra became worried as his power seemed to increase day after day. Indra sent beautiful young women to seduce Trisiras, but nothing tempted him from his path of asceticism. Eventually, Indra decided to kill him and struck him down with his thunderbolt. However, even then the boy continued to radiate such a splendid light over the entire world that Indra's fears were unallayed.

Tvashtri, the boy's father, determined to avenge the death of his son and created a huge and terrifying demon called Vritra. The demon challenged Indra to a battle, and a bloody and terrifying onslaught ensued. Eventually, Vritra swallowed the god. The assembly of deities was horrified and decided to make the demon open his mouth. As soon as Vritra did so, Indra jumped out, and the battle began again.

Eventually, a great *RISHI*, or sage, was consulted and, with the help of *VISHNU*, a truce was agreed upon. Vritra promised to make peace, provided that Indra never attacked him with a weapon of wood, stone or iron, nor with anything wet or dry, nor during the night or day. Indra agreed, but he continued to plot his revenge on the demon.

At sunset one evening he saw a pillar of foam, neither wet nor dry nor wood, stone, nor iron, arising from the sea. He took the pillar and threw it at Vritra, who immediately fell dead. After slaying the demon, Indra liberated the waters, the sun, the sky and the dawn.

VISHNU, *the supreme cosmic principle, forms a triad of great gods with Brahma and Shiva.* (STONE, 10TH CENTURY.)

VISHNU, *attended by his consort, Lakshmi, sleeps on the world snake, Sesha, while Brahma, the creator, emerges from the lotus growing from Vishnu's navel.* (MINIATURE, RAJASTHAN, 18TH CENTURY.)

Y

YAKSHAS *(left) are Hindu nature spirits. The female spirits, yakshis, though graceful, can be spiteful and sometimes eat children.* (SANDSTONE BRACKET, 2ND CENTURY AD.)

THE YAKSHAS, according to Hindu mythology, are followers of the god of riches, Kuvera. They live in the Himalayas and guard hidden treasure. The yakshas are usually depicted with short limbs and pot bellies. They are often benign, and are worshipped as protective spirits and bringers of fertility. Female yakshas are known as yakshis. In Buddhism, the yakshas are sometimes wild creatures who haunt lonely places and show hostility towards people by disturbing their meditations.

In Tibet, the yakshas are known as gnod-sbyin. Regarded as semi-divine beings, they resemble nature spirits and protect Buddha and the Buddhist law. According to one tradition, Tibet was originally ruled over by a succession of beings, the first of whom were the black and warlike gnod-sbyin.

YAMA appears in the *Rig Veda*, the ancient sacred hymns of Hinduism. He is the guardian of hell and is regarded as "King of the Dead". A fierce deity, he is usually said to be the son of Vivasvat, the sun, and the brother of *MANU*, the only survivor of the great flood. Yama's companion and sister was Yamuna, or Yami.

The brother and sister are sometimes said to have been the first human couple, and Yama to have been the first man who died. According to one story, Yama set out to explore the world and discovered a path to heaven. As a result, mortality was introduced to the world. As the guardian of the dead, Yama was originally regarded as a friendly deity. However, by the time of the *Brahmanas*, the Hindu texts, which were commentaries on the Veda, or "Sacred Knowledge", Yama had become a sinister and destructive force. He developed into the terrifying punisher of human beings, and was depicted armed with a noose and a mace, green in colour, and with two four-eyed dogs as companions. These dogs would sometimes wander the world, gathering together the souls of the dying.

When the soul leaves the body, it is said to cross the river Vaitarani to the land of the dead, where it proceeds towards the judgment room. There, an account of the soul's deeds is read out, whereupon Yama makes his judgment. The soul will be sent either to a paradise, to one of many hells, or back to the world of the living, where it will be reborn.

One myth tells how the devoted Savitri persuaded Yama to give her back her husband Satyavan. Yama, impressed by her love, offered to grant her a wish as long as she did not ask him to restore Satyavan to life. She agreed, but wished for more sons fathered by her husband, so Yama had to send him back to keep his promise.

In Buddhist mythology, Yama is the ruler of the hells. Originally he was a king of Vaishali, a city in north-eastern India. During a ferocious battle, the king wished that he was the ruler of hell and was reborn as Yama. He was accompanied to hell by his eight generals and 80,000 soldiers. There, he has molten copper poured into his mouth three times a day. The punishment will last until all Yama's deeds have been atoned for. In the meantime, he inflicts disease and old age on humans, to prevent them from living immoral lives.

Yama's sister, Yami, is said to rule over the females in hell. In Tibetan Buddhism, Yama is often shown accompanied by Yami and is sometimes regarded as one of the *DHARMAPALAS*, or "Protectors of the Teaching".

YAMA *(right) with Naciketas, a man to whom Yama taught the secret of immortality. Yama is regarded as the guardian of hell and "King of the Dead".*

YAMA *with his shakti, Yami, goddess of death. They stand in the posture of Yab-Yum on Yama's attendant animal, a black buffalo. Yama is a guardian of the south, the direction associated with the dead.*

YAMANTAKA, or "He Who Puts an End to Yama", is one of Buddhism's *VIDYARAJAS*, or kings of mystical knowledge. He conquers *YAMA*, god of the dead, and is sometimes shown trampling him. A wrathful manifestation of the buddha *AKSOBHYA*, he is one of the *BODHISATTVAS* who welcome the faithful into Aksobhya's paradise. He is also regarded as a *DHARMAPALA*, or "Protector of the Teaching", and is said to fight pain.

Yamantaka is often shown with six arms and legs as well as six horribly contorted faces, each with three eyes. He is usually represented seated on a white cow, although he sometimes rests on a rock. His body is coloured black, dark blue or green, and he is surrounded by flames. In Tibet, he is sometimes shown holding an axe and a skull, and he may wear a tiara of skulls, a belt of skulls and carry a human corpse.

YAMI; YAMUNA see *YAMA*.

YASHODA see *KRISHNA*.

THE YIDAMS are the tutelary deities of Tibet. There are numerous yidams since each deity in the Tibetan pantheon can be adopted as a tutelary god. Their name means "Firm Mind". The yidams are invoked by people for protection, but they are more usually regarded as deities who can help in an individual's transformation. They are nearly always depicted with their *SHAKTI*, their corresponding female energies, and are usually coloured blue. The male yidams are divided into bhagavats, dakas and herukas, whereas the female yidams are divided into bhagavatis and *DAKINIS*.

THE YUGAS are Hinduism's cycles, or ages of the world. Each yuga lasts for thousands, even millions, of years.

The yugas decline in length through the cycle, reflecting the decline in righteousness. The Krita Yuga, lasting 1,728,000 human years, was the golden age, when there were no gods, demons or diseases and when human beings were saints. The Treta Yuga lasted 1,296,000 years and was the age when sacrifices began and people became less virtuous. The Dwapara Yuga was a decadent age, lasting 864,000 years, when virtue lessened even more and desire, disease and disasters entered the world. The Kali Yuga, 432,000 years long, is the degenerate age, when only a quarter of virtue remains and people have sunk into wickedness. The Kali Yuga is the age in which we are currently living.

More than four million human years make up a Maha Yuga, or great age, and one Maha Yuga equals a day and a night in the life of Brahma. Each Maha Yuga is preceded and followed by periods of twilight, which last a tenth of the length of a Maha Yuga. During this time, *BRAHMA* sleeps.

ZHANG ZHUNG see *GSHEN-RAB*.

YAMANTAKA *is a wrathful guardian deity of Tibetan Buddhism, depicted in the posture of embrace, or Yab-Yum, with his shakti, Vidyadhara.*

THE MYTHS OF
EAST ASIA

INTRODUCTION

THE GREAT WORLD religions founded in West and Central Asia gradually spread eastwards until they encountered the gods and goddesses of the Far East. To a greater or lesser extent, Hinduism, Buddhism and Islam all influenced the indigenous beliefs of East and South-east Asia. However, the host countries tended to make the encroaching deities their own, embracing them within their own mythologies by a process of adaptation and assimilation.

China, the so-called "Mother Civilization of East Asia", did not view the incoming gods and goddesses as a threat. The immensely stable structure of Chinese society meant that, rather than feeling threatened by outside beliefs, the Chinese were able to modify and absorb outside influences while maintaining their own culture.

China has its origins in the second millennium BC, when the Shang kings founded a state which formed the basis for all subsequent development. During the ancient Shang dynasty, ancestor worship was already in evidence, and numerous gods were also venerated, including the great Shang Di. Worshipped as the ancestor of the dynasty, Shang Di came to have an important role in Chinese religious thought. The Zhou invaders, who overthrew the Shang dynasty in about 1050 BC, worshipped a deity known as Tian, or "Heaven".

In the sixth century BC, Confucianism emerged, although it was not until the Han dynasty (206 BC–AD 220) that it became the philosophy of the state. Founded by Master Kong (551–479 BC), Confucianism propounded a belief in a highly structured society and stressed the importance of the bonds of family life. Master Kong remained, however, noncommittal about the existence of supernatural beings.

BUDDHA *was widely venerated in China, especially during the Tang dynasty between the seventh and ninth centuries AD. Buddhism offered a consoling message about the transience of suffering and the possibility of eventual salvation.* (BUDDHA PREACHING, BANNER FROM DUNUANG CAVES, CHINA, 8TH CENTURY AD.)

Whereas Confucianism drew its adherents from all social classes, Daoism, which emerged at about the same time, tended to appeal to the underprivileged. Daoists seek out the Dao, or "Way", a type of divine

EAST ASIA
SIBERIA
Lake Baikal
Oikhon Is.
MONGOLIA
Mt. Kunlun
R. Yellow
CHINA
R. Yangtze
KOREA
Sea of Japan
JAPAN
Yellow Sea
East China Sea
Pacific Ocean
INDIA
BURMA
LAOS
VIETNAM
THAILAND
CAMBODIA
South China Sea
Luzon
PHILIPPINES
Mindanao
MALAYSIA
Celebes Sea
Indian Ocean
Borneo
Sumatra
INDONESIA
Bali
Java

principle underlying nature. Its followers aim to achieve harmony with the principle by stilling and emptying the mind. During the first millennium AD, Daoism developed an elaborate pantheon of gods and goddesses. Its principal deity was the "Jade Emperor", whose heaven, modelled on that of the earthly emperor, contained numerous ministries and officials.

Around the beginning of the Christian era, Buddhism entered China, introduced by Buddhist monks travelling along the ancient trade route, known as the Silk Road, from India and Central Asia. It was a peaceful invasion, since Buddhism did not feel it necessary to reject the gods and spirits of popular religion, provided that people realized that only the Buddha could offer true salvation. What made the incursion of Buddhism even smoother was the fact that the incoming religion had similarities with Daoism: both Buddhism and Daoism aimed to control mental processes. As a result, there came to be an interplay between the two faiths after Buddhism's arrival in China.

China had a widespread cultural influence on its neighbouring countries, including Japan. Shinto, the early religion of Japan, took

YU HUANG (below), the "Jade Emperor", was the chief deity of the Daoist pantheon. His supremacy in heaven mirrored that of the emperor on earth, with whom he was said to correspond directly. (CHINESE WALL PAINTING, C. 1325.)

CONFUCIUS *is known in the West by the Latin rendering of his name, Kong Fuzi. Benevolence was central to his doctrine, which was adopted by the state during the Han dynasty.* (Chinese drawing.)

much of its cosmology, including that of an egg-shaped cosmos, from Chinese sources. However, whereas the Chinese regarded their "Jade Emperor" as a reflection of the earthly emperor, the Japanese claimed that the members of the imperial family were descended from their chief deity, the sun goddess Amaterasu, giving them a divine right to govern. In the sixth century AD, Buddhism entered Japan, spreading from China and Korea. Japan adopted Buddhism and used it to complement Shintoism, so that it still remains unclear whether some deities are Shinto or Buddhist. The overlap of Shinto and Buddhist ideas gave Japanese Buddhism its own distinctive flavour.

Chinese civilization also influenced South-east Asia, in particular Vietnam. However, Burma, Thailand, Cambodia, Laos, peninsular Malaysia and the Indonesian islands of Sumatra, Java and Bali were all affected by the advance of Indian culture, and especially by the cults of the great Hindu gods Vishnu and Shiva. On the island of Bali, Shiva and Buddha were sometimes worshipped as a joint deity.

From the beginning of the 17th century, Islam became the dominant religion of insular South-east Asia, carried there by Muslim traders. However, despite the impact of these major religions, indigenous beliefs persisted. For example, on Bali, where Hinduism is the official religion, mediums still communicate with deities and spirits; among the peoples of Borneo, the indigenous animistic beliefs continue to produce a mythology peopled by ghosts and spirits connected with natural phenomena.

In other areas of East Asia, traditional beliefs have been lost under the force of incoming religions. Many of the shamanic myths of Mongolia were lost after the introduction of Buddhism to the country in the 13th century. In Siberia, shamanism came under threat from Muslim missionaries from the tenth century onwards. However, while Islam won many converts, a reverse process also took place, with certain Central Asian Sufi orders being influenced by shamanism. Later; shamanism declined in the face of the missionary activity of the Russian orthodox church in the 19th century and, after the Russian revolution of 1917, Siberian shamans were persecuted by the Communists. Today, however, there are movements to revive shamanism to the level of influence it held in times gone by .

In general, the countries of East Asia have contributed to the already rich mythologies of the religions to which they have become hosts. In China, the goddess of mercy,

SHAMANS *of Mongolia perform ritual dances with the use of drums to induce a trance state. These charismatic figures have the power to control spirits and to make journeys out of their bodies to the upper and lower spirit worlds. They are central figures in many communities, combining the functions of priest and doctor.* (Illustration from Le Tour du Monde, c. 1850.)

Guanyin, evolved out of the Indian bodhisattva Avalokiteshvara and became a powerful mother goddess. Amitabha, the buddha of boundless light, became an important deity in both China and Japan. As Omito Fu in China and as Amida in Japan, he came to have an immense impact, in particular on the Japanese mind.

Initially identified with the great Shinto goddess Amaterasu, Amida became the focus of a school of Buddhism that teaches that all of those who call on the Buddha in faith will gain entry to his wondrous paradise. By confidently looking forward to a glorious hereafter, Chinese and Japanese devotees came to view earthly life as simply transitory. The figure of Omito Fu/Amida thus demonstrates the manner in which an incoming deity can both be transformed by and, in turn, come to transform the society in which it makes its home.

A

THE ABAASY, according to the Yakut people of Siberia, are evil supernatural beings who live in the lower world and are ruled over by the malevolent spirit *ULU TOYO'N*. The son of the chief Abaasy is said to have only one eye and iron teeth.

AIZEN-MYOO is regarded as the god of love in popular Japanese belief. He is a deity of both physical and intellectual desire and represents love transformed through the desire for enlightenment. His body is red and he has six arms holding various weapons, three eyes and the head of a lion in his hair. Despite his frightening appearance, he shows great compassion for humankind.

AJYSYT see *ITCHITA*.

AMATERASU is the sun goddess of Japanese mythology and one of the most important deities within the Shinto pantheon. Her full name, Amaterasu-O-Mi-Kami, means "August Person who Makes the Heavens Shine". Amaterasu was brought into being when *IZANAGI*, the male half of the primal couple, washed his face after returning from *YOMI*, the land of the dead. The sun goddess emerged from Izanagi's left eye and the moon god *TSUKIYOMI* from his right. Izanagi told Amaterasu that she should rule the high plains of heaven and gave her his sacred bead necklace.

The storm god *SUSANO-WO*, who had been born from Izanagi's nose, angered his father by saying that, rather than rule over the waters as Izanagi had decreed, he wanted to join his mother *IZANAMI* in Yomi. As a result, Izanagi banished Susano-Wo. Before leaving, Susano-Wo said that he wanted to say goodbye to Amaterasu, his sister. However, Amaterasu suspected that her brother wanted to take her kingdom from her, so she prepared for battle. Arming herself with a bow and two quivers of arrows, she shook her bow in challenge and stamped the earth beneath her feet. Susano-Wo claimed that he had no wish to usurp Amaterasu's power. Instead, he said that they could prove which of them was the most powerful by seeing who could produce male deities.

Amaterasu began the contest by breaking her brother's sword into three, chewing the pieces, then spitting them out. A mist appeared from her mouth, soon taking the form of three goddesses. Susano-Wo then took the fertility beads with which Amaterasu bound her hair and arms. He cracked the beads with his teeth, and from them produced five male gods. He then announced that he had won the contest. However, Amaterasu said that because the gods had come from her own jewels, she had won the contest. Susano-Wo ignored her protest and celebrated his victory by wreaking havoc on earth. He destroyed the rice fields, filled in the irrigation ditches and

***AIZEN-MYOO** sits on a blossoming lotus, a symbol of enlightenment. He is popularly seen as the god of romantic and erotic love.* (JAPANESE SCULPTURE, C. 12TH CENTURY.)

AMATERASU *(above), hearing the commotion outside her cave, looked out in curiosity and light returned to the world.* (Woodblock print by Taiso Yoshitoshi, 1882.)

finished his rampage by skinning a young pony and hurling it through the roof of the sacred weaving hall, where Amaterasu and her attendants sat weaving. One of the maidens died of fright, and Amaterasu fled in terror and fury.

The goddess hid in a cave, thereby casting the world into darkness. The evil gods were delighted, as the darkness enabled them to perform their wicked deeds undetected. However, the good deities beseeched Amaterasu to return to the world. The goddess refused, and so the deities hatched a plot. They found the cock whose crow precedes the dawn and made a mirror strung with jewels. Then, after setting the cock and the mirror outside Amaterasu's hiding place, they asked the goddess *AME-NO-UZUME* to dance on an upturned tub. The cock began to crow and the goddess began to dance, her feet creating a frenzied drumming noise. Eventually, the goddess was carried away by the ecstasy of her dance and removed her clothes, whereupon all the gods began to laugh. Unable to contain her curiosity, Amaterasu emerged from the cave and caught sight of her reflection in the mirror. As she was lured out to gaze at her own beauty, the world was again lit by the sun.

Amaterasu and her attendants are said to have been weaving the garments of the gods, or those of the priestesses who officiate at ceremonies associated with the sun goddess's cult. Another theory argues that the women were weaving the fabric of the universe, which remained incomplete.

Until 1945, Amaterasu was worshipped as a sacred ancestor of the Japanese imperial family, and a mirror forms part of the imperial regalia. A major shrine to the goddess at Ise is visited by millions of pilgrims each year. (See also *CREATION MYTHS*)

AME-NO-UZUME, or simply Uzume, is the dawn goddess and the goddess of laughter, according to the Shinto mythology of Japan. She helped to tempt *AMATERASU* out of a cave after the sun deity, enraged by the behaviour of the storm god *SUSANO-WO*, had taken shelter there. Ame-No-Uzume danced at the entrance to the cave, eventually becoming so carried away by her antics that she flung off all her clothes. The assembled gods burst out laughing, and the disturbance caused Amaterasu to look out of her hiding-place to see what was happening. As a result, her light returned to the world.

Another myth tells how Ame-No-Uzume distracted a local solar deity, the "Monkey Prince", who had attempted to block the descent from heaven of *NINIGI* or Honinigi, Amaterasu's grandson. In due course, Ame-No-Uzume and the Monkey Prince were married.

AME-NO-UZUME *(below) helped to lure Amaterasu out of a cave by arousing her curiosity with an erotic dance.* (Illustration from Myths and Legends of Japan.)

B

AMIDA is a Japanese deity who derives from the buddha Amitabha, or "Boundless Light", who postponed his own entry into nirvana in order that he might save humankind. In China, Amida is known as Omito Fu. He is the central figure in the "Pure Land" sects of Buddhism. The devotees believe that, by invoking the buddha at the hour of their death, they may be reborn in the Pure Land, Amida's western paradise. Once in the Pure Land, the faithful remain free from pain and desire until the time for their final enlightenment arrives.

Amida was originally identified with *AMATERASU*, the sun goddess and the most important Shinto deity. He is often represented welcoming the faithful to his Pure Land, surrounded by numerous bodhisattvas and celestial beings.

ANTABOGA is the world serpent of Balinese mythology. At the beginning of time, only Antaboga existed. By means of meditation, the great serpent created the world turtle, *BEDAWANG*. Two snakes lie on top of the world turtle, as well as the Black Stone, which forms the lid of the underworld.

The underworld is ruled by the goddess *SETESUYARA* and the god *BATARA KALA*, who created the light and the earth. Above the earth lies a layer of water and, above the water, a series of skies. *SEMARA*, the god of love, lives in the floating sky, and above that lies the dark blue sky, home to the sun and moon. Next is the perfumed sky, which is full of beautiful flowers and is inhabited by Tjak, a bird with a human face; the serpent Taksaka; and a group of snakes known as the Awan, who appear as falling stars. The ancestors live in a flame-filled heaven above the perfumed heaven, and beyond that is the abode of the gods.

ARA is a spirit who features in a creation myth of the Iban, one of the Dayak peoples of Borneo. The story tells how, at the beginning of time, Ara floated in the form of a bird above a boundless ocean together with another spirit, *IRIK*. The birds eventually plucked two enormous eggs from the water. From one of the eggs, Ara formed the sky, and from the other, Irik formed the earth. However, because the earth was too large for the sky, the two spirits had to squash it until it became the right size. During the process, mountains and valleys, rivers and streams were created. Plants began to appear, and then the two spirits decided to create human beings. At first they tried to make them from the sap of trees but, when this proved unsuccessful, they used the soil. After fashioning the first humans, they gave them life with their bird-song.

AS-IGA, according to the Ostyak people of Siberia, is a benevolent spirit. His name means "Old Man of the Ob", the great river that runs through Siberia.

THE BA XIAN, or Pa Hsien, or "Eight Immortals", are symbols of good luck and important figures within the Daoist mythology of China. They are not, however, gods, although they are often viewed as such. The Ba Xian are said to have achieved immortality through the practice of the Dao, or "Way". Although accounts of how they became immortal did not appear until the 15th century, some of the Ba Xian featured in earlier myths.

***AMIDA** sits on a lotus, emitting rays of golden light, with an aura larger than a billion worlds.* (WOOD SCULPTURE, 18TH CENTURY.)

The first figure to achieve immortality was Li Tieguai ("Li with the Iron Crutch"). An ascetic, Li Tieguai was taught by Laozi, said to be the founding father of Daoism, who descended from heaven in order to help him. One day, soon after gaining immortality, Li decided to visit a sacred mountain. He left his body behind, asking his disciple to look after it for seven days and telling him that, if by then he had not returned, the disciple was to burn it.

On the sixth day, the disciple's mother fell ill. Anxious to visit her, the disciple burned Li's body. When Li's soul returned, it found only a heap of ashes, and so entered the body of an ugly beggar with a crippled leg who had died of hunger. Although Li did not want to live in such a horrible body, Laozi persuaded him to do so and gave him a crutch to help him to walk. According to another tale, Li was given the crutch by *XI WANG MU*, the "Queen Mother of the West", who healed a wound on Li's leg and taught him how to become immortal. Li is usually depicted as a beggar leaning on an iron crutch.

Li Tieguai is said to have instructed Zhong-li Quan in the Daoist doctrine. According to one tradition, Zhong-li Quan found instructions for gaining immortality behind the wall of his dwelling when it collapsed one day. Zhong-li Quan followed the guidelines, whereupon he disappeared to the heavens on a cloud. Another tale tells how, during a famine, Zhong-li Quan miraculously produced silver coins and gave them to the poor, thereby saving them from starvation. Zhong-li Quan was fat, bald and sported a long beard. He was

THE BA XIAN included Zhang Guolao, who is represented here, riding his mule back-to-front, in a paper model outside a temple during a festival in Taiwan.

often represented with a fan made from feathers or palm leaves. After gaining immortality, he became a messenger of heaven.

Lu Dongbin was born in the tenth century AD. While still a student, he met a fire dragon who gave him a magic sword with which he could conceal himself in heaven. Later, Lu Dongbin visited an inn where he met a man called Han Zhongli. While Han Zhongli warmed up a pot of wine, Lu fell asleep and saw the whole of his future life in a dream. He dreamt that he would enjoy good fortune for 50 years but then his luck would run out, his family ruined and he himself killed by bandits.

When Lu Dongbin woke up, he became convinced of the worthlessness of earthly ambition and decided to renounce the world. He followed Han Zhongli into the mountains in order to seek the Dao and achieve immortality. Lu Dongbin is said to mingle with ordinary mortals, rewarding the good and punishing the wicked. He uses his sword to conquer ignorance, passion and aggression. He is the patriarch of many Chinese sects and the most popular immortal in Chinese culture.

Han Xiang is usually said to be a nephew of a Tang dynasty philosopher. He became a disciple of Lu Dongbin, who took Han to heaven and showed him the tree that bears the peaches of eternal life. Han began to climb the tree but slipped and crashed to earth. Just before landing, he achieved immortality. Han Xiang is said to have a wild temper and supernatural powers. On one occasion, he caused peonies to blossom in the middle of winter. A prophecy was written on their petals and, though at the time the words appeared to mean nothing, they later came true. Han is traditionally portrayed carrying a peach, a flute or a bouquet of flowers.

Cao Guojiu was a brother of Empress Cao of the Song dynasty. He lived in the 11th century AD and is said either to have become disillusioned by the corrupt life of the court or to have been overwhelmed with shame when his brother was found to be a murderer. Whatever the reason, he disappeared into the mountains in pursuit of the Dao.

On coming to a river, Cao tried to persuade the boatman to carry him across by showing him the golden tablet that had allowed him entrance to court. The boatman was unimpressed and Cao, ashamed, threw the tablet into the river. The boatman turned out to be Lu Dongbin in disguise. Lu Dongbin adopted Cao as his disciple and instructed him in the Dao.

Another version of the story tells how the emperor gave Cao a golden medal, which had the ability to allow its owner to overcome all obstacles. When Cao showed the medal to the boatman, a priest asked him why he found it necessary to use such methods of persuasion. Ashamed, Cao threw the medal into the river, whereupon the priest revealed himself as Lu Dongbin and promised to help Cao gain immortality.

Zhang Guolao was an old man who lived at the time of the Empress Wu of the Tang dynasty, in the eighth century AD. He is often shown riding back-to-front on a white mule. The mule was said to be capable of travelling thousands of miles each day and, when not being ridden, could be folded up and put in a bag. To bring the mule back to life, Zhang just sprinkled it with water.

The emperor grew intrigued by Zhang and asked a Daoist master to tell him his true identity. The master replied that he was afraid to answer the emperor's question because he had been told that if he did so, he would immediately die. He finally agreed to reveal who Zhang was, on condition that the emperor promised afterwards to go barefoot and bareheaded to Zhang and ask him to forgive the master for his betrayal. The emperor agreed, whereupon the master said that Zhang was an incarnation of the chaos that existed at the beginning of time. The master died, but when the emperor went to ask Zhang for forgiveness, he was brought back to life.

Zhang could endow the childless and the newly married with children. He is sometimes shown holding the peaches of eternal life or the bag that contains his mule.

Lan Caihe was either a girl or a man who looked like a woman. In summer she wore a thick overcoat and in winter only light clothing. She wore a belt made of black wood and a boot on only one foot. Her family dealt in medicinal herbs. One day, when she was collecting herbs, Lan Caihe met a beggar dressed in filthy rags, his body covered in boils. The girl looked after the beggar, who turned out to be Li Tieguai in disguise. For her kindness, Li Tieguai rewarded the girl with immortality. Lan Caihe then toured the country singing songs and urging people to seek the Dao. One day, she took off her coat, boot and belt, and rose into the sky riding on a crane. She is sometimes represented carrying a basket of fruit or flowers.

He Xiangu became immortal after grinding and eating a mother-of-pearl stone. After swallowing the stone, He Xiangu became as light as a feather and found that she was able to fly over the mountains gathering fruits and berries. One day the emperor summoned her to his court, but she became immortal and disappeared. She is usually depicted holding either a peach or a lotus blossom. (See also *THE EIGHT IMMORTALS*)

The Bajang is an evil spirit who, in the folk-tales of the Malay-speaking people of South-east Asia, appears when a disaster or illness is about to occur. He usually takes the form of a giant polecat (ferret) and is particularly harmful to children.

The master of the household is said to be able to catch the Bajang and keep him in a container. If the master feeds the Bajang milk and eggs, the spirit becomes friendly and will cause the master's enemies to fall ill. However, if the master fails to feed the spirit, he will attack him.

Barong, according to Balinese mythology, is the leader of the forces of good and the enemy of *Rangda*, the demon queen. He is regarded as the king of the spirits and traditionally takes the form of a lion. Ritual battles, usually ending in Rangda's defeat or a compromise, are staged between the two beings. (See also *Demons*)

Basuki is a giant serpent of Balinese mythology. He lives in the underworld cave that is ruled over by the god *Batara Kala* and the goddess *Setesuyara*.

Batara Guru is the name by which the Hindu god Shiva was known in South-east Asia before the arrival of Islam. He was the omnipotent sky god and was also viewed as a god of the ocean. Shiva was introduced to Java, Sumatra, Bali and the Malay peninsula sometime before the fifth century AD.

The Malay people added their own stories to the Indian tales of the great god's exploits. In Sumatra, for example, Batara Guru was said to have created the earth by sending a handful of soil to his daughter, *Boru Deak Parudjar*, who had jumped from heaven into a vast ocean in order to avoid the unwelcome advances of the god Mangalabulan. A swallow told Batara Guru what had happened, and the god sent the bird down to earth with the soil. When the girl threw the soil into the water, it immediately formed an island. This so annoyed the sea serpent *Naga Padoha* that he arched his back, causing the island to float away. Batara Guru then sent down more soil, as well as an incarnation of himself in the form of a hero. The hero managed to keep the serpent still by placing an iron weight on his back so that he sank to the lower depths. Try as he might, Naga Padoha was unable to move the huge weight, but his writhings caused the formation of mountains and valleys.

***Benkei** was the companion of the hero Yoshitsune. They were once attacked by a ghostly company of the Taira clan.*

(Illustration from Myths and Legends of Japan.)

After he had created the islands of the South-east Asian archipelago, Batara Guru sprinkled them with seeds, from which arose all animals and plants. Boru Deak Parudjar and the hero then produced the first human beings.

BATARA KALA, according to the creation myth of the Balinese, is the god who rules over the underworld cave together with the goddess *SETESUYARA*. Batara Kala created the light and the earth.

BEDAWANG is the Balinese world turtle whom the world serpent *ANTABOGA* created through meditation. Two snakes lie on top of the world turtle as well as the Black Stone, which forms the lid of the underworld. The god *BATARA KALA* and the goddess *SETESUYARA* rule over the underworld.

BENKEI, according to Japanese mythology, is the companion of the hero *YOSHITSUNE*. He is said to have been conceived by a *TENGU*, or demon. He soon grew to a great height and became very strong. None the less, Yoshitsune succeeded in overpowering Benkei in a duel, whereupon the giant became the hero's servant.

BENTEN, or Benzai, was one of the *SHICHI FUKUJIN*, or seven deities of good fortune or happiness, an assembly of immortals grouped together in the 17th century by a monk who intended them to symbolize the virtues of a man of his time. Benten was said to be the sister of the king of the Buddhist hells. Later, due to a mistake, she was attributed with the virtues of good luck and was included in the group of seven deities of happiness.

Benten helps human beings acquire material gains. She is said to have married a dragon in order to render him harmless, and is sometimes represented riding a dragon or sea serpent. She is associated with the sea. The goddess is also believed to be an exemplar of the feminine accomplishments, and she is often shown playing a musical instrument. Venerated by gamblers and jealous women, as well as by speculators and tradesmen, Benten is believed to bring good luck in marriage and is the patron saint of the geishas. (See also *THE SHICHI FUKUJIN*)

BENTEN *holding a zither and riding on a dragon, is visited in her cave at Enoshima by a nobleman asking her to grant prosperity to his house. The goddess is associated with material wealth.* (GOLD LACQUER SCREEN, 19TH CENTURY.)

BENZAI see *BENTEN*.

BISHAMON is a Japanese god who was derived from Vaishravana, one of the Guardian Kings of Buddhism. Bishamon, like Vaishravana, was originally the heavenly guardian of the north, but he later became the protector of the law who guarded people from illness and demons. He was also a god of war. Bishamon is believed to possess enormous wealth and to dispense ten sorts of treasure or good luck. As a result, he was included in the list of *SHICHI FUKUJIN*, the seven deities of happiness or good luck, an assembly of immortals grouped together in the 17th century by a monk who intended them to symbolize the virtues of a man of his time.

Bishamon is normally represented as a blue-faced warrior clad in full armour, and his attributes include a spear and a pagoda, a symbol of religious devotion. He is sometimes known by the name Bishamon-tenno or Bishamonten, and is often shown trampling two demons. In the sixth century, Prince Shotoku called upon the god to help him in his crusade against anti-Buddhist factions. (See also *THE SHICHI FUKUJIN*)

BORU DEAK PARUDJAR, according to the mythology of Sumatra, is the daughter of the god *BATARA GURU*, the name by which the Hindu god Shiva was known in South-east Asia before the arrival of Islam. Batara Guru is said to have created the earth by sending a handful of soil to his daughter, Boru Deak Parudjar, who had jumped from heaven into a vast ocean in order to avoid the unwelcome advances of the god Mangalabulan. A swallow told Batara Guru what had happened, and the god sent the bird down to earth with the soil. When Boru Deak Parudjar threw the soil into the water, it immediately formed an island. This so annoyed the sea serpent *NAGA PADOHA* that he arched his back, making it float away.

Batara Guru then sent down more soil, as well as an incarnation of himself in the form of a hero. The hero managed to keep the serpent still by placing an iron weight on his back so that he sank to the depths. Try as he might, Naga Padoha was unable to move the weight, but his writhings caused the formation of mountains and valleys.

After he had created the islands of the South-east Asian archipelago, Batara Guru sprinkled them with seeds from which arose all the animals and plants. Boru Deak Parudjar and the hero then produced the first human beings.

BISHAMON is a Japanese god of war whose attributes include a spear and a pagoda, a symbol of religious devotion. He is shown here with a ministering demon. (WOODBLOCK PRINT BY ISAI, 19TH CENTURY.)

BOTA ILI, according to the Kedang people of eastern Indonesia, was a wild woman who lived at the top of a mountain. Her body was covered with hair, and she had long, pointed fingernails and toenails. She ate lizards and snakes and would cook them over a fire, which she lit by striking her bottom against a stone.

One day, a man called *WATA RIAN* noticed the smoke of Bota Ili's fire and set off to find its source. He took with him a fish to eat and some wine. When he reached the top of the mountain, Wata Rian climbed a tree and waited for Bota Ili to return with her catch of reptiles. The wild woman struck her bottom against a rock to start a fire, but to no effect. Looking up, she saw Wata Rian and shrieked at him to come down from the tree so that she could bite him to death. Wata

THE CITY GOD stands resplendent on his altar in the City God Temple in Xi Gang in Taiwan.

Rian, unafraid, told her to calm herself or he would set his dog on her. The two of them lit a fire and cooked their food together.

Bota Ili drank so much wine that she fell asleep, whereupon Wata Rian shaved the hair from her body and discovered that she was really a woman. The two were eventually married.

BUJAEGN YED is a culture hero of the Chewong, a Malayan people. One day, Bujaegn Yed, a hunter, was eating the food he had caught when *YINLUGEN BUD*, an ancient spirit, appeared to him. The spirit warned the hero that he was committing a terrible sin in failing to share his food. Bujaegn Yed took heed of the warning and took some of the food home to give to his wife, who was pregnant.

When Bujaegn Yed's wife was about to give birth, the hero was on the point of cutting open her stomach to allow the baby out, as was customary at that time, when Yinlugen Bud again appeared. The spirit showed Bujaegn Yed how to deliver a baby in the correct manner, and also taught him the rules and rituals of childbirth. Then, after teaching Bujaegn Yed's wife how to breastfeed a baby, the spirit disappeared. From that time on, women did not have to die when their children were born.

CAO GUOJIU see *BA XIAN.*

CHANG E see *ZHANG E.*

CHIYOU or Ch'iyu, is variously described as a son, descendant or minister of *SHEN NONG*, the ancient Chinese god, or culture hero, associated with medicine and agriculture. Chiyou rebelled against *HUANG DI*, the "Yellow Emperor", in a struggle for the succession. After Chiyou had driven Huang Di's forces on to an immense plain, the enemies engaged in a tremendous battle.

Huang Di's army was composed of bears, tigers and other ferocious animals, whereas Chiyou's army was composed of demons. Chiyou was also supported by Chi Song Zi, the "Master of Rain", and Fei Lian, the god of wind. With their help he smothered Huang Di's soldiers in a thick, black fog, whereupon the latter invented the compass in order to find his whereabouts. Chiyou then called down the wind and rain, whereupon Huang Di summoned the goddess of drought, Ba, to clear the skies. Eventually, Chiyou was defeated and decapitated, although his headless body continued to run across the battlefield before finally falling down dead.

Chiyou was said to have invented warfare and weapons and was also a renowned dancer. Although his body was that of a human being, he had the feet of an ox. He was said to have four eyes and six arms, pointed horns, a head made from iron and hair as sharp as spears. He lived on a diet of sand and stones.

CH'IYU see *CHIYOU.*

CHORMUSTA see *QORMUSTA.*

CHU JONG see *ZHU RONG.*

THE CITY GOD was the impersonal tutelary deity of walled cities and towns, responsible to *YU HUANG*, the "Jade Emperor", in heaven. In each town, his temple was regarded as the "yamen", or celestial court, the counterpart to the terrestrial state yamen with its human mandarin responsible to the emperor in Beijing. The City God performed the same duties "on the other side", controlling harmful ghosts and spirits with his retinue of tamed demons within the city bounds. Prayers were addressed to him on behalf of a deceased, asking him to intercede with the ten judges of the purgatorial courts in the underworld, reflecting the widespread Buddhist concept of reincarnation.

DAIKOKU, one of the gods of good fortune, performs a New Year dance carrying his bulging sack of rice. Tucked into his belt is his rice mallet, which grants wishes and from which money spills when it is shaken. (FUNDAME INRO, C. 1850.)

DAIKOKU was one of the *SHICHI FUKUJIN,* or seven gods of good fortune, a group of deities assembled in the 17th century by a monk who intended them to symbolize the virtues of a man of his time.

Daikoku was regarded as the god of wealth and a patron of farmers. He is often depicted standing or sitting on bales of rice, which are sometimes being eaten away by rats. Daikoku remains untroubled by the rats' greed because he is so wealthy. He usually carries a mallet, with which he is able to grant wishes. His picture was sometimes placed in kitchens, and he is sometimes said to have provided for the nourishment of priests. (See also *THE SHICHI FUKUJIN*)

DAINICHI-NYORAI is the Japanese form of the buddha Mahavairocana, or the "Great Illuminator". He was introduced to Japan at the beginning of the ninth century, together with numerous other Buddhist figures. He became the supreme deity of some esoteric sects and is sometimes regarded as the "Primordial Buddha". *YAKUSHI-NYORAI,* the divine healer, is sometimes seen as an aspect of Dainichi-Nyorai.

DAISHO-KANGITEN see *SHOTEN*.

DEMONG, according to the Iban of Borneo, governed the ancestors of the Iban people after they had been led from a country near Mecca to their present home. Demong married the daughter of a local ruler in order to ensure good relations with the existing inhabitants of Borneo. The woman, Rinda, had several children. When Demong was about to die, he ordered that a boundary stone be erected in order to mark the Ibans' territory. The stone stands to this day, and it is said that whoever attempts to move it risks incurring the wrath of Demong.

DIDIS MAHENDERA was a fabulous creature who, according to the Dayak people of Borneo, appeared together with *ROWANG RIWO* during the first epoch of creation, when a part of the universe was brought into being with each successive clash of the two cosmic mountains. The creature had eyes made from jewels.

DIMU see *DIYA*.

DIYA and Tian-Long were attendants of *WEN CHANG*, the Chinese god of literature. Diya, whose name means "Earthly Dumb", and Tian-Long, meaning "Heavenly Deaf", helped Wen Chang with the setting and marking of his examination papers, since, being deaf and dumb, they could be relied on not to leak the questions in advance. Another myth mentions these two as the primal couple, who gave rise to human beings and all other creatures. Diya was sometimes known as Dimu, meaning "Earth Mother".

DIZANG WANG, or *TI-TS'ANG WANG,* is one of the four great bodhisattvas ("buddhas-to-be") of Chinese buddhism. Long ago, Dizang Wang vowed that he would become a buddha, but only when he had liberated all creatures on earth from the relentless cycle of death and rebirth.

In one of his existences, he was a girl whose mother killed animals for food. Through meditating, the girl succeeded in saving her mother from hell. Dizang Wang is believed to succour all those who are detained in the courts of hell. He is depicted as a monk holding a metal staff which opens the gates of hell, and is often surrounded by the ten judges. He is the equivalent of the Indian bodhisattva Kshitigarbha and the Japanese *JIZO-BOSATZU.*

DONGYUE DADI, or Tung-yüeh Ta-ti, is the "Great Emperor of the Eastern Peak" according to Chinese mythology. He assists the "Jade Emperor" *YU HUANG* and supervises all areas of earthly life.

There are 75 departments within Dongyue Dadi's offices. One lays down the time for the births and deaths of all creatures, another determines people's social

DAIKOKU stands on two bulging bales of rice to symbolize his prosperity, and holds his magic mallet. As the patron of agriculture he was the protector of the soil and he was also seen as a friend of children. (JAPANESE SCULPTURE.)

standing, another their wealth and another the number of children they will have. Dongyue Dadi's offices are staffed by the souls of the dead. His daughter, Sheng Mu, looks after women and children. Dongyue Dadi is usually represented sitting down and wearing the garments of an emperor.

THE EARTH GOD, the ubiquitous local territorial deity, is the closest to the lives of villagers and is amongst those most frequently seen on the altars of the common people. The Earth God is not looked upon as powerful or fearsome. He is a celestial deity, the lowest ranking official in the bureaucracy of the celestial pantheon, and is the tutelary god of each sector of a large village or suburb; the protector of the well-being of both town and country dwellers. He has control over the wealth and fortune of the people.

The Earth God is almost universally thought to be an impersonal spirit. People appeal to him for anything that affects their lives and livelihoods. In times of peril, images of the Earth God have sometimes been taken from their shrines to be shown the cause of a problem, such as drought, flood, frost, caterpillars, locusts or mildew, to enable the deity to understand fully what his devotees are suffering.

EBISU, in Japanese mythology, was one of the *SHICHI FUKUJIN*, or seven gods of good fortune or happiness, an assembly of deities grouped together in the 17th century by a monk who intended them to symbolize the virtues of a man of his time. Ebisu himself is credited with the virtue of candour.

***THE EARTH GOD** (right) sits on the altar of a local temple, clutching his staff and tael of gold, symbolizing wealth.*

***DAINICHI-NYORAI** (below), the "Great Sun Buddha", was the supreme deity of the Shingon sect. Its members held that the esoteric teachings of the Buddha were too obscure to be expressed in writing, but could be presented in painting.* (PAINTING ON SILK, 13TH CENTURY.)

He is said to be the patron of labourers, wealth and prosperity, and to promote hard work. Ebisu is believed to have originated in Shinto belief as the son of *OKUNINUSHI*, the mythical hero. He is also sometimes identified with the third son of *IZANAGI AND IZANAMI*, the primal couple, and as such is regarded as one of the ancestors of the first people of Japan.

In some areas of Japan, the god of farms is called Ebisu; fishermen also invoke the god before going to sea. Ebisu is symbolized by a large stone, which a boy must retrieve from the bottom of the water. He is usually represented dressed as a peasant and smiling. He holds a fishing rod in one hand and a sea bream (sunfish), a symbol of good luck, in the other hand. (See also *THE SHICHI FUKUJIN*)

EC, according to the Yenisei people of Siberia, is the supreme god. He regularly descends to earth in order to ensure the well-being of creation. Ec drove his wife, *KHOSADAM*, out of the sky in punishment for being unfaithful to him with the moon.

THE EIGHT IMMORTALS see *BA XIAN*.

YIN AND YANG

DAOIST PHILOSOPHY CENTRED ON the principle of unity in the cosmos and the belief that a natural order, based on balance and harmony, determined the behaviour of everything in existence. Two interacting forces held the Chinese universe in delicate balance: yin, the female element, was associated with coldness, darkness, softness and the earth. It originally referred to the shady side of the mountain. Yang, the sunny side, was the male principle, associated with light, warmth, hardness and the heavens. The two forces were opposites but mutually dependent, and needed to be in equilibrium for harmony to exist. They were present in every aspect of the world, in contrasting pairs such as life and death, or good and evil, as well as in everyday activities, objects, animals and human characters. In the ancient Chinese creation myth, yin and yang were held inside the cosmic egg until the struggle of the opposing forces cracked the shell.

THE YIN/YANG SYMBOL (above) expresses the interaction between opposites that gives rise to the universe and everything in it. The dark section (yin) and the light section (yang) are directly opposed, yet interlocking and mutually dependent. Together they form a perfect circle. The two small spots show that each opposing force contains a small seed of the other within it. (CARVED CHINESE JOSS BOARD.)

THE BAGUA (left) were discovered by Fu Xi, the legendary emperor, who saw them inscribed on the back of a tortoise he found on the banks of the Yellow River in about 3000 BC. The constantly changing interactions of yin and yang gave rise to the infinite variety of patterns of life, symbolized in the three-line symbols of the eight trigrams. The top line of each trigram represents heaven, the bottom is earth and the middle line is humankind. (ILLUSTRATION FROM SUPERSTITIONS EN CHINE, 1915.)

THE YIN/YANG SYMBOL *(below), surrounded by the trigrams of the bagua, was hung on the house door as a protective amulet to prevent the entry of devils. With it might hang a picture of the immortal Liu Hai with his three-legged bowl, who brought good luck to those involved in commercial ventures. He carried a string of gold pieces to remind him of a visitor who had piled them up with eggs to demonstrate the precariousness of his high office at court.* (ILLUSTRATION FROM SUPERSTITIONS EN CHINE, 1915.)

THE PEI TOU IMMORTALS *(above) were star spirits of which the most important were the "Three Stars of Happiness": Shou Lao, the god of longevity; Fu Shen, the god of luck; and Cai Shen, the god of wealth. They are shown here contemplating the yin/yang symbol on a scroll, and surrounded by symbolic figures of long life and immortality: the pine tree with Shou Lao's white crane, the stag and a child presenting a peach.* (CHINESE SILK EMBROIDERY, 17TH CENTURY.)

THE DRAGON *(right) and the phoenix were often used together decoratively. For the Chinese, dragons represented the male, yang element and were a beneficent force of nature, even though they had fiery tempers. The mythical phoenix represented the female, yin element. The dragon was the emblem of the Chinese emperor, and the phoenix of the empress, and together the two creatures were used to symbolize marital harmony.* (JADE RITUAL DISC WITH DRAGON AND PHOENIX, C. 481–221 BC.)

F

EMMA-O *(left), the king of hell, was no match for the strong man Asahina Saburo, and was humiliated by having to crawl between his legs.* (KINJI INRO, 19TH CENTURY.)

EMMA-O *(right) wears a magistrate's hat to indicate his office as judge of the dead.* (NASHIJI INRO, 18TH CENTURY.)

EMMA-O, according to Japanese Buddhism, is the ruler of hell and the judge of the dead. He is identified with the Chinese deity *YANLUO WANG* and derives from the Hindu god of death, Yama.

Emma-O rules over the underground hell Jigoku, where he is surrounded by 18 generals and thousands of soldiers as well as demons and guards with horses' heads. The underworld is divided into eight hells of fire and eight of ice. According to one tradition, death begins as a journey across a vast, empty plain. In other versions of the tale, infernal beings guard the dead during their journey. At the entrance to hell lies a steep mountain, which the deceased have to climb before encountering, on the other side of the mountain, a river with three crossings. One of the crossings is a shallow ford, which those who have committed only minor sins may cross. Another is a bridge over which good people may pass. The third is a horrific torrent filled with monsters, through which evil sinners must struggle. At the other side of this third crossing waits a horrible old woman who strips her victims naked. They are then taken before Emma-O by the guards of hell. Emma-O judges only men; his sister decides the fate of women. The god sits between two severed heads, and a magic mirror reflects all the sinner's past wrongdoings. Emma-O then judges the individual's sins and allocates them to the appropriate hell. The souls of the dead can, however, be saved with the help of a bosatsu, the Japanese form of the bodhisattva.

ERLIK, according to the Altaic people of southern Siberia, is the king of the dead, an adversary of the supreme god *ULGAN*. He incurred Ulgan's wrath by leading the first men to commit sin. The great sky god sent the saviour *MAIDERE* down to earth in order to teach men to respect and fear him, but Erlik succeeded in killing him. Flames shot forth from the saviour's blood, eventually reaching up to heaven and destroying Erlik and his followers. Erlik was then banished to the underworld. Erlik is regarded both as the first man and as the elder brother of the creator. He is depicted as a terrifying being, having taken on some of the characteristics of Yama, the Buddhist god of the underworld. He sometimes appears as a bear.

ES is the sky god of the Ket people of Siberia. Although he is invisible, he is depicted as an old man with a long black beard.

Es created the world and made the first human beings from clay. When he threw clay with his left hand towards the right, it became a woman; when he threw clay with his right hand towards the left, it became a man.

ESEGE MALAN TENGRI, or "Father Bald-head Tengri", is the sky god of the Buriat people of Siberia.

FANGCHANG see *PENGLAI*.

FU HSI see *FU XI*

FU XI, or Fu Hsi, according to Chinese mythology, is the brother and husband of *NU GUA*. Whereas Nu Gua rules over the earth, Fu Xi rules over the sky. They are both represented with the tails of dragons.

One popular myth tells how, long ago, a man was labouring in his fields when he heard a rumble of thunder. He ordered his son and daughter into his house, hung an iron cage under its eaves and stood in wait, holding a large iron fork. All at once, there was an enormous clap of thunder and a flash of lightning, and the monstrous thunder god, *LEI GONG*, appeared wielding a huge axe. The man attacked Lei Gong with his fork, pushed him into the iron cage and slammed the door shut. Immediately, the rain and wind ceased.

FU XI's (above) legacy to Chinese civilization included the invention of the calendar, the fishing net and the bagua, or eight trigrams. (19TH CENTURY ILLUSTRATION.)

The following morning, the man prepared to journey to the local market in order to buy spices with which to pickle the thunder god. Before leaving home, he warned his children not to give Lei Gong anything to eat or drink. As soon as the man had left, Lei Gong began to beg the children for just the merest drop of water. At first the children heeded their father's instructions, but eventually they relented. As soon as the water touched his lips, Lei Gong became strong again and burst out of his cage. Before leaving, he thanked the children for helping him and gave them one of his teeth, which he told them to plant in the ground. The children planted the tooth and, within a few hours, it grew into a plant bearing a gourd.

It began to rain, and by the time the man returned from market, the rain had covered the whole earth. The man told his children to climb inside the gourd for safety, then he built a boat and rose up to heaven on the swelling water. There, he knocked on the door and begged the lord of heaven to end the flood. The lord of heaven commanded the water god to put an end to the flood, but the god was so diligent that the water immediately subsided, and the man's boat crashed down to earth, killing him. However, the children were unharmed because the gourd cushioned their fall.

The children proved to be the only survivors of the flood. They became known as Fu Xi. When they grew up, the young man suggested that they have children. The young woman was reluctant, since they were brother and sister, but agreed on condition that her brother was able to catch her in a chase. Fu Xi caught his sister, and so began the custom of marriage. The woman then changed her name to Nu Gua.

According to another version of the tale, although the two beings wanted to marry and have children, they knew that they would first have to be granted permission from the gods because, being brother and sister, the marriage would be incestuous. The couple climbed a sacred mountain, and each built a bonfire on its summit. The smoke from the two fires mingled, and Nu Gua and Fu Xi took this to mean that they had been granted permission to marry. Time passed and eventually Nu Gua gave birth to a ball of flesh. Fu Xi chopped the ball into numerous pieces with an axe and carried the fragments up a ladder to heaven. A gust of wind scattered the pieces of flesh all over the earth; when they landed, they became human beings. In this way, the earth was repopulated. (See also *CREATION MYTHS; YIN AND YANG*)

FU XI (below centre) became the first of the legendary emperors of China, followed by Shen Nong and Huang Di.

FUDO-MYOO (left), a terrifying deity who protects Buddhism and its adherents, holds a sword in one hand and a rope in the other. (SCULPTURE, 12TH–14TH CENTURY.)

FUDO-MYOO is the most important of the five great Japanese myoos, the equivalent of Indian Buddhism's vidyarajas, terrifying emanations of the five "Great Buddhas of Wisdom". Fudo-Myoo corresponds to the Buddha *DAINICHI-NYORAI*. He is usually portrayed with a terrifying face half-concealed by long hair and surrounded by a halo of flames. The flames are believed to consume the passions. In one hand, he holds a sword, which is used to conquer greed, anger and ignorance, and in the other hand he holds a rope with which he catches those who oppose the Buddha.

FUGEN-BOSATSU is the Japanese form of the bodhisattva or "buddha-to-be", Samantabhadra. He represents innate reason and is believed to be able to prolong people's lives. One tale tells how Fugen-Bosatsu appeared before a monk disguised as a courtesan with the intention of demonstrating that the nature of Buddha was latent in even the most sinful of women. Fugen is often depicted sitting on a white elephant with six tusks, or sometimes riding four elephants. He may be shown with 20 arms.

FUKUROKUJU is one of the *SHICHI FUKUJIN*, the seven gods of good fortune or happiness, a group of deities assembled in the 17th century by a monk who intended them to symbolize the virtues of a man of his time.

Fukurokuju himself symbolizes the virtue of popularity as well as wisdom, longevity, virility and fertility. He is usually depicted with a very long, thin head to indicate his intelligence and a short, fat body. He is sometimes accompanied by a crane, a stag or tortoise, all creatures which symbolize longevity. Fukurokuju is of Chinese origin

FUDO-MYOO (above) is surrounded by a halo of flames, the symbol of his virtues. (PAINTING, C. 13TH CENTURY)

FUGEN-BOSATSU (below) sits on a lotus blossom carried by a white elephant. (JAPANESE SILK PAINTING, 14TH CENTURY)

and may have been a Daoist sage. He is the godfather of *JUROJIN*, the god of longevity and happy old age. (See also *THE SHICHI FUKUJIN*)

FUXING see *SAN XING*

GAO YAO, or Ting-jian, was an ancient Chinese god of judgement. His accompanying animal, a mythical one-horned goat, helped him to detect injustice.

GIMOKODAN is the name that the Bagobo people of the Philippines give to the underworld. The Bagobo are a hill tribe living on the island of Mindanao. According to tradition, Gimokodan, the land of the dead, lies below the earth and is divided into two parts. One part is reserved for brave warriors who die in battle, the other part houses everyone else. A giantess lives in the second section and feeds the spirits of dead children with milk from her many breasts. Most of the spirits, however, turn to dew as soon as it is daylight and only become spirits again at night. A river lies at the entrance of Gimokodan, and all those who bathe in it forget their former lives.

GONG-GONG appears in Chinese mythology as a terrible monster who brings about a disastrous flood. He takes the form of a black dragon and is attended by a nine-headed snake. As the sworn enemy of the legendary benevolent emperor *YAO*, Gong-Gong decided to impale Mount Buzhou with his horn, thereby disturbing the balance of the earth and causing the rivers to overflow. He then tore a hole in the sky, disturbing the course of the sun. The monster is thus held responsible for all irregularities of weather and light.

According to another version of the tale, Gong-Gong and ZHU RONG, the divine lord of fire, decided to fight each other in order to determine which of them was the most powerful. The battle continued for several days. Eventually, the two creatures fell out of heaven, and Gong-Gong was defeated. Gong-Gong was so humiliated by having lost the battle that he determined to kill himself by running head first at Mount Buzhou, one of the mountains which supported the sky. When Gong-Gong struck the mountain, a great chunk fell off, a huge hole was torn in the sky and enormous cracks appeared in the earth. Fire and water gushed out, and a massive flood covered almost the entire surface of the world. The few areas that escaped the flood were destroyed by fire.

The goddess *NU GUA* selected some coloured stones from the bed of a river and melted them down. She then patched the sky with the melted stones and propped up the four points of the compass with the legs of a tortoise. However, when Gong-Gong collided with the mountain, he caused the heavens to tilt towards the northwest, which is why all the great rivers of China flow eastwards.

GAO YAO'S (above) assistant in his pursuit of justice was a mythical one-horned animal, sometimes described as a qilin, or unicorn, who butted the guilty but spared the innocent. (SINO-TIBETAN ENAMEL QILIN.)

***FUKUROKUJU** (left), the god of long life and wisdom, is portrayed as a benevolent old man with an enormous brain.* (JAPANESE LACQUERED VASE, 19TH CENTURY)

GUAN DI *was worshipped as the protector of state officials in thousands of temples throughout China, in which the swords of public executioners were housed.* (CHINESE PORCELAIN, 16–17TH CENTURY.)

GUAN DI, or Kuan-ti, is the Daoist patron deity of soldiers and policemen. He protects the realm and looks after state officials. During the Chinese Qing dynasty (1644–1912), Guan Di was venerated for his warlike functions. In other periods he was regarded as the guardian of righteousness who protects men from strife and evil. In popular belief, Guan Di was famed for casting out demons. He was also called upon to provide information about people who had died and to predict the future.

Guan Di was originally a general called Guan Gong or Guan Yo, who lived in the third century AD, during a time of turmoil at the close of the Han dynasty. He was renowned for his military skill, but he also came to be admired for his great courage and loyalty, since he was eventually executed by his enemy as a prisoner of war because he refused to change his allegiance. Because of his many virtues he was later deified, being officially recognized as a god at the end of the 16th century. Guan Di is represented as a giant dressed in green with a long beard and a red face. He is often depicted standing next to his horse and clad in full armour.

GUANYIN, or Kuan Yin, is Chinese Buddhism's goddess of mercy or compassion. She developed from the male bodhisattva, or "buddha-to-be", Avalokiteshvara, known in Japan as KWANNON, and helps all beings on earth to attain enlightenment. Guanyin was herself originally regarded as male but increasingly gained female characteristics. Believed to bless women with children, she is sometimes depicted holding a child in her arms. However, she may also be represented as a bodhisattva with a thousand arms and a thousand eyes. She sometimes appears in the company of a young woman holding a fish basket, standing on clouds or riding on a dragon in front of a waterfall.

Guanyin is believed to live on a mountain or an island in the Eastern Sea. She is said to have introduced humankind to the cultivation of rice, which she makes wholesome by filling each kernel with her own milk. The goddess comes to the aid of all those who need her help, especially when they are threatened by water, demons, fire or the sword. She is sometimes said to stand on a cliff in the middle of flaming waves and rescue shipwrecked people from the sea, the symbol of samsara, the ceaseless round of earthly existence.

The 14th-century novel *Journey to the West*, which is said to provide a popular record of Chinese mythology, tells how the "Monkey King" went up to heaven where he stole the peaches of immortality from the garden of XI WANG MU, the "Queen Mother of the West". The monkey incurred the wrath of all the gods and was finally taken captive by Buddha. However, Guanyin interceded on the monkey's behalf and he was allowed to accompany a Buddhist pilgrim during his journey to India.

Another myth tells how Guanyin was the third daughter of King Miao Zhong. She entered a religious order against the wishes of her father, who did all he could to persuade her to remain in the outside world. Eventually, the king decided that he would have to kill her. However, YANLUO WANG, lord of death, appeared and led Guanyin away to his underworld kingdom. There, Guanyin soothed the damned and transformed hell

GUAN DI *is sometimes portrayed as a mandarin, sitting unarmed, stroking his beard.* (SOAPSTONE FIGURE, 17–18TH CENTURY.)

GUANYIN (above), Chinese Buddhism's goddess of mercy and compassion, is often depicted holding a willow branch and a vase filled with the dew of compassion.

GUANYIN (right) helps all beings attain enlightenment. Originally a male deity, she increasingly gained female characteristics. (CHINESE PORCELAIN, 13–14TH CENTURY.)

into a paradise. Yanluo Wang then released Guanyin, and she was reborn on an island where she protected seafarers from storms. Her father then fell ill, and Guanyin healed him by cooking a piece of her own flesh for him to eat. In gratitude, the king ordered a statue of his daughter to be made. However, the sculptor misunderstood the king's instructions and made a statue with a thousand arms and a thousand eyes.

Guanyin is also credited with the ability to release prisoners from their chains, remove poison from snakes and deprive lightning of its power. She is believed to be capable of curing almost every sickness. A very popular goddess, her image is often found in people's homes and the festivals of her birth and enlightenment are endowed with great significance by Buddhists.

GUEI, or Kuei, according to Chinese mythology, are spirits formed from the *YIN*, or negative essence, of people's souls. These spirits or emanations are always feared because they are said to take their revenge on those people who ill-treated them when they were alive. They can be identified because they wear clothes which have no hems and their bodies cast no shadows.

H

HACHIMAN is the Japanese god of war. However, he is also a god of peace, and sometimes serves as a god of agriculture and protector of children. A historical figure, he is the deified form of the Emperor Ojin, who died at the end of the fourth century AD and was famed for his military deeds and bravery. Within the Shinto religion, Hachiman became a very popular deity, although his name does not appear in the sacred texts of Shintoism. He came to be regarded as a protector of Buddhism and is viewed by Buddhists as a bosatsu, the Japanese form of a bodhisattva, or "buddha-to-be". His sacred creature is the dove.

HAN XIANG see *BA XIAN*.

HE XIANGU see *BA XIAN*.

HIKOHOHODEMI is the great-grandson of the Japanese sun goddess *AMATERASU* and the son of *NINIGI*, or Honinigi, and his wife, Kono-Hana-Sakuyu-Hime.

Hikohohodemi's name means "Fireshade". His brother is called *HONOSUSERI*, or "Fireshine". Hikohohodemi hunted land animals, whereas his brother was a fisherman. One day the brothers tried to swap their means of livelihood but discovered that neither was able to perform the other's tasks. Honosuseri returned the bow, but Hikohohodemi had lost Honosuseri's fish hook and so offered him another in its stead. Honosuseri, however, refused to accept the replacement.

Upset, Hikohohodemi visited the sea god Watatsumi-No-Kami at the bottom of the ocean. Having previously found the fish hook in the mouth of a fish, the sea god returned it to Hikohohodemi. Meanwhile, Watatsumi-No-Kami's daughter had fallen in love with the young god. The couple were married and lived together for many years. Eventually, Hikohohodemi decided to return home. Before leaving, Hikohohodemi's father-in-law gave him two jewels, which made the tide rise and fall; he also gave him a friendly crocodile to transport him on his journey.

Back on land, the god returned the fish hook to Honosuseri, who, despite this gesture, continued to pester his brother. Eventually, Hikohohodemi lost all patience and made the tide rise. When Honosuseri was almost covered by the sea, he begged forgiveness and promised to serve Hikohohodemi, whereupon the latter caused the tide to go out.

The daughter of the sea god joined Hikohohodemi on land and announced that she was about to have his child. She made Hikohohodemi promise not to look at her while she gave birth,

***HACHIMAN** is the Japanese god of war, the deified form of the Emperor Ojin. Centuries after his death, a vision of a child appeared at his birthplace, identifying itself with an ideogram representing the name Hachiman.* (STATUE BY KAIKEI, 13TH CENTURY.)

but the god was unable to resist the temptation and peeped through a crack in the wall of his wife's hut. There, he saw his wife transformed

HIKOHOHODEMI was the grandfather of Jimmu-Tenno, the first emperor of Japan.

into an enormous dragon. Afterwards, Hikohohodemi's wife returned to the sea and sent her sister to look after the child.

When the boy grew up, he married his aunt, the sea-god's daughter Tamayori-Hime, who had brought him up. They produced a son with two names, Toyo-Mike-Nu and Kamu-Yamato-Iware-Hiko. After his death, the boy was known as *JIMMU-TENNO*. He was the first emperor of Japan.

HINKON, according to the Tungu people of Siberia, is the god of hunting and lord of animals.

HKUN AI is a hero of Burmese mythology. He married a dragon who had taken the form of a beautiful woman. During each water festival, the woman became a dragon again, and Hkun Ai eventually became upset by his wife's metamorphoses. He decided to leave her, but before he did so, she gave him an egg. In due course the egg cracked open to reveal a son whom Hkun Ai called Tung Hkam.

When the boy grew up, he fell in love with a princess who lived on an island. Tung Hkam could not find a way to cross over the water to reach his beloved, until one day his mother appeared and formed a bridge with her back. Tung Hkam eventually became a great king.

HOMOSUBI see *KAGUTSUCHI*.

HONINIGI see *NINIGI*.

HONOSUSERI, according to the Shinto mythology of Japan, was the elder brother of *HIKOHOHODEMI*. Honosuseri was a great fisherman, while his brother hunted animals on land. Honosuseri's name means "Fireshine", and his brother's name means "Fireshade". The brothers are the great-grandsons of the sun goddess *AMATERASU* and the sons of *NINIGI*, or Honinigi, and his wife Kono-Hana-Sakuyu-Hime.

HOTEI is one of the *SHICHI FUKUJIN*, or seven Japanese gods of good fortune or happiness. He is represented as a Buddhist monk and is recognizable by his bald head and vast belly, a symbol both of his wealth and friendly nature and of a soul that has achieved serenity through Buddhism. Hotei is often shown leaning on a large sack, which is said to contain endless gifts for his followers. He is regarded as a friend of the weak and of children. He may have originated as a Chinese hermit called Budaishi who lived in the 10th century AD and was believed to be an incarnation of Maitreya. (See also *THE SHICHI FUKUJIN*)

HSI HO see *XI-HE*.

HSI WANG MU see *XI WANG MU*.

HSIEN see *XIAN*.

HSÜAN TSANG see *XUAN ZONG*.

HOTEI is depicted as a smiling monk with a large belly, which signifies contentment, not greed. He carries a fan and a sack. (IVORY NETSUKE, LATE 19TH CENTURY.)

CREATION MYTHS

MYTHS OF THE CREATION OF THE WORLD begin with emptiness, darkness, a floating, drifting lack of form or a fathomless expanse of water. Out of this dim swirl comes a more tangible object which holds the promise of both solid land and human life. The egg is a potent symbol of creation, and features in mythologies all over the world, including those of China and South-east Asia. According to the folklore of the Iban in Borneo, the world began with two spirits floating like birds on the ocean, who created the earth and sky from two eggs. In Sumatra, a primordial blue chicken, Manuk Manuk, laid three eggs, from which hatched the gods who created the world. A Chinese creation myth, which may have originated in Thailand, begins with the duality governing the universe – yin and yang – struggling within the cosmic egg until it splits, and the deity Pangu emerges.

IZANAGI AND IZANAMI were the primal couple in the Japanese creation myth. The gods arose in a remote heaven far above the floating world, and generations of gods and goddesses were born before these two were instructed to complete and solidify the world below. As a result of their union Izanami gave birth to all the islands of Japan and numerous gods and goddesses, including the fire god Kagutsuchi who burnt her so badly that she died. These rocks off the Japanese coast, near Ise, are known as the Myoto-Iwa, or wedded rocks, and symbolize Izanagi and Izanami. They are bound together by a rice-straw rope.

PANGU *(above) grew 3 metres (10 feet) every day, pushing the earth and sky apart. He lived for 18,000 years and when he died his body formed the world, each part becoming one of its elements. His flesh became the soil, his hair the vegetation, his perspiration the dew, and so on. Finally, the fleas and other parasites inhabiting his body became the first humans. He was said to be responsible for the weather: when he smiled the sun shone, but if he was sad or angry, storms would ensue.* (LITHOGRAPH, 19TH CENTURY.)

AMATERASU *(above) the sun goddess, was born from the left eye of Izanagi as he washed his face. The unruly behaviour of her brother, the storm god Susano-Wo, frightened and angered her so much that she hid in a cave, plunging the whole world into darkness. All the other gods assembled in front of the cave and lured her back out by showing her her own glorious reflection in a divine mirror. As she emerged, the sun reappeared.* (UTAGAWA KUNISADA, THE GODDESS AMATERASU EMERGING FROM EARTH, WOODBLOCK PRINT, 1860.)

FU XI *(top centre) was the creator god who figured in the oldest Chinese myths, but when legendary dynasties were devised in accounts of ancient history, he became the first emperor, and was said to have reigned from 2852–2737 BC. He taught his subjects how to make fishing nets and rear domestic animals, and discovered the bagua inscribed on the shell of a tortoise. These were the eight trigrams, based on combinations of the symbols for yin and yang, which formed the basis of Chinese calligraphy.* (MA LIN, FU XI, 13TH CENTURY.)

SUSANO-WO *(top right) was the storm god, the brother of Amaterasu. Sometimes known as the "Raging Male", he caused chaos in the world with his unpredictable behaviour, and the gods punished him by throwing him out of heaven. Once living on earth, his conduct improved, and he killed a terrible eight-headed serpent to win the hand of his beautiful wife, Kushi-Inada-Hime. While chopping through the serpent's tail, he discovered the legendary sword called Kusanagi, or "Grass Mower", which he sent to heaven as a gift for his sister.*

I

HUANG DI, or Huang Ti, is the legendary "Yellow Emperor" of Chinese mythology who is said to have lived in the 3rd millennium BC. According to one story, Huang Di came into being when the energies that instigated the beginning of the world merged with one another, and created human beings by placing earthen statues at the cardinal points of the world and leaving them exposed for 300 years. During that time, the statues became filled with the breath of creation and eventually began to move. Huang Di allegedly received his magical powers when he was 100 years old. He achieved immortality and, riding a dragon, rose to heaven where he became one of the five mythological emperors who rule over the cardinal points. Huang Di himself rules over the fifth cardinal point, the centre. (See also *CHINA'S SACRED PEAKS*)

HUANG TI see *HUANG DI.*

IDA-TEN, according to Japanese mythology, is a god who protects monks and is the guardian of their good conduct. He is depicted as a young man wearing armour and holding a sword. Ida-Ten is the Japanese equivalent of the Hindu warrior god Skanda, or Karttikeya, and was adopted by Buddhism in the seventh century.

HUANG-DI is worshipped as one of the founders of Chinese culture and is said to have invented writing, the compass and the pottery wheel, and instituted the breeding of silkworms.

ILA-ILAI LANGIT is a mythical fish who features in the creation story of the Dayak people of Borneo. The tale tells how, at the beginning of time, all creation was enclosed in the mouth of a gigantic snake. Eventually, a gold mountain arose and became home to the supreme god of the upper region, while a jewel mountain arose and became home to the supreme god of the lower region. The two mountains collided together on numerous occasions, each time creating part of the universe. This period has become known as the first epoch of creation, when the clouds, the sky, the mountains, the cliffs, the sun and moon were made. Afterwards, the "Hawk of Heaven" and the great fish Ila-Ilai Langit were brought into being, followed by two fabulous creatures: *DIDIS MAHENDERA*, who had eyes made of jewels, and *ROWANG RIWO*, who had golden saliva. Finally, the golden headdress of the god *MAHATALA* appeared.

In the second epoch of creation, *JATA*, the divine maiden, created the land. Soon afterwards, hills and rivers were formed. In the third epoch of creation, the tree of life appeared and united the upper and lower worlds.

INARI is the god of rice, according to the Shinto mythology of Japan. His cult is extremely widespread since he is believed to ensure an abundant rice harvest and therefore brings prosperity.

In popular belief, Inari is represented as an old, bearded man sitting on a sack of rice, but the deity also appears in female form, with flowing hair. He, or she, is accompanied by two foxes. It is sometimes said that the god lives

HUANG DI (far left) was the third of the legendary emperors described in the Han dynasty to explain early Chinese history. Fu Xi and Shen Nong preceded him.

INARI's shrine at Kobe. Inari was the god of rice and is sometimes referred to as the god of food. He came to be regarded as a god of prosperity and is invoked by tradespeople. (THE SHRINE OF INARI AT KOBE BY WALTER TYNDALE, CANVAS, C. 1910.)

in the distant mountains and that the foxes act as his messengers. Alternatively, the god himself is occasionally regarded as a fox. Images of foxes are found in front of all of his shrines. Inari's wife was the food goddess *UKE-MOCHI*. When *SUSANO-WO* or, according to some versions of the myth, *TSUKIYOMI*, killed Uke-Mochi for producing food from her orifices, Inari took over her role as the deity of agriculture.

IRIK is a spirit who features in a creation myth of the Iban, one of the Dayak peoples of Borneo. Together with another spirit, *ARA*, Irik floated in the form of a bird above a boundless ocean. The birds eventually plucked two enormous eggs from the water. From one of the eggs, Irik formed the earth and from the other, Ara formed the sky. However, because the earth was too large for the sky, the two spirits had to squash it until it was the right size. During the process, mountains and valleys, rivers and streams were created. Immediately, plants began to appear. The two spirits then decided to create human beings. At first they tried to make them from the sap of trees, but, when this proved unsuccessful, they used the soil. After fashioning the first humans, they gave them life with their bird-song.

ISSUN BOSHI is a diminutive hero of Japanese mythology whose name means "Little One-Inch". His parents, despite being married for many years, had failed to conceive a child. In desperation, they prayed that they might be given a son even if he were only as tall as a fingertip. The gods took the couple literally and gave them a tiny child.

When Issun Boshi was 15 years old, he set off for Kyoto, taking with him a rice bowl, a pair of chopsticks and a needle stuck in a bamboo sheath. He paddled down the river, using the rice bowl as a boat and the chopsticks as oars. After arriving at Kyoto, Issun Boshi secured a job in the service of a noble family. For many years, he worked hard and his employers were pleased with him.

One day, the young hero accompanied the daughter of the house to the temple. On the way there, two giant *ONI*, horned devils, jumped out at them. Issun Boshi immediately attracted their attention so that the daughter could escape. One of the oni succeeded in swallowing Issun Boshi. Undeterred, the tiny man drew his needle out of its sheath and stabbed the devil in the stomach. As he crawled up the devil's throat, he continued to stab him until, with huge relief, the oni spat him out. Immediately, the other oni prepared to attack Issun Boshi, whereupon the hero leapt up and began attacking its eyes with his needle. Both oni soon fled, leaving behind them a mallet, an object of good luck. Issun Boshi and the girl struck the mallet on the ground and made a wish. Immediately, Issun Boshi grew into a full-size samurai. The couple returned home, and the girl's father agreed to allow them to be married.

ITCHITA, according to the Yakut people of Siberia, is an earth goddess and an aspect of the great mother goddess. She keeps sickness away from human beings, and is attended by the spirits of the grass and trees. She herself lives in the white beech tree. Other aspects of the great mother are the goddess Ynakhsyt, who protects cattle, and Ajysyt, who looks after children and helps women in childbirth. Ajysyt constantly sways backwards and forwards, thereby encouraging the growth of the life force.

J

IZANAMI AND IZANAGI, standing on the "Floating Bridge of Heaven", stir the sea with the heavenly jewelled spear to create the world. (WOODBLOCK PRINT, 19TH CENTURY.)

IZANAGI AND IZANAMI, according to Shinto belief, were the eighth pair of deities to appear after heaven and earth had been created out of chaos. Their full names, Izanagi-No-Mikoto and Izanami-No-Mikoto, mean "The August Male" and "The August Female".

Izanagi and Izanami were ordered to create the islands of Japan. They stood side by side on the "Floating Bridge of Heaven", lowered the heavenly jewelled spear into the sea and began to stir. When they lifted the spear out of the water, droplets fell from its tip and became an island, the first solid land. The two gods then descended on to the island and built a heavenly pillar and a splendid palace.

One day, the deities realized that each of their bodies differed from that of the other. Izanami said that her body was not fully formed in one place and Izanagi said that his body had been formed in excess in one place. Izanagi then suggested that they bring these two parts together. The two deities circled around the heavenly pillar until they met one another and joined their bodies together. Izanami bore a child, but he was a deformed creature called Hiruko, or "Leech Child", whom the couple immediately abandoned at sea. The gods decided that the child had been born imperfect as a result of Izanami having spoken first during the couple's courting ritual. Once again, the couple circled the pillar and this time, Izanagi spoke first.

Izanami subsequently gave birth to the islands of Japan as well as to the gods and goddesses of waterfalls, mountains, trees, plants and the wind. While giving birth to the god of fire, *KAGUTSUCHI*, Izanami was so badly burned that she died. However, even while dying she continued to bear more and more gods. Eventually, she disappeared to *YOMI*, the land of the dead.

Izanagi was desperately upset. Many deities were formed from his tears, and when he sliced off the fire god's head, even more deities came into being. Izanagi determined to follow his wife to Yomi, but by the time he arrived there she had already eaten the food of the dead. Although Izanami tried to persuade the gods to allow her to return to the land of the living, they refused her request. Izanagi then stormed into the hall of the dead and, after lighting a tooth of his comb and using it as a torch, he saw Izanami. She was horribly transformed: her corpse was squirming with maggots and eight thunder deities had taken up residence in her body.

Horrified at the sight of his wife, Izanagi fled back home. His behaviour infuriated Izanami, who sent the hags of Yomi, together with numerous thunder deities and warriors, to hunt him down. However, by employing various magic tricks, Izanagi succeeded in escaping them. When the god finally reached the outer edge of the land of the dead, he found three peaches. Picking them up, he threw them at the hags, who immediately ran away. Izanagi told the peaches that from that time onwards they would save mortals, just as they had saved him.

At length, Izanami, who by now had herself become a demon, set off in pursuit of Izanagi. In order to block her way, her husband pushed a huge boulder into the passage that separated Yomi from the land of the living. The husband and wife stood on either side of the boulder, and Izanami told Izanagi that in punishment for his behaviour she would strangle a thousand people each day. Izanagi replied that, each day, he would ensure that 1,500 people were born.

The god then purified himself by washing in a river. When he removed his clothes, a new deity came into being as each garment fell to the ground. Finally, Izanagi washed his face and, in so doing, brought into existence the sun goddess *AMATERASU*, the moon god *TSUKIYOMI* and the storm god *SUSANO-WO*. Izanagi decided to divide his kingdom equally among these three deities. (See also *CREATION MYTHS*)

JAR-SUB, according to the ancient Turkic and modern Altaic peoples of Siberia, personifies the

JIZO-BOSATSU (above) is sometimes represented as a monk. He carries a staff with rings whose jingling warns small creatures of his approach so he will not step on them. (CARVED WOOD, 11TH CENTURY.)

combination of earth and water. Jar-Sub can refer either to the universe as a whole, or to the native land.

JATA, according to a creation myth of the Dayak people of Borneo, was a divine maiden who made the land and the hills during the second epoch of creation. In the first epoch of creation, the clouds, the sky, the mountains, the cliffs, the sun and moon all came into being. Afterwards, the "Hawk of Heaven" and the great fish *ILA-ILAI LANGIT* were created, followed by two fabulous creatures, *DIDIS MAHENDERA* with the jewel eyes and *ROWANG RIWO* with the golden saliva. Finally, the golden headdress of the god *MAHATALA* appeared. In the third epoch of creation, the tree of life arose, thereby uniting the upper and lower worlds.

JIMMU-TENNO, according to Japanese mythology, was the first Emperor of Japan and thus the founder of the Imperial line. He was said to be the descendant of the sun goddess *AMATERASU* and the grandson of *HIKOHOHODEMI*. During his life, Jimmu-Tenno was known by two names, Toyo-Mike-Nu and Kamu-Yamato-Iware-Hiko; it was only after his death that he became known as Jimmu-Tenno. Jimmu-Tenno was said to have acceded to the throne in 660 BC.

One story tells how, while moving east with his troops in search of new territories and a place from which to rule his kingdom, he was bewitched by a god who took the form of a bear and caused the invaders to fall asleep. One of Jimmu-Tenno's followers dreamt of a magic sword sent by Amaterasu to help Jimmu-Tenno pacify the land now known as Yamato. When he awoke, the soldier found the sword and gave it to his leader. The forces continued on their journey, led by a crow. When they reached Yamato, Jimmu-Tenno built a magnificent palace and married a local princess.

JIZO-BOSATSU is the Japanese form of Kshitigarbha, the bodhisattva or "buddha-to-be" who protects children. He is also said to help pregnant women and travellers. His cult is extremely popular in Japan, where he tends to be regarded as a venerable person rather than as a deity. Each year, his devotees confess their faults to him in the ceremony known as the "Confession of Jizo".

According to one tale, dead children whose parents simply lament their deaths, rather than offering up prayers to help them to be reborn, are sent to a sandy beach or river bank in hell. There, they spend their time building shrines, which are destroyed each night by demons. However, Jizo eventually appears to console the children. He wraps them in the folds of his robe and tells them that he is their father and mother.

JIMMU-TENNO (below) was the legendary first emperor of Japan, from whom the Japanese Imperial family claims direct descent. (DRAWING, ANON. 20TH CENTURY.)

K

JUROJIN (left) is shown as a small old man with a long white beard. One of the Shichi Fukujin, or seven gods of good fortune or happiness, he holds the promise of happiness in old age. (IVORY NETSUKE.)

JUROJIN is one of the *SHICHI FUKUJIN* or seven gods of good fortune or happiness, an assembly of deities gathered together in the 17th century by a monk who intended them to symbolize the virtues of a man of his time.

Jurojin was the god of longevity and happy old age. He is depicted as a small old man with a long white beard and is shown in the company of a crane, tortoise or deer, all symbols of longevity. The god also carries a staff to which is attached a scroll or book, which is said to contain the wisdom of the world. He is said to be extremely fond of rice wine. (See also *THE SHICHI FUKUJIN*)

KADAKLAN, according to the mythology of the Tinguian people of Luzon in the Philippines, is the god of thunder. He lives in the sky and beats his drum to create thunder. His dog Kimat is the lightning; he bites whatever Kadaklan chooses.

KAGUTSUCHI, or Homosubi, is the fire god of Japanese Shinto mythology. He is the son of *IZANAMI*, the female half of the primal couple. When she gave birth to him, the goddess was so badly burned that she died. In revenge, *IZANAGI*, Kagutsuchi's father, attacked the fire god, slicing off his head. In doing so, Izanagi created several more deities. Kagutsuchi was greatly feared by the Japanese.

KAMI was the word used in ancient Japan to refer to anything mysterious or sacred. Its range of application covered everything from objects of folk cults to important deities. The kami came to be regarded as supernatural beings with human qualities. Sometimes, they are nature deities such as mountains, trees and rivers; sometimes they embody values or ideals. They may be protective deities or important men. The Buddha was thought of as the kami of China, and, later on, local kami came to be regarded as protectors of Buddhism. Some became identified with Buddhist deities.

KAMI-MUSUBI see *OKUNINUSHI*.

KANNON see *KWANNON*.

THE KAPPA, according to Japanese mythology, are a race of monkey-like demons. They live in ponds and rivers, and lure human beings, as well as other creatures, down into the depths of the water where they then feed on them. As well as being particularly fond of blood, the kappa like cucumbers.

They are malicious creatures who can, however, sometimes be appeased or bargained with. For example, if a cucumber is inscribed with the names and ages of a particular family and thrown into the water where a kappa lives, the creature will not harm that family. The kappa also display a certain vulnerability. They always return a low bow, and in doing so they spill the water, which empowers them, from the saucer-shaped depressions in the tops of their heads.

Because they are very knowing, they can sometimes prove helpful to human beings. According to one tale, a kappa persuaded a man on a horse to play tug-of-war with him. As soon as they had grasped hold of one another, the man spurred on his horse, and the water began to spill from the top of the kappa's head. The kappa begged the man to stop, promising that if he did so, he would teach him how to mend bones. The rider agreed, and his family became renowned for their knowledge of bone-setting.

The kappa have monkey-like faces, webbed hands and feet and yellow-green skin. They wear shells like tortoises.

KARITEI-MO see *KISHIMO-JIN*.

THE KAPPA (above) are demons who drag animals or people into rivers to feed on. They resemble monkeys but stink of fish. (ILLUSTRATION FROM MYTHS AND LEGENDS OF JAPAN.)

KHADAU see *MAMALDI*.

KHORI TUMED is a hero of Mongolian shamanism. One day, he saw nine swans fly on to the island of Oikhon on Lake Baikal. The swans removed their feathered garments and revealed themselves to be beautiful women. Believing that they were alone, they bathed naked in the lake. However, while the women were bathing, Khori Tumed stole one of their dresses and so, when they left the water, one of them was unable to fly away.

Khori Tumed married the swan woman and they lived happily together, eventually producing 11

KUNLUN, beyond the western limits of the ancient Chinese empire, was home to the "Queen Mother of the West".

sons. However, the time came when the swan woman asked Khori Tumed to give her back her feathers. The hero refused, but his wife continued to ask him for her dress, assuring him that she would not fly away. Eventually, Khori Tumed relented and allowed her to try the dress on. Immediately, she flew up and out of a window in their tent. Before she finally escaped, Khori Tumed persuaded her to name their sons. The swan woman did so and then flew around the tent, bestowing blessings on the tribes.

KHOSADAM, according to the Yenisei people of Siberia, is the wife of *EC*, the supreme god. Ec drove her out of the sky after discovering that she had been unfaithful to him with the moon. Khosadam is an evil, destructive deity and appears as a devourer of souls.

KHUN K'AN see *THENS*.

KHUN K'ET see *THENS*.

KIMAT see *KADAKLAN*.

KISHIMO-JIN, or Karitei-Mo, is Japanese mythology's "Goddess Mother of Demons". She is said to eat children and to have destroyed a town in India while Gautama Buddha was living there. When the townspeople begged the Buddha to save them, he hid Kishimo-Jin's son beneath his begging bowl. The demoness was distraught and finally asked the Buddha for help. The Buddha converted her by explaining that the pain she felt at the loss of her son was similar to that she wilfully inflicted on other people. Kishimo-Jin was thus converted to Buddhism and became a protector of children. She is often represented seated on a chair and holding a child in her arms.

KUNLUN, where Gautama Buddha sits enthroned, is regarded as a kind of earthly paradise by both Buddhists and Daoists. (BUDDHIST SCROLL.)

KUAN-TI see *GUAN DI*.

KUAN YIN see *GUAN YIN*.

KUEI see *GUEI*.

K'UN LUN see *KUNLUN*.

KUNLUN, or K'un Lun, is a mountain range in western China that is regarded as a Daoist paradise. It is said to be the home of *XI WANG MU* and the immortals. As well as rising above the ground, it is said to descend underground, thereby connecting the realm of the dead with that of the gods. Xi Wang Mu, the "Queen Mother of the West" is said to grow the peaches of immortality in the garden of her splendid palace on Kunlun.

THE EIGHT IMMORTALS

DAOISM EMERGED AS A philosophical system at about the same time as Confucianism, around the sixth century BC. Later, in response to the growing popularity of Buddhism, it acquired all the trappings of a religion, including a mythology. The "Eight Immortals" were central figures in Daoist myth and Chinese folk religion. They had all gained eternal life through seeking the Daoist "Way", and each set an example of ideal behaviour that could be followed by ordinary people to gain enlightenment. Though they were not gods, their immortality gave them superhuman powers: they practised magic and could fly through the air at great speed. They had many adventures while pursuing their mission to banish evil from the world, and were all cheerfully addicted to wine, so that they were sometimes described as the Jiu-zhong Ba Xian – the "Eight Drunken Immortals".

LI TIEGUAI (far left, above) was the first immortal. His body was prematurely cremated while his soul was visiting a sacred mountain. As his own body was no longer available to him, his soul had to inhabit that of a lame beggar, and he used an iron crutch to support himself. Li later revived his disciple's dead mother with a phial of magic medicine, and came to be regarded as the patron of pharmacists. (RELIEF TILE, QING DYNASTY.)

HE XIANGU (second from right), the patron of unmarried girls, was a young woman herself who acquired immortality when a spirit appeared to her on the mountain where she lived and instructed her to grind and eat a mother-of-pearl stone. The stone made her weightless and able to fly over the mountains. She is usually shown carrying a peach or a lotus blossom. (RELIEF TILE, QING DYNASTY.)

CAO GUOJIU (far left) carried a golden tablet which allowed him admission to the imperial court, because he was the brother of the empress. He left the court to seek the Daoist "Way" but, when he found he had no money to pay a ferryman, he tried to impress him with his court credentials. The ferryman, who was Lu Dongbin in disguise, pointed out his folly, and Cao threw the tablet into the river. As an immortal, Cao Guojiu was the patron of the nobility. (RELIEF TILE, QING DYNASTY.)

SHOU LAO *(left) the Daoist god of longevity, was visited by the "Eight Immortals" on one of their journeys together. Originally a stellar deity, the "Old Man of the South Pole", he had evolved into an old man who carried a gourd containing the water of life. He rode on a stag, a symbol of happiness.* (CHINESE DISH, C. 1680.)

HAN XIANG *(left), Lu Dongbin's disciple, was said to be the great-nephew of a Daoist philosopher. He was a wandering minstrel who played the flute. During the sea voyage of the "Eight Immortals", Ao Bing, son of the "Dragon King of the Eastern Sea", tried to steal the flute and take Han Xiang prisoner. There was a great battle to rescue Han Xiang, in which the immortals were, naturally, victorious.* (IVORY FIGURE, MING DYNASTY.)

LU DONGBIN's *(below) blessing on parents was believed to bestow intelligent children, so Chinese scholars regarded him especially highly, and he was the guardian of ink makers. When the "Eight Immortals" decided to cross the sea, they each threw down an object on which to ride, which each turned into a sea monster. Lu Dongbin used his magic sword.* (LU DONGBIN RIDING ON A KRAKEN, FROM SUPERSTITIONS EN CHINE, 1915.)

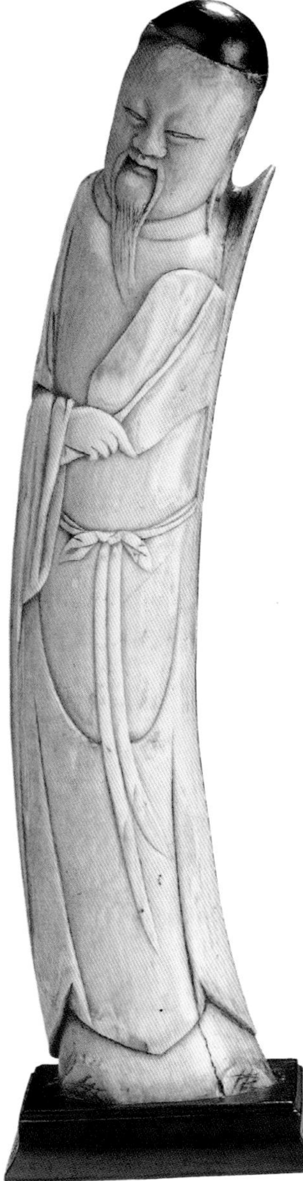

LAN CAIHE *(above) was either a girl or an effeminate man. She was the patron of the poor, because she gained her immortality by her kindness in attending to the needs of a filthy beggar, whose wounds she washed and dressed. The beggar turned out to be Li Tieguai, the first of the "Eight Immortals". Lan Caihe was sometimes shown with a basket of flowers, because of her skill in growing marvellous blooms from a small pot of earth.* (FRESCO, QING DYNASTY.)

ZHANG GUOLAO *(above) rode on a white mule, sometimes sitting facing the animal's tail. He was a great necromancer, and his mule had extraordinary powers. It could travel over vast distances but, when no longer required, it could be folded up like a sheet of paper and kept in a bag. Zhang Guolao is often depicted with the bag containing his mule, or hitting a bamboo drum. He granted both happy marriage and the gift of children.* (IVORY AND BRONZE FIGURE, MING DYNASTY.)

ZHONG-LI QUAN *(left) learnt the "Way" of Daoism from Li Tieguai, then disappeared into the clouds on achieving immortality and became the messenger of heaven. Bald, with a long beard, he carried a feather fan and was the patron of soldiers. Zhong-li Quan was sometimes also shown holding a peach. The peaches of Xi Wang Mu, the "Queen Mother of the West" ripened every 3,000 years, when the immortals ate them to renew their immortality.* (IVORY FIGURE, MING DYNASTY.)

L

KWANNON *(above) lived in a cave in the Iwai Valley.* (WOODBLOCK PRINT BY HIROSHIGE, ANDO OR UTAGAWA, 1853.)

KWANNON *(right), the Japanese god or goddess of mercy, could assume 33 different forms, including this one with 11 heads.* (WOOD SCULPTURE, 12TH CENTURY.)

KWANNON, or Kannon, according to Japanese Buddhist belief, is the god or goddess of mercy. She is the Japanese form of the Chinese goddess *GUANYIN*, or Kuan Yin, who herself derives from the Indian male bodhisattva Avalokiteshvara. The feminization of Kwannon is relatively modern. Kwannon, as a bosatsu, or bodhisattva, is a "buddha-to-be" who has decided to remain on earth in order to help other people to achieve enlightenment. She is known as the "Lady Giver of Children" and is a very popular deity, the protector of women and children. Kwannon is said to have been born from a ray of light, which emerged from the right of the Buddha Amitabha. There is also a Kwannon with a horse's head and one with numerous arms. According to one tradition, Kwannon could assume 33 different forms, which gave rise to a great ritual pilgrimage to 33 sanctuaries dedicated to her.

LAN CAIHE see *BA XIAN*.

LAO CHÜN see *LAO JUN*.

LAO JUN, or Lao Chün, is the name given to the deified form of Laozi, who, by tradition, wrote the Dao-de Jing, the text which forms the basis of Daoism. He is believed to have lived in the sixth century BC; his deification began in the second century BC. Lao Jun became one of the most important Daoist gods and was sometimes said to have arisen from the primordial chaos. According to another legend, he emerged from his mother's side after a gestation of 80 years.

LEI GONG, or Lei Kung, is the god of thunder in China's Daoist pantheon. Known as "My Lord Thunder", or "Thunder Duke", he is depicted as a horribly ugly man with wings, claws, and a blue body. He carries a drum, and in his hands he holds a mallet and a chisel. Lei Gong attacks any human being

LAO JUN *(above) is said to have been a contemporary of Confucius and a teacher of the Buddha.* (PAINTED SCROLL, 18TH CENTURY.)

LAO JUN *(above right), who was reputed to have been born with white hair and the power of speech, lived to a very great age.* (PAINTING BY QIAN GU, 16TH CENTURY.)

guilty of an undetected crime or who remains beyond the reach of the earthly law.

One story tells how a fierce storm arose in the middle of a thick forest. A hunter looked up into the trees and saw a child holding a flag. Lei Gong, the thunder god, approached the child but as soon as the child waved the flag, he retreated. Immediately, the hunter realized that the child must be an evil spirit and that the flag must be made of some unclean material, since all deities dislike impure objects. The hunter shot down the flag, and Lei Gong instantly struck the tree in which the child was perched. Unfortunately, being so close to the tree, the hunter was also struck by the thunder. However, when he came round, the hunter found a message on his body saying that his life had been prolonged for 12 years in thanks for having assisted with the work of heaven. At the foot of the tree, the hunter found the body of a vast lizard, the real form of the child.

LEI GONG *(above), the winged thunder god, harasses sheep and swine in a storm of thunder clouds and explosive lightning flashes.* (WOODBLOCK PRINT, 19TH CENTURY.)

M

LEI KUNG see *LEI GONG*.

LI NAZHA see *NAZHA*.

LI TIEGUAI see *BA XIAN*.

THE LIGHTNING GODDESS is one of the nature deities referred to in early Chinese legends. She is the wife of the god of thunder, *LEI GONG*, and carries a pair of mirrors which she uses to create flashes of lightning and, occasionally, fires. The gods of thunder, lightning, wind and rain were invoked by the people during times of drought.

LING CHIH see *LING ZHI*.

LING ZHI, or Ling Chih, according to Daoist belief, is a plant of immortality. Its name means "magic herb". Ling zhi is believed to be either a type of grass or a mushroom. It grows on the three islands of the immortals, and anyone who eats it is said to gain immortality for at least 500 years.

LONG WANG, or Lung Wang, are "Dragon Kings" according to Chinese mythology. They are the servants either of Yuanshi Tian-Zong, the "Celestial Venerable of the Primordial Beginning", or *YU HUANG*, the "Jade Emperor", who was Yuanshi Tian-Zong's assistant and later came to surpass him in power. According to Daoist belief, there are different varieties of Long Wang: the celestial dragon kings, the dragon kings of the five cardinal points and the dragon kings of the oceans. Each of the dragon kings of the oceans has responsibility for one of the four oceans, helped by an army of sea creatures. The Long Wang bring rain.

LU DONGBIN see *BA XIAN*.

THE LIGHTNING GODDESS holding her two mirrors, which she flashes to cause lightning.

LUNG WANG see *LONG WANG*.

LUXING see *SAN XING*.

MAHATALA is the supreme god of the Dayak people of Borneo. He rules over the upper regions and lives on Jewel Mountain.

MAIDERE, according to the Altaic people of Siberia, was the saviour whom the great sky god *ULGAN* sent to earth in order to protect human beings from the evil ways of the god and first man *ERLIK*. Erlik succeeded in killing Maidere, whereupon the saviour's blood gave rise to vast flames, which leapt up to the skies, destroying Erlik's heaven.

MAIN is a mythical hero of the Evenk people of Siberia. One story tells how a great elk ran to the top of a hill in the upper world and impaled the sun on its antlers. Immediately, human beings, who lived in the middle world, were subjected to continual darkness. The hero Main flew to the upper world on a pair of skis and proceeded to hunt down the elk. He eventually succeeded in shooting

LONG WANG *(above), a dragon king, holds court in this modern mural in a mountain temple in Shanxi province in northern China. It is said that the dragon kings live in their own crystal palaces beneath the water.*

the animal with an arrow, whereupon sunshine returned to the middle world of human beings. Main remained in the upper world, guarding the sun. According to Evenk tradition, each evening the elk catches the sun and each night, Main pursues the elk and reclaims the sun in order to rise the next morning.

MAMALDI, according to the Amur people of Siberia, created the continent of Asia. She and her husband, Khadau, are regarded either as the first human couple or as the parents of the first shaman. Whereas Khadau created the souls of shamans, Mamaldi breathed life into them. She was eventually killed by Khadau.

LONG WANG *(left), a celestial dragon king. Because they were the bringers of rain, dragon kings controlled life and death.*

MANUK MANUK, according to Sumatran mythology, is a fabulous blue chicken, which belonged to the supreme god. One day, the chicken laid three gigantic eggs from which emerged three gods. The gods created the three levels of the universe: the upper world, or heaven; the middle world, or the earth; and the underworld.

MARISHI-TEN is Japanese Buddhism's goddess, or sometimes god, of war and victory. In the Middle Ages, Japanese warriors believed that Marishi-Ten made them invisible. She is depicted either sitting or standing on a boar or herd of boars. She sometimes has as many as eight arms in which she holds numerous weapons.

LING ZHI *(right), the fabled mushrooms of immortality, being gathered by a boy.* (DRAWING BY ZHANG LING, 16TH CENTURY.)

MEN SHEN consist of a pair of Chinese gods who look after entrances and doorways. One of the gods is usually represented with a red or black face, the other with a white one. They are armed with weapons and magic symbols, and guard houses as well as palaces. During the New Year festivities, paper images of the gods are stuck on doors to protect those that live within from evil demons.

Although their origins are supposed to lie in the ancient past – when they were said to prevent spirits escaping from hell – one pair of Men Shen was later said to represent two historical generals who heroically guarded the palace of a Tang dynasty emperor against demons. According to one myth, the emperor had promised to look after a dragon king who had made a mistake while distributing the rain and had been condemned to death by the "Jade Emperor", *YU HUANG*. However, the emperor was unable to keep his promise and the spirit of the dragon king held him responsible for his death. Each night, the dragon king would come and cause a commotion outside the palace gates. Unable to sleep, the emperor fell ill, so his two generals guarded the doors. Eventually, the dragon king was driven away.

MIROKU-BOSATSU is the Japanese form of Maitreya, the future buddha. He currently lives in the Tushita heaven awaiting his future birth as a human being and finally as a buddha.

MOMOTARO is a Japanese hero who was born from a peach and was renowned for conquering demons. An elderly couple, who had been unable to have children, found a peach floating in a stream. When they cut the fruit open, they found a tiny baby boy inside. The baby sat up and ate the peach, whereupon the delighted couple called him Momotaro or "Peach Child". They raised Momotaro to be a brave and noble boy.

When he was 15, he decided to repay his parents and friends for looking after him, and determined to rid a neighbouring island of the *ONI*, or devils, which were persecuting them. Momotaro pocketed three dumplings, which the old woman had cooked, and set off for the island. He soon encountered a dog, a pheasant and a monkey, each of whom agreed to accompany him on his quest in return for a dumpling. The four adventurers then took a boat and crossed over to the island. There, they found numerous girls who had been taken prisoner by the oni. Momotaro attacked the castle of the oni and, together with his companions, succeeded in killing all the devils. He then piled his boat high with the treasure that the oni had stolen from the village people, helped the captive girls on board and returned home a hero.

MEN SHEN *(above left), one of a pair of entrance gods, guards a Chinese temple door in Yogjakarta, Java.*

MEN SHEN *(above), guarding a temple entrance, are sometimes represented as two generals, Heng and Ha, whose weapons include poisonous breath and fire.*

MONJU-BOSATSU is the Japanese form of the bodhisattva, or "buddha-to-be", Manjushri. His name means "he whose beauty

MOMOTARO (left), before his battle with the oni, enlisted the help of a pheasant in exchange for a dumpling. (ILLUSTRATION FROM MYTHS AND LEGENDS OF JAPAN.)

charms", and he personifies wisdom, compassion and contemplation. Monju-Bosatsu is often shown accompanied by a lion and is usually seated, holding the sword of intelligence, which cuts through ignorance.

MOYANG KAPIR is a civilizing hero spirit, according to the Ma'Betisek people of Malaysia. He stole the bag that contained the rules of civilized human behaviour from the ferocious spirit *MOYANG MELUR* and then distributed them among his people in order that they might no longer commit murder, cannibalism and incest.

MOYANG MELUR, according to the Ma'Betisek people of Malaysia, is a spirit being who guarded the rules of civilized behaviour. He is said to live on the moon and to be half-human, half-tiger. For a long time, Moyang Melur kept the rules of civilized behaviour to himself and, as a result, human beings constantly committed murder, incest and cannibalism.

One night, Moyang Melur was so enthralled by the chaos and destruction that was taking place below him that he leaned right out of the moon in order to take a closer look. However, he leaned too far and fell to earth. There, he met a hunter called *MOYANG KAPIR*. Moyang Melur told Moyang Kapir that unless he was able to return to the moon immediately, he would kill every single human being. Moyang Kapir promptly threw a rope to the moon, and they both climbed up it.

Moyang Melur was looking forward to killing and eating Moyang Kapir, but the latter quickly slid back down to earth, taking with him the rules of civilized behaviour, which he had found hidden in a bag under a mat. The hunter then distributed the rules among his people.

MONJU-BOSATSU (above right), the Japanese form of Manjushri, with the Buddha (seated in the centre) and the bodhisattva Fugen-Bosatsu. (14TH CENTURY.)

MIROKU (left), the future buddha, sits in contemplation, awaiting the time of his coming on earth. (JAPANESE SCULPTURE.)

SHAMANS OF MONGOLIA

In many traditional communities, the shaman is a central figure combining the function of priest and doctor. He or she has the power to control spirits which, though neither good nor evil, may be destructive: to protect the community he or she incorporates them in him or herself. The shaman's ability to make out-of-body journeys to the upper and lower spirit worlds is also part of a protective role in the tribe. In shamanistic myths the world was once peopled by beings who could easily travel between heaven and earth, but after the bridge between the two was broken, most people lost their original wisdom. Eventually only a few – the shamans – were able to reach heaven, and they could do so only in spirit, by separating their souls from their bodies. Shamanistic myths, passed down through successive generations in an oral tradition, tell of a process of decline, from a golden age, when great spirits brought knowledge to the world, to the present, when not even all shamans can fly away from it.

DRUMMING (above) is used to induce a trance state in which the shaman's soul can leave his body. The drum beat excludes other stimuli while its insistent rhythm works on the consciousness. According to Mongolian legend, early shamans could use their drums to call back the souls of the dead. The lord of the dead, fearing that he would lose all his subjects, ordained that the shamans' drums, originally double-headed, should have only a single head to reduce their power.

ANIMALS (left) are used by Siberian Yakut shamans as receptacles for their souls. Each shaman keeps his chosen animal far away from other people, so that its life is protected and his spiritual well-being ensured. However, once a year, when the last snow melts, the animals are said to come down from the mountains and walk into the villages. The most powerful shamans keep their souls in horses, elks, bears, eagles or boars; the weakest keep them in dogs. Sometimes the animals fight, and if one is harmed, its shaman will fall ill or die.

YAKUT SHAMANS *(above) claim descent from a primordial shaman who rebelled against the supreme god and was condemned to eternal fire. His body, which was composed of reptiles, was consumed, but a single frog escaped the flames and gave rise to a line of shamanic demons from whom Yakut shamans are still drawn.* (LITHOGRAPH, C. 1835.)

A SHAMAN *(left) enacts a healing ceremony over a sick man. Illness is thought to be due to the loss of the person's soul, which may have wandered to the land of the dead in error, looking for its home. The shaman's task is to retrieve the soul and for this he or she needs to be able to fly to the underworld and persuade it to return. The shaman may also massage, stroke or blow on the patient, and suck harmful material out through the skin.* (A SHAMAN OF YAKUTIA, C. 1805.)

N

MUCILINDA *(left) coiled his body under the Buddha beneath the sacred fig tree at Bodhi-gaya* (STONE CARVING, 3RD CENTURY AD.)

MUCILINDA's *(left) multiple heads, with their cobra-like hoods, spread out like an umbrella to shelter the seated Buddha, here represented by an empty seat.* (STONE CARVING.)

MUCILINDA is the king of the serpent deities, or water spirits, known as *NAGAS*. According to a legend, Mucilinda sheltered the Buddha with the outspread hoods of his seven heads during a downpour that lasted for seven days. When the sun returned, the serpent was transformed into a young prince who proceeded to pay homage to the Buddha. In India, and especially in South-east Asia, Mucilinda is often depicted protecting the Buddha.

NAGA PADOHA is the great sea serpent of South-east Asian mythology. In the tale of creation, *BATARA GURU*, a form of the great Hindu god Shiva, created the first solid land whereupon Naga Padoha sought to destroy it by writhing and thrashing about in the ocean. However, Batara Guru, in his incarnation as a hero figure, managed to control the serpent, pressing him down with a vast iron weight so that he descended to the lower regions of the cosmos.

NAGAS, according to the mythology of South-east Asia, are supernatural beings who take the form of serpents. The great serpent Sesha, on whose coils the god Vishnu rested in the intervals between creation, was served by nagas. In Buddhist belief, the serpent *MUCILINDA* was a naga king who sheltered Gautama Buddha from the weather. In Tibetan Buddhism, the nagas are said to guard the Buddhist scriptures. (See also *DEMONS*)

NAZHA, the "Third Prince" and *enfant terrible* of Chinese mythology, is an exorcising spirit and a deity of popular religion. Nazha is also said to have been a powerful deity in his own right, dispatched down to the human world by *YU HUANG*, the "Jade Emperor", to subdue or destroy the demons raging through the world. He was incarnated as the third son of Li Jing, a general who fought for the Zhou dynasty in the 12th century BC. Nazha grew up to be full of mischief and the numerous legends surrounding his life are probably better known to Chinese peasants than recent imperial history.

NGA, according to the mythology of the Samoyed Yuraks of Siberia, is the god of death and hell, and one of the two great demiurges, or supreme deities. One tale relates how the earth threatened to collapse, so a shaman visited *NUM*, the other great demiurge, and asked him for advice. Num instructed the shaman to descend below the earth and call upon Nga. The shaman did so and married Nga's daughter. He then supported the earth in his hand and became known as the "Old Man of the Earth".

NINIGI, or Honinigi, is the grandson of the great *AMATERASU*, the sun goddess of Japanese Shinto

NAGAS *(below) are spirits in the form of serpents. They may be benevolent and protective, like Mucilinda sheltering the Buddha from the rain.* (THAI BRONZE, 1291.)

mythology. Amaterasu had been trying for some time to find someone to rule over earth. At first, she decided to send her son, Ame-No-Oshido-Mimi, down from the heavens. However, the god looked over the Floating Bridge of Heaven, saw the many disturbances happening below, and refused to go.

The gods all met together in order to decide what to do and eventually determined to send down Ame-No-Hohi. Three years passed but the gods heard nothing from Ame-No-Hohi. They then decided to send down his son, Ame-No-Wakahiko. Before he left, they gave him a bow and arrows.

Ame-No-Wakahiko descended to earth and soon married Shitateru-Hime, the daughter of OKUNINUSHI, the god of medicine and magic. This time, eight years passed without the gods hearing any news. At the end of that time, they sent down a pheasant to find out what Ame-No-Wakahiko had

NAZHA (above), the "Third Prince" and son of Li Jing, is the enfant terrible of Chinese Mythology. Numerous popular legends are told about his escapades.

been doing. The pheasant perched on a tree outside the god's house.

One of the women of the house noticed the bird and told Ame-No-Wakahiko that it was an evil omen. Immediately, the god shot it with his bow and arrow. The arrow passed straight through the bird, entered heaven and fell at the feet of Amaterasu and the god Takami-Masubi. The god recognized the arrow and, in fury, flung it back down to earth where it killed Ame-No-Wakahiko. Shitateru-Hime, his wife, was devastated.

The gods then sent two of their number down to visit Okuninushi. They told him that they had been sent by the sun goddess in order to bring the land under her command. Okuninushi spoke to his two sons. The older son agreed to worship Amaterasu, but the younger son tried to resist. However, the two gods soon overpowered the younger son, who then promised not to put up any resistance against the sun goddess. Okuninushi also agreed to the sun goddess's rule, on condition that a place should be reserved for him among the major deities worshipped at the famous shrine at Izumo. Amaterasu agreed to this.

At last, Amaterasu sent her grandson, Ninigi, down to earth. Before leaving heaven, Ninigi was given various divine objects, including the mirror into which the sun goddess had gazed after emerging from hiding in the cave, the heavenly jewels that had produced Amaterasu's sons and the sword Kusanagi, which the storm god SUSANO-WO had found in the tail of the eight-headed snake, Yamato-No-Orochi. These three items became the emblems of Japanese imperial power.

NAZHA's (above) father, Li Jing, was a commander who fought during the mythological wars between dynasties in the 12th century BC.

Ninigi married Kono-Hana-Sakuyu-Hime, the daughter of a mountain god. When Kono-Hana-Sakuyu-Hime conceived on the first night that she slept with her husband, Ninigi suspected her of having been unfaithful to him. In response, Kono-Hana-Sakuyu-Hime built a house with no doors, and, when she was about to give birth, she entered the house and set it alight saying that if she had been unfaithful, her child would die. As it turned out, Kono-Hana-Sakuyu-Hime produced three sons. One of them, HIKOHOHODEMI, married the daughter of the sea god. Their child later fathered a boy who, after his death, became known as JIMMU-TENNO. Jimmu-Tenno was the founder of the imperial line of Japan.

O

THE NIO, according to Japanese Buddhism, are the two guardian kings, or kings of compassion. They are usually represented as giants who guard the entrances to temples and monasteries, and are dressed either in sarongs or in armour. They are believed to banish evil spirits and thieves, and to protect children.

NU GUA or Nü Kua, is an ancient Chinese creator deity who, after the great flood, became the consort of *FU XI*. Her name is derived from the words for gourd or melon, a symbol of fertility, and she is sometimes known as the "Gourd Girl". Nu Gua is said to have been half-human and half-serpent or dragon and to have had the ability to change her shape at will. She is sometimes shown holding a pair of compasses while Fu Xi holds a set square, symbolizing their part in the creation. Nu Gua is also said to have invented the flute.

According to one story, Nu Gua descended to earth after it had been separated from the sky, and after the mountains, rivers, animals and plants had been created. She tamed the wild animals and, together with other mythological figures, taught humankind how to irrigate the land. However, Nu Gua is most famous for having created human beings out of clay or mud.

One day, as Nu Gua wandered through the world, she began to feel that something was missing and longed to have some companionship. She sat down on the bank of a river and, gazing at her reflection in the water, she began to play with some mud from the riverbed. Almost without thinking, she began to model the clay into a little figure. However, rather than giving the figure a tail like herself, she gave it legs and feet. When Nu Gua had finished moulding the figure, she stood it on the ground and it immediately came to life, dancing and laughing with happiness.

THE NIO (left) are the two guardian kings or kings of compassion. They are usually represented as temple guardians, with fierce expressions which are designed to deter evil spirits from entering the sacred precinct.

Nu Gua was so happy with her creation that she decided to fill the whole world with people. She worked until it grew dark, and as soon as the sun rose the next morning, she set to work once more. Although the people wandered off, Nu Gua could still hear their voices and so she never again felt lonely. Before long, Nu Gua realized that she could not possibly create enough people to populate the whole earth. She decided to call on her magic power and, taking a length of vine, she trailed it in the mud and then whirled it about in the air. As soon as the drops of mud touched the ground, they were transformed into human beings.

It is sometimes said that those people whom Nu Gua fashioned with her hands became rich and fortunate, whereas those who were created when the drops of mud fell to the ground were the poor and humble people.

NU GUA'S (left) image on a Chinese temple altar in Singapore. She is known as the "Dark Lady of the Ninth Heaven".

Realizing that her little people might eventually die and become extinct, Nu Gua divided them into male and female so that they could bear children.

Nu Gua and Fu Xi are also renowned for having saved the world from a flood. One tale tells how the world had become wild and chaotic: human beings were eaten by wild animals, immense fires raged continuously and water flowed without ceasing. Nu Gua mended the skies with melted stones, supported the heavens with the legs of a turtle and piled ashes of reeds on a river bank to dam the waters until, at last, everything became calm again.

NÜ KUA see *NU GUA*.

NUM and *NGA*, according to the mythology of the Samoyed Yuraks of Siberia, are the two great demiurges, or supreme deities. At the beginning of time, Num sent several birds one after the other to explore the endless stretches of water. Eventually, one of the birds returned with a small piece of sand or mud,from which Num created a floating island.

Another tale relates how the earth threatened to collapse, whereupon a shaman visited Num and asked him for advice. Num instructed the shaman to descend to Nga, the god of death and hell, who lived beneath the earth. The shaman did as instructed and married the daughter of Nga. He then supported the earth in his hand and became known as the "Old Man of the Earth". Num lives in a place of light, but he regularly visits earth to ensure it is secure.

OGETSU-NO-HIME see *UKEMOCHI*.

***OKUNINUSHI** is seen here with the white hare of Inaoa, who foretold his success in his quest for the hand of Yakami.*

OKUNINUSHI, according to Japanese Shinto mythology, is the god of medicine and magic. His name means "Great Land Master", and he ruled the earth after its creation until *AMATERASU* sent her grandson *NINIGI* to take his place. As god of medicine, he is credited with having invented therapeutic methods of healing.

Okuninushi had 80 brothers, all of whom wanted to marry the beautiful princess *YAKAMI* or Ya-Gami-Hime. While the brothers were on their way to visit the princess, a flayed hare stopped them and asked them for help. The brothers told the hare to wash in the sea and then dry itself in the wind. The hare suffered excruciating pain and distress. The creature then met Okuninushi who, feeling sorry for it, told it to bathe in fresh water and then roll around in the pollen of kama grass. The hare did as Okuninushi advised and immediately felt better. In gratitude, the hare, who was really a god, told Okuninushi that the beautiful princess Yakami would be his.

Okuninushi's brothers were furious. They heated a vast rock until it was white-hot and rolled it down a mountain towards their brother. Okuninushi mistook the rock for a boar, caught hold of it and was burned to death. However, with the help of his mother, Kami-Musubi, he was brought back to life. The brothers then crushed Okuninushi to death. This time, Kami-Musubi advised her son to avoid further attacks by taking refuge in the underworld.

There, Okuninushi met the storm god *SUSANO-WO* and his daughter Suseri-Hime. The couple fell in love. When Susano-Wo discovered this, he sent Okuninushi to sleep in a room full of snakes. However, the god was protected by a scarf, which Suseri-Hime had given him. The following night, Susano-Wo sent him to sleep in a room full of centipedes and wasps, but again Okuninushi was protected. Susano-Wo then fired an arrow into the middle of an enormous field and told Okuninushi to look for it. When Okuninushi reached the middle of the field, Susano-Wo set fire to the grass. However, a mouse showed Okuninushi a hole in which he could take shelter from the fire and then brought the arrow to him.

By this time, Susano-Wo was beginning to approve of Okuninushi. He asked him to wash his hair and then went to sleep. While Susano-Wo was sleeping, Okuninushi tied the storm god's hair to the rafters of his palace and fled with Suseri-Hime. He took with him Susano-Wo's sword, bow and arrows and his harp, called Koto. As Okuninushi and Suseri-Hime made their escape, the harp brushed against a tree, and the noise of its strings awoke Susano-Wo. The god jumped up and in so doing pulled down his house with his hair.

Okuninushi hurried onwards. Eventually, at the borders of the underworld, Susano-Wo almost caught up with the elopers and called out to them, advising Okuninushi to fight his brothers with Susano-Wo's weapons in order that he might rule the world. It seems that Okuninushi's trickery had finally convinced the storm god that he would make a suitable husband for Suseri-Hime, because he then asked the god to make Suseri-Hime his wife and to build a palace at the foot of Mount Uka. Okuninushi became ruler of the province of Izumo.

***ONI** are horned demons responsible for a variety of ills and misdeeds. This woman is using an oni puppet to frighten a child.* (JAPANESE LACQUERED SWORD GUARD.)

THE ONI are giant horned demons. They are said to have come to Japan from China with the arrival of Buddhism, and Buddhist priests perform annual rites in order to expel them. The oni can be a variety of colours and have three fingers, three toes and sometimes three eyes. They are usually cruel and lecherous, and they are said to sweep down from the sky in order to steal the souls of people who are about to die. One story tells how the diminutive hero *MOMOTARO* freed numerous young girls whom the oni had captured and raped.

The oni of hell have the heads of oxen or horses; they hunt down sinners and take them away in their chariot of fire to *EMMA-O*, the ruler of the underworld. Some oni are held responsible for illness and disease, and others are said to have once been mortal women whose jealousy or grief transformed them into demons.

OT, the fire queen of the Mongols, is said to have been born at the beginning of the world, when the earth and sky separated. Her blessing is invoked at weddings and her radiance is said to penetrate throughout all the realms. Ot is believed originally to have been identical with *UMAI*, mother goddess of the Turkic people of Siberia.

OTSHIRVANI, according to Siberian mythology, is a god of light. He was sent by the supreme god to fight Losy, a monstrous serpent who killed all mortal beings by covering the world with poison. Otshirvani took the form of an enormous bird and, seizing Losy in his claws, threw him against the world mountain, killing him.

PA HSIEN see *BA XIAN*.

PAMALAK BAGOBO, according to the Bagobo people of Mindanao in the Philippines, is the god who created human beings. According to tradition, monkeys once behaved and looked like humans and only acquired their current appearance when Pamalak decided to create humankind as a separate race.

P'AN-KU see *PANGU*.

PANGU, or P'an-ku, is the cosmic giant of Chinese mythology. He is said to be the child of *YIN* and

***PANGU** is the giant who emerged from the cosmic egg when it split to form the earth and sky. He held the two apart to create the world.*

PANGU, the cosmic creator and mythological deity, on an altar in a temple in Tainan, in southern Taiwan.

YANG, the vital forces of the universe. The myth of Pangu's birth tells how, at the very beginning of time, only chaos existed. Chaos took the form of a primordial egg, and eventually Pangu took shape inside its shell. The creature slept and grew inside the egg for 18,000 years until, eventually, he woke up and stretched. The light part of the egg, which was pervaded by yang, rose up to become the sky; the heavy part, pervaded by yin, sank down and became the earth.

Pangu, fearing that the earth and sky might merge together again, stood between them, his head keeping the sky aloft and his feet treading down the earth. For 18,000 years, the distance between heaven and earth increased at a rate of 3 metres (ten feet) a day. Pangu grew at the same rate to continue to hold heaven and earth apart.

Eventually, when Pangu considered that there was no risk of the earth and sky rejoining, he fell asleep and eventually died. The giant's enormous corpse gave rise to all the elements. His breath became the wind and clouds, his voice became the thunder and lightning, his left eye became the sun, and his right eye became the moon. His four limbs and his trunk were transformed into the cardinal directions and the mountains, his blood became the rivers and his veins the roads. His flesh became trees and soil, the hair on his head and his beard became the stars in the sky, and the hairs on his body were transformed into grass and flowers. His teeth and bones became metal and stones, and his sweat produced the dew. Finally, the fleas and parasites on his body became the ancestors of the different races of human beings.

Many later tales elaborate the story of Pangu. According to one, the alternation of night and day occurs when Pangu opens and closes his eyes. Another version of the myth tells how Pangu was born from the five basic elements and formed heaven and earth with a chisel and hammer. Pangu is still worshipped by some of the people of South China. (See also *CREATION MYTHS; CHINA'S SACRED PEAKS*)

PENG LAI, or P'eng-lai, according to Daoist belief, is an island in the East China Sea inhabited by the immortals or *XIAN*. The plant of immortality, *LING ZHI*, grows there. Many explorers have attempted to discover the mythical island, but all expeditions have failed – sometimes, it is said, because the island sinks beneath the waves. Everything on the miraculous island is made of gold and jewels: the trees are made of pearl and coral, and the animals and birds are glittering white.

The two other islands of the immortals are Fangchang and Yingzhou. Originally, there were five islands, but a giant caused two of them to break away from their moorings and sink without trace. Fangchang, lying off the east coast of China, is said to be inhabited by dragons and to boast marvellous palaces made of gold, jade and crystal. Thousands of immortals live there, cultivating the plant of immortality. Yingzhou is also credited with a marvellous appearance and inhabitants.

P'ENG-LAI see *PENG LAI*.

POLONG, according to Malayan and Indonesian tradition, is a flying demon created from the blood of a murdered man. Whoever owns the Polong can order it to attack his enemies. The victims tear their clothes, go blind and eventually lose consciousness. However, the Polong also feeds on the blood of its owner.

PU LANG SEUNG see *THENS*.

CHINESE DRAGONS

THE CHINESE DRAGON CAME FIRST in the mythical hierarchy of 360 scaly creatures, and was one of the four animals who symbolized the cardinal points. Associated with the east, the dragon stood for sunrise, spring and fertility and was opposed by the white tiger of the west, who represented death. Daoist dragons were benevolent spirits associated with happiness and prosperity, and were kind to humans. However, when Buddhism became popular, their character was modified by the Indian concept of the naga, which was a more menacing creature. In folk religion, the Long Wang

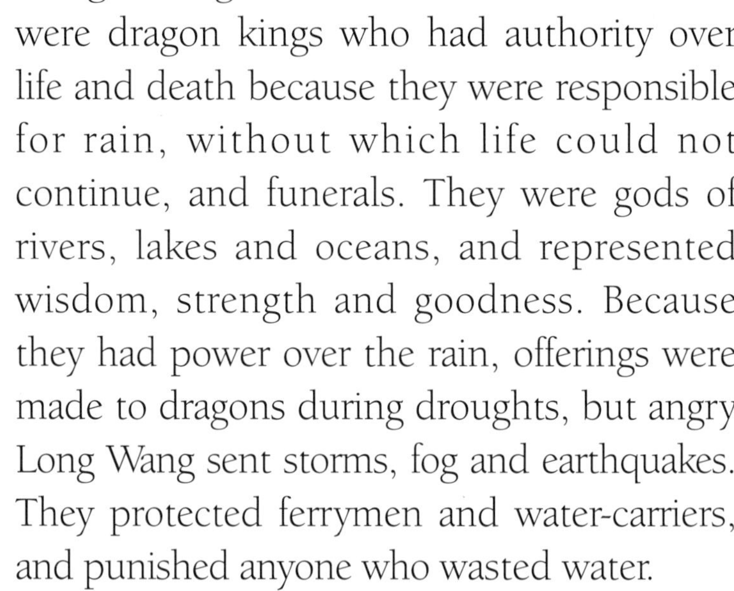

were dragon kings who had authority over life and death because they were responsible for rain, without which life could not continue, and funerals. They were gods of rivers, lakes and oceans, and represented wisdom, strength and goodness. Because they had power over the rain, offerings were made to dragons during droughts, but angry Long Wang sent storms, fog and earthquakes. They protected ferrymen and water-carriers, and punished anyone who wasted water.

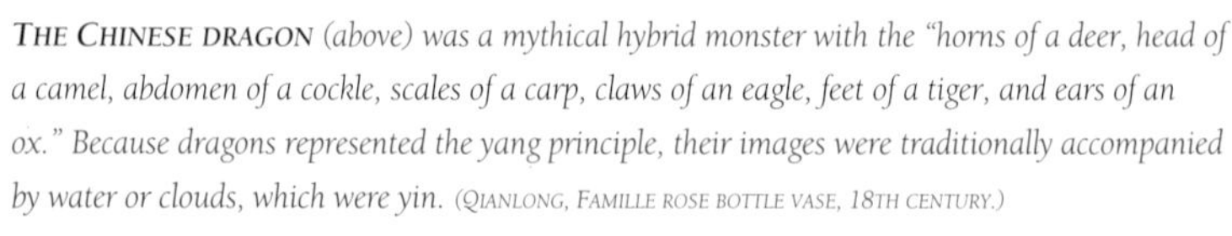

THE CHINESE DRAGON *(above) was a mythical hybrid monster with the "horns of a deer, head of a camel, abdomen of a cockle, scales of a carp, claws of an eagle, feet of a tiger, and ears of an ox." Because dragons represented the yang principle, their images were traditionally accompanied by water or clouds, which were yin.* (QIANLONG, FAMILLE ROSE BOTTLE VASE, 18TH CENTURY.)

DRAGON PROCESSIONS *(left), which were held all over China in spring, welcomed the annual return of these generous creatures and ensured fertility. Dragons spent the winter underground, emerging on the second day of the second lunar month. Their arrival, announced by claps of thunder, coincided with the beginning of the spring rains, and this was the time to go out into the fields and begin the year's cultivation. As bringers of rain, dragons were coloured blue-green.* (HSTE YANG, PROCESSION OF THE BLUE DRAGON.)

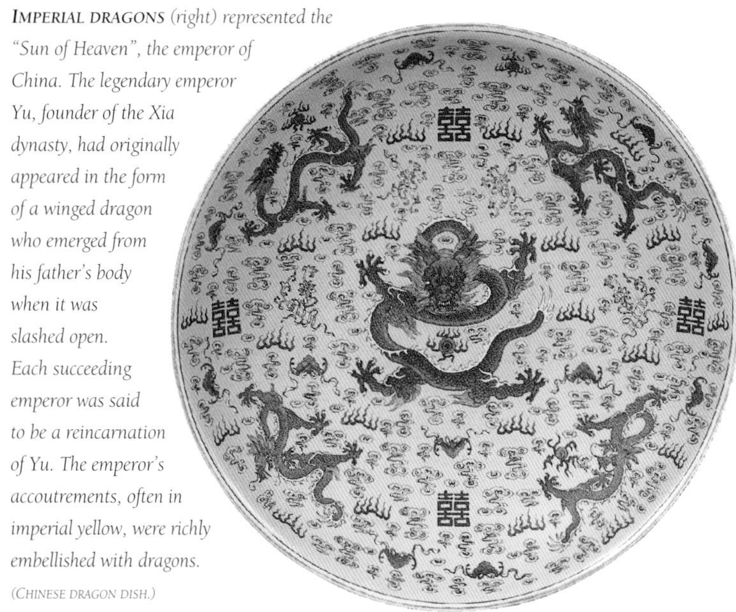

Imperial dragons *(right) represented the "Sun of Heaven", the emperor of China. The legendary emperor Yu, founder of the Xia dynasty, had originally appeared in the form of a winged dragon who emerged from his father's body when it was slashed open. Each succeeding emperor was said to be a reincarnation of Yu. The emperor's accoutrements, often in imperial yellow, were richly embellished with dragons.* (Chinese dragon dish.)

A dragon *(above) was often depicted playing with a flaming pearl or ball, which symbolized thunder. It was this heavenly sport which was thought to cause the rain to fall. Only imperial dragons were represented with five claws on each foot. Those with four claws signified the status of a prince, while court officials were allowed only three claws for the dragons embroidered on their robes and other possessions.* (Chinese pillar rug.)

Hui-neng *(right), the Chinese Buddhist patriarch, persuaded a fierce dragon to shrink so small that it would fit into a tiny rice bowl and was thus able to subdue it. The magic powers of dragons included the ability to make themselves invisible at will and change their shape and size. They could shrink to the size of a silkworm or swell to fill all the space between heaven and earth.* (Illustration from *Superstitions en Chine*, 1914.)

R

PUDAI (left), in the "Cave of the Laughing Buddha" in Zhejiang Province, China, is portrayed with a fat belly and a wide grin.

PUDAI (right), also known as the "Hempbag Monk", on a temple altar in Tainan, in southern Taiwan.

PU-TAI see *PUDAI*.

PUDAI, or Pu-tai, was a Chinese monk who is said to have lived in the tenth century AD and whose original name was Qizi. He is said to have earned his name, which means "Hempen Sack", from his habit of wandering through towns with a beggar's sack on his back. He was believed to be able to predict the weather, and his life was filled with miraculous events. At his death, he revealed himself to be an incarnation of Maitreya, the future Buddha. Pudai is often represented as the "Laughing Buddha", the Chinese style of depicting Maitreya.

PULANG GANA, according to the Iban people of Borneo, is an earth spirit who ensures the abundant growth of rice. According to tradition, a long time ago the Iban began to clear the jungle in order to create the first rice farm. However, when they arose the next morning, they found that all the trees had grown back. The same happened after their next attempt to clear the jungle, and the next. At last, the Iban decided to keep watch during the night in order to try and solve the mystery.

That night, they saw Pulang Gana coax the trees back to life and ensure that they became rooted in the soil once more. They tried to catch the spirit, who explained that he owned the earth and everything that grew in it, and that he alone could ensure that the plants flourished. When the people asked the spirit what they should do before cultivating rice, he told them that they should offer up gifts to him.

QORMUSTA, or Chormusta, according to Mongolian belief, is king of the Tengri, the realms of heaven. The supreme god, he lives in the centre of the world and is associated with the creation of fire.

RADIN is a mythical hero of the Iban people of Borneo. One tale tells how, after winning a battle, Radin began to be troubled by a hungry ghost. When the ghost introduced smallpox to Radin's tribe, the hero determined to kill it. One night, Radin hid inside a roll of matting, and when the ghost approached, he jumped out and cut it into pieces with his sword. Before falling asleep again, Radin heard something fall to the ground and, when daylight came, he found a carving of a hornbill, a sacred bird, lying on the ground in pieces. Radin realized that this signified that the ghost was far too powerful a being to overcome, so he and his people moved to another area.

THE RAIN SPIRIT is one of the early nature gods who were referred to in Chinese legendary stories. In his struggle with *HUANG DI*, the "Yellow Emperor", *CHIYOU* begged the "Wind God" and the "Master of Rain" to bring on a major storm, with gales and torrential rains to help him. Along with the *LIGHTNING GODDESS* and the God of Thunder, these nature spirits were invoked during times of drought. The Goddess of Lightning flashes the two mirrors she carries to cause lightning, while thunder is made by the thunder god with his hammer and drums, and has the power to kill. The Master of Rain is said to own a mysterious one-legged bird, which can drink the seas dry.

THE RAIN SPIRIT (left), with his vase of water, sometimes also holds a dragon on a plate, since the dragon is a symbol of rain.

RANGDA (right), the Balinese demon queen, is represented by a terrifying mask.

RANGDA is the terrifying demon queen of Bali. She leads an army of evil witches against *BARONG*, the leader of the forces of good. The evil demon is usually represented as scantily clad, with long hair and with claws in place of fingernails and toenails.

It is sometimes suggested that Rangda derived from an 11th-century Balinese queen who was exiled

by the king for practising witchcraft against his second wife. In revenge, Rangda attempted to destroy the kingdom. Half the population died of plague before she was overcome by the superior powers of a holy man. The name Rangda means "widow". (See also *DEMONS*)

ROWANG RIWO is a fabulous creature who, according to the Dayak people of Borneo, appeared during the first epoch of creation with *DIDIS MAHENDERA*. Rowang Riwo had golden saliva and Didis Mahendera had eyes of jewels.

THE SAN QING DAOZU's *senior deity is Yuanshi Tian-zong, "Jade Pure", who is invisible and eternal.*

THE SAN GUAN DADI, or San Kuan Ta-ti, are the "Three Great Primordial Rulers" and "Controllers of Heaven, Earth and the Waters". Also known as the San Yuan Dadi, they are of mythical origin and are revered as the source of all happiness and forgiveness of sins, able to avert calamities and sickness. Legend has it that *YU HUANG*, the "Jade Emperor", sent them down to earth to govern it, and observe men's good and evil thoughts and deeds.

SAN-HSING see *SAN XING*.

THE SAN QING DAOZU's *second deity is Ling-bao Tian-zong, who regulates time and yin and yang.*

SAN KUAN TA-TI see *SAN GUAN DADI*.

THE SAN QING DAOZU, or, as they are sometimes known, "The Three Pure Ones", are the supreme deities of the orthodox Daoist pantheon, ruling the entire cosmos from the highest heaven. In the "Doctrine of the Three Pure Ones", they are the symbolic personification of the three life principles: breath, vital essence and spirit. They are prayed to as a group for assistance in coping with the problems of life.

THE SAN QING DAOZU's *third deity is Lao Jun. He is the deified form of the legendary founder of Daoism, Laozi.*

SAN GUAN DADI, *the three great primordial rulers, are transcendent powers who bestow happiness, forgive sins and protect from evil.*

The first is the "Perfect One", or "Jade Pure", Yuanshi Tian-zong, the deity of the beginning representing primeval origins. He is in charge of the "Heaven of the Heavenly Ones" and is said to have formulated the heavens and earth and dominated the first phase of creation.

The "Highest Holy One", Ling-bao Tian-zong, the "High Pure", represents energy and activity. He is in charge of the "Heaven of the Perfect Ones", Zhenren, and is said to have devised the rules for calculating time and controlling the interaction of *YIN* and *YANG*, as well as the doctrine for the heavens and earth. He is the guardian of magical writings. Ling-bao dominated the second phase of creation.

The "Greatest Holy One", the "Supreme Pure", *LAO JUN*, representing humankind, is the deified philosopher Laozi who is in charge of the third and lowest heaven, that of the immortals. He is said to have dominated the third phase of the creation of the cosmos, and inspired the formation of religious Daoism at a later stage.

THE SAN XING (left) are the most important spirits of the stars of the constellation Ursa Minor. (CHINESE PORCELAIN DISH, 18TH CENTURY.)

THE SAN XING, or San-hsing, or "Three Stars", are the three Chinese gods of good fortune. They were historical figures who were given divine status in recognition of their special merits. Fuxing or "Lucky Star" is usually depicted alongside a child or as a bat, a symbol of good luck. He is the god of happiness. Luxing or "Star of Honour" is the god of salaries and is often shown as a deer. Shouxing, "Star of Longevity", is shown with the face of an old man, a white beard and eyebrows, a high bald head and holding a knotty staff, a symbol of the immortals.

Fuxing is said to have been a government official called Yang Cheng who lived during the sixth century BC. He came from a village whose inhabitants were all very short in height. Each year, the emperor, who enjoyed surrounding himself with dwarfs, would call a number of the villagers to his court and insist that they remain there. As a result, as time went by, the population of the village began to dwindle. Eventually, Yang Cheng asked the emperor to take pity on the village folk. The emperor was impressed by Yang Cheng's petition and so ceased his demands.

Luxing is sometimes identified with *WEN CHANG*, the god of literature, or is said to have been Shi Fei, a servant of the founder of the Han dynasty, who lived at the end of the third century BC.

Shouxing came to be known as *SHOU LAO*, the god of long life and "Old Man of the South Pole". He is said to fix the date of everyone's death, writing it down beforehand. However, although the digits of the appointed date cannot be changed, they can sometimes be juggled.

According to one tale, a child called Zao Yan was told that he had only 19 more years to live. One day, the boy was told to go to a field, taking with him some food and wine. There, he would find two men playing a game of draughts (checkers) under a mulberry tree. Zao Yan was advised to offer the men food and drink but to refuse to answer any of their questions. The boy did as he was told. He gave the two men the food and drink, then waited quietly while they argued over how they should thank him. The men finally decided to reverse the order of the digits of the number of years Zao Yan was to live, thereby decreeing that he should live for a further 91 years. Zao Yan later discovered that one of the men had been Shou Lao.

THE SAN XING (above) are usually portrayed as three good-humoured old men, surrounded by symbols of good fortune, longevity and immortality. (PAINTED SILK SCROLL BY WANG CHAO, C. 1500.)

THE SAN XING Luxing and Fuxing are dressed as mandarins, while Shouxing, the god of longevity, holds a sprig of Ling Zhi, the plant of immortality. (JADEITE FIGURES, LATE QING DYNASTY.)

SEMARA, according to the mythology of the Balinese, is the god of love who lives in the floating sky, one of a series of skies that lies above the layer of water hanging over the earth.

SENGALONG BURONG see *SURONG GUNTING*.

SETESUYARA, according to Balinese mythology, is the goddess who rules over the underworld together with the god *BATARA KALA*.

SHAKA-NYORAI is the Japanese name for the Buddha Shakyamuni Gautama. Although Shaka is worshipped in Japan, the dominant form of Buddhism is the "Pure Land" school, whose followers chiefly venerate the buddha *AMIDA* or Amitabha.

SHAKA-NYORAI, the Japanese buddha, preaching at Ryoj-Usen Mountain. (WALL PAINTING, 8TH CENTURY.)

SHANG DI, or Shang Ti, was worshipped as the ancestor of China's Shang dynasty, established around 1500 BC. The supreme god, he ruled over heaven and controlled natural phenomena such as the thunder, lightning, wind and rain. He was also regarded as the god of agriculture and was believed to determine people's fates. He was sometimes known simply as Di, which means "Lord" or "God".

SHANG TI see *SHANG DI*.

SHEN NONG, or Shen Nung, is an ancient Chinese god of medicine, health, agriculture and forestry. Together with *FU XI* and *HUANG DI*, he was one of the San Huang, or "Three Nobles", legendary emperors of China. He was sometimes referred to as the "Divine Husbandman", although, as god of the hot winds, he could also bring harm. Shen Nong is said to have invented the plough to improve the lives of the ancient Chinese. He taught them how to grow food and revealed the medicinal properties of plants.

Because he had a transparent stomach, he was able to observe the effect of food and drink on his body. However, while investigating the effect of an unusual piece of grass, he turned black and died.

SHENG MU see *DONGYUE DADI*.

THE SHICHI FUKUJIN are the seven Japanese gods of good fortune or happiness. Their names are *DAIKOKU*, *EBISU*, *BENTEN*, *BISHAMON*, *FUKUROKUJU*, *JUROJIN* and *HOTEI*. Among the group are deities from Buddhism, Japanese folklore and Chinese Daoism. The group was assembled in the 17th century by the monk Tenkai, who intended the gods to symbolize the virtues of fortune, magnanimity, candour, dignity, popularity, longevity and amiability. The deities are said to travel together on a treasure ship and are sometimes portrayed thus. (See also *THE SHICHI FUKUJIN*)

SHEN NONG (below left), with Huang Di, another legendary emperor of China.

SHEN NONG (below) is portrayed dressed in green leaves to symbolize his close association with plants as god of medicine and agriculture.

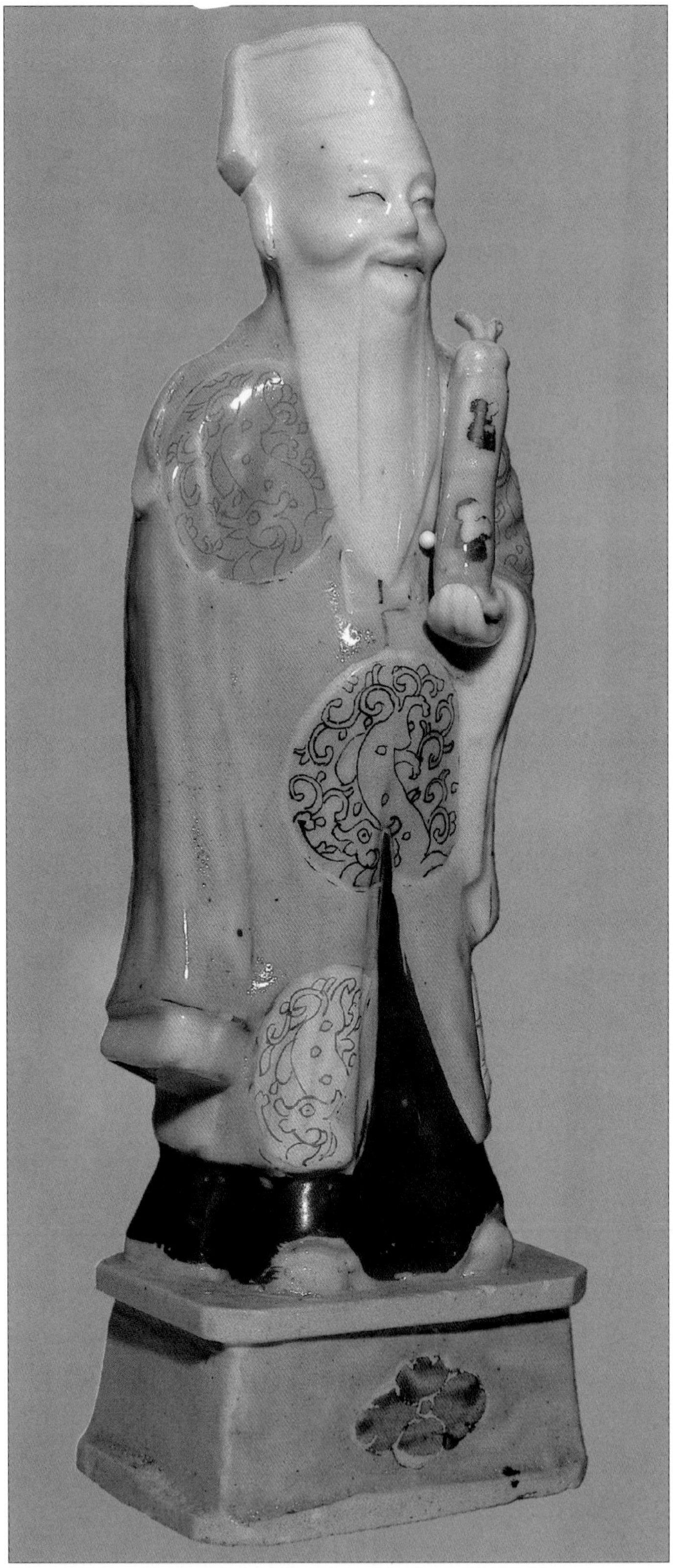

SHOTEN, or Daisho-Kangiten, is a Japanese form of the Indian elephant-headed god Ganesha, who was adopted by certain Buddhist sects. His cult was introduced to Japan in the ninth century. Shoten both creates obstacles and overcomes them. He is worshipped by esoteric sects, and the god's tremendous power is believed to help people to gain enlightenment.

SHOU LAO is the Daoist god of long life. Originally known as Shouxing, he was one of the *SAN XING* or Chinese gods of good fortune. In due course, he came to rule over the department of the heavens that decrees the life-span of human beings. The god is usually shown with a large head and carrying a staff as well as a gourd, which holds the water of life. In his other hand, he holds the peach of eternal life. His creature is the white crane, a symbol of immortality. (See also *THE EIGHT IMMORTALS*)

SHOUXING see *SHOU LAO*.

SHUN is one of the five legendary emperors, or Wu Di, of Chinese mythology. The emperor *YAO* chose Shun, rather than his own son, as his successor. Shun was said to be a potter who travelled throughout the four directions and banished all the threatening creatures guarding their entrances. He is said to have lived in the third century BC and to have been succeeded by *YU*.

SUKU-NA-BIKONA, a dwarf deity, assisted *OKUNINUSHI*, one of Japan's great mythological heroes. He is regarded as a benevolent deity who is learned in both healing and cultivation.

After Okuninushi had settled in his palace with his wife, Suku-Na-Bikona arrived in a tiny boat on the crest of a wave. Okuninushi put the dwarf in the palm of his hand in order to examine him, whereupon the creature leapt up and bit the hero on his cheek. Okuninushi was annoyed and told the gods what had happened. One of the gods realized that the dwarf must be his son, a mischievous child who had fallen to earth. The god asked Okuninushi to look after his child, who proceeded to help the hero to establish his rule. Eventually, however, Suku-Na-Bikona disappeared.

SURONG GUNTING is a culture hero of the Iban people of Borneo. He went to visit his grandfather, a spirit called Sengalong Burong and, during his journey, the stars taught him about the agricultural cycle. When he reached his destination, his grandfather taught him about rituals and omens.

SHOU LAO (left) wears the robes and hat of a mandarin in his capacity as the heavenly official who determines human life-spans. (CHINESE PORCELAIN, 18TH CENTURY.)

SHOU LAO (right), the Daoist god of long life, has a large head and carries a staff. (JADE CARVING, 17TH CENTURY.)

In due course Sengalong Burong threw the young man out of his house in punishment for having slept with his aunt, Dara Chempaka Tempurong. According to Sengalong Burong, if people of adjacent generations slept with one another there would be a terrible harvest. Surong Gunting returned to his home and taught his people all that he had learned.

SUSANO-WO is the storm god of Japanese Shinto mythology. He came into being when *IZANAGI*, the male half of the primal pair, washed his face after returning from the land of the dead. Susano-Wo emerged from Izanagi's nose.

Izanagi divided his kingdom between his three children, the others being the sun goddess *AMATERASU* and the moon god *TSUKIYOMI*. To Susano-Wo he allocated rulership of the ocean. Susano-Wo was dismayed with his lot and protested, saying that he wanted to join his mother *IZANAMI* in the underworld. Izanagi immediately banished Susano-Wo.

Before leaving, Susano-Wo visited his sister Amaterasu. He challenged her to a contest in order to determine which of them was the most powerful. The task was to see who of them could give rise to male deities. Susano-Wo took Amaterasu's fertility beads from her hair and arms and, breaking them with his teeth, blew them out as five male deities. He then pronounced himself victorious. Amaterasu disagreed, saying that the beads belonged to her, and therefore she had won the contest. Susano-Wo ignored his sister's protests and proceeded to celebrate

his victory by causing devastation on earth. He finished his riotous activities by throwing a flayed pony through the roof of the sacred weaving hall where Amaterasu sat with her attendants. Amaterasu was so angry that she hid in a cave, thereby bringing darkness to the world. Although Amaterasu was eventually lured out of the cave, the gods decided that Susano-Wo ought to be punished. They ordered him to give them numerous gifts and cut off his beard and the nails of his hands and feet. Finally, the gods threw Susano-Wo out of heaven.

According to another tale, Susano-Wo ordered the food goddess *UKE-MOCHI* to give him something to eat. The goddess responded by pulling food from her nose, mouth and rectum whereupon the disgusted Susano-Wo killed her. From her corpse sprouted all the basic food crops: rice seeds grew from her eyes, millet from her ears, wheat from her genitals, red beans from her nose and soy beans from her rectum. In some versions of the legend, it is the moon god Tsukiyomi, rather than Susano-Wo, who kills the food goddess.

When Susano-Wo arrived on earth he set out to find some human beings. He soon came across an elderly couple and a beautiful young woman. The couple, weeping, told Susano-Wo that an eight-tailed, eight-headed monster called Yamato-no-Orochi had eaten seven of their eight daughters and was about to take their youngest daughter too. Susano-Wo promised to kill the monster and in return asked to be allowed to marry the daughter.

The couple agreed, whereupon Susano-Wo turned the daughter into a comb, which he fastened in his hair. The god then told the man and woman to place eight large tubs of rice wine on eight platforms and to surround the platforms with a fence containing eight openings. When the monster approached, it began to drink up the wine with its eight heads and soon fell down drunk. The god then chopped up the monster's body with his sword, discovering in the process the famous sword called Kusanagi or "Grass Mower" in its tail. (See also *CREATION MYTHS*)

SUSERI-HIME see *OKUNINUSHI.*

T'AI-I see *TAIYI.*

TAI SUI, the "President of the Celestial Ministry of Time" and "Ruler of the Year", is an arbiter of human destiny worshipped to avert calamities. He rules the cycle of 60 years, each of which is controlled by one of the subsidiary Tai Sui.

Astrology concerns human fortune, and the stellar deity Tai Sui presides over dates and times, auspicious or otherwise. Astrologers match a person's birth date and time with the cycle to provide a guide to auspicious and inauspicious years. Tai Sui was an early deity honoured at the beginning of spring by the official religion and the official class in imperial China, as well as by Daoists. He is one of the fiercest gods in the pantheon and must be placated whenever ground is disturbed for any reason.

TAIYANG DIJUNG see *YI.*

TAIYI, or T'ai-i, has various meanings within Daoism. Sometimes it is said to be identical with the Dao, but over time it came to be personified as the highest deity within the Daoist pantheon. Taiyi is sometimes said to live in the polar star and to be served by the five mythical emperors.

TAIYI TIANZUN, or T'ai-i T'ien-tsun, is an early Daoist deity who is the saviour of sufferers and unfortunates. He is one of the more senior and significant of the Daoist gods, and is said to be equal to the "Jade Emperor" in rank.

Before the time of *HUANG DI*, the "Yellow Emperor", Taiyi Tianzun had been regarded as the supreme deity. He became the medical adviser to the "Yellow Emperor".

***TAI SUI** is surrounded by some of the 60 images which portray the annual Tai Sui. These are all subsidiary deities of the "Lord of Time".*

THE SHICHI FUKUJIN

SEVEN POPULAR JAPANESE DEITIES, the Shichi Fukujin, were considered to bring good luck and happiness. Each one personified a different aspect of good fortune. Although they were included in the Shinto pantheon, only two of them, Daikoku and Ebisu, were indigenous Japanese gods. Others were versions of popular Buddhist gods imported from China, while Benten and Bishamon originated as Hindu deities, and Hotei as a Daoist god. Buddhism was declared the official religion of the Japanese imperial court in AD 593, but instead of trying to stamp out the existing faith, Buddhist missionaries in Japan drew parallels between the two faiths and proclaimed the identities of the deities to be the same. Because of this peaceable marriage of the two faiths, it was easy for attractive and popular Buddhist gods, such as those of good fortune, to be assimilated with the innumerable kami of the old religion.

BISHAMON *(above) the god of war, came from the Hindu pantheon. He stood for benevolent authority. He was a warrior and always wore full armour, so that he was forever ready for battle. He is always shown carrying a lance and a miniature pagoda to symbolize his dual virtues as a soldier and a missionary.* (HERIAN PERIOD FIGURE, 11TH CENTURY.)

THE SEVEN GODS *(above left) were often depicted travelling together on their treasure ship* Takara-Bune, *representing a cargo of all the good luck anyone could ask for in life. The ship carried various magical articles on board, such as a hat which rendered the wearer invisible, and a purse that was always full of money.* (HIROSHIGE, TREASURE SHIP WITH SEVEN GODS OF GOOD FORTUNE, WOODBLOCK PRINT, 19TH CENTURY.)

BENTEN *(left), the only goddess in the group of seven, was a goddess of love, and was believed to bring good luck in marriage. She rode on a dragon or a sea serpent and was associated with the sea, so her shrines were often located by the sea or on islands. She was a patron of music and played a stringed instrument called a* biwa. (GILDED KOMAI BOX, LATE 19TH CENTURY.)

FUKUROKUJU *(left), perhaps originally a Daoist sage, was the god of long life, wisdom and popularity. He was a little old man with a short body and legs and a very long, narrow bald head, which indicated his intelligence. His traditional companions were animals associated with longevity: a crane, a stag or a tortoise.* (JAPANESE IVORY NETSUKE, 18TH CENTURY.)

HOTEI *(left) was a fat, bald monk who carried a large sack and a small screen. His enormous belly was meant to indicate his contentment and serene good nature, rather than greed. He is often depicted seated comfortably on his sack, laughing merrily.* (ARITA MODEL, LATE 17TH CENTURY.)

JUROJIN *was the godson of Fukurokuju, and also promised long life and a happy old age. He had a long white beard to indicate his great age and was portrayed carrying a staff to which was attached a scroll containing all the wisdom of the world, including the life-span of each individual.* (JAPANESE INRO, 19TH CENTURY.)

DAIKOKU *was the god of wealth and agriculture. He was portrayed wearing a cap and hunter's clothes, surrounded by the symbols of prosperity. Standing or sitting on a bag of rice, he carried another large sack of rice over his shoulder and a rice mallet in his hand, with which he granted wishes. He was sometimes said to be the father of Ebisu.* (SATSUMA MODEL, LATE 19TH CENTURY.)

EBISU *was the Shinto god of work. The most popular of the seven gods, he was a fisherman, and was fat and cheerful. He was usually shown holding a large fish. Later, he became associated with profit and could bring good luck to commercial ventures. Ebisu was deaf, so he did not join the other gods for the Shinto festival at Izumo which takes place in October. Instead, his festival was held in his own temple.* (SATSUMA MODEL, LATE 19TH CENTURY.)

TARVAA was one of the first shamans of Mongolia. As a young man, he fell ill, and his relatives assumed he was dead. Tarvaa was so displeased at this presumption that his soul left his body and flew up to the spirit world. There, he met the judge of the dead who demanded to know why he had arrived so early. The judge, impressed that the youth possessed the courage to visit his kingdom, offered to give him a present before he returned to the land of the living. Tarvaa, rather than choosing wealth or glory, asked to be given knowledge of all the marvels that he had encountered in the spirit world, together with the gift of eloquence. He then returned to his body. However, he found that in his absence, birds had pecked out his eyes, and so he spent the rest of his days unable to see. He became famous for his wisdom and his tales of the spirit world.

TAWARA-TODA is a hero, possibly of historic origins, who features in the mythology of Japan. He defeated an enormous centipede which had been ravaging the territory of the king of the dragons. In gratitude, the king gave Tawara-Toda several supernatural gifts, including a bag of rice which constantly refilled itself.

THE TENGRI, according to the mythology of the Buriats of Siberia, are a type of spirit being. It is said that 54 good-natured Tengri live in the west, whereas 45 bad-natured Tengri live in the east. The Tengri are also regarded as realms, all of which are interconnected, and which together form a cosmic tree.

THE TENGU are creatures of Japanese mythology who are said to live in trees and mountainous areas. Part human, part bird, they have long noses and are sometimes depicted wearing cloaks of feathers or leaves. Although they play tricks, they are not outrightly evil.

TEVNE, according to traditional Mongolian belief, is a hero who managed to appropriate the yellow book of divination from the king. The king had a beautiful daughter whom he desperately tried to protect by keeping her hidden from the outside world. All the king's servants knew that if they revealed the princess's whereabouts, the yellow book of divination would reveal their guilt. As a result, for many years the princess remained in hiding.

One day, Tevne decided that he would attempt to confuse the book. He dug a deep hole in the ground and trapped one of the princess's servants in it. He then built a fire on top of the hole, placed a kettle over the fire and, taking a piece of iron piping, passed it through the kettle. Then, speaking through the pipe, he asked the woman how he could find the princess. The woman told Tevne how the beautiful girl could be identified, so he released her.

Later, Tevne succeeded in picking out the princess from girls of similar appearance. Although the king was furious, he was forced to allow Tevne to marry her. In order

TIAN (above), the sky or heaven, is symbolized by a ceremonial Bi disc. (CHINESE JADE, 3RD–2ND CENTURY BC.)

THE TENGU (left), though wicked, could also be helpful, and rescued the hero Tameto from a giant fish. (WOODBLOCK PRINT BY KUNIYOSHI, 19TH CENTURY.)

to discover who had revealed the secret of his daughter's identity, the king sought advice from his yellow book. The book told him that he had been tricked by a man with earthen buttocks, a body of fire, lungs of water and an iron pipe for vocal cords. The king decided that the book's abilities had deserted it, and so he burned it. Sheep licked up the ashes and thereby acquired divinatory powers.

THE THENS, according to the people of Laos and northern Thailand, are the three divine ancestors who, together with three great men, Pu Lang Seung, Khun K'an and Khun K'et, established human society.

The Thens lived in the upper world, whereas the three great men ruled over the lower world, living by means of fishing and growing rice. A vast bridge joined together the two worlds.

One day, the Thens suddenly announced that all human beings should give them a portion of their food before they sat down to eat a meal. When the people refused, the Thens caused a huge flood to cover the earth. The three great men built a raft on top of which they constructed a house. Taking women and children with them, they travelled over the flood to the upper world in order to seek a reprieve from the chief Then.

The king of the Thens told the travellers to seek shelter in heaven with one of his relatives, Grandfather Then Lo. However, the three great men noticed that the flood was beginning to recede, and they told the king that they would rather return to the lower kingdom, since in heaven they were unable to walk or run because there was no solid ground. The king gave the divine ancestors a buffalo and sent them back down to earth.

Three years passed, after which time the buffalo died. A plant began to grow from its nostrils, and before long gave rise to three gourds. A strange noise issued from the gourds, whereupon one of the great men bored a hole in each of the fruit. Immediately, human beings began to emerge from the plants. The first people to emerge were the aboriginal slaves, followed in due course by the Thai people.

The three great men taught the people how to cultivate fields and how to weave. Later, Then Teng and Then Pitsanukukan descended from the upper world in order to teach the Thais about time as well as how to make tools, weave cotton and silk and prepare food.

Finally, the king of heaven sent the lord of the divine musicians to teach the people how to make and play instruments, and how to sing and dance. When the divine musician had finished his work he returned to heaven, and the bridge that connected the two worlds was destroyed.

TI see *SHANG DI*.

TI TS'ANG WANG see *DIZANG WANG*.

TIAN, or T'ien, is the Chinese word that refers both to the sky, or heaven, and to its personification as a deity. According to Daoism, there are 36 heavens, which are arranged on six levels. Each level is inhabited by different deities. The highest heaven is that of the "Great Web", which is sometimes said to be the home of the "Celestial Venerable of the Primordial Beginning", Yuanshi Tianzun.

From ancient times, Tian, or Tian Di, was regarded as a supreme being who had the power to influence the destiny of human beings, bringing order and calm, or catastrophe and punishment. The Chinese emperor is regarded as the "Son of Heaven", or Tianzi, and is believed to mediate between Tian and humankind.

TIAN DI see *TIAN*.

U

TIAN LONG see *DIYA*.

T'IEN see *TIAN*.

TING-JIAN see *GAO YAO*.

TOKOYO, according to Japanese mythology, was the daughter of a samurai called Oribe Shima who had displeased the emperor and been banished from the kingdom. Oribe Shima set up home on a desolate group of islands known as the Oki Islands.

He was extremely unhappy as he missed his daughter. Tokoyo was also miserable at being separated from her father and determined to find him. She sold all her property and set out for a place called Akasaki on the coast, from where the Oki Islands could just be seen. Although Tokoyo tried to persuade the fishermen to row her out to the islands, they all refused, since it was forbidden to visit anyone who had been sent there.

One night, Tokoyo took a boat and sailed out to the islands alone. She fell asleep on the beach, and the next morning she began to search for her father. The young woman soon encountered a fisherman and asked him if he had seen her father. He replied that he had not, and warned her not to ask anyone where he was as it might cause immense trouble. As a result, Tokoyo wandered all over the islands, listening to what people were saying, but never asking the whereabouts of her father.

One evening, she came to a shrine of the Buddha and after praying to him, fell asleep. She was soon woken by the sound of a girl crying and looking up she saw a young girl and a priest. The priest led the girl to the edge of the cliffs and was about to push her into the sea when Tokoyo ran up and stopped him. The priest confessed that he was forced to carry out the ritual in order to appease the evil god *OKUNINUSHI*. If he were not sent a young girl each year, the god would become very angry and cause great storms and many fishermen would drown.

Tokoyo offered to take the girl's place, saying that she was so unhappy without her father that the loss of her life meant nothing to her. Then, Tokoyo prayed to the Buddha again and, with a dagger between her teeth, dived into the ocean intending to hunt down the evil god and kill him.

At the bottom of the ocean, Tokoyo spied a marvellous cave. Inside, instead of the evil god, she found a statue of the emperor who had banished her father. She began to destroy the statue, but then thought better of it and, tying it to herself, she began to swim back. Just as she was leaving the cave, Tokoyo found herself confronted by a serpentine creature. Unafraid, she swam up to it and stabbed it in the eye. Blinded, the creature was unable to gain entrance to the cave, and Tokoyo succeeded in attacking it until finally she killed it.

When Tokoyo arrived at the shore, the priest and the girl carried her to town, and word of her heroic deeds soon spread. The emperor himself, who had suddenly found himself cured of an unknown disease, heard what had happened and realized that Tokoyo must have released him from an evil spell. He ordered the release of Oribe Shima, and the father and daughter returned to their home town.

TOMAM, according to the Ket people of Siberia, is a goddess who looks after migratory birds.

TOKOYO succeeded in killing a monstrous sea serpent and thus freed the emperor from an evil curse. (ILLUSTRATION FROM MYTHS AND LEGENDS OF JAPAN.)

TSAO-CHÜN see *ZAO JUN*.

TS'AO KUO-CHIU see *BA XIAN*.

TSUKIYOMI, in Shinto mythology, is the god of the moon. His name means "Counter of the Months". Tsukiyomi is said to have come into being when *IZANAGI*, the male half of the primal couple, purified himself after visiting the underworld. When he washed his face, Tsukiyomi appeared from Izanagi's right eye, the sun goddess *AMATERASU* from his left eye and the storm god *SUSANO-WO* from his nose. Izanagi divided his kingdom between his three offspring, allocating to Tsukiyomi the realms of the night.

According to one version of the myth relating how the staple crops of Japan were created, Tsukiyomi asked the food goddess *UKE-MOCHI* for a meal, but when she produced the food from her orifices, he was so disgusted that he killed her. The basic foodstuffs then appeared from the corpse of the goddess. When Amaterasu learned what had happened, she was displeased and said that she would never set eyes on her brother again. It is for this reason that the sun and the moon inhabit the sky at different times.

TUNG-YÜEH TA-TI see *DONGYUE DADI*.

UKE-MOCHI, or Ogetsu-No-Hime, is the food goddess, according to the Shinto mythology of Japan. She is married to *INARI*, the god of rice. The storm god *SUSANO-WO* or, in some versions of the story, the moon god *TSUKIYOMI* ordered the food goddess to give him something to eat. The goddess responded by pulling food from her nose, mouth and rectum

***URASHIMA** returned from his stay under the ocean riding on the back of a turtle.*
(WOODBLOCK PRINT BY TAISO YOSHITOSHI, 1882.)

whereupon the god, disgusted, killed her. From Uke-Mochi's corpse sprouted all the basic food crops: rice seeds grew from her eyes, millet from her ears, wheat from her genitals, red beans from her nose and soy beans from her rectum. She is also said to have produced a cow and a horse.

ULGAN is the great sky god of the Altaic people of Siberia. He sent the saviour *MAIDERE* to earth in order to teach men to respect the true god. Maidere was slain by the evil *ERLIK*, but flames arose from his blood and reached up to heaven, destroying Erlik and his followers. Ulgan is sometimes depicted surrounded by rays of light.

ULU TOYO'N is the malevolent creator spirit of the Yakut people of Siberia. He lives in the third sky and rules over the *ABAASY*, evil beings who live in the lower world. Ulu Toyo'n is also the lord of thunder and is said to have given fire to human beings, as well as one of their three souls.

UMAI is the mother goddess of the Turkic people of Siberia. She is said to have 60 golden tresses, which resemble the rays of the sun, and to look after newborn babies and help couples to conceive. Sometimes known as Ymai, or Mai, she is believed to have originally been identical with *OT*, the fire queen of the Mongols.

URASHIMA was a young fisherman who features in the mythology of Japan. One day, when out fishing, he caught an old turtle. Rather than killing the creature, he took pity on it and threw it back into the water, whereupon a beautiful girl emerged from the spray. The girl stepped into Urashima's boat, told him that she was the daughter of the sea god, a dragon king, and invited him to come and live with her in their palace under the ocean. The palace was made of seashells, pearls and coral, and Urashima found himself waited upon by seven golden-tailed dragons.

For four years, Urashima lived in perfect happiness with his wife, the dragon princess. However, one day he began to long to see his parents and the streets where he used to play. Before he left for his former home, Urashima's wife gave him a casket, telling him that, provided it remained closed, it would enable him to return to her. When Urashima reached his homeland, he found that everything looked strange to him. Eventually, he asked an old man if he knew the whereabouts of Urashima's cottage. The old man replied that Urashima had drowned 400 years ago while out fishing. Urashima was so shocked that he failed to remember his wife's instructions and opened the casket. Immediately, a puff of white smoke escaped from the casket and drifted towards the sea. Urashima himself suddenly began to grow old. His hair grew white and his hands shook, until finally he became no more than a pile of dust and was blown away on the wind.

USHIWAKA see *YOSHITSUNE*.

UZUME see *AME-NO-UZUME*.

WEN CHANG, the god of literature, is dressed as a mandarin and holds a sceptre as a symbol of his official position in the heavenly hierarchy. (CHINESE BLANC-DE-CHINE FIGURE, 17TH CENTURY.)

VIZI-ANYA see *VIZI-EMBER.*

VIZI-EMBER, according to the mythology of the Magyars of Siberia, is a water spirit who lives in lakes and rivers. He devours human beings and, if none are forthcoming, he will call out, demanding to be satisfied. Those who hear his voice know that someone is about to drown.

There are also two female water spirits, the water mother Vizi-anya and the water maiden Vizi-leany. Whenever one of these spirits appears to humankind, the vision signifies that something unfortunate is about to happen.

VIZI-LEANY see *VIZI-EMBER.*

WAKAHIRU-ME, according to Japanese Shinto belief, is the younger sister of the sun goddess *AMATERASU*. She is said to have been sitting with Amaterasu in the divine weaving hall when the storm god *SUSANO-WO* threw a flayed horse into the chamber.

The divine weaving hall was the place where Amaterasu and her attendants were said to weave garments, for the gods themselves or for the priestesses of the sun goddess. Alternatively, the deities were said to be weaving the unfinished parts of the universe.

WATA RIAN, according to the Kedang people of eastern Indonesia, was the hero who civilized the wild woman *BOTA ILI*. Bota Ili lived on top of a mountain; her body was covered with hair and the nails of her fingers and toes were long and pointed. She ate lizards and snakes, and would cook them over a fire, which she lit by striking her bottom against a stone. One day, Wata Rian noticed the smoke of Bota Ili's fire and set off to find its source.

When he reached the top of the mountain, Wata Rian climbed a tree and waited for Bota Ili to return with her catch of reptiles. In due course, the wild woman returned. She struck her bottom against a rock to start a fire, but to no effect. Looking up, she saw Wata Rian and shrieked at him to come down from the tree in order that she might bite him to death. Wata Rian, unafraid, told her to calm herself or he would set his dog on her. The two of them lit a fire and cooked their food together. Bota Ili drank so much wine that she fell asleep, whereupon Wata Rian shaved the hair from her body and discovered that she was a woman. The couple were eventually married.

WEN CHANG is the Daoist god of literature. Originally a stellar deity, he descended from his home in the stars and lived through 17 lives, each of which was filled with remarkable events and achievements. At the end of this time, Wen Chang was finally rewarded by the "Jade Emperor" with the title "Grand Emperor of Literature".

According to one story, a student was disappointed with his performance in an examination and, fearing he had failed, begged Wen Chang to help him. That night, while he was asleep, the student saw the god throwing several essays into a fire. Among them, the student recognized his own. After the essays had disintegrated into tiny pieces of ash, the god transformed them. Wen Chang gave the student his corrected essay, and the young man memorized it.

The following morning, the student discovered that a fire had destroyed the building where all the essays had been kept and that he would have to repeat the examination. This time, he wrote the essay as the god had instructed him and passed.

The deity is usually represented sitting down, wearing the robes of a mandarin and holding a sceptre. Wen Chang is in fact a constellation of six stars. When the stars are bright, literature is said to flourish. He is accompanied by several officials who set and mark exam papers and bear tidings to those who pass. They include *DIYA* and Tian Long.

THE WIND GOD, an impersonal nature deity, assumed human form as Feng Po during the Tang or Song dynasties. Images in mainland China portrayed him as an

THE WIND GOD is a nature spirit, like the gods of rain, thunder and lightning. He is portrayed as an old man carrying a sack of wind.

elderly man carrying a sack of cold wind which he pointed in the direction he wished wind to blow. In northern and central China he was sometimes portrayed astride a tiger, and was also often depicted holding a pair of open fans with which he produced gentle breezes. He was accompanied by a shrimp spirit carrying a vase filled with rainwater which he sprinkled as he went.

THE WU DI, or Wu Ti, are the "Five Perfect Emperors" of Chinese mythology who are said to have lived during the third century BC. They are the "Yellow Emperor" (*HUANG DI*), Zhuan Xu, Du Gu, *YAO* and *SHUN*. One of the five elements is associated with each emperor.

XI-HE, or Hsi Ho, according to Chinese mythology, is the mother of the ten suns and the wife of Taiyang Dijun, the god of the eastern sky. Each morning, Xi-He would carry one of her sons to the edge of the sky in her chariot in order that he might spend the day lighting up the world. Eventually, the suns rebelled against their ordered existence and appeared in the sky together, thus causing devastation on earth. Nine of them were shot down by the divine archer *YI*.

XI WANG MU, or Hsi Wangmu, is described in ancient Chinese texts as a monster with a human face, the teeth of a tiger and a leopard's tail. She ruled over the demons of the plague and was known as the goddess of epidemics. However, by the first century AD she had become a noble lady. Known as the "Queen Mother of the West", she was said to rule over the western paradise of the immortals in the Kunlun Mountains where she was attended by the "Jade Girls" and three-legged birds.

Xi Wang Mu is portrayed as a beautiful woman wearing a royal gown and sometimes riding on a crane. She is said to live in a palace of jade, nine storeys high and surrounded by a golden wall more than a thousand miles long. The male immortals live in the right wing of her palace and the female immortals in the left.

In her garden, Xi Wang Mu grows the peaches of immortality, which release all those who eat them from death. However, the tree bears fruit only once every 3,000 years. When the peaches are ripe, Xi Wang Mu invites all the immortals to a feast during which they eat the marvellous fruit.

Xi Wang Mu is said to have given a peach of immortality to several ancient Chinese rulers. In the myth of the divine archer *YI* and his wife *ZHANG E*, Yi is given the elixir of immortality by the "Queen Mother of the West", but Zhang E drinks it all up, thereby condemning her husband to life as a mortal. According to some versions of the tale of the immortal Li Tieguai, it was the Queen Mother of the West who taught him the secret of immortality.

In popular mythology, she is regarded as Wang Mu Niangniang, the wife of the "Jade Emperor", *YU HUANG*. Once a year, she is said to meet her consort, Dong Wang Gong, who lives in the east. The occasion is believed to symbolize the union of *YIN* and *YANG*.

***XI WANG MU**, with other deities, rides through the heavens in a celestial chariot drawn by cranes.* (CAVE PAINTING AT DUNHUANG, CHINA, C. AD 535–556.)

DEMONS

DEMONS APPEARED IN ALL KINDS OF mythologies as servants and ministers of deities, including the ruler of the underworld. They usually personified forces of evil, and appeared on earth to wreak havoc among mortals by bringing disease and famine, or inhabiting the living. In the afterlife, they existed to punish the wicked with cruelly appropriate tortures for the sins they had committed in life. For a Buddhist, this state of torment could not be everlasting because rebirth continued, but the time in Naraka (the underworld) represented the lowest point of the soul's journey. In Japan, demons were called oni. Most were invisible, though some appeared in the form of animals, and they were the source of sin and misfortune. Even so, they were not viewed as wholly evil. The fox oni, for instance, was considered especially dangerous, yet was the companion of Inari, the rice god, who was popular and benevolent.

HELL *(above) for the Chinese was divided into ten levels, presided over by the "Kings of the Law Courts". Souls had first to appear before Yanluo Wang, the supreme master, who heard their case then sent them on to each court in turn for their punishments to be decided. The kings, dressed like emperors, presided over the ghastly tortures that were carried out by demons. Souls could avoid hell only by living blameless lives and by making regular offerings to Guanyin, goddess of mercy.* (ILLUSTRATION FROM SUPERSTITIONS EN CHINE, 1914.)

JIGOKUDAYU *(left), the "Lady from Hell", was a Japanese courtesan who experienced enlightenment when she looked in her mirror and, instead of her reflection, saw a vision of a skeleton gazing back at her. She became a disciple of the 15th-century Zen master Ikkyu Sojun, the "Holy Madman" who frequented inns and brothels and danced in the street with a skull on a pole. Here, two laughing demons hold up a mirror for her to see her vision.* (JIGOKUDAYU SEES HERSELF IN A MIRROR, BY TAISO YOSHITISHI, WOODBLOCK PRINT, 1882.)

Barong *(above) the spirit king, is the opponent of Rangda, the demon queen, in the great battle between good and evil, which is presented as a dance in Bali and other parts of South-east Asia. He takes the form of a lion, representing day, light and the forces of goodness. During their battle, the humans who try to help Barong are put under a spell by Rangda, which makes them turn their weapons on themselves, but Barong keeps them from harm.* (Balinese stone carving.)

Rangda *(left), the ferocious female demon of Bali, had a lolling, fiery tongue, pendulous breasts and rolling eyes. A creature of darkness, sickness and death, she was the leader of a band of witches. Her name means "widow", and she may derive from an 11th-century Balinese queen exiled for practising sorcery. In revenge she tried to destroy the kingdom, and half the population died of plague before a holy man put an end to her black magic.* (Balinese ritual mask.)

Nagas *(right) are dragon-like demons, and were dangerous and destructive spirits. Of Indian origin, their mythology spread with Buddhism into China and beyond. Some are half-human, half-snake, while others are monstrous water creatures who guard the depths of lakes. Naga Padoha is the serpent ruler of the underworld who, according to the mythology of South-east Asia, was confined there by the creator god Batara Guru when he tried to destroy the earth.* (Naga sculpture in a Balinese shrine fountain.)

Y

THE XIAN were said to live in the Kunlun Mountains, the location of the sacred peach garden where Xi Wang Mu, the "Queen Mother of the West", grew the peaches of immortality which they ate to ensure eternal life. (PAINTING, C 14TH CENTURY.)

THE XIAN, or Hsien, according to Chinese mythology, are beings who have gained immortality. They are not deities, but have been granted the gift of eternal life.

The immortals are either celestial or terrestrial. Celestial immortals live in Tian, the Daoist heaven, or on the isles of the immortals situated in the Eastern Sea, or in the Kunlun Mountains. They can change their appearance at will and are often represented riding on the backs of cranes. The terrestrial immortals live in forests and mountains.

XUAN ZANG, or Hsüan Tsang, was a celebrated Buddhist monk of the seventh century AD. Said to have been commissioned by the emperor of China, he journeyed to the source of Buddhism in India in quest of instruction, and returned with Buddhist scriptures. Some of his bones are still revered in temples in China and Japan.

Xuan Zang's great pilgrimage was immortalized in the 16th-century novel *Xi You Ji (The Journey to the West)* by Wu Zheng-en. According to this story, the monk was accompanied by four aides on his hazardous journey. Of the four, the most important and active was the "Monkey King". The other three were part players, the illiterate and slow-witted monk Sha; Piggy; and the White Horse on which Xuan Zang rode.

YA-GAMI-HIME see *YAKAMI*.

YAKAMI, or Ya-Gami-Hime, was a beautiful princess of Japanese mythology who lived at Inaba, a province near Izumo. The 80 brothers of the great hero *OKUNINUSHI* all wished to marry the princess. On their way to woo her, they met a hare that had been flayed. The brothers cruelly advised the hare to cure itself by bathing in the sea and drying itself in the wind. Naturally, this caused the animal to suffer severe pain. Later, when Okuninushi came across the hare, he told it to bathe in fresh water and then roll in the pollen of kama grass. On doing so, the hare found itself cured. It revealed itself to be a deity and told Okuninushi that he would marry Yakami.

YAKUSHI-NYORAI was one of the first buddhas to be venerated in Japan and became one of the most important. While still a bodhisattva, he is said to have made 12 vows, including promising to find a cure for all illnesses.

His name means "Master with Remedies", and he is commonly known as the "King of Medicines", or the "Divine Healer". Yakushi also vowed to transform his body into beryl in order that he might light up the whole world with his radiance. His home, situated in the east, was known as the "Land of Pure Beryl".

Yakushi-Nyorai is usually shown carrying a medicine bowl, and miraculous powers are attributed to his effigies.

THE XIAN included figures such as Han Shan, one of "The Four Sleepers" who is usually depicted holding a scroll. He would explain its contents to his fellow sleeper, Shi De, in unintelligible gibberish. (PAINTED SILK SCROLL, 14TH CENTURY.)

YAMATO TAKERU is a hero who features in the mythology of Japan. Originally called O-Usu-No-Ikoto, he was the son of Emperor Keiko. The emperor told his other son to bring two beautiful young women to him, but the son made the maidens his own wives and sent two other women in their place. The emperor, who was planning to punish his son, ordered Yamato Takeru to bring his brother to dine.

After five days, there was still no sign of the brother. Puzzled, the emperor asked Yamato Takeru what had happened to him. Yamato replied that he had crushed his brother to death and pulled off his limbs. The emperor, impressed at his son's strength, sent Yamato Takeru to destroy some rebels who threatened his kingdom.

For his first quest, the hero was sent to the west to slaughter two brothers. The palace of the brothers was surrounded by countless

warriors, so Yamato Takeru disguised himself as a girl and entered the palace during a feast. While everyone was busy eating and drinking, Yamato Takeru caught hold of one of the brothers and stabbed him. The other brother tried to escape, but Yamato Takeru seized and killed him, too. As the second brother lay dying, he named his killer Yamato Takeru or "Brave One of the Yamato".

On his journey home, Yamato Takeru brought all the mountain, river and sea deities under control. However, he had not been at home long when the emperor sent him off on another mission. Yamato Takeru complained to his aunt Yamato Pime that he needed time to rest, as well as more protection, and so his aunt gave him a sword and a bag, which she told him to open only in an emergency. The hero then did as his father, the emperor, had asked and killed many more enemies.

Eventually, a man lured Yamato Takeru into a trap. He begged the hero to go to a pond in the middle of a vast plain and kill a deity who lived in its waters. Once Yamato Takeru was in the middle of the plain, the man set fire to the area, trapping the hero. Undeterred, Yamato Takeru cut down the grass with his magic sword. Then, opening the bag his aunt had given him, the hero found it contained a flint. Immediately, he lit another fire, which overcame the first, killing the man and all his followers.

Yamato Takeru performed many other brave and glorious deeds. On his long homeward journey, while crossing the sea in a boat with his wife Oto Tatiban Pime or Miyazu-Hime, the sea deity began to stir up the waves. Oto Tatiban Pime offered to sacrifice herself in order to save her husband and, stepping out of the boat, disappeared beneath the waves. Once on shore again, Yamato Takeru broke his journey by a mountain pass in order to eat some food. Seeing a deer, the hero threw the remains of his meal at the animal, not realizing that it was the deity of the pass. The deer fell down dead. Soon afterwards, Yamato Takeru encountered another deity in the form of a white boar and broke a taboo by saying that he would kill it. A fearsome hailstorm then descended, dazing the hero. None the less, Yamato Takeru struggled onwards until eventually he fell down dead. His soul was transformed into a huge white bird.

XUAN ZANG *(above), the fabled travelling monk, is accompanied by his aides, the Monkey King, Piggy, the slow-witted She and the White Horse.*

YAKUSHI-NYORAI *(below) is the "Divine Healer" of Japanese Buddhism. Effigies of the buddha are credited with miraculous curative powers.* (GILT BRONZE, 8TH CENTURY.)

YAN DI see *SHEN NONG*.

YAN WANG see *YANLUO WANG*.

YANG, according to Daoist belief, originally stood for the mountain slope facing the sun, and was associated with light and warmth. This ancient concept came to be viewed as one of the two cosmic forces, the other being *YIN*, which interacted to produce the universe. Yang represents masculinity, activity, heat, dryness and hardness. It is believed that yang may have originally been a sky deity. (See also *YIN AND YANG*)

YANLUO WANG is the senior king of the ten courts of the Chinese underworld. He investigates the past lives of the dead and sends them on to the other kings for punishment in the hells which are attached to each court. Eight of the "Kings of the Law Courts" punish particular souls while the remaining king allocates souls to bodies in preparation for their reincarnation. However, according to some versions of the tale, every soul has to appear before each of the courts in turn.

Horrific tortures await serious offenders: corrupt officials are forced to swallow molten gold, and the worst offenders are plunged into boiling oil, crushed by stones or cut in half.

YAO is one of the five legendary emperors of Chinese mythology. He is said to have ruled over China during the third century BC. Within Confucianism, Yao is regarded as the examplar of a good ruler. He is credited with having established the calendar, and with introducing official posts whose holders were responsible for making correct use of the four seasons of the year.

It was during his reign that the divine archer *YI* shot nine of the ten suns out of the sky and that a huge flood threatened to destroy the world. Yao made *SHUN* his successor, subjecting him to a series of tests before allowing him to take over the reins of power.

***YANLUO WANG** is the terrifying king of hell who presides over the judgement and punishment of souls.* (CHINESE CERAMIC, 1523.)

YI is the divine archer of Chinese mythology. He performed many brave deeds, including shooting nine of the ten suns from the sky, obtaining the elixir of immortality from *XI WANG MU*, and bringing under control the winds which plagued the "Yellow Emperor".

The ten suns lived in a giant mulberry tree known as Fu Sang, which grew in a hot spring beyond the eastern ocean. They were the children of Taiyang Dijun, the god of the east and lord of heaven, and *XI-HE*, goddess of the sun. Xi-He ordained that only one sun should appear in the sky at a time so, each morning, she would drive a sun to the edge of the sky in her chariot, and at the end of the day would return it to the Fu Sang tree. In this way, light and warmth were brought to the world.

After a thousand years, the ten suns grew tired of their ordered way of life and decided to rebel. One day, they all appeared in the sky together. They were delighted with themselves, but their continual presence in the sky caused devastation on earth: the soil dried up, the crops withered and died and even the rocks began to melt. Soon there was scarcely anything left to eat or drink. Monsters and wild animals came out of the forest in search of food and began to devour human beings.

Eventually, the people begged their ruler, *YAO*, to help them. Yao prayed to Taiyang Dijun to take pity on humankind. Taiyang Dijun and Xi-He heard Yao's prayers and ordered nine of the suns to return to the Fu Sang tree. However, their entreaties fell on deaf ears.

Taiyang Dijun then called on the divine archer Yi for help. The great god gave Yi a red bow and a quiver of white arrows, and told him to bring his sons under control and to kill the wild animals. Yi, together with his wife *ZHANG E*, proceeded to do as Taiyang Dijun had instructed him. However, whereas Dijun had intended Yi merely to frighten the suns into submission, Yi decided that the only solution was to kill them. Taking an arrow from his quiver, he fired it high into the sky. Immediately, a huge ball of

fire appeared, and the air was filled with flames. On the ground lay a three-legged raven. Yi then shot another arrow at the sky, and another; each time, one of the suns was extinguished and fell to earth as a three-legged raven.

Yao realized that if Yi carried on, no light or warmth whatsoever would be left, so he told one of his courtiers to steal one of Yi's arrows so that he could destroy only nine of the ten suns. When there was only one sun left in the sky, Yi began to kill the wild animals and monsters that were devouring human beings.

Peace returned to the earth, and everyone praised Yi. The divine archer returned to heaven with Zhang E. However, to Yi's surprise, and Zhang E's anger, the god Taiyang Dijun spurned Yi for having killed his sons and ordered him and his wife to leave heaven and live on earth as mortals.

Yi was happy enough, hunting in the forests, but Zhang E grew bored and worried that now, one day, she would die. As a result, Zhang E persuaded Yi to visit the "Queen Mother of the West" and ask her for the elixir of immortality. The Queen Mother agreed to help Yi and Zhang E. She gave them a box containing enough elixir to enable them to live for ever, but said that there was only sufficient elixir for one of them to gain complete immortality.

Zhang E swallowed all of the elixir herself, and was punished by being stranded on the moon. When Yi discovered his wife's treachery, he was dismayed. However, he decided that, since he was to die, he should pass on his skills. He took a pupil, Peng Meng, who soon became an expert archer, although not so proficient as Yi. In time, Peng Meng grew jealous of Yi's superior ability and killed him. Another version tells how Yi was finally forgiven by the gods and returned to heaven.

YIN, according to Daoist belief, originally referred to the mountain slope facing away from the sun. Together with *YANG*, Yin was viewed as one of the two cosmic forces whose interaction produced the universe. Yin represents the female principle – the cold, the dark and softness – and may have originated as an earth deity. (See also *YIN AND YANG*).

YINGZHOU see *PENG LAI*.

YINLUGEN BUD, the ghost of the tree trunk, is an ancient spirit of the Chewong people of Malaysia. He taught the hero *BUJAEGN YED* how to deliver children and instructed him in many other rituals associated with childbirth. He also warned Bujaegn Yed that it was sinful not to share his food when he ate a meal.

YMAI see *UMAI*.

YNAKHSYT see *ITCHITA*.

YOMI is the land of the dead in Japanese Shinto mythology. It is a land of filth rather than of punishment, and it is known as the "Land of Darkness", or the "Land of Roots". *IZANAGI*, the male half of the primal couple, followed his wife *IZANAMI* to Yomi, but failed to secure her release.

YOSHITSUNE, also known as Ushiwaka, is a hero who features in Japanese mythology. He was trained in the art of warfare by the Tengu and then succeeded in avenging the defeat of his people, the Minamoto clan. He defeated the giant *BENKEI* in a duel whereupon the giant became his servant.

YOSHITSUNE *was trained in swordplay by the Tengu, the bird-like imps of Japanese myth.* (WOODBLOCK PRINT BY KUNISADA, C. 1815.)

YAO*, fourth of the legendary emperors of China, was the pattern of the good ruler.* (PAINTING BY MA LIN.)

YU was the hero of the flood in Chinese mythology. He is revered for his dedication to hard work. Yu was sometimes shown as half-dragon, half-human, but eventually he came to be represented as entirely human.

Yu laboured for 13 years to put an end to the flood. He controlled and directed all the waters of the earth by cutting holes through the mountains, creating rivers, springs and estuaries. Eventually, his hands and feet grew callused, and he became so exhausted, he could scarcely walk. However, he struggled on, building an irrigation system in order to drain the flood waters into the sea.

In the course of his mammoth drainage work, he made the land fit for cultivation and connected the nine provinces of China to one another. The ruling emperor was so grateful that he abdicated and gave the throne to Yu, who became the first emperor of the Xia dynasty. Yu is said to have reigned from 2205 to 2197 BC. Each succeeding emperor was seen as an incarnation of the dragon Yu.

Another myth tells how, in order to carry out his work, Yu would transform himself into a bear. Each day, when the time came for him to eat, he would beat his drum, and his wife would carry out food for him. One day, when Yu was breaking up rocks, his wife mistook the sound for the beating of his drum. She rushed out with his food, but as soon as she saw the bear she fled. Yu ran after her but, being pregnant, she fell to the ground exhausted and turned to stone. The stone continued to grow and, when the time of the expected birth arrived, Yu split it open, whereupon his son, Qi, was born.

YU HUANG (above), the "Jade Emperor" or "August Personage of Jade" is the supreme ruler of heaven and earth.

YU DI was another name given to *YU HUANG*, the so-called "Jade Emperor" of Chinese mythology.

YU HUANG, or the "Jade Emperor", came to be regarded as the supreme ruler of heaven in Chinese mythology. He was responsible for determining events both in the heavens and on earth, and he had a vast number of underlings to carry out his commands. Yu Huang's chief assistant was *DONGYUE DADI*, or "Great Emperor of the Eastern Peak". Dongyue Dadi alone had 75 gods to help him in his work.

At the beginning of each year, Yu Huang would summon all the deities to his palace, which was in

YU (left) the Lord of the Flood, was given the task of controlling and draining the waters that covered the plains of China.

the highest of the heavens, and was guarded by the "Transcendental Official". The deities would then be allocated new positions, according to how they had performed their duties during the previous year. The various ministries oversaw everything, from water and time, to war and wealth.

The heavenly administration was a replica of the earthly one. If, for example, there was a flood, the earthly official would warn the heavenly official – the deity – that his work was substandard and, if necessary, he would be fired. New deities would be confirmed by the Daoist priests. The "Jade Emperor" was said to deal directly with the emperor of China, whereas his attendants dealt with less important human beings. In the 11th century AD, when the emperor of China was losing his power, he attempted to regain support by claiming to be in direct communication with heaven and to have received a letter from Yu Huang.

One myth tells how before Yu Huang was born, his mother dreamt that *LAO JUN*, the deified form of Laozi, the putative founding father of Daoism, handed her a child. The young Yu Huang succeeded his father, the king, to the throne but abdicated after a few days in order to retire to the mountains and study the Dao. He attained perfection and, for the rest of his life, he instructed the sick and poor in the Dao. Eventually, he became an immortal and after millions more years was transformed into the "Jade Emperor". Yu Huang is usually depicted sitting on his throne wearing the ceremonial robes of an emperor, embroidered with dragons.

The "Queen Mother of the West", *XI WANG MU*, who is known by many titles, including Wang Mu Niangniang, was said to be the wife of Yu Huang. He has a large family of sisters, daughters and nephews, and a celestial dog, who helps to protect the heavenly household from evil spirits.

YUANSHI TIAN-ZONG see *SAN QING DAOZU*.

YUQIANG, or Yü-ch'iang, in Chinese mythology, is the god of the sea and of ocean winds. As a god of the sea, he is represented with the body of a fish and riding two dragons. As a god of the winds, he is represented with the body of a bird and a human face.

According to one tale, Yuqiang was ordered by the king of heaven to anchor the five floating islands of the immortals. Yuqiang succeeded in the task by enlisting the help of 15 giant tortoises. He allocated three of the tortoises to each island and ordered them to take it in turns to carry one of the islands on their backs. Each turn was to last 60,000 years. Unfortunately, a giant caught six of the tortoises, and so two islands were set adrift. They floated away and sank, leaving only three.

YU HUANG *(left) is said to know 72 ways of transforming himself, and numerous temples are dedicated to him.*

YUQIANG *(below), the god of the ocean winds, listens to the Buddhist doctrine.* (PAINTING BY ZHAO BOZHU, SONG DYNASTY.)

CHINA'S SACRED PEAKS

THE GREAT CREATOR PANGU lived for 18,000 years, growing every day and filling the space between the earth and the sky. When he died, his body formed the world. In one version of the myth, his head became Tai Shan mountain in the east; his feet, Hua Shan in the west; his right arm, the northern Heng Shan; his left arm, the southern Heng Shan; and his stomach Song Shan, the mountain of the centre. These were the five sacred Daoist mountains of China. They were worshipped as deities in their own right: pilgrims climbed stairways to the summits and made sacrifices to them. In the heavenly bureaucracy of the Chinese pantheon, the "Ministry of the Five Sacred Mountains" was controlled by Tai Shan, the grandson of Yu Huang, the "Jade Emperor".

TAI SHAN's (above) summit is reached by climbing the "Stairway to Heaven", which consists of about 7,000 steps lined with shrines and temples. Sacrifices were offered at the top of the mountain by the emperor each spring, but he could not presume to do this unless his reign was a successful one. Successive emperors made ceremonial journeys to the holy mountains that marked the limits of the empire, to assert their claim to their territory.

TAI SHAN (left), the holiest peak, is the sacred mountain of the east. Its presiding deity ("Lord of the Yellow Springs") ruled the earth and regulated birth and death, while his daughter Bixia Shengmu ("Princess of Streaked Clouds") protected women and children. Souls left the mountain at birth and returned there at death. The mountain was granted various noble titles by the Jade Emperor.

A PAGODA (right) stands at the summit of Mount Song Shan, the mountain of the centre, in the heart of the ancient Chinese empire.

HUANG DI (below left) the "Yellow Emperor", was the third and most splendid of the legendary emperors of China, preceded by Fu Xi and Shen Nong. Huang Di ordered roads to be built and mountain passes to be cut throughout his empire. When he journeyed to Tai Shan to make sacrifices, his chariot was drawn by six dragons. Tigers and wolves preceded it, serpents slithered beside it, phoenixes flew overhead and spirits followed behind. The road ahead was cleaned and swept by the gods of wind and rain.

HUA SHAN (above) was the sacred mountain of the west. The hero Yu, who controlled the great flood of China, visited the four corners of the world, marked by the sacred peaks. At Hua Shan he found people who drank dew and ate the air, who had three faces each but only one arm. Daoists believed that mountain-tops brought them closest to the Dao and built many of their temples on or near the summits of the sacred mountains.

HENG SHAN (left) in Shanxi Province, has a monastery clinging precariously to the sheer rock face. This is the northern Heng Shan, said to have been formed from the right arm of the giant Pangu.

ZAO JUN, the kitchen god, is honoured with fire crackers during the New Year celebrations. (CHINESE PAINTING, 19TH CENTURY.)

ZAO JUN, or Tsao-chun, is a Daoist kitchen god, worshipped since at least the second century BC. He is still widely worshipped, and his picture is placed above the kitchen stove. At New Year, his spirit is offered a meal of meat, fruit and wine, and his lips are smeared with honey. The portrait is then burned in order to help the god on his way to heaven. The honey is supposed to keep Zao Jun sweet for when he reports on each family's conduct to *YU HUANG*.

According to one story, Zao Jun was once a poor man who, because he was unable to support his wife, or because of a trick she played on him, had to allow her to marry someone else. He wandered far and wide begging. One day, he realized he had come to the home of his former wife and was so ashamed that he tried to hide in the hearth, where he was burned to death.

Another version of the tale tells how, before he became a deity, Zao Jun was a man called Zhang Lang. He was married to a good and faithful woman but left her for a young girl. Things went badly for him. In due course, the young girl became bored with Zhang Lang; he lost his sight and had to beg for food.

One day, Zhang Lang appeared at the door of his former wife. However, being blind, he did not know her. The woman invited Zhang Lang in and gave him his favourite meal. He was reminded of his wife and told the apparent stranger his story. His wife told Zhang Lang to open his eyes, and when he did so, he found he was able to see again. However, Zhang Lang was so ashamed at his former behaviour that he jumped into the hearth and was burned to death. His wife managed to seize one of his legs, which is why the fire poker is described as "Zhang Lang's leg".

ZHANG E, or Chang O, according to Chinese mythology, is the wife of the divine archer *YI*. The lord of heaven, Taiyang Dijun, condemned Yi and Zhang E to live on earth as mortals in punishment for killing nine of his ten sons. Zhang E was furious and persuaded Yi to obtain the elixir of immortality from *XI WANG MU*, who lived on Mount Kunlun. The myth varies slightly, but, according to one version, the Queen Mother took pity

ZHANG E *(left) stole the elixir of eternal life from her husband Yi, and fled to live on the moon.* (CHANG E FLEES TO THE MOON, BY TAISO YOSHITISHI, WOODBLOCK PRINT, 1885.)

on Yi and gave him enough elixir to enable two people to live for ever, but only sufficient for one person to gain complete immortality. Yi returned home with the elixir, and Zhang E immediately began to toy with the idea of swallowing all the elixir herself. However, she was worried that the gods might be angry with her if she abandoned her husband, so she consulted an astrologer. The astrologer suggested that Zhang E should travel to the moon where she would be free both from the accusations of the gods and the hardships of life as a mortal. He also promised that Zhang E would be miraculously transformed.

Zhang E was immediately persuaded by the astrologer's suggestion. She stole the elixir of immortality from where it was hidden in the rafters of her house and swallowed it. Immediately, she began to float up to the moon. However, when she tried to call out, she discovered that she could only croak: she had been transformed into a toad.

Zhang E's companions on the moon were a hare and an old man who constantly attempted to chop down a tree. According to one version of the myth, Zhang E did finally regain her human appearance and lived the rest of her life in the palace of the moon. She is often shown wearing regal garments and carrying the disc of the moon in her right hand. She is regarded as a symbol of *YIN*, the female principle.

ZHANG GUOLAO see *BA XIAN*.

ZHONG-LI QUAN see *BA XIAN*.

ZHU RONG, or Chu Jong, according to Chinese mythology, is regent of the southern quarter of heaven and the divine lord of fire. He helped to divide heaven and earth from each other. One myth tells how Zhu Rong and the ferocious monster *GONG-GONG* decided to fight each other in order to determine which of them was the most powerful. Zhu Rong managed to defeat Gong-gong, who was so ashamed that he tried to kill himself and in the process caused a massive flood.

ZHU RONG *(below), the God of Fire, on a temple altar in Taipei, Taiwan.*

Egypt / Mesopotamia / Iran

THE DESCENDANTS OF RA

The Egyptian creator god Ra and his descendants are known collectively as the Ennead, or "Nine Gods" of Heliopolis, the site of Ra's principal sanctuary. Ra needed no consort, but spat or sneezed out Shu and Tefnut and later, from his own tears, created humanity. The children of Nut were two pairs of twins.

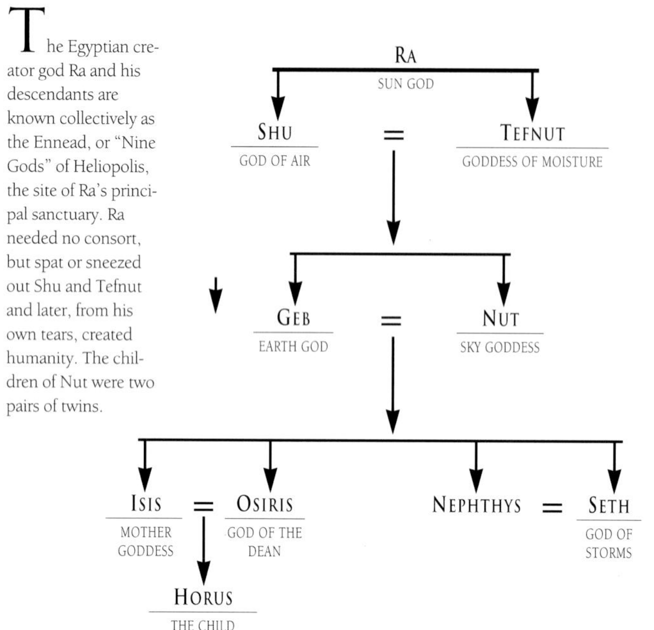

EXPLANATORY NOTE
The following family trees have been laid out to illustrate the various unions and children between important gods and goddesses described in this book. The = sign denotes sexual relationships and lines descending from the sign shows the child or children of that union.

THE SUMERIAN PANTHEON

The Sumerians, living in Mesopotamia in the fourth and third millennia BC, developed a religious framework which was adapted by the Akkadians, Babylonians and other later civilizations in the region. Sumerian deities were organized into a settled pantheon by priests, who inscribed their myths on clay tablets.

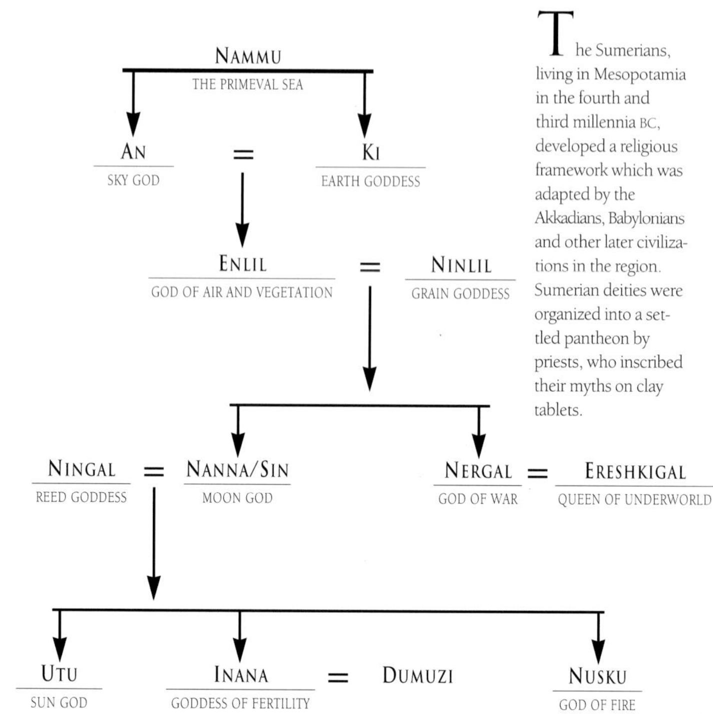

THE BABYLONIAN PANTHEON

The great gods born to Anshar and Kishar disturbed the repose of their ancestors Apsu and Tiamat, who determined to destroy them. Marduk undertook to conquer Tiamat on condition that the other gods made him pre-eminent, and from her corpse he created the heavens, earth and humanity.

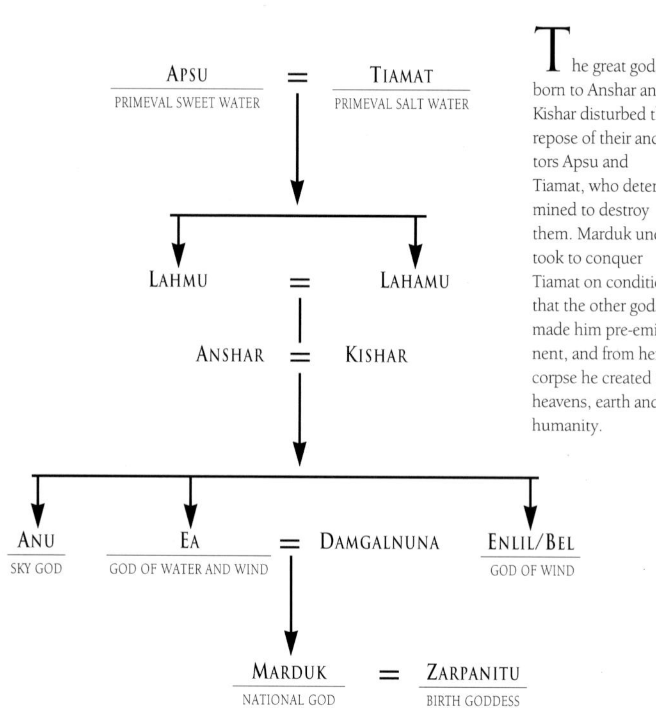

THE ZOROASTRIAN HEAVENLY HIERARCHY

AHURA MAZDA/SPENTA MAINYU
THE WISE LORD

HUMANITY

AMESA SPENTAS
SONS AND DAUGHTERS OF, OR ASPECTS OF, GOD

VOHU MANO	ASHA VAHISHA	SPENTA ARMAITI	KHSHATHRA VAIRYA	HAURVATAT	AMERETAT
GOOD THOUGHT *animals/cattle*	RIGHTEOUSNESS *fire*	DEVOTION *earth*	DOMINION *sun and heavens*	WHOLENESS *waters*	IMMORTALITY *plants*

YAZATAS
PROTECTIVE SPIRITS

ANAHITA	ATAR	HAOMA	SRAOSHA	RASHNU	MITHRA	TISHTRYA
WATER, FERTILITY	FIRE	HEALING PLANTS	OBEDIENCE, THE HEARER OF PRAYERS	JUDGMENT	TRUTH	THE DOG-STAR, SOURCE OF RAIN AND FERTILITY

In the Zoroastrian tradition, Ahura Mazda alone is worthy of worship. The seven Amesa Spentas are his creations and act as intermediaries between Ahura Mazda and his devotees. Many of the Yazatas were ancient Iranian deities who were included in the reformed religion as the servants of Ahura Mazda.

India / Japan

SHIVA'S FAMILY

Shiva is both the creator and the destroyer, and Parvati is the gentle aspect of his shakti, or creative energy. She is also an aspect of the great goddess, Devi, and a reincarnation of Shiva's wife Sati, who committed suicide. In her subservience to her husband, Parvati is a model for mortal devotees of Shiva.

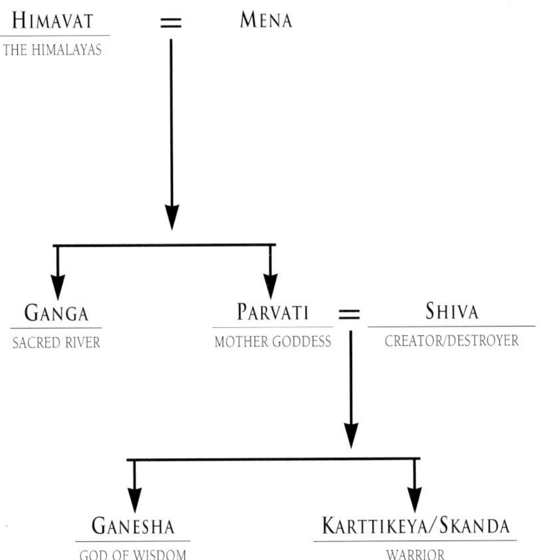

VEDIC CREATION MYTH

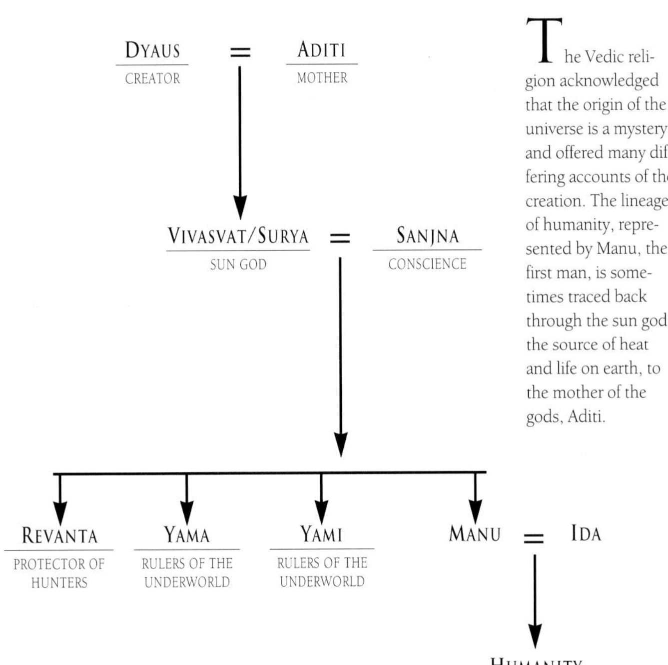

The Vedic religion acknowledged that the origin of the universe is a mystery, and offered many differing accounts of the creation. The lineage of humanity, represented by Manu, the first man, is sometimes traced back through the sun god, the source of heat and life on earth, to the mother of the gods, Aditi.

HIERARCHY OF VEDIC DEITIES

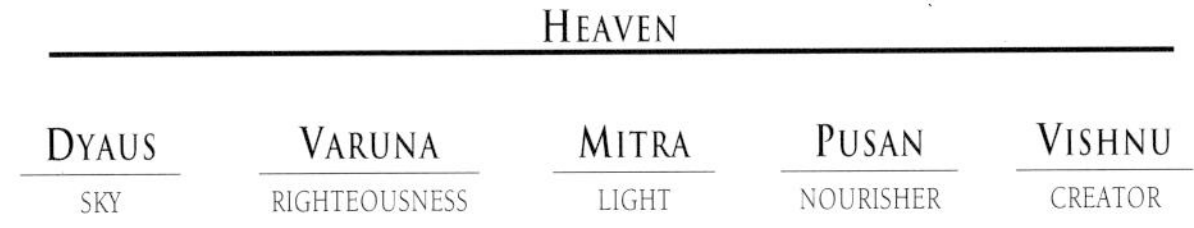

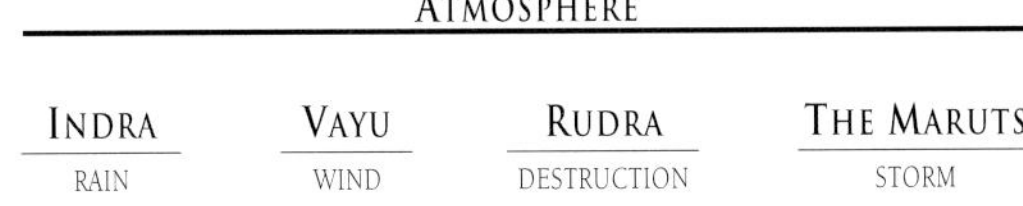

The ancient heavenly deities were endowed with universal power, but were remote figures, whereas Indra and the other gods of the atmosphere exert a more direct influence over human life. Agni is the god of the sacrificial fire, and is therefore an intercessor between the gods and humankind.

SHINTO CREATION MYTH

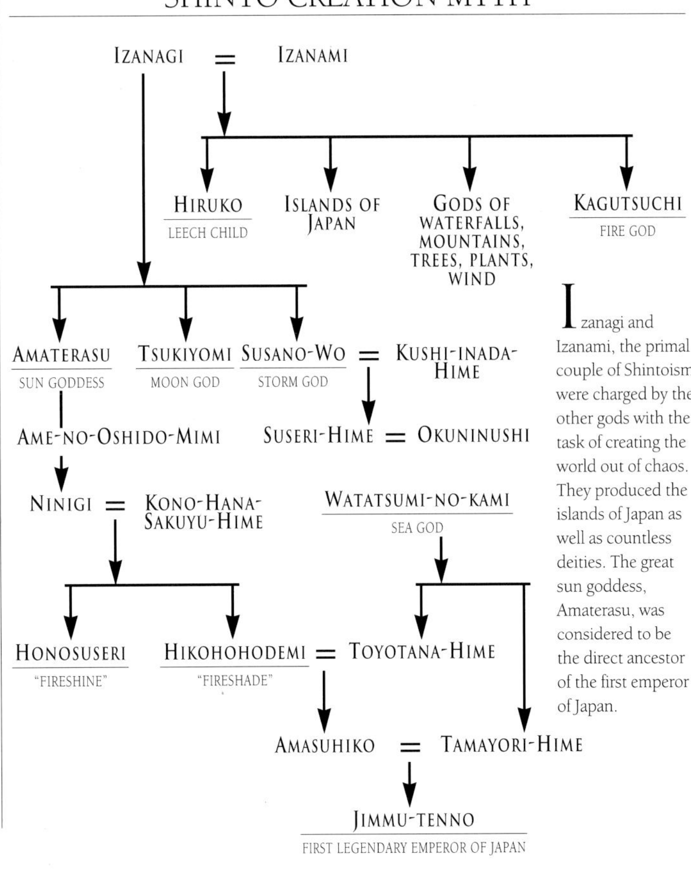

Izanagi and Izanami, the primal couple of Shintoism, were charged by the other gods with the task of creating the world out of chaos. They produced the islands of Japan as well as countless deities. The great sun goddess, Amaterasu, was considered to be the direct ancestor of the first emperor of Japan.

PICTURE ACKNOWLEDGEMENTS

The Publishers are grateful to the agencies listed below for kind permission to reproduce the following images in this book.

AKG, London: p3l and p63 National Museum, Cairo; p10 Kunsthistorisches Museum, Vienna; p11 Haifa University; p14br Musee du Louvre, Paris; p16t National Museum, Damascus; p21tr Kunsthistorisches Museum, Vienna; p21bl Musee du Louvre, Paris; p23tl National Museum, Cairo; p24 Museo Naxionale Romano delle Terme, Rome; p25br Musee du Louvre, Paris; p27tr Museo Ostiense, Ostia; p28tr Hosios Loukas Monastery, Greece; p30bl Museo Capitular de la Catedral, Gerona; p31tr Neuburg Monastery, Austria; p32tl Nationalmuseum, Aleppo; p33r Galleria degli Uffizi, Florence; p35 Icon Gallery, Sveti Kliment; p39; p49tr Kunsthistoriches Museum, Vienna; p51b Musee du Louvre, Paris; p55 British Museum, London; p57 Bibliotheque Municipale, Dijon; p58; p60b Aegyptishes Museum, Berlin; p61 Kunsthistoriches Museum, Vienna; p62tl Musee du Louvre, Paris; p64 Egyptian Museum, Cairo; p65t; p67tr Musee du Louvre, Paris; p67bl Musee du Louvre; p67br Museo Nazionale Romano delle Terme, Rome; p68 Haifa University; p72 Mossul Museum; p75 Royal Collection, Copenhagen; p79 National Museum, Cairo; p85tl Serbian Monastery of Hilandar; p89b Yale University Art Gallery, New Haven; p92 SMPK, Berlin; p95tr; p96t Sammlung G.W. Essen, Hamburg; p98l private collection; p99r State Hermitage, St Petersburg; p114t J. Speelman Ltd, London; p114b State Hermitage, St Petersburg; p115tl; p115tr State Hermitage, St Petersburg; p115br; p117t Musee Guimet, Paris; p120t; p126t; p127t Lucknow Museum; p127b; p129b Rose Art Museum, Waltham, Mass,; p135; p149br SMPK, Berlin; p153t State Hermitage, St Petersburg; p159tl Musee Guimet, Paris; p162t Fine Arts Museum, Ulan Bator; p164 State Hermitage, St Petersburg; p169b; p195 Nationalmuseum, Peking;

Ancient Art and Architecture: p14bl; p16b; p17tl; p18b; p27tl; p29bl; p32br; p36; p38tl; p42tr; p42bl; p45; p46bl; p47b; p51tr; p52tl; p52b; p54b; p59bl; p70t; p70b; p73b; p78t; p82; p95tl; p104t; p106t; p109t; p111tl; p121; p125tl; p129t; p137br; p139t; p143tl; p159br; p159tr; p165b; p169t; p171b; p184; p186b; p192br; p194tl; p196; p204tl; p207tr; p208r; p213tr; p216tl; p216tr; p218t; p227tl; p227bl; p229t; p230tr; p230m; p232; p241b.

Ancient Egypt Picture Library: p21mr; p23br; p26bl; p34b; p38tr; p38bl; p41mr; p46bl; p51tl; p54tr; p60t; p65b.

Duncan Baird Publishing/Japanese Gallery, London: p202.

Bildarchiv Foto, Marburg: p205b.

Bridgeman Art Library: p4 and p97b Victoria & Albert Museum, London; p6l Musee du Louvre, Paris; p15tl Museo Diocesano de Solsona, Lerida; p22 Lauros-Giraudon; p26tl Fitzwilliam Museum, Cambridge; p33 private collection; p34t Beatty Library, Chester; p43bl Giraudon; p100 Musee Guimet, Paris; p107 Victoria & Albert Museum, London; p110 private collection; p117br Ashmolean Museum, Oxford; p119t National Museum of India, New Delhi; p120br National Museum of India, New Delhi; p122t Christie's; p131t National Museum of India, New Delhi; p132t British Library, London; p132br National Museum of India, New Delhi; p133tr National Museum of India, New Delhi; p133br Dinodia Picture Agency, Bombay; p136t National Museum of India, New Delhi; p137t private collection; p146t Oriental Museum, Durham University; p147 Victoria & Albert Museum, London; p148t Fitzwilliam Museum, University of Cambridge; p152tl National Museum of India, New Delhi; p152tr National Museum of India, New Delhi; p155t British Library, London; p156t Victoria & Albert Museum, London; p156b Victoria & Albert Museum, London; p157b National Museum of India, New Delhi; p160tl Victoria & Albert Museum, London; p161bl National Museum of India, New Delhi; p168 Freud Museum, London; p201 Chris Beetles Gallery, London; p203tl Victoria & Albert Museum, London; p208l Blackburn Museum and Art Gallery; p220t private collection; p224br Museum fur Volkerkunder, Basle.

The British Museum: p199tl; p209b.

Christie's Art Gallery: p26br; p41tr; p41br; p77bl; p77br; p84tl; p84br; p85tr; p86; p90 and 133mt; p105tr; p118; p124t; p125tr; p133bl; 150bl; p151t; p151bl; p154t; p180; p183; p186t; p190tl; p190tr; p193l; p193Tr; p197b; p206b; p207bm; p207br; p211b; p222t; p223tl; p223tr; p226bl; p230b; p231tl; p231tr; p231br; p231bm; p231bl; p236t; p240tr.

Corbis: p3r and p216b Luca I. Tettoni; p15br Mimmo Jodice; p17br Gianni Dagli Orti; p31tl Bettmann; p48t Charles & Josette Lenars; p66t The State Russian Museum; p80 Nik Wheeler; p82 Paul Almasy; p83r Gianne Dagli Orti; p84tr Michael Nicholson; p85bl Bettman; p87; p89 Paul Almasy; p97tl Historical Picture Agency; p101b Nik Wheeler; p105tl Luca I. Tettoni; p109b Gian Berto Vanni; p141b Luca I. Tettoni; p142t Angelo Hornak; p150br Luca I. Tettoni; p159bl Charles & Josette Lenars; p163t Angelo Hornak; p165t Historical Picture Agency; p167br Luca I. Tettoni; p172/3 and p237 Pierre Colombel; p176 Royal Ontario Museum; p178 Sakamoto Photo Research Laboratory; p179tl Asian Art & Archaeology, Inc.; p189br Asian Art & Archaeology, Inc.; p192tl Sakamoto Photo Research Laboratory; p192tr Sakamoto Photo Research Laboratory; p198 Ric Ergenbright; p205t Keren Su; p210b Adam Woolfitt; p213b Sakamoto Photo Research Laboratory; p215t Christel Gerstenberg; p219 Macduff Everton; p224t Keren Su; p226tr Kimbell Art Museum; p233 Royal Ontario Museum; p235 Asian Art & Archaeology, Inc.; p238b Asian Art & Archaeology, Inc.; p239t Jack Fields; p239br Michael Freeman; p239bt Morton Beebe, S.F.; p240tl Asian Art & Archaeology, Inc.; p242 Royal Ontario Museum; p245t Brian Vikander; p246t Lowell Georgia; p246b Lowell Georgia; ;247tr Lowell Georgia; p247mr Keren Su; p247b Keren Su; p249t Asian Art & Archaeology, Inc..

CM Dixon: p18t; p21ml; p37; p56b; p97tr; p104b; p117bl; p170t; p177tl; p194br; p206t; p207tl; p226tl; p228; p248.

Edimedia: p1 and 17lt; p108t; p128.

ET Archive: p2 and p53 San Vitale Ravenna, Italy; p6t; 7t; 7tb; p12bl; p19br; p20t Musee du Louvre, Paris; p20b Egyptian Museum, Cairo; p21tl Archeological Museum, Cairo; p37; p41mr; p44tr Musee du Louvre, Paris; p46tr Hittite Museum, Ankara; p50 Christie's; p71l Musee du Louvre; p88; p94 Musee Guimet, Paris; p96b Victoria & Albert Museum, London; p98r Musee Guimet, Paris; p103tr Victoria & Albert Museum, London; p105b Victoria & Albert Museum, London; p108b British Library, London; p123 Musee Guimet, Paris; p130t Victoria & Albert Museum, London; p134t British Library, London; p138 Musee Guimet, Paris; p140t Musee Guimet, Paris; p140b Musee Guimet, Paris; p145b Lucien Biton Collection, Paris; p149t Victoria & Albert Museum, London; p167t Musee Guimet, Paris; p174 British Museum; p189tl; p199b; p209tl British Museum, p209tr British Museum; p222b; p243t; p248.

Mary Evans: p8/9 and p59t; p31br; p40t; p40b; p41tl; p41bl; p47t; p48b; p49bl; p49bm; p74b; p76b; p77tr; p77tl; p81b; p84bl; p85mr; p124b; p177tr; p188b; p189tr; p203br; p207bl; p215b; p223b; p238r.

Michael Holford: p19tr; p69t; p73t; p76tr; p76ml; p115bl; p158; p188t.

Hutchison Library: P142b J Horner; p143b Gail Goodger.

Icorec: p220b.

Image Solutions: P144t, p144b; p145tl; p166t.

Images of India: P154b.

Icorec: P220b.

National Palace Museum, Tapei: P243b; p245b.

Panos Pictures: p66b Jean-Léo Dugast.

Royal Asiatic Society, London: P113b; p113t.

K Stevens: p181; p185; p187t; p210t; p211t; p212tr; p212tl; p217r; p217l; p218b; p221; p224bl; p225tr; p225tl; p225br; p225bm; p225bl; p229b; p236b; p241t; p244b; p244t; p249b.

Jacket Credits:
Front: E.T. Archive, left, right and background; Edimedia, middle.
Back: E.T. Archive, bottom, bottom left and top right; Edimedia, bottom right.
Both flaps: E.T. Archive.

INDEX